Computer-Aided Design of User Interfaces V

T0181129

COMPUTER-AIDED DESIGN OF USER INTERFACES V

Proceedings of the Sixth International Conference on Computer-Aided Design of User Interfaces CADUI'2006 6-8 June 2006, Bucharest, Romania

edited by

Gaëlle Calvary
Université Grenoble 1
Grenoble, France

Costin Pribeanu
National Institute of Research & Development in Informatics
Bucharest, Romania

Giuseppe Santucci
Università degli Studi di Roma "La Sapienza"
Roma, Italy

and

Jean Vanderdonckt
Université catholique de Louvain
Louvain-la-Neuve, Belgium

 Springer

A C.I.P. Catalogue record for this book is available from the Library of Congress.

ISBN 978-94-017-8487-0 (HB)
ISBN 978-1-4020-5820-2 (eBook)

Published by Springer,
P.O. Box 17, 3300 AA Dordrecht, The Netherlands.

www.springer.com

Printed on acid-free paper

TABLE OF CONTENTS

Sponsors vii

Programme Committee Members ix

Acknowledgements xi

Keynote Paper

1. Generating User Interfaces from Conceptual Models:
   A Model-Transformation Based Approach 1
   Ó. Pastor

Multimodal User Interfaces

2. Towards Object Oriented, UIML-based Interface
   Descriptions for Mobile Devices 15
   R. Schaefer and S. Bleul
3. Towards a System of Patterns for the Design
   of Multimodal Interfaces 27
   G. Godet-Bar, S. Dupuy-Chessa, and L. Nigay
4. Design Options for Multimodal Web Applications 41
   A. Stanciulescu and J. Vanderdonckt
5. A Generic Approach for Pen-based User Interface Development 57
   S. Macé and E. Anquetil

Virtual and Mixed Reality User Interfaces

6. Participatory Design Meets Mixed Reality Design Models:
   Implementation Based on a Formal Instrumentation
   of an Informal Design Approach 71
   E. Dubois, G. Gauffre, C. Bach, and P. Salembier
7. A Method for Developing 3D User Interfaces of Information Systems 85
   J.M. González Calleros, J. Vanderdonckt, and J. Muñoz Arteaga
8. GestAction3D: A Platform for Studying Displacements
   and Deformations of 3D Objects Using Hands 101
   *D. Lingrand, Ph. Renevier, A.-M. Pinna-Déry, X. Cremaschi,
   S. Lion, J.-G. Rouel, D. Jeanne, Ph. Cuisinaud, and J. Soula*

User Interfaces for Multi-Device Environments

9. Designing and Developing Multi-user, Multi-device Web Interfaces 111
   F. Paternò and I. Santos
10. A System to Support Publishing, Editing, and Creating
    Web Content for Various Devices 123
    M.M. Silva and E. Furtado
11. Transformational Consistency 137
    K. Richter

12. Rapid Prototyping of Distributed User Interfaces 151
    J.P. Molina Massó, J. Vanderdonckt, P. González López,
    A. Fernández-Caballero, and M.D. Lozano Pérez
13. The Comets Inspector: Manipulating Multiple User
    Interface Representations Simultaneously 167
    A. Demeure, G. Calvary, J. Coutaz, and J. Vanderdonckt

User Interface Layout in Multi-Device Environments

14. A Generic Approach for Multi-device User Interface
    Rendering with UIML 175
    K. Luyten, K. Thys, J. Vermeulen, and K. Coninx
15. Device Independent Layout and Style Editing Using
    Multi-level Style Sheets 183
    W. Dees
16. Automatic Interface Generation through Interaction,
    Users, and Devices Modeling 191
    E. Bertini, G. Santucci, and A. Calì

User Interface Design Support

17. The Meta Sketch Editor: A Reflexive Modeling Editor 201
    L. Nóbrega, N.J. Nunes, and H. Coelho
18. A Hybrid Tool for User Interface Modeling and Prototyping 215
    H. Trætteberg
19. Towards a Support of User Interface Design by Composition Rules 231
    S. Lepreux and J. Vanderdonckt
20. IDEALXML: An Interaction Design Tool:
    A Task-based Approach to User Interface Design 245
    F. Montero and V. López-Jaquero
21. Integrating Model-based and Task-based Approaches to
    User Interface Generation 253
    S. España, I. Pederiva, and J.I. Panach

User Interface Usability Evaluation

22. Automated Repair Tool for Usability and Accessibility
    of Web Sites 261
    A. Jasselette, M. Keita, M. Noirhomme-Fraiture, F. Randolet,
    J. Vanderdonckt, Ch. Van Brussel, and D. Grolaux
23. Automating Guidelines Inspection: From Web Site Specification
    to Deployment 273
    J. Xiong, M. Diouf, Ch. Farenc, and M. Winckler
24. Remote Web Usability Evaluation Exploiting Multimodal
    Information on User Behavior 287
    F. Paternò, A. Piruzza, and C. Santoro

SPONSORS

Official CADUI Web site

Computer-Aided Design of User Interfaces
http://www.isys.ucl.ac.be/bchi/cadui

Corporate Sponsors

CARE Technologies
http://www.care-t.com

DefiMedia
http://www.defimedia.be

IBM Belgium
http://www.ibm.com/be

OlivaNova Model Execution Software
http://www.care-t.com/products/index.asp

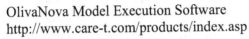

RedWhale Software Corporation
http://www.redwhale.com

SAP AG
http://www.sap.com

Scientific Sponsors

ACM Special Interest Group on Computer-Human
Interaction (SIGCHI)
http://www.sigchi.org

ACM SIGCHI Belgian Chapter (BelCHI)
http://www.belchi.be

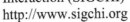

ACM SIGCHI Romanian Chapter (RoCHI)
http://www.ici.ro/chi-romania

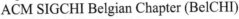

Association Francophone d'Interaction Homme-
Machine (AFIHM)
http://www.afihm.org

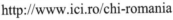

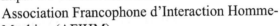

Belgian Laboratory of Computer-Human Interaction
(BCHI)
http://www.isys.ucl.ac.be/bchi

Sponsors

COST Action n°294 – MAUSE: Towards the MAturation of Information Technology USability Evaluation
http://www.cost294.org

European Cooperation in the field of Scientific and Technical Research (COST)
http://www.cost.esf.org

European Science Foundation (ESF)
http://www.esf.org

Institut d'Administration et de Gestion
http://www.uclouvain.be/iag

National Institute for Research and Development in Informatics (ICI)
http://www.ici.ro

The Open Interface Foundation
http://www.openinterface.org

SIMILAR: The European research taskforce creating human-machine interfaces SIMILAR to human-human communication
http://www.similar.cc

Sixth Framework Program, European Commission
http://cordis.europa.eu/fp6

Université catholique de Louvain
http://www.uclouvain.be

Université Grenoble 1, Equipe IIHM
http://iihm.imag.fr/site

Universita' degli Studi di Roma "La Sapienza"
http://www.uniroma1.it

Università di Roma
"La Sapienza"

USIXML

UsiXML (USer Interface eXtensible Markup Language) Consortium
http://www.usixml.org

PROGRAMME COMMITTEE MEMBERS

Silvia Abrahao, Polytechnic University of Valencia, Spain
Sabin-Corneliu Buraga, UAIC Iasi, Romania
Gaëlle Calvary, Université Grenoble 1, France
Joëlle Coutaz, Université Grenoble 1, France
Olga De Troyer, Vrije Universiteit Brussel, Belgium
Emmanuel Dubois, IRIT Toulouse, France
Antonio Fernández-Caballero, University of Castilla-La Mancha, Spain
Peter Forbrig, University of Rostock, Germany
Elizabeth Furtado, University of Fortaleza, Brazil
Pascual Gonzalez, University of Castilla-La Mancha, Spain
Philip Gray, University of Glasgow, UK
James Helms, Harmonia, Inc., USA
Geert-Jan Houben, Vrije Universiteit Brussel, Belgium
Robert J.K. Jacob, Tufts University, USA
Anthony Jameson, DFKI, Germany
Herman Kaindl, Vienna University of Technology, Austria
Nora Koch, University of Munich, Germany
Christophe Kolski, Université de Valenciennes, France
James Lin, IBM Almaden, USA
Victor López-Jaquero, University of Castilla-La Mancha, Spain
Jesús Lorés, University of Lleida, Spain
Maria-Dolorès Lozano, University of Castilla-La Mancha, Spain
Kris Luyten, University of Hasselt, Belgium
Mark T. Maybury, The Mitre Corp., USA
Francisco Montero, University of Castilla-La Mancha, Spain
Laurence Nigay, Université Grenoble 1, France
Erik G. Nilsson, SINTEF, Norway
Monique Noirhomme, Facultés Universitaires N.-D. de la Paix, Belgium
Nuno J. Nunes, University of Madeira, Portugal
Luis Olsina, University Nacional de La Pampa, Argentina
Philippe Palanque, IRIT Toulouse, France
Fabio Paternò, ISTI-CNR, Italy
Paolo Pinheiro da Silva, Stanford University, USA
Horia D. Pitariu, UBB Cluj-Napoca, Romania
Costin Pribeanu, ICI, Romania
Angel Puerta, RedWhale Software Corp., USA
Kai Richter, Computer Graphics Center (ZGDV), Germany
Giuseppe Santucci, Universita' degli Studi di Roma "La Sapienza", Italy
Kevin A. Schneider, University of Saskatchewan, Canada
Daniel Schwabe, PUC Rio de Janeiro, Brazil

ACKNOWLEDGEMENTS

The editors would like to particularly thank the authors, the reviewers, the participants, and the sponsors for their support of the CADUI'2006 edition. We also warmly thank Prof. O. Pastor for giving the keynote address of this conference.

The editors would like to thank Cristian Voicu, who significantly helped in the preparation and the editing of the final version of this book, and Teodora Voicu for her support to the conference participants. This book was supported by the SIMILAR network of excellence, the European research taskforce creating human-machine interfaces SIMILAR to human-human communication (www.similar.cc), funded by the 6th Framework Program, IST Program of the European Commission, under contract FP6-IST1-2003-507609. The editors are also grateful to Juan Manual Gonzalez Calleros for the two first images on the cover and José Pascual Molina for the picture of the multi-monitor display.

Chapter 1

GENERATING USER INTERFACES FROM CONCEPTUAL MODELS: A MODEL-TRANSFORMATION BASED APPROACH

Óscar Pastor

Department of Information Systems and Computation, Valencia University of Technology,
Camino de Vera s/n, 46071 Valencia (Spain)
E-Mail: opastor@dsic.upv.es – Web: http://oomethod.dsic.upv.es/anonimo/
memcontactinfo.aspx?idMember=2
Tel.: +34- 963877794 – Fax: +34- 963877359

Abstract   Traditionally, the Software Engineering community has been interested in defining methods and processes to develop software by specifying its data and behavior disregarding user interaction. On the other hand, the Human-Computer Interaction community has defined techniques oriented to the modeling of the interaction between the user and the system, proposing a user-oriented software construction. This paper aspires to reconcile both visions by integrating them in a whole software production process. An approach based on conceptual-schema centric software development is presented, where conceptual primitives intended to specify static, dynamic and interaction aspects are properly provided. Furthermore, Model Transformation techniques are proposed to go from the problem space, represented by the Conceptual Schema, to the solution space, represented by the corresponding final software product. This proposal is underpinned by some current MDA-based technology, which makes user-oriented, model-based software generation a reality

Keywords: Conceptual modeling of user interface, Functional requirements, Model-based code generation, User Interaction and Model-driven approach

1.   INTRODUCTION

Traditionally, modeling an Information System from a Software Engineering (SE) perspective basically consists in specifying its static (data-oriented) and dynamic (function-oriented) architecture. A lot of methods and techniques have been provided in the past to solve this specification problem,

1

G. Calvary et al. (eds.), Computer-Aided Design of User Interfaces V, 1–14.
© 2007 Springer.

including well-known data modeling techniques (e.g., the Entity-Relation-ship Model [5] and its extensions), and process modeling approaches (e.g., Structured Analysis, Data Flow Diagrams). Object-Oriented Modeling was seen in the nineties as the way to encapsulate statics (data) and dynamics (behavior) under the common notion of object, and new methods [3,24] and languages (e.g., UML [2]) have been proposed under this unified paradigm. The focus at the modeling step has always been put on those data and functional system aspects, while one very important issue was normally left at least for design time: the user interaction. Why interaction modeling is not considered at the same level than data and behavior modeling in the vast majority of SE-based software production methods? Isn't interaction an essential part of the world description, as system data and functionality are?

It has been remarkable to realize that, even if the design and the implementation of User Interfaces (UIs) are recognized to be the most time-consuming step of any software production process, its modeling was rarely considered at the same level of data and function modeling when specifying a system. A whole community emerged to face that problem: the Human-Computer Interaction community (HCI).

To face and solve this dichotomy, one challenging goal in the context of both SE and HCI is to provide proper bridges between their best-known software production methods and techniques. Starting from the idea that SE is considered to be strong in specifying data and functional requirements, while HCI is centered on defining user interaction at the appropriate level of abstraction, a sound software production process must provide ways for specifying in a precise way data, functionality and interaction, all together. If any of those aspects is not properly faced, the whole software production process will fail, because the reality to be modeled is a mix of data, functionality and interaction. Consequently, software production methods that combine the most data-oriented and functional-oriented, conventional requirements specification, with the more interaction-oriented, UI modeling aspects are strongly required.

In this context, Model Transformation technologies (i.e., MDA approaches [13]) make possible to provide a global software process where all the relevant aspects of the analyzed problem (structure, behavior and user interaction) are specified from the beginning (Requirements Model). Those resulting models are first projected onto a Conceptual Schema and onto the final software product later. Based on the use of this Model Transformation approach, the intended contribution of this work is to provide the basis to build such a software production process, with two basic principles in mind:

1. Model Transformation is used as the basic software production paradigm, to automate the conversion of a source Requirements Model into its corresponding Conceptual Model and then converting this conceptual model

into the System Design and Implementation. A Model Compiler should be the responsible of implementing the corresponding mappings.

2. Each modeling step provides appropriate methods to deal properly with the specification of structural, functional and interaction properties. To do that, the conceptual primitives (conceptual constructs) that constitute the basic building blocks of the required models must be properly identified. The definition of Conceptual Patterns constitutes a good strategy to define those conceptual primitives in detail.

Taking advantage of the current research on Model Transformation methods and tools (where we find MDA [13], Extreme Non-Programming [15], and Conceptual-Schema Software Development), we will focus on the Conceptual-Model-to-Software-Product Model Transformation Process. Interaction patterns at the conceptual level of modeling will be introduced, and how to convert them into UIs will be shown, providing an MDA-based approach where not only data models and process models are properly converted into database and programs, but also UIs are created from their corresponding interaction model. How to go from the problem space to the solution space in an automated way will be commented based on the OlivaNova Model Execution (ONME) tool [4], an MDA-based tool that generates a software product that corresponds to the source Conceptual Schema. We intend to demonstrate that conceptual modeling is more powerful when user interaction and system data and behavior are modeled within a unified view at the conceptual level.

To fulfill those goals, the paper is structured as follows. Section 2 presents an overview of model-based UI development environments proposed in the literature. Section 3 introduces an object-oriented, model-based software production process, where system statics, dynamics and interaction aspects are specified in a unified framework. In particular the interaction patterns required for modeling system interaction are introduced in detail, while in Section 4 how to go from the interaction model to the final UI is shown. Finally, the conclusions, some lessons learned derived from the process application, and future works are presented.

2. RELATED WORK

If we look for approaches to design and implement UIs based on modeling, there are two main groups of proposals in the HCI area:

- **MB-UIDEs**: From an HCI point of view, there is a number of model-based UI development environments reported in the literature. In da Silva's survey [6], several MB-UIDEs are reviewed, distinguishing two generations of tools. The aim of the first generation was to provide a run-time environment for UI models; some examples are COUSIN [9], HUMANOID [20] and MIKE [17]. The second generation aimed to provide support for interface modeling at a high level of abstraction. Examples of these environments include ADEPT [12], GENIUS [10], MASTERMIND [21], MECANO [19], TADEUS [8], and TRIDENT [1]. Many of the second generation of MB-UIDEs rely on a domain model. This model is often a description of the domain entities and relationships between them, which are represented as a declarative data model (as in MECANO), an entity-relationship data model (as in GENIUS), or an object-oriented data model (as in TADEUS). Some MB-UIDEs like ADEPT, TADEUS, TRIDENT and UsiXML [11,22] propose task models as a primary abstract interaction modeling, from which the abstract interface models (or its equivalent dialogue models) are later derived. It is important to remark that UsiXML is an XML-based interface description language that is supported by a suite of tools [23], ranging from creating UI sketches to generating the final UI. Therefore, we will consider UsiXML [11] as an MB-UIDE for the purposes of this review.

- **UML-based approaches**: WISDOM [16] is a UML-based SE method that proposes a use case-based, evolutive method in which the software system is iteratively developed by incremental prototypes until the final product is obtained. The UML notation has been enriched with the necessary stereotypes, labeled values and icons to allow a user-centered development and a detailed UI design. Three of its models are concerned with interaction modeling at different steps: the Interaction Model, at the analysis stage; and the Dialog Model and the Presentation Model during the design stage, as refinements of the Interaction Model. Another important proposal is UMLi [7]. It is a set of UI models that extends UML to provide greater support for UI design. UMLi introduces a new diagram: User Interface Diagram. UMLi is the first reliable proposal of UML to capture the UI formally. However, the models have so detailed that do the modeling very difficult. Problems of middle size are very difficult to specify, that is what probably explains why UMLi is not adopted in industrial environments.

When we compare the reviewed approaches, in general we find a poor lifecycle support in most MB-UIDEs, and a lack of integration between models to provide a full software production process. In addition, none of the reviewed MB-UIDEs allow the specification of the system functionality. The result is that the application being modeled cannot be completely generated. There are some efforts leading to properly map the elements of a task model to the elements of a domain and interface models by defining a transformation model and the corresponding support tools, but although there are tools that deal with the final UI generation, no business layer is generated due to the lack of a precise functional model.

The UML-based approaches try to solve the problem by integrating all the different perspectives through the use of UML. But being UML so imprecise in terms of semantics of its conceptual primitives, what they finally provide is a mess of models and notations where model transformation is not possible because the formal semantics of those basic building blocks of the different models are not precisely defined.

From a SE point of view, some development methods and environments have been proposed. They normally use a class diagram-like model to capture the system structure and a process model to fix the functionality that the system is supposed to provide. In addition, in recent years some CASE tools (e.g., Together, Rational Rose, Poseidon) have been proposed with the objective of providing some kind of automation to manage these models. Anyway, interaction modeling is not a usually key issue when requirements and conceptual modeling is represented in a software production process.

Being how to achieve this whole integration in a model transformation-based platform a basic goal, in the next section we are going to see how all those modeling pieces (data, behavior, and user interaction) can be properly put together in a sound Software Production Process.

3. MODEL-BASED INTERFACE DEVELOPMENT WITH OLIVANOVA MODEL EXECUTION

In this section, we present a complete software production process that combines functional requirements specification, user interaction design, and implementation. It is defined on the basis of the OO-Method [18] and the OlivaNova Model Execution (ONME) tool [4], an implementation of the OO-Method. OO-Method is a model-based environment for software development that complies with the MDA paradigm [13] by defining models of a different abstraction level. Fig. 1 shows the parallelism between the models proposed by MDA and the models dealt with in OO-Method [18].

At the most abstract level, a Computation-Independent Model (CIM) describes the IS without considering if it will be supported by any software application; in OO-Method, this description is called the *Requirements Model*. The Platform-Independent Model (PIM) describes the system in an abstract way, having in mind that it will somehow be computerized but still disregarding the underpinning computer platform; this is called the *Conceptual Model* in OO-Method. ONME implements an automatic transformation of the Conceptual Model into the *source code* of the final user application. This is done by a *Model Compilation* process that has implicit knowledge about the target platform. This step is equivalent to the Platform Specific Model (PSM) defined by MDA. In the following, we explain the main steps of such a software production process, focusing on the Conceptual Model to final Software Product transformation.

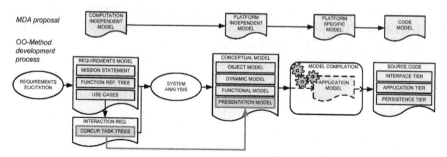

Figure 1. An MDA-based development framework for UI development

3.1 Modeling Data and Behavior

In order to cover the data and behavior perspectives, OO-Method defines a PIM called *Conceptual Model* consisting of: the Object Model, the Dynamic Model, and the Functional Model, which can all be designed using the Requirements Model as input. The *Object Model* specifies the object structure and its static interactions. It is modeled as an extended UML class diagram. The *Dynamic Model* represents the control, the valid sequences of events and the interaction between the objects. The *Functional Model* specifies how events change the object states. Therefore, the behavior of the system is modeled by the Functional and Dynamic Models working together.

Detailed information of the Conceptual Patterns required specifying data and behavior through these three models can be found in [18]. In this paper, we want to emphasize how to do a similar work from the system interaction point of view. This means that we are going to work with Interaction Model. This Interaction Model will be the last component of the Conceptual Modeling step, and we are going to see which basic building blocks are required to construct a correct specification. It must be remarked that each interaction pattern exists because a corresponding software component counterpart is associated to it. This is why the design and implementation of a Model Compiler will be the logical consequence of the approach.

3.2 Modeling Interaction

To model the interaction between the system and the user, OO-Method incorporates an *Interaction Model*. Based on a set of basic interaction patterns, it allows describing the interaction by means of three levels of presentation patterns as shown in Fig. 2.

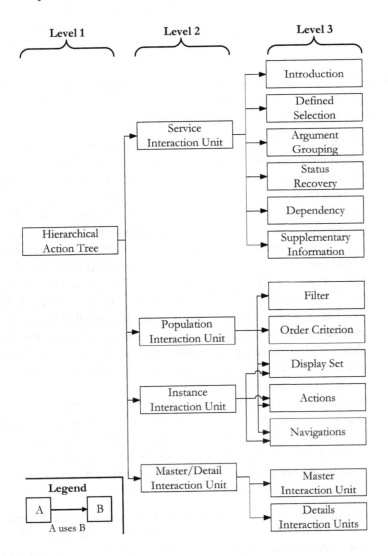

Figure 2. Interaction patterns and their use relationships

These three levels are:

- **Level 1. Hierarchy of Actions Tree (HAT):** It organizes in a tree the functionality that will be presented to the different users who access the system. Each intermediate node of the tree acts as a container with a label. Each leaf node contains a label and a link to an interaction unit. As we will see later, under a model transformation perspective, these data will be automatically mapped to menus (in windows environments) or pages and links (in web environments) in the implementation phase. Using a tree structure is a good technique to support the *Gradual Approach*. The interaction units referenced in the tree leaves are those basic, level 2 interaction units that are described next.

- **Level 2. Interaction Units (IUs):** They represent abstract interface units that the user will interact with to carry out his/her tasks. There are three main types of interactions to be considered:

  1. **Service UI**. A Service IU models a dialogue whose objective is to help the user execute a service. Normally, the need of a Service IU is the consequence of the existence of a functional requirement - coming from the Requirements Model- that the modeler will identify as a service associated with a certain class. In terms of specification, the Service IU encapsulates the interaction unit to supply a service in the interface. In this context, the service specification can be completed asking the user: *What input data are needed for this service?, How should input data be grouped?, Are the input fields inter-related?, What kind of feedback do you need for each selected object?*, etc. The answers to these questions will be specified by using other auxiliary simple patterns that are the lower level interaction patterns –level 3, introduced next–. Being the service argument the main granule, the questions to be answered are related to: *Introduction* aspects (constraining the edition of values), *Defined Selection* (defining by enumeration the valid values), *Population Selection* (expressing how to select objects for OO arguments), *Dependency* (expressing dynamic interdependencies among UI components), *Supplementary Information* (providing extra feedback for object identifiers), *Status Recovery* (recovering argument values from attributes), and *Grouping* (logical grouping of arguments).

  2. **Instance UI**. It specifies how to visualize one selected instance of a class. An Instance IU models the data presentation of a class instance and supports the required interaction with it. It is oriented to object manipulation. In user terms, the Instance IU arises from the necessity to observe single objects. In addition, the user may want to change the state of the selected object (by means of services) and/or to navigate to related objects. In the problem domain the analyst identifies a certain class, e.g., Vehicle. Once the class is defined, he could ask the user the following questions: *Which attributes of the object do you wish to view? What actions can be done on the object? Which additional info (relationships) do you want to reach in the*

interface by navigation? Again, the answer to these questions is provided by the lower-level, auxiliary interaction patterns (level 3), that will fix the concrete functionality. In particular, the specification of the Instance Pattern is defined using three elementary patterns: a *Display Set* (fixing what properties to show), *Actions* (specifying what services could be executed by the instance) and *Navigation* (defining the links to the association/aggregation relationships which can be reached from the corresponding instance). In OVID, the concept of view plays a similar role to the Instance Presentation Pattern.

3. **Population UI.** This interaction pattern deals with the necessity of working with object collections. It allows specifying how to filter and search among the selected objects, how to order them when presented to the user, how to navigate from a selected object of the collection to others attached to it, and what actions can be executed from an object. Again, these properties are dealt with through the use of the corresponding lower-level patterns –elementary patterns–. We will introduce a *Filter,* an *Order Criterion,* a *Display Set,* a *Navigation path,* and a list of *Actions* respectively. From the methodological point of view, the modeler identifies a class with its attributes, services, and relationships that will be used as component bricks for the specification of this kind of user interaction. More complex interaction can be specified based on combinations of the previous ones. For instance, a Master/Detail IU could be defined as a complex interaction unit that deals with master/slave presentations.

- **Level 3. Elementary Patterns (EPs):** These patterns constitute the primitive building blocks of the UI and allow the restriction of the behavior of the different interaction units. In the current OO-Method Interaction Model proposal there are 11 Elementary Patterns, which have been introduced associated with their corresponding relevant Interaction Unit. As a matter of example, let us see how to characterize the Filter EP. A filter is a criterion specified for searching for objects. Once a class has been picked, the user needs to search for objects satisfying a given condition. Example, searching cars by fare or color in a Car Rental Service. By fixing the required attributes to be used for the query, and their intended values –if any-, the system can create the corresponding filter criterion. If the modeler has identified the Vehicle class in the problem domain, he can ask the user: *How do you need to search for Vehicles?* Each answer from the user constitutes a component of the filter criterion to be built. Example, the formula for searching red cars with special fare is: color="red" and fare.code="special".

4.   GENERATING THE SYSTEM

Generating the System is better understood if tools are used. As OO-Method has ONME tool as implementation, we will use it to explain the model-based code generation strategy. As we are focusing on User Interaction, we will center the presentation on how to generate the UIs. How to generate the Database and the set of programs that implement the system data and functionality respectively can be seen in detail in [18] from a more theoretical point of view, and in [4] from a more industrial-oriented perspective.

In MDA terms, once we have completed the PIM, the next step is to take advantage of ONME automatic production of the *source code* (Code Model). Nowadays, ONME implements a *Model Compilation* process to automatically transform the information described in the *Conceptual Model* into a full software system in the following platforms: Visual Basic, C#, ASP .NET, Cold Fusion and JSP; using as a repository SQL server 2000, ORACLE or DB2. This results in a three-layer application that includes the interface tier, the business tier, and the persistence tier. As an explanation of the transformation patterns implemented by the ONME, Table 1 shows the correspondences between PIM elements and concrete widgets for the Visual Basic platform [14].

Table 1. Some Transformation Patterns

Presentation model	VB component
Hierarchical action tree (HAT)	Application menu
Interaction unit	MDI child form
Service IU	MDI child form with entry controls
Simple type service argument	Entry control
Object-valued service argument	Generic control OIDSelector
Filter	Filter control
Filter variable	Entry control
Actions	Button panel
Action item	Button
Service throw	"Accept" button and code to validate and invoice the service
Cancellation	"Cancel button" and code to close the formulary
Services invocation	Code for linking business logical layer with service invoice
Data presentation	Code for formatting and data recovery

To better understand the UI Generation Process, let's comment how a concrete Service IU specification (at the Problem Space level) is properly transformed into a Concrete User Interface (at the Software Space level).

From a conceptual perspective, when specifying a class service in the Class Model –as for instance, a New Expense Report service as shown in Fig. 3–, we have a set of arguments of a corresponding type. For such a service argument, a couple of label and text edit controls will be introduced. Position, format and length are interaction properties that can be incorporated in this specification level. Additionally two buttons will be added: one for activating the service (ok) and another to cancel it (cancel).

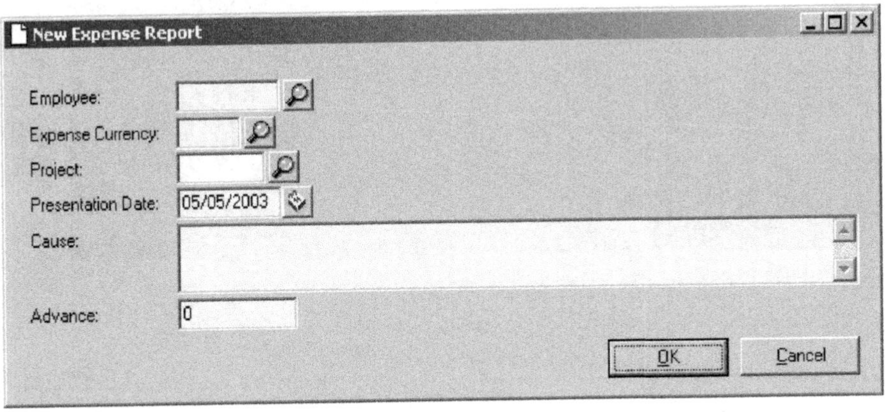

Figure 3. A Service UI

Additionally, some service arguments will provide the facility of value selection from a given condition, defined on the corresponding target class attributes. In this case, a population selection EP is specified determining those attributes to be used for building the selection condition. The transformation process will indicate this situation using a magnifying glass icon. An associated execution semantics fixes the final implementation. Clicking this icon, a selection window will allow the user to introduce the desired values for the attributes of the condition to be built, and the corresponding query will be triggered to obtain the set of potential valid values; one of them will be selected as a service argument. The following table shows each interaction model component that is used to define a class service window and its interface component implementation.

Table 2. Correspondences between the Presentation Model and the Final Interface

Presentation model	Final interface
Hierarchical action tree (HAT)	File Changes Others Window
Service IU	The whole window
Service throw and Cancellation	OK Cancel
Simple type service argument	Identifier:
Introduction pattern for a date field	Code for validating date format

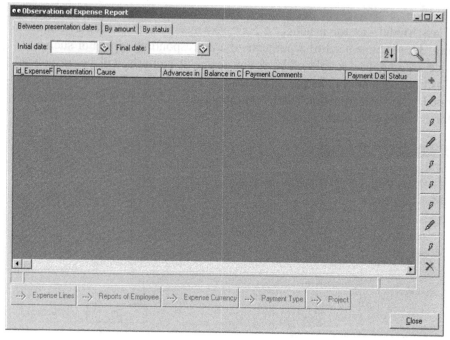

Figure 4. A Population UI

As a second example let's analyze the software representation of a Population IU at the Solution Space. As said before, what we have to specify in this case at the modeling step is which class attributes are to be seen, what filters could be required to help with the process of selecting instances, which actions could be activated when a given instance is selected, and what navigation is feasible in terms of other's class information reachability. We can see in the previous figure a concrete representation of those interaction patterns in terms of a UI, where

1. The specified filters are in the top of the window.
2. The main screen includes the area where the data (attributes) of the objects that satisfy the corresponding filter condition are shown.
3. The available actions for a particular instance are represented in the set of icons aligned vertically at the right part of the window.
4. And where finally the valid navigation options are represented in the lower part of the window.

There are many other options, but as soon as a particular template for the final UI is defined, it is possible to implement a model transformation process where full automation becomes a real chance.

5.   SUMMARY AND FUTURE WORK

Software production methods need a complete software production process that properly integrates system functionality, behavior, and user interaction from the early stages of the system lifecycle. This process should also allow the modeling, and implementation of UIs, properly integrated with the more conventional, SE-oriented modeling and implementation of system data and functionality. In accordance with these ideas, we have presented the basic principles to embed user interaction modeling as an essential part of the Conceptual Modeling phase, and converting the resulting conceptual schema into a final software product where all UIs, programs and database are properly generated; a Model Transformation-Based approach has been proposed, where the automatic generation of the complete, final software becomes an affordable dream. Some lessons learned while applying the proposed software production process include the need of providing design capabilities to face the "beautification" of the "to-be, final UI", while modeling the higher-level interaction aspects. One open issue is to which degree interaction properties can be fully included in an Interaction Model. With the help of tools as ONME that already incorporates the proposed ideas into industrial, Model-Transformation-based Software Production, the proposed process is being empirically validated to prove its effectiveness.

REFERENCES

[1] Bodart, F., Hennebert, A.-M., Leheureux, J.-M., and Vanderdonckt, J., *A Model-based Approach to Presentation: A Continuum from Task Analysis to Prototype*, in Proc. of 1st Int. Workshop on Design, Specification, and Verification of Interactive Systems DSV-IS'94 (Bocca di Magra, June 1994), Springer-Verlag, Berlin, 1995, pp. 77–94.

[2] Booch, G., and Jacobson, I., *The Unified Modeling Language*, Addison-Wesley, New York, 1999.

[3] Booch, G., *Object-oriented Analysis and Design with Applications*, 2nd ed., Benjamin Cummings, Redwood City, 1993.

[4] Care Technologies, Denia, Spain, 2006, accessible at http://www.care-t.com.

[5] Chen, P.P., *The Entity-Relationship Model - Toward a Unified View of Data*, ACM Transactions on Database Systems, Vol. 1, No. 1, March 1976, pp. 9–36.

[6] da Silva, P.P., *User Interface Declarative Models and Development Environments: A survey*, in Ch. Johnson (ed.), Proc. of 7th Int. Workshop on Design, Specification, and Verification of Interactive Systems DSV-IS'2000 (Limerick, 5-6 June 2000), Lecture Notes in Computer Science, Vol. 1946, Springer-Verlag, Berlin, 2000, pp. 207–226.

[7] da Silva, P.P., and Paton, N.W., *User Interface Modeling in UMLi*, IEEE Software, Vol. 20, No. 4, July/August 2003, pp. 62–69.

[8] Elwert, T., and Schlungbaum, E., *Modelling and Generation of Graphical User Interfaces in the TADEUS Approach*, in Ph. Palanque, R. Bastide (eds.), in Proc. of 2nd Int. Workshop on Design, Specification, and Verification of Interactive Systems DSV-IS'95 (Château de Bonas, 7–9 June, 1995), Springer-Verlag, Vienna, 1995, pp. 193–208.

[9] Hayes, P., Szekely, P., and Lerner, R., *Design Alternatives for User Interface Management Systems Based on Experience with COUSIN*, in L. Borman, B. Curtis (eds.), in Proc. of the ACM Conf. on Human Factors in Computing Systems CHI'85 (San Francisco, 14–18 April 1985), ACM Press, New York, 1985, pp. 169–175.

[10] Janssen, C., Weisbecker, A., and Ziegler, J., *Generating User Interfaces from Data Models and Dialogue Net Specifications*, in Proc. of the ACM Conf. on Human Factors in Computing Systems INTERCHI'93 (Amsterdam, 24–29 April 1993), ACM Press, New York, 1993, pp. 418–423.

[11] Limbourg, Q., Vanderdonckt, J., Michotte, B., Bouillon, L., and Lopez, V., *UsiXML: A Language Sup-porting Multi-Path Development of User Interfaces*, in Proc. of 9th IFIP Working Conf. on Engineering for Human-Computer Interaction EHCI-DSVIS'2004 (Hamburg, July 11–13, 2004), Lecture Notes in Computer Science, Vol. 3425, Springer-Verlag, Berlin, 2005, pp. 200–220.

[12] Markopoulos, P., Pycock, J., Wilson, S., and Johnson, P., *Adept - A Task Based Design Environment*, in Proc. of the 25th Hawaii Int. Conf. on System Sciences HICSS'92, IEEE Computer Society Press, Los Alamitos, 1992, pp. 587–596.

[13] Model-Driven Approach (MDA), accessible at http://www.omg.org/mda.

[14] Molina, P., *User Interface Specification: From Requirements to Automatic Generation*, Ph.D. thesis, DSIC, Universidad Politécnica de Valencia, Valencia, March 2003.

[15] Morgan, T., *Doing IT Better*, in Proc. of 3rd Annual Conf. on Information Systems Technology and its Applications ISTA'2004 (Salt Lake City, 15–17 July 2004), Lecture Notes in Mathematics, Springer-Verlag, Berlin, 2004.

[16] Nunes, N.J., and Cunha, J.F., *Wisdom: A Software Engineering Method for Small Software Development Companies*, IEEE Software, Vol. 17, No. 5, 2000, pp. 113–119.

[17] Olsen, D., *A Programming Language Basis for User Interface Management*, in K. Bice, C. Lewis (eds.), Proc. of the ACM Conf. on Human Factors in Computing Systems CHI'89 (Austin, 30 April-4 May 1989), ACM Press, New York, 1989, pp. 171–176.

[18] Pastor, O., Gómez, J., Insfrán, E., and Pelechano, V., *The OO-Method Approach for Information Systems Modeling: from Object-Oriented Conceptual Modeling to Automated Programming*, Information Systems, Vol. 26, No. 7, November 2001, pp. 507–534.

[19] Puerta, A., *The MECANO Project: Comprehensive and Integrated Support for Model-Based Interface Development*, in J. Vanderdonckt (ed.), Proc. of the 2nd Int. Workshop on Computer-Aided Design of User Interfaces CADUI'96 (Namur, 5–7 June 1996), Presses Universitaires de Namur, Namur, 1996. pp. 19–36.

[20] Szekely, P., *Template-Based Mapping of Application Data to Interactive Displays*, in Proc. of the 3rd Annual Symposium on User Interface Software and Technology UIST'90 (Snowbird, 3–5 October 1990), ACM Press, New York, 1990, pp. 1–9.

[21] Szekely, P., Sukaviriya, P., Castells, P., Muthukumarasamy, J., and Salcher, E., *Declarative Interface Models for User Interface Construction Tools: the MASTERMIND Approach*, in Proc. of the 6th IFIP TC 2/WG 2.7 Working Conf. on Engineering for Human-Computer Interaction EHCI'95, Chapman & Hall, London, 1995, pp. 120–150.

[22] Vanderdonckt, J., Limbourg, Q., Michotte, B., Bouillon, L., Trevisan, D., and Florins, M., *UsiXML: a User Interface Description Language for Specifying Multimodal User Interfaces*, Proc. of W3C Workshop on Multimodal Interaction WMI'2004 (Sophia Antipolis, 19–20 July 2004).

[23] Vanderdonckt, J., *A MDA-Compliant Environment for Developing User Interfaces of Information Systems*, in O. Pastor, J. Falcão e Cunha (eds.), Proc. of 17th Conf. on Advanced Information Systems Engineering CAiSE'05 (Porto, 13–17 June 2005), Lecture Notes in Computer Science, Vol. 3520, Springer-Verlag, Berlin, 2005, pp. 16–31.

[24] Yourdon, E., *Object-Oriented Systems Design an Integrated Approach*, Yourdon Press, 1993.

Chapter 2

TOWARDS OBJECT ORIENTED, UIML-BASED INTERFACE DESCRIPTIONS FOR MOBILE DEVICES

Robbie Schaefer[1] and Steffen Bleul[2]
[1]C-LAB, Paderborn University, Fuerstenallee 11 – D-33102 Paderborn (Germany)
E-Mail: robbie@c-lab.de – Web: http://www.c-lab.de
Tel.: +49 5251 606107 – Fax: +49 5251 606065
[2]Distributed Systems Group FB16 - Elektrotechnik/Informatik, Kassel University
Wilhelmshöher Allee 73 – D-34121 Kassel (Germany)
E-Mail: bleul@uni-kassel.de – Web: http://www.vs.uni-kassel.de/~bleul/
Tel.: +49 561 804 6276 – Fax: +49 561 804 62 77

Abstract To avoid multiple works in designing user interfaces for different devices and interaction modalities, the use of a meta-language like UIML seems to be appropriate in order to start with a general UI description and provide mappings to different target devices. For the support of mobile devices and to improve re-usability of user interface definitions, we introduce the language DISL that modifies several parts of UIML and propose object oriented extensions with the conceptual language ODISL

Key words: Mobile devices, Re-usability, User Interface Markup Language

1.   INTRODUCTION

Mobile devices and disappearing computers rise significant challenges in User Interface (UI) development as each device comes with different characteristics which require different interfaces. In order to avoid the development of a new interface for each available platform, a model-based approach is required to abstract from platform specific details. In fact even abstractions from certain interaction modalities are useful. Since many mobile devices have severe limitations regarding memory and processing power, further constraints have to be considered.

For these reasons, a renaissance of model-based UI development can be observed for example in [6], where several techniques are described or in

15

G. Calvary et al. (eds.), Computer-Aided Design of User Interfaces V, 15–26.

[12], where a task model is used to provide different interfaces for varying platforms.

Being a meta-language, the User Interface Markup Language (UIML) [2] uses the approach of separating the interface from the logic and presentation, where the presentation for different platforms is made available through dedicated mappings. While this proved to be feasible, UIML can be improved in order to support UI development for mobile devices: reducing the amount of connections to the backend, providing means to describe UIs modality independent and allowing the re-use and refinement of UI objects. This is achieved by focusing on abstract interface elements and a powerful dialog model that is the basis for the behavioral description.

After having reflected the related works we present the language DISL which simplifies UIML in order to provide renderers for different modalities and which can be optimized for handsets with limited capabilities. By improving the dialog model, foundations are laid for an object oriented version which is introduced with the conceptual language ODISL. Followed by some examples, the architecture and implementation of a DISL-based rendering system for mobile devices is sketched and the chapter closes with some conclusions.

2. RELATED WORK

Model based approaches for UI development often start at a high level, e.g., with a task model as in [12]. UIML however is already too specific as it provides presentation elements and a behavioral section which implements an event based dialog model. Nevertheless, a sound dialog model provides a perfect abstraction from the concrete UI while being fine grained enough to model the human system interaction.

Several classical approaches exist which focus on the description of user dialogs like Dialogue-Nets [9], Petri Nets [15], UAN (User Action Notation) [7], and DSN (Dialog Specification Notation) [5]. They refer all to the same principle concepts, are based on variants of parallel Finite State Machines, and mainly differ in their description means and hierarchical decomposition into components. They define the user dialog by means of states and state transitions, which are triggered by events from the UI elements. An interesting observation is that several of these approaches provide or have been extended with object oriented features, for example as hierarchical Petri Nets [8] or with ODSN [18].

Much research has been dedicated to introduce UI development in object oriented frameworks which makes perfectly sense since for example the separation of application logic and the presentation encourages such an approach. The Model View Controller Concept [16] may serve as an early and well known example. More recently, efforts have been done to include UI modeling methods in the UML family as in [11] and [13].

As we are particularly interested in the reusability of User Interface Objects with all their axes, the PAC model [4] provides valuable insights: There, an interactive application is structured into abstraction, presentation and control which can be recursively applied. In contrast, UIML is more oriented towards the MVC as it is based on the Meta Interface Model which can be considered as a finer grained version of the MVC. An important part of this model is the behavioral section, which describes the control model and can be based on one of the previously introduced dialog models. In the next section we discuss how UIML can be improved by integrating object oriented concepts and abstractions from concrete views.

3. UIML FOR DIFFERENT DEVICES AND MODALITIES

UIML can be used to build multi-platform UIs [1]: first, a generic vocabulary is used to specify a more abstract UI and in a second step, the generic UI is transformed to a concrete UI representation such as Java Swing or HTML. This principle works well, for different platforms that share the same interaction philosophy, as UIML supports linear mapping with the peers section and a generic vocabulary can thus be transformed quite straightforwardly. For example all widgets of an HTML-Form are available with most APIs for Graphical User Interfaces. So if a generic vocabulary supports forms, a mapping to other platforms is mostly a matter of diligence.

Problems occur however, when we include platforms with completely different interaction modalities such as voice and gestures. In this case not only the naming of widgets and their properties have to be changed, but sometimes also the complete structure of the interface, which can be hardly achieved with UIML in its current form. Therefore we propose to abstract the vocabulary even more and combine it with an external transcoding approach or the usage of an interpreter for the required modality. Both will be detailed in the next subsection.

3.1 DISL - An Extended Subset of UIML

In order to allow generic and modality independent dialog descriptions, we used UIML as a base, simplified it by removing the capability of being a meta-language and improved the behavioral part for storing and processing several local UI- and system states. The changes which resulted in the language DISL (Dialog and Interaction Specification Language) are motivated and explained in the next paragraphs.

As one design goal was the support for mobile devices, we intended to allow renderers on the device. Therefore there was a need to simplify UIML. Being a meta-language, UIML uses a vocabulary which is needed to map UIML to concrete interfaces. For DISL we wanted to avoid different vocabularies, so that one UI model can be used and an interpreter for devices with limited storage and processing power could render the model. For devices where there is no DISL renderer available, we rely on external transformations e.g., DISL to WML.

As we do not have a vocabulary-based mapping from UIML to toolkit specific widgets, we defined modality independent *generic widgets* which are inspired amongst others by [14]. This concept does not describe real widgets but only general interaction elements for input, output and logical grouping. For example we defined a *variablefield* for output that could be rendered as text in a GUI, synthesized speech in a voice driven interface, or as beeps or light flashes.

Even more important are changes done to the behavioral part of UIML, as we introduced variables and arithmetic operations. The variables can be used to store system states, which allow processing multiple states together with events and compares to dialog models which allow parallel transitions. In fact, the control model of DISL is based on the DSN [5] notation.

By allowing basic arithmetic operations on variables representing system states, a UI can have some logic directly in its behavior. The aim is not to weaken the separation of concerns but to minimize unnecessary calls to the backend application. As a simple example consider a small interface which shows the number of button presses. For each button press, the backend application has to be called in order to provide an updated counter. So, on a mobile phone, the UI freezes every time the button is pressed. If the increment of the counter is implemented in the interface, the backend has only to be called when important input has to be transmitted or the event processing requires synchronization.

3.2   ODISL - Towards Object Oriented UIML

For re-using parts of a UI specification, UIML supports templates which can be defined for the most important parts of a UI description, amongst others presentation, structure, style, content, behavior and logic. Templates in UIML form a viable concept which is in some aspects close to the object oriented paradigm for the following reasons:

- Templates support the principle of inheritance, as a template may consist of other templates which are included via the source attribute. So, UIML documents could be defined as a template which serve as a base class and through inclusion of this base template, another UIML document can inherit from the first document.
- Parts of a template can be specified as *hidden*.
- In principle, polymorphism is supported through UIML templates, as the *restructure* element has *cascade* and *replace* attributes which can be used to modify "inherited" properties.

However, object oriented features are only implicitly available through the UIML template concept and since they are not designed by purpose to be object oriented, some difficulties occur as described in the open issues document by the UIML standardization committee [3]. For example, there should be a way to restrict access to certain elements of a template by making them immutable or making parts of a template optional could be desired. Another open issue is addressing the parameterization of templates in order re-use the behavior specification. We think that a profound introduction of real object orientation to UIML will solve the issues described before. As templates only support some aspects of object orientation, they fail in other aspects, when it comes to apply real objects that are instances of classes, since the sub classing of templates constitutes mainly of a textual changes to the UI-tree via *replace, union* and *cascade*.

Key to an object oriented UI markup language is the possibility to inherit and encapsulate the behavior of the UI. Therefore the behavioral extensions proposed by DISL prove to be very useful, as we now have a way to capture states and describe behavior that is intrinsic to local UI objects. All that is needed is a way to really encapsulate these parts and make them accessible to child objects and allow instantiation of UI objects. So, DISL has been modified and UIs are now referred to as interfaceclasses which can be instantiated through their identifier. Interfaceclasses may inherit from other interfaceclasses.

```
<method id="setVisible" access="public">
  <params>    <param id="visible" type="boolean"> </params>
  <returns>
  <return id="isVisible" type="boolean"/>
  </returns>
  <action>
    <statement>
      <variable-content id="isVisible"/> <param-content id="visible"/>
    </statement>
  </action>
```

```
<afterresolving>
  <statement>
    <return-content id="isVisible"/>
    <property-content generic-widget="showValue" id="visible"/>
  </statement>
</afterresolving>
</method>
```

Figure 1. A method definition in ODISL

Each interfaceclass consists of the elements structure, style, behavior and methods. If such an element is not stated in the *interfaceclass*, the class inherits the element from the parent class. If an element is specified, the content extends the inherited content. Furthermore, access rights as *public* or *private* can be set for most DISL-elements. Methods are introduced to operate on the elements of the interfaceclass they where defined in. They take a list of input parameters and return values. Inside a method, an action part is used to set values or trigger events. A similar part is needed to specify how the result values are constructed e.g., by assignments with the content of internal variables. Since this can happen only after the action part is resolved, this element is called "afterresolving". The code excerpt in Fig. 1 shows how a method is constructed in ODISL.

4.   IMPLEMENTATION AND EXAMPLES

In order to visualize the concepts of the previous sections, some examples are provided, after having detailed a client-server architecture that provides UI descriptions for mobile devices. This architecture allows controlling applications on the mobile device, on the server or using the device as a universal remote control as it is done within the pebbles project [10]. Having a UI server allows also a more flexible handling of UI descriptions as they can be transformed into specific target formats for mobile devices, which do not have dedicated DISL renderers.

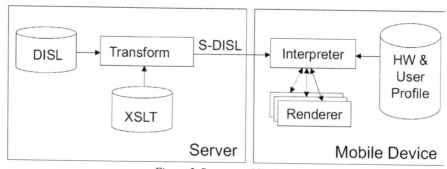

Figure 2. System architecture

In fact, our DISL renderer for mobile phones also requires a pre transformation, which is done server side in order to establish a highly efficient parsing process on the client device. Fig. 2 shows a simplified view of the architecture for use with mobile devices that are equipped with DISL (or more specifically serialized DISL) renderers. For systems without DISL or S-DISL renderers, e.g., simple WAP-phones, the transformation component has to generate other target formats. However, in that case some of the advances by using DISL may be lost.

The first example (Fig. 3) shows, how a part of the behavioral section of the volume control of a media player can be modeled in DISL and how variables are used to keep the state information. First, variables for the current volume and a value for increasing the volume are assigned. The rule IncVolume implements the condition that evaluates to true, if the widget IncVolume is selected. After the conditions of each rule are evaluated we have to decide which transitions will be fired. This is done for every transition, where the condition of the if-true tag is true, and then a set of statements is processed in the action part. There, incVolumeValue is added to the previous set volume, and statements update the UI, e.g., setting a yes and cancel control. The resulting interface for a mobile phone is shown in Fig. 5 where several parts of the UI (more than just the previously discussed volume control) are rendered in an emulator.

```
<behavior>
  <variable id="Volume" internal="no" type="integer">128  </variable>
  <variable id="incVolumeValue" internal="no" type="integer">
    20
  </variable>...
  <rule id="IncVolume">
    <condition>
      <equal>
        <property-content generic-widget="IncVolume"
          id="selected">
          yes
        </property-content>
      </equal>
    </condition>
  </rule>...
  <transition>
    <if-true rule-id="IncVolume"/>
    <action>
      <statement assignment="add">
```

```
        <variable-content id="Volume"/>
        <variable-content id="incVolumeValue"/>
      </statement>
      <statement>
        <property-content id="visible" generic-widget="Apply">
            yes
        </property-content>
      </statement>...
    </action>
   </transition>
  <behavior>
```

Figure 3. Behavior of volume control in DISL

Applying the previously discussed concept of generic widgets, we are also able to use further devices and modalities with the media player. For example, we implemented a simple gesture control, where the SoapBox [17] (a small wireless multisensor) is used to detect vertical and horizontal hand movements for controlling the player. Fig. 4 illustrates how the media player is controlled by multiple interaction means.

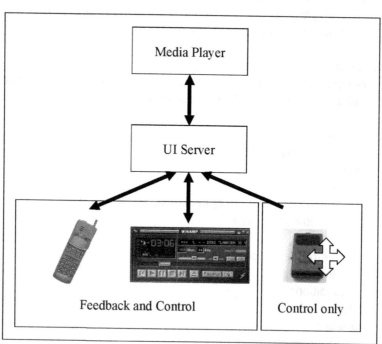

Figure 4. Multi device control of a media player

The second example shows how the previously discussed object oriented extensions are applied in the conceptual language ODISL. Consider for this the volume control from the first example: Changing the volume is an operation which is intrinsic to several applications as TV Control, music player etc. and could be triggered by different means such as simple key presses with the mobile phone or more appealing UIs on different devices. A slider to set the volume is modeled in Fig. 6. Such a slider can inherit of course from a generic volume control.

Figure 5. UI rendered on Mobile Phone

For defining a UI object, ODISL introduces the notion of an interfaceclass where all subparts belong to the class. Classes by inherit by default from their parent class, marked by the extends-attribute. As in DISL, interfaceclasses consist of structure, style and behavior, which all can be referenced, but they have an additional *method* element which will be explained later. These parts can be referenced also by other classes unless they are marked as *private*. The *style* section in the example shows that inherited sections can be extended by adding new parts. Within the behavior section, a new transition is added to the existing ones which fires on the event when the slider has been moved, meaning a new value is available. In that case, the SliderValue property of the generic widget VolumeValue is assigned the new value multiplied by the IncrementValue.

```
<odisl>
  <interfaceclass id="VolumeSlider"
  extends="VolumeControl">
    <structure name="VolumeSliderStructure"
      extends="VolumeControlValue"/>
    <style name="VolumeSliderStyle"
      extends="VolumeControlStyle">
    <part generic-widget="VolumeValue">
      <property id="IncrementValue">20</property>
      <property id="SliderMoved">false</property>
      <property id="SliderValue">3</propert>
    </part></style>
    <behavior name="VolumeSliderBehavior"
      extends="VolumeControlBehavior">
      <transition id="newSliderValue" access="private">
        <condition>
          <equal>
            <property-content generic-widget="VolumeValue"
            id="SliderMoved"/>
            <constant>true</constant>
          </equal></condition>
        <action>
          <statement assignment="set">
            <property-content generic-widget="VolumeValue"
            id="value"/>
            <expression assignment="mul">
              <property-content generic-widget="VolumeValue"
                id="IncrementValue"/>
              <property-content generic-widget="VolumeValue"
                id="SliderValue"/>
            <expression/>
          </statement></action>
      </transition></behavior>
    <methods name="SliderDisplayMethods"
              extends="EditableDisplayMethods"/>
  </interfaceclass>
</odisl>
```

Figure 6. Volume slider in ODISL

Since the transition is marked as private, it is not visible for other classes but can only be accessed through methods of this class. So methods provide an access mechanism to private elements and thus encapsulation of UI elements consisting of structure, style and behavior can be ensured. In this example, the internal behavior of the slider is of no interest to the using class of the slider, so we only inherit the editableDisplay-Methods without extending them, where the display in this case is just a field to show the value of a variable. Having methods as a means to access private elements from an interface class is a quite powerful concept because a user of the interface class does not have to deal with the internal behavior of the interface elements and can easily access relevant properties e.g., through get- and set functions.

5.   CONCLUSION

In this paper we introduced the language DISL and its object oriented version ODISL, in order to improve UI development for mobile devices with potentially different modalities. This is achieved by the application of modality independent widgets and improvements in the dialog model. A proof of concept implementation shows that such a renderer can be build for limited devices. Since the design of DISL is still quite close to UIML, some parts of the DISL specification such as the usefulness of variables or basic support of arithmetic operations are already acknowledged by the UIML community and currently under discussion for inclusion in the upcoming standard of UIML. The object oriented features of ODISL could eventually pave the path for an even more reusable UIML than it is now with the use of templates.

ACKNOWLEDGMENTS

This work has been partly funded by the EU within the 6th Framework Program project UBISEC.

REFERENCES

[1] Ali, M.F., Pérez-Quiñones, M.A., Abrams, M., and Shell, E., *Building Multi-Platform User Interfaces with* UIML, in Ch. Kolski, J. Vanderdonckt (eds.), "Computer-Aided Design of User Interfaces III", in Proc. 4th Int. Conf. on Computer-Aided Design of User Interfaces CADUI'2002 (Valenciennes, 15–17 May 2002), Kluwer Academics Pub., Dordrecht, 2002, pp. 255–266.

[2] Abrams, M., Phanouriou, C., Batongbacal, A.L., Williams, S.M., and Shuster, J.E., *UIML: An Appliance-Independent XML UI Language*, Computer Networks, Vol. 31, 1999.

[3] Abrams, M., Luyten, K., Schaefer, R., Vanderdonckt, J., Vermeulen, J., Shabanov, D., and Helms, J. (eds.), *Open Issues in the UIML 3.1 Specification*, Working Draft 02, OASIS Working Draft, 14 November 2005, accessible at http://www.oasis-open.org/committees/documents.php?wg_abbrev=uiml.

[4] Coutaz, J., *PAC: An Object Oriented Model for Implementing User Interfaces*, SIGCHI Bulletin, Vol. 19, No. 2, October 1987, pp. 37–41.

[5] Curry, M.B., and Monk, A.F., *Dialogue Modelling of Graphical User Interfaces with a Production System,* Behaviour and Information Tech., Vol. 14, No. 1, 1995, pp. 41–55.

[6] Eisenstein, J., Vanderdonckt, J., and Puerta, A., *Applying Model - Based Techniques to the Development of UIs for Mobile Computers,* in Proc. of ACM Conf. on Intelligent User Interfaces IUI'01 (Santa Fe, 14–17 January 2001), ACM Press, New York, 2001, pp. 69–76.

[7] Hartson, H.R., Siochi, A.C., and Hix, D., *The UAN: A User-oriented Representation for Direct Manipulation Interface Designs*, ACM Transactions on Information Systems, Vol. 8, No. 3, July 1990, pp. 181–203.

[8] He, X., *A Formal Definition of Hierarchical Predicate Transition Nets*, in Proc. of 17th Int. Conf. on Application and Theory of Petri Nets (Osaka, 24–28 June 1996), pp. 212–229.

[9] Janssen, C., *Dialogue Nets for the Description of Dialogue Flows in Graphical Interactive Systems*, in Proc. of Software-Ergonomie'93 (Bremen, 15–17 March 1993), Vol. 39, Teubner, Stuttgart, 1993.

[10] Nichols, J., Myers, B.A., Higgins, M., Hughes, J., Harris, T.K., Rosenfeld, R., and Pignol, M., *Generating Remote Control Interfaces for Complex Appliances*, in Proc. of ACM Symposium on User Interface Software and Technology UIST'02 (Paris, 27–30 October 2002), ACM Press, New York, 2002, pp. 161–170.

[11] Nunes, N.J., and Cunha, J.F., *WISDOM: A UML Based Architecture for Interactive Systems*, in Proc. of 7th Int. Eurographics Workshop on Design, Specification, Verification of Interactive Systems DSV-IS'2000 (Limerick, 5–6 June 2000), Lecture Notes in Computer Science, Vol. 1946, Springer-Verlag, Berlin, 2000, pp. 191–205.

[12] Paternò, F., and Santoro, C., *One Model, Many interfaces*, in Ch. Kolski, J. Vanderdonckt (eds.), "Computer-Aided Design of User Interfaces III", in Proc. 4th Int. Conf. on Computer-Aided Design of User Interfaces CADUI'2002 (Valenciennes, 15–17 May 2002), Kluwer Academics Pub., Dordrecht, 2002, pp. 143–154.

[13] Pinheiro da Silva, P., and Paton, N.W., *User Interface Modelling with UML*, in Proc. of the 10th European-Japanese Conf. on Information Modelling and Knowledge Representation (Saariselka, May 2000), IOS Press, Amsterdam, 2000.

[14] Plomp, J., and Mayora-Ibarra, O., *A Generic Widget Vocabulary for the Generation of Graphical and Speech Driven User Interfaces*, International Journal of Speech Technology, Vol. 5, No. 1, January 2002, pp. 39–47.

[15] Roché, P., d'Ausbourg, B., and Durrieu, G., *Deriving a Formal Model from UIL Description in order to Verify and Test its Behavior*, in D.J. Duke, A.R. Puerta (eds.), Proc. of 6th Int. Eurographics Workshop on Design, Specification, Verification of Interactive Systems DSV-IS'99 (Braga, 2–4 June 1999), Springer-Verlag, Vienna, 1999.

[16] Reenskaug, T., *Thing-Model-View-Editor: An Example from a planning system*, Xerox PARC Technical Note, May 1979, accessible at http://heim.ifi.uio.no/~trygver/1979/mvc-1/1979-05-MVC.pdf.

[17] Tuulari, E., and Ylisaukko-oja, A., *SoapBox: A Platform for Ubiquitous Computing Research and Applications*, in F. Mattern, M. Naghshineh (eds.), in Proc. of First Int. Conf. on Pervasive Computing (Zürich, August 2002), Lecture Notes in Computer Science, Vol. 2414, Springer-Verlag, Berlin, 2002, pp. 125–138.

[18] Szwillus, G., *Objektorientierte Dialogspezifikation mit ODSN*, in Proc. of Software-Ergonomie'97 (Dresden, March 1997), Berichte des German Chapter of the ACM, Teubner, Vol. 49, Stuttgart, 1997, pp. 285–295.

Chapter 3

TOWARDS A SYSTEM OF PATTERNS FOR THE DESIGN OF MULTIMODAL INTERFACES

Guillaume Godet-Bar, Sophie Dupuy-Chessa, and Laurence Nigay

CLIPS-IMAG-IIHM, BP 53, F-38041 Grenoble Cedex 9 (France)
E-Mail: {guillaume.godet, sophie.dupuy, laurence.nigay}@imag.fr –
Web: http://iihm.imag.fr/site/
Tel.: + 33 4 76 63 59 70 – Fax: +33 4 76 44 66 75

Abstract   Since R. Bolt's seminal "Put that there" demonstrator, more and more robust and innovative modalities can be used and empirical work on the usage of multiple modalities is now available for guiding the design of efficient and usable multimodal interfaces. This paper presents a system of patterns for capitalizing and formalizing this design knowledge about multimodal interfaces as patterns. Patterns are used for illustrating our system of patterns

Keywords: Patterns, Multimodal interaction

1.   INTRODUCTION

The first multimodal interface was designed more than twenty years ago, with the seminal demonstrator of Bolt [2] combining speech and gesture: the "Put that there" interaction paradigm. Since then modalities as well as the knowledge on how to design and develop multimodal interfaces have evolved. Indeed, in addition to more and more robust and innovative modalities such as the Phicons [10], conceptual and empirical work on the usage of multiple modalities [17] is now available for guiding the design of efficient and usable multimodal interfaces. However, most of the results on the design of multimodal interfaces have not yet been formalized or included in a tool for helping a non-specialist to design a multimodal interface.

Our work addresses the problem of capitalizing and formalizing good design practices so as to help designers to design efficient and usable multimodal interfaces. Towards this goal we have chosen a pattern-based approach

G. Calvary et al. (eds.), Computer-Aided Design of User Interfaces V, 27–40.

because patterns provide an efficient way for addressing the problem of capturing experiences related to recurring design problems. Their goal is to provide solutions general enough to be adapted to different contexts. Patterns have become a well-known way of organizing knowledge and experiences in various design domains.

In this paper, we focus on patterns for multimodality as a means of both facilitating multimodal interaction design and providing a basic tool support for multimodal interface design process. Following a review on interaction patterns in the Computer-Human Interaction domain in Section 2 we recall the criteria that a system of patterns should fulfill. We then present our system of patterns in Section 3 that we illustrate by considering two patterns.

2.   INTERFACE DESIGN: THE PATTERN APPROACH

2.1   Existing Systems of Patterns for Interaction Design

Several pattern catalogs are dedicated to interaction design. Most of them focus either on traditional WIMP interface design or on web application design. These patterns include those described in [3,6,20,21]. They are generally classified according to usability criteria. None of them take into account multimodal interaction design.

Complementary to those patterns dedicated to interaction design, we also found patterns for the software design of the interfaces. For example, Bass *et al.* [1] identify patterns that relate a usability scenario with an architectural mechanism. As opposed to Gamma *et al.* [8], Bass *et al.* [1] propose architectural mechanisms that do not provide a software design solution but rather a set of requirements that must be addressed for the software design. Their goal is "to couple specific aspects of usability and architecture". Again such software patterns do not cover the case of multimodal interaction.

Patterns described in [22] constitute the first approach to structured multimodal interface design and software design, defining patterns dedicated to output multimodality for presenting large information spaces. Several patterns for output multimodal interaction design are presented and linked with software patterns based on the PAC-Amodeus software architecture model [14]. Output multimodality has also been studied by Nesbitt [13]: a large set of multi-sensory interface guidelines (the MS-Guidelines) are defined as usability and design rules along with a process for multi-sensory output design (the MS-Process). Such results therefore do not follow the problem/solution structure usually found in patterns.

To sum up, in Human-Computer Interaction, several pattern catalogs have been proposed for interaction design or software design. The existing patterns for multimodality are dedicated to output multimodal interaction and none of the existing system of patterns addresses the design of multimodal interaction as a whole, i.e. input and output multimodal interaction.

For defining a system of patterns for multimodality, the first step consists of adopting a suitable pattern language. One approach could be to extend one of the existing systems of patterns to the case of multimodality. Nevertheless although the above-mentioned systems of patterns differ in terms of formalisms, none of them is adequate for our goal to encompass both multimodal design products and processes and to integrate the patterns in a tool:

- The patterns are presented in a narrative way [1,6], or are loosely structured [3,20,22]. It is therefore difficult to navigate in the set of patterns.
- The solutions provided by the patterns require a great deal of adaptation to be instantiated by the designer to her/his specific needs. Moreover the solutions provided by the patterns are not formal enough. Patterns are therefore difficult to formalize and consequently complex to integrate into tools.
- Patterns are often related by dependence links [3,6,20,21,22]. Those links participate in creating a hierarchal map of the patterns, and to a larger extent a pattern language, as explained by [18]. However there is no refinement to those dependencies, i.e. the links are not typed. This tends to create a loose pattern language structure, giving less opportunity for the designer to explore alternatives, refinements, etc.

As opposed to the above-mentioned studies, we aim at addressing the issue of interaction/software design for input and output multimodality, using a structured pattern-based approach.

2.2   System of Patterns for Multimodality: Criteria

Schmidt *et al.* [19] highlighted a set of criteria for useful and usable patterns. We have adapted them to our specific goals.

1. The patterns should attempt to federate good practices in multimodal interaction design. Such results in multimodality must be proven to increase the usability of the interactive system either by increasing the productivity, the comfort, the flexibility or the robustness of the interaction.
2. The patterns should be aimed at designers knowledgeable in traditional interface design, but lacking insight on multimodal interface design. The patterns should also provide sufficient knowledge concerning psycho-cognition, usability, and examples, so as to help make informed decisions about the design of a multimodal system.
3. The system of patterns should offer a set of process patterns that are independent of a specific development process. It should be possible to

integrate the system of patterns into any kind of development process, using both the links between patterns and the contextual information provided by each pattern.
4. Solutions should be presented in a formal way when possible, using well-established formalisms, in order to provide the designer with semi-automatic evaluation and code generation tools.

We show in the following section how our system of patterns fulfills the above criteria by first presenting the adopted P-Sigma formalism and then the system of patterns illustrated by two patterns.

3.   A SYSTEM OF PATTERNS FOR MULTIMODAL INTERACTION DESIGN

3.1   The P-Sigma Formalism

For describing our patterns, we apply the P-Sigma formalism [4]. P-Sigma is a structured approach for describing patterns that supports extensions in order to match specific domain-related needs. The P-Sigma formalism allows the description of three types of patterns: product, process and documentation. Process patterns address methodological problems and are usually used to break down development methods into smaller steps that in turn are also described using patterns. Product patterns answer design problems at any level of abstraction by proposing structuring models. For example, patterns by Gamma *et al.* [8] provide product patterns that describe solutions with the class diagrams. Additionally, the three types of P-Sigma patterns rely on the same problem/solution structure that is typically found in pattern description. Indeed, each pattern is divided into three major sections: Interface, Realization and Relations, which allow efficient internal navigation.

- The Interface section includes elements for selecting a pattern: a description of the designer's problem, of the context in which the pattern may be used (in terms of available products or patterns already applied), its strengths, how it classifies into the pattern language. Those aspects can be expressed either in textual form or more formally.
- The Realization section defines a solution as a product or a process, depending on the pattern type. This section can be described textually or formally by providing models, either by applying well-known formalisms or by using less defined descriptions. This section also describes application cases and consequences.
- The Relation section enables us to position a pattern with regard to other patterns within the system, thus allowing external navigation amongst the

patterns of the system. This section of the patterns also defines the overall organization of the patterns as a hierarchy. Internal and external navigation as well as the pattern hierarchy contribute to a definition of a system of patterns as defined in [18]. Additionally, P-Sigma supports relation typing. The relation types are: use, refinement, requirement and alternative. A "Use" relation acts as a pointer to another pattern referenced in the Realization section. A "Refinement" relation can be used to describe the current pattern as a specialization of another one. A "Requirement" relation shows which patterns need to be applied before using the current pattern. An "Alternative" relation points at patterns that respond to the same problem as the current one, but with different forces.

3.2   Our Patterns

In P-Sigma, patterns are classified explicitly in the "Classification" section of each pattern so as to facilitate the navigation amongst patterns: the classification (product/process/documentation) reflects the type of solution (methodology, models, etc.) that will be applied when using the pattern. We refine this classification to be specific to multimodal interfaces and we also add the position of the pattern according to the software design phases. Currently most of our patterns are dedicated to the specification phase. The elements of classification specific to our system of patterns are described below:

Product patterns are divided into:
- Interaction design patterns that describe the interaction between the user and the system, using specific models and constraints,
- Software design patterns akin to Gamma *et al.* [8] that describe the software design techniques supporting the interaction techniques.

Process patterns are separated into:
- Consistency patterns that aim at helping to check the overall consistency of the interactive system model,
- Methodological guidelines that fill in the procedural loopholes between the models either deduced from previous phases of development or extracted from product patterns.

Documentation patterns include:
- Patterns that provide sufficient theoretical basis for non-specialists to understand the taxonomies and models used within the product and process patterns. For example, one of the documentation patterns describes the ASUR formalism [7] that we apply to depict interaction design techniques in our product patterns.

- Patterns related to cognitive models of user's behavior, which are useful when designing multimodal interfaces. For example, one of the documentation patterns explains why the user tends to interact with a system in a multimodal way when manipulating a large number of concepts [17].

Our main contribution concerns the set of product and process patterns that we describe in the following sections.

3.2.1   Product patterns

As explained above, our system of patterns includes two types of product patterns, which target different stages in the design (i.e. interaction design and software design). Interaction design patterns define interaction techniques according to different criteria that include:

- **User tasks**. For example, if the user has to perform critical tasks, information feedback and redundancy (see the CARE properties [15]: Complementarity, Assignment, Redundancy and Equivalence as relationships between modalities) are predominant design issues. For example we have defined a pattern that enforces the redundancy property by giving indications on how to add redundant modalities for the accomplishment of a task.
- **Concept domains**. For example, what would be an efficient interaction technique if the user has to manipulate objects on a 2D representation, e.g., a map. Fig. 1 provides an effective solution to such a problem.

The identification of the above criteria usually results from the application of process patterns, as explained in the following section (Section 3.2.2 on process patterns). Additionally, the "Context" section in Fig. 1 describes which elements from the prior development phases will be necessary when applying the pattern.

Software patterns complement interaction patterns in that their solutions represent typical software design choices. However the developer is not limited to those and may provide her/his own software design. Indeed, the models and constraints detailed in the interaction design patterns offer sufficient information so as to allow the designer to build her/his own software architecture for supporting the designed interaction.

The distinction between interaction and software patterns is specified in the "Classification" section. For example, in Fig. 1, the "Classification" section defines that the pattern is a product interaction pattern, which can be used during the specification phase of a design process. Additionally, the section defines that the pattern addresses a task and/or a concept-specific problem.

Additionally, the formal solutions provided by both types of product patterns rely on a common formalism. Although still under study, its current form, which is based on the ASUR formalism [7], already constitutes a solid base for modeling user interaction and its software counterpart. The "Formal model" section of Fig. 1 includes an example of solution described using ASUR:

- It describes interaction in terms of abstract modalities (i.e. abstract devices and abstract interaction languages as defined in [14], thus representing only the main characteristics that need to be integrated into the future system. As described in Fig. 1, an efficient way to manipulate objects on a map would be speech inputs combined with pen inputs as well as graphical outputs.
- Physical proximity between devices is represented by a (=) relation. In Fig. 1, such a relation is specified between the pen input device and the graphical output device.

The "Textual solution" section provides additional constraints that, among others, specify the nature of the coupling between the devices. The use of text is due to the limits of our actual description formalism. These constraints will also be integrated into the "Formal model" section. The "Application cases" section gives examples of systems which feature a spatial input interaction. We also provide references to the sources that contributed in identifying the strengths of the interaction pattern. The "Application consequences" section of Fig. 1 provides additional support for implementing the fusion of the speech and pen-input modalities, as well as details on alternatives that the developer may wish to explore.

Identifier	Spatial input interaction
Classification	{Product ˆ Specification ˆ Task or concept-specific ˆ Interaction}
Context	{Projected task tree ˆ Domain concepts ˆ Deployment environment ˆ Usability prescriptions}
Problem	One needs to design a multimodal input interaction adapted to tasks that involve the expression of spatial information. Such information includes: selecting objects in a 2D space (e.g., a map), modifying spatial attributes of an object (including position, size and orientation), designating points in a 2D space (e.g., a specific place on a map).
Strength(s)	• Increases the compactness of input expressions (efficiency) • Brings person-system interaction closer to person-person interaction (naturalness) • Allows the user to change modalities when realizing the tasks in an opportunistic way (flexibility)
Formal strength(s)	{Efficiency ˆ Naturalness Flexibility}

Solution	
Formal model	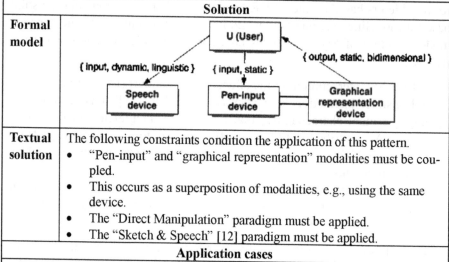
Textual solution	The following constraints condition the application of this pattern. • "Pen-input" and "graphical representation" modalities must be coupled. • This occurs as a superposition of modalities, e.g., using the same device. • The "Direct Manipulation" paradigm must be applied. • The "Sketch & Speech" [12] paradigm must be applied.
Application cases	
Geographic Information Systems (GIS) are good examples of interactive systems with spatial tasks. Users of such systems need to designate places, add objects on a map and move them around, give directions [16] or describe places and itineraries [12], using the "Sketch & Speech" paradigm.	
Application consequences	
• The designer may want to provide the user with a hand-free interaction model, using gesture recognition techniques that could allow her/him to directly interact on a large display with hands, as described in the pattern "Gesture-based input interaction". • The designer may want to use the pattern "Software aspects of spatial input interaction" for details on how to implement this interaction model.	

Figure 1. An example of an interaction product pattern

3.2.2 Process patterns

Our system pattern includes two types of process patterns: the consistency and methodological patterns. The consistency patterns define methods to check the consistency of the interaction model in term of usability. For instance, one process pattern focuses on how to evaluate whether the selected input modalities may be conflicting, e.g., when two parallel tasks use the same input modality, thus creating ambiguities in input expressions to be interpreted by the system. The methodological process patterns provide the designer with indications on how and when to apply product and process patterns. The methodological patterns also allow the designer to adopt different types of development: either fast-paced design or more thorough design processes. The former implies only domain concept analysis (e.g., which concept attributes will be manipulated and which modalities would fit these attributes) while the latter includes a detailed analysis of the user's tasks and therefore allows us to define more specific product patterns, such as the one described in the previous section.

Fig. 2 presents an extract of our root pattern, whose aim is to help the designer decide whether designing a multimodal input interface is appropriate. The elements of the "Classification" section help situate the pattern in the system and also characterize its generic aspect. In the "Context" section of Fig. 2, it is specified that the domain concepts, task tree and usability prescriptions have already been described in prior development phases. The "Formal steps" section's activity diagram states that an analysis should be conducted on the artifacts specified in the "Context" section, while the "Textual steps" section gives indications on this analysis, more specifically on what criteria need to be fulfilled and on how to evaluate whether a given system would benefit from the application of multimodal input interaction.

Let us apply the activity diagram of Fig. 2 to a simple example. For instance, we consider the case where the user's task analysis (as specified in the "Formal steps" section of Fig. 2) leads the designer to identify that the most often performed task is to view a small set of images (e.g., photographs) displayed on a grid. Based on the criteria described in the "Textual steps" section of Fig. 2, the designer may conclude that the user would probably not benefit from multimodal input interaction. We now consider the same system, but with a large set of images: The user may need to scale up or down, reorient and move images. By applying the criteria of the "Textual steps" section, the evaluation of the analysis clearly shows that, depending on the complexity of the tasks (e.g., the user might need to apply several transformations to a single image, scaling it down while rotating it), using a multimodal input interface might increase the efficiency and usability of the interactive system.

Identifier	Applicability of multimodal input interaction
Classification	{Process ˆ Specification ˆ Generic ˆ Consistency}
Context	{Task tree ˆ Domain concepts ˆ deployment environment ˆ usability prescriptions}
Problem	One needs to decide if, given a set of user's tasks, a multimodal input interface needs to be designed.
Strength(s)	• Increases command expression density (efficiency) • Allows the user to change modalities depending on the context of use (flexibility) • Allows the integration of equivalent modalities, selected by the user according to her/his needs (flexibility) • Increases input and output data confidence, when they are expressed by different modalities (robustness) • Allows the user to interact with the system in a more intuitive and/or natural way (naturalness)

Solution	
Formal steps	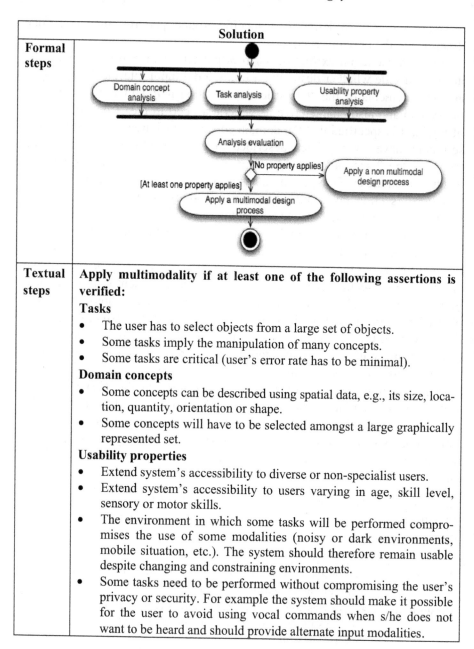
Textual steps	**Apply multimodality if at least one of the following assertions is verified:** **Tasks** • The user has to select objects from a large set of objects. • Some tasks imply the manipulation of many concepts. • Some tasks are critical (user's error rate has to be minimal). **Domain concepts** • Some concepts can be described using spatial data, e.g., its size, location, quantity, orientation or shape. • Some concepts will have to be selected amongst a large graphically represented set. **Usability properties** • Extend system's accessibility to diverse or non-specialist users. • Extend system's accessibility to users varying in age, skill level, sensory or motor skills. • The environment in which some tasks will be performed compromises the use of some modalities (noisy or dark environments, mobile situation, etc.). The system should therefore remain usable despite changing and constraining environments. • Some tasks need to be performed without compromising the user's privacy or security. For example the system should make it possible for the user to avoid using vocal commands when s/he does not want to be heard and should provide alternate input modalities.

Figure 2. An example of a methodological process pattern

3.2.3 Pattern relations

As stated in Section 3.1, the P-Sigma formalism allows us to link patterns in different ways (i.e. the four relation types: use, refinement, requirement and alternative). Fig. 3 shows examples of relations amongst our patterns. We can observe within this small sample of pattern relations that different levels within the hierarchy of patterns emerge: high-level process patterns, interaction design patterns and then software design patterns. Each level represents different phases within the design process of a system. Likewise, those relations clearly illustrate the external navigability between the patterns of our system.

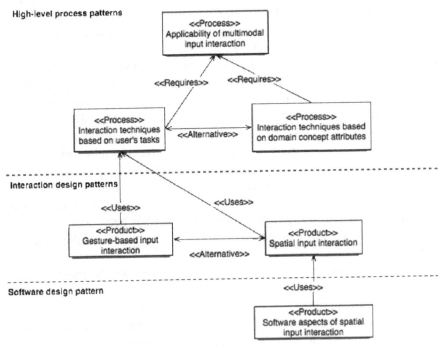

Figure 3. Sample of the relations between patterns

4.   CONCLUSION AND FURTHER WORK

We have introduced our system of patterns for the design of multimodal interfaces. As a starting point for our system of patterns, we have described 15 patterns: 5 product patterns, 5 process patterns and 5 documentation patterns using the P-Sigma formalism. These patterns are structured as follows:

- **5 product patterns:** Spatial input interaction, Software aspects of spatial input interaction, Gesture-based input interaction, Input modalities for critical tasks, Modality availability.
- **5 process patterns:** Applicability of multimodal interaction, Interaction techniques based on user's tasks, Interaction techniques based on domain

concept attributes, Input disambiguation, Consistency of input modalities for parallel user tasks.

- **5 documentation patterns**: Modality description, ASUR formalism, ASUR formalism for interaction techniques, ASUR formalism for software aspects of multimodal interaction, User behaviour and multimodal input.

Our current process and product patterns constitute the basis of a generic method for designing multimodal input interaction. Also, we have formalized some more specific interaction techniques. Our system of patterns fulfills the criteria described in Section 2.2:

- Our patterns implement good practices in multimodal interaction design since they are based on the domain literature (including the proceedings of the International Conference on Multimodal Interaction) and especially empirical results on usability such as the "ten myths of multimodal interaction" [16]. Based on the literature, we identified recurring practices that we formalized using the P-Sigma formalism. Novel multimodal interaction techniques may also be included into our system of patterns if they provide more efficient and usable techniques.

- Our system of patterns includes documentation on psycho-cognition, usability and insightful examples, similar to what has been done in [13], so as to help make informed decisions about the design of a multimodal system.

- Our patterns are independent from a particular development process. Nevertheless, they can be included in one. An ideal situation would be the development process described using P-Sigma, such as in [9].

- Solutions are presented in a formal way. Depending on the pattern type, different formalisms are used. Processes are represented using UML activity diagrams and products are described using a specific formalism.

While the format of the patterns is finalized and the way to formalize the patterns with the P-Sigma language is established, further work needs to be done on the models that are provided to the designer including their semantics and their description completeness as well as on the various classification schemes used for interaction design such as the user's task classification, and the modality classification.

Adopting the P-Sigma pattern language formalism enables us to employ our system of patterns using the AGAP tool [5]. AGAP supports the description of any pattern language as long as its grammar can be formally described. In addition, to support the specification of patterns, AGAP provides extraction of patterns to define browsable methodological guides. Once our patterns will be specified in AGAP, we will use its generation capability to obtain a website. This website can be used by designers on its own or can also be linked to other guides via HTML hyperlinks. For instance, we plan to integrate it within an extension to the development process described in [9], for post-WIMP interactive systems [11]. That will be a first attempt to validate our system of patterns.

However validating a system of patterns is a difficult task: since the very first system of patterns (e.g., [8]), validation has consisted of recognizing the patterns as a successful federation of accepted practices. Therefore our aim is to evaluate whether our system of patterns does indeed provide "logical" solutions for designing multimodal interfaces, and whether its use does help in creating usable and efficient multimodal systems. Towards this goal we plan to test our system of patterns on different case studies. Additionally, we envision conducting an experiment with masters students: for the design of an interactive system, we plan to provide one group of students with the entire system of patterns, instrumented with the AGAP tool, while another group will only rely on design methods as taught during the multimodal HCI course.

ACKNOWLEDGMENTS

This work is partly funded by the multidisciplinary French project VERBATIM and by the SIMILAR network of excellence, the European research task force creating human-machine interfaces similar to human-human communication of the European Sixth Framework Programme (FP6-2002-IST1-507609 - http://www.similar.cc).

REFERENCES

[1] Bass, L., John, B.E., Juristo, N., and Sanchez-Segura, M.-I., *Usability-supporting Architectural Patterns*, in Proc. of 26th Int. Conf. on Software Engineering ICSE'2004 (Edinburgh, 23–28 May 2004), IEEE Computer Society, Los Alamitos, 2004, pp. 716–717.

[2] Bolt, R.A., *"Put-that-there": Voice and Gesture at the Graphics Interface*, in Proc. of the 7th Annual ACM Conf. on Computer Graphics and Interactive Techniques SIGGRAPH'80 (Seattle, 14–18 July 1980), Computer Graphics, Vol. 14, No. 3, 1980, pp. 262–270.

[3] Borchers, J.O., *A Pattern Approach to Interaction Design*, in Proc. of ACM Conf. on Designing Interactive Systems: Processes, practices, methods, and techniques DIS'2000 (New York, 17–19 August 2000), ACM Press, New York, 2000, pp. 369–378.

[4] Conte, A., Fredj, M., Giraudin, J.-P., and Rieu, D., *P-Sigma: un formalisme pour une représentation unifiée de patrons*, in Proc. of XIXth Congrès Informatique des Organisations et Systèmes d'Information et de Décision INFORSID'2001 (Martigny, 24–27 May 2001), 2001, pp. 67–86.

[5] Conte, A., Fredj, M., Hassine, I., Giraudin, J.-P., and Rieu, D., *AGAP: an Environment to Design and Apply Patterns*, in Proc. of IEEE Int. Conf. on Systems, Man and Cybernetics SMC'2002 (Hammamet, 6–9 October 2002), Vol. 7, IEEE Computer Society Press, Los Alamitos, 2002, pp. 135–146.

[6] Coram, T., and Lee, J., *Experiences–A Pattern Language for User Interface Design*, in Proc. of Joint Pattern Languages of Programs Conferences PLOP'96 Workshop on Patterns (Allerton Park, 4–6 September 1996), 1996, accessible at http://www.maplefish.com/todd/papers/Experiences.html.

[7] Dubois, E., Nigay, L., and Troccaz, J., *Assessing Continuity and Compatibility in Augmented Reality Systems*, International Journal on Universal Access in the Information Society, Vol. 1, No. 4, 2002, pp. 263–273.

[8] Gamma, E., Helm, R., Johnson, R.E., and Vlissides, J., *Design Patterns: Elements of Reusable Object-Oriented Software*, Addison-Wesley, Reading, 1995.

[9] Hassine, I., Rieu, D., Bounaas, F., and Seghrnouchni, O., *Symphony: A Conceptual Model Based on Business Component*, in Proc. of IEEE Int. Conf. on Systems, Man and Cybernetics SMC'2002 (Hammamet, 6–9 October 2002), Vol. 3, IEEE Computer Society Press, Los Alamitos, 2002.

[10] Ishii, H., and Ullmer, B., *Tangible Bits: Towards Seamless Interfaces between People, Bits and Atoms*, in Proc. of ACM Conf. on Human Factors in Computing Systems CHI'97 (Atlanta, 22–27 March 1997), ACM Press, New York, 1997, pp. 234–241.

[11] Juras, D., Rieu, D., and Dupuy-Chessa, S., *Vers une méthode de développement pour les systèmes mixtes*, in Proc. of Journée NEPTUNE'2006 (Paris, 16 May 2006), to appear.

[12] Lee, B.-W., and Yeo, A.W., *Integrating Sketch and Speech Inputs Using Spatial Information*, in Proc. of 7th Int. Conf. on Multimodal Interfaces ICMI'2005 (Trento, 4–6 October 2005), ACM Press, New York, 2005, pp. 2–9.

[13] Nesbitt, K.V., *Multi-sensory Display of Abstract Data*, Ph.D. thesis, School of Information Technology, University of Sidney, Sydney, 2003.

[14] Nigay, L., and Coutaz, J., *A Generic Platform for Addressing the Multimodal Challenge*, in Proc. of the ACM Conf. on Human factors in computing systems CHI'95 (Denver, 7–11 May 2005), ACM Press, New York, 1995, pp. 98–105.

[15] Nigay, L., and Coutaz, J., *Multifeature Systems: The CARE Properties and their Impact on Software Design*, in J. Lee (ed.), Proc. of First Int. Workshop on Intelligence and Multimodality in Multimedia Interfaces: Research and Applications IMMI'1 (Edinborough, 1995), AAAI Press, 1995.

[16] Oviatt, S., *Ten Myths of Multimodal Interaction*, Communications of the ACM, Vol. 42 No. 11, 1999, pp. 74–81.

[17] Oviatt, S., Coulston, R., and Lunsford, R., *When do we Interact Multimodally? Cognitive Load and Multimodal Communication Patterns*, in Proc. of 6th ACM Int. Conf. on Multimodal Interfaces ICMI'2004 (State College, 13–15 October 2005), ACM Press, New York, 2004, pp. 129–136.

[18] Salingaros, N., *The Structure of Pattern Languages*, Architectural Research Quarterly, Vol. 4, 2000, pp. 149–161.

[19] Schmidt, D.C., Fayad, M., and Johnson, R.E., *Software patterns,* Communications of the ACM, Vol. 39, No. 10, October 1996, pp. 37–39.

[20] Tidwell, J., *Designing Interfaces*, O'Reilly & Associates, 2005.

[21] van Welie, M., and Trætteberg, H., *Interaction Patterns in User Interfaces*, in Proc. of 7th Pattern Languages of Programs Conference PLoP'2000 (Monticello, 13–16 August 2000), Washington University Technical Report No. wucs-00-29, accessible at http://jerry.cs.uiuc.edu/~plop/plop2k/proceedings/Welie/Welie.pdf.

[22] Vernier, F., *La multimodalité en sortie et son application à la visualisation de grandes quantités d'information*, Ph.D. thesis, University of Grenoble, Grenoble, 2001.

Chapter 4

DESIGN OPTIONS FOR MULTIMODAL WEB APPLICATIONS

Adrian Stanciulescu and Jean Vanderdonckt

School of Management (IAG), Université catholique de Louvain
Place des Doyens, 1 – B-1348 Louvain-la-Neuve (Belgium)
E-mail: {stanciulescu, vanderdonckt}@isys.ucl.ac.be – Web: http://www.isys.ucl.ac.be/bchi
Tel: +32 10 47{8349, 8525} – Fax: +32 10 478324

Abstract   The capabilities of multimodal applications running on the web are well de-lineated since they are mainly constrained by what their underlying standard mark up language offers, as opposed to hand-made multimodal applications. As the experience in developing such multimodal web applications is growing, the need arises to identify and define major design options of such application to pave the way to a structured development life cycle. This paper provides a design space of independent design options for multimodal web applications based on three types of modalities: graphical, vocal, tactile, and combined. On the one hand, these design options may provide designers with some explicit guidance on what to decide or not for their future user interface, while exploring various design alternatives. On the other hand, these design options have been implemented as graph transformations per-formed on a user interface model represented as a graph. Thanks to a transformation engine, it allows designers to play with the different values of each design option, to preview the results of the transformation, and to obtain the corresponding code on-demand

Keywords: Design decision, Design option, Design rationale, Design space, Multimodal user interface, User interface extensible mark up language, Web interface

1.   INTRODUCTION

The combination of design options forms a *design space*. The *design space analysis* [9] represents a significant effort to streamline and turn the open, ill-defined, and iterative [13] interface design process into a more formalized process structured around the notion of design option. A design space consists of a *n*-dimensional space where each dimension is denoted by

41

G. Calvary et al. (eds.), Computer-Aided Design of User Interfaces V, 41–56.
© *2007 Springer.*

a single design option. For this space to be orthogonal, all dimensions, and therefore all their associated design options, should be independent of each other. This does not mean that a dimension cannot be further decomposed into sub-dimensions. In this case, the design space becomes a snowflake model. Design options often involve various stakeholders representing different human populations with their own preferences and interests. Consequently, design decisions often result from a process where the various des-ign options are gathered, examined, and ranked until an agreement is reach among stakeholders. This decision process is intrinsically led by con-sensus since stakeholders' interests may diverge and by trade-off between multiple criteria, which are themselves potentially contradictory. Design options present several important advantages:

- When they are explicitly defined, they clarify the development process in a structured way in terms of options, thus requiring less design effort and striving for consistent results if similar values are assigned to design options in similar circumstances.
- Defining a design option facilitates its incorporating in the development life cycle as an abstraction which is covered by a software, perhaps rely-ing on a model-based approach. Ultimately, every piece of development should be reflected in a concept or notion which represents some abstrac-tion with respect to the code level as in a design option. Conversely, each design option should be defined clearly enough to drive the implementa-tion without requiring any further interpretation effort.

On the other hand, design options also suffer from some shortcomings: design options could be very numerous, even infinite in theory. But in prac-tice, it is impossible to consider a very large amount of design options bec-ause of several reasons: they are too complex or expensive to implement, they do not necessarily address users' needs and requirements, they are out-side the designer's scope of understanding, or imagination, or background, their decision is not always clear and when they are decided, they may vio-late some other usability principle or guideline.

We believe that it is important to define such a design space for multi-modal web applications because of several reasons: the languages in which they are implemented (e.g., XHTML, VoiceXML, X+V) restrict the amount of possible interfaces to obtain and directly set the CARE properties [6] to assignment and equivalence. In addition, the interaction styles [2] supported by these languages make them appropriate for certain types of applications (e.g., information systems), but totally inadequate for other types (e.g., air traffic control) [11]. Multimodal web applications typically combine three interaction modalities: graphical (e.g., a XHMTL web page in a web browser), vocal (e.g., a VoiceXML application through a multimodal web browser), tactile (e.g., a X+V application running on an interactive kiosk equipped with a tactile screen). These modalities could be combined together, thus multiplying the combination of design options which are specific to each modality and complexifying the entire design space. Sometimes, a design option which was estimated relevant for a particular modality (say the graphical channel) may become totally irrelevant when this modality is combined with another one (say with the vocal channel). The fusion/fission mechanism is generally the one implemented in the browser with which the multimodal web application is run. Independently of any implementation or tool support, having at hands a design space where a small, but significant, set of design options could be envisaged is a contribution which could be useful to any designer of a multimodal web application. This provision avoids designers to replicate the identification and definition of these design options, while leaving them free to consider other options or to overwrite existing ones.

After arguing for the importance of a design space for Multimodal Web User Interfaces (MWUIs) in this section, the next section reviews some efforts devoted to supporting the development life cycle of multimodal web applications and identifies the shortcomings to be addressed in this paper. Section 3 defines the so-called design space for MWUIs, channel by channel, in a way that is independent of any implementation. Section 4 explains one method for implementing this design space in MultiXML, an assembly of software modules for computer-aided design of MWUIs, based on UsiXML [10]. Section 5 exemplifies a case study developed according to the method supported by the MultiXML software. Section 6 summarizes the experience gained with this method and its associated software.

2.   RELATED WORK

MWUIs are usually materialized as off-line or on-line applications for which we would like to address the following requirements, which have been mostly used in isolation in the state of the art, but not simultaneously: usage of models to produce the multimodal interface (e.g., [2]), description of these models with a specification language (e.g., DISL [12], D3ML [5], MXML–www.macromedia.com, RIML [17], UIML–www.uiml.org), XISL [8]), explicit design options for multimodal dialog (e.g., CARE properties [6]), task-based design of multimodal applications [4]).

A representative example of a complete environment for producing several Multimodal Web Applications is MONA (Mobile multimOdal Next generation Applications – http://mona.ftw.at/index.html). It involves a presentation server for a wide range of mobile devices in wireless LAN and mobile phone networks that transforms a single MWUI specification into a graphical or multimodal UI and adapts it dynamically for diverse devices: WAP-phones, Symbian-based smart phones or PocketPC and PDAs. The application design process is based on use cases that allow to refine and validate the design of multimodal UI prototypes for each device. These prototypes are further submitted to a heuristic evaluation performed by evaluators with design experience.

ICARE [3] is a component-based approach for the design and development of multimodal interfaces, composed of elementary components that describe pure modalities. The composition components are: complementarity, redundancy, and equivalence. An editor was designed in order to allow users to graphically assemble components. It offers the possibility of automatic generation of the code supporting the CARE properties [6] in the fusion.

Teresa [4] automatically generates X+V MWUIs in the following way: the initial task model for the envisioned system is transformed into a system task model that is specific for a multimodal platform, that is in turn transformed into an abstract user interface, a concrete user interface, and the code of a final user interface. Designing such UIs implies the use of several par-ameters, with their associated values, but the authors do not identify a coherent and explicit set of design options that can be combined in a design space. In Teresa, all transformations are hard coded, embedded, and unique, whereas they are made explicit, thus visible and modifiable, executable and multiple in the present approach. All transformations implemented according to the expected design decision are written in the same specification language as for the models (i.e., UsiXML) and could then be modified.

MOST (Multimodal Output Specification Platform) [13] is a platform that allows the design of output multimodal systems (i.e., graphical, vocal and tactile modalities) based on a cycle model composed of three steps (i.e., analysis, specification and simulation). After identifying the necessary output interaction components (i.e., mode, modality and medium) in the analysis step, the specification step formalizes the results of the previous step based on a series of attributes and criteria assigned to each specific output interaction component. Further, depending on the current state of the interaction context, a behavioral model allows the identification of the most suitable output form that can be used in order to present each interaction component. The behavioral model is expressed under the form of a set of election rules that produces an adapted multimodal presentation.

The above described models and tools do not respond to all the requirements identified at the beginning of this section regarding an integrated set of design options for multimodal web applications. In the following sections we present our work that combines the design option requirements presented above into one single, systematic approach.

3.   DESIGN OPTIONS FOR MULTIMODAL WEB USER INTERFACES

3.1   Design Options for Graphical UIs

Design options for graphical user interface are described according to the five parameters specified in Fig. 1.

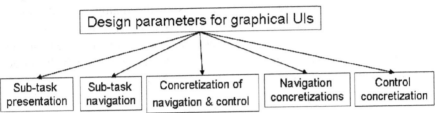

Figure 1. Design parameters for graphical user interfaces

Sub-task presentation parameter specifies the appearance of each sub-task in the final user interface. The possible values are illustrated in Fig. 2. The presentation of each sub-task can be either separated or combined. Separated presentation identifies the situation when each sub-task is represented in different containers (e.g., different windows), while the combined value identifies the situation when all sub-tasks are presented in the same container. In the last case, three different types of combinations are possible:

- *One by one*: only one sub-task is presented at a time (e.g., in combined box, in tabbed dialog box, in float window).
- *Many at once*: multiple sub-tasks are presented in the same time (e.g., in float window).
- *All in one*: all sub-tasks are presented in the same time (e.g., in areas with separators, in group boxes, in bulleted list, in numbered list).

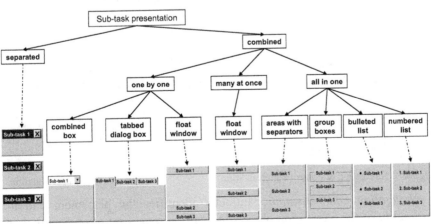

Figure 2. Final representation of sub-task presentation parameters

Sub-task navigation parameter is an extension of the notation introduced in [16]. It specifies the way in which the dialog control is transferred from one sub-task to another. Fig. 3 illustrates the two possible values: *sequential* or *asynchronous*. The sequential navigation, also called synchronous, restricts the transfer of the dialog control only to a neighbor presented sub-task. The asynchronous type offers more flexibility in transferring the dialog control by eliminating the above restriction and allowing a transfer from any source sub-task to any target sub-task. Passing the dialog control from a source sub-task to a target sub-task implies two simultaneous actions: *deactivate* the container in which the source sub-task is executed (represented here with a yellow bulb) and *activate* of the container in which the target sub-task is executed (represented here with a red bulb).

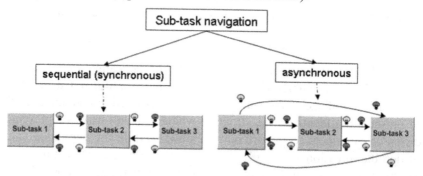

Figure 3. Types of navigation between sub-tasks

Concretization of navigation and control is a parameter specifying whether the navigation and control are ensured by the same object. In Fig. 4, the *separated* value identifies the situation in which the control and the navigation between the sub-tasks are attached to different objects/logically grouped set of objects. When the same object ensures simultaneously both the navigation and control, the parameter is set to *combined*.

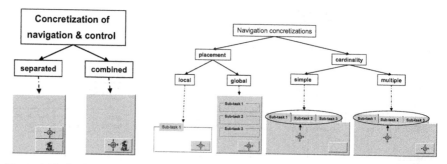

Figure 4. Navigation & control concretization   Figure 5. Types of navigation

Navigation concretization parameter identifies the placement and the cardinality of the navigation objects/logically grouped set of objects that ensure the navigation. Fig. 5 illustrates the different values of this parameter.

There are two *types of placement* for the navigation objects are: *local placement* (specifies the existence of a navigation object attached to each presented sub-task) or *global placement* (a general object ensuring the whole navigation between the sub-tasks). The cardinality specifies the number of objects hosting the navigation. We have identified two *types of cardinality*: *simple* (the navigation is ensured by a single object like an OK button or a single logically grouped set of objects like the (NEXT, PREVIOUS) group of buttons) or *multiple* (the navigation is ensured simultaneously by two or more objects/logically grouped set of objects like a group of tab items in a tabbed dialog box and the (NEXT, PREVIOUS) group of buttons).

Control concretization parameter identifies the placement and cardinality of the control objects. Fig. 6 illustrates the different values of this parameter. There are two *types of placement* of the control objects: *local placement* (specifies the existence of a control object attached to each presented sub-task) or *global placement* (a general object controlling each sub-task). The cardinality specifies the number of objects that assure the control. We have identified two *types of cardinality*: *simple* (the navigation is ensured by a single object like an OK button or single logically grouped set of objects like a group of tab items in a tabbed dialog box) or *multiple* (the navigation is ensured simultaneously by two or more objects/logically grouped set of objects like a group of tab items in a tabbed dialog box and the (NEXT, PREVIOUS) group of buttons).

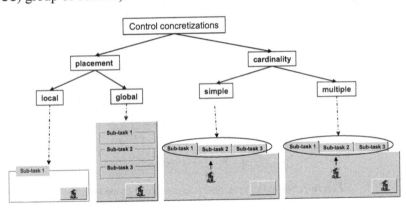

Figure 6. Types of control concretization

In order to exemplify (Fig. 7) the design options for graphical UIs, we present a car rental system that is sub-divided into three sub-tasks: providing Personal information, selecting the Car's features and filling in the Payment information. The following values for the design options were set to:

- Sub-task presentation: is *combined all in one*. All sub-tasks are combined into their corresponding group box in the same window.
- Sub-task navigation: is *sequential*. Once the user has fulfilled the information required in the group box corresponding to sub-task 1, he can

activate only the sub-task 2 (see navigation *a*). From the group box associated to sub-task 2, he has two possibilities: returning to the sub-task 1
group box (see navigation *c*) or continue with the sub-task 3 (see navigation *b*). From sub-task 3 group box the user can activate only the sub-task
2 group box (see navigation *d*).

- Concretization of navigation and control: is *combined*. The (OK, CANCEL)
  logically grouped set of buttons assures in the same time the navigation
  between the group boxes as well as the control.
- Navigation concretization: is of type *global placement* because for all the
  sub-tasks there is a general logically grouped set of objects that assures
  the navigation (i.e., (OK, CANCEL) buttons) and has a *simple cardinality*
  because the navigation is assured by only one logically grouped set of
  objects (i.e., (OK, CANCEL) buttons).
- Control concretization: is of type *global placement* because for all the
  sub-tasks there is a general logically grouped set of objects that assures
  the control (i.e., (OK, CANCEL) buttons) and has a *simple cardinality*
  because the control is assured by only one logically grouped set of objects
  (i.e., (OK, CANCEL) buttons).

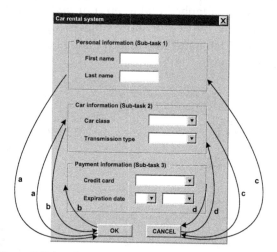

Figure 7. Sub-tasks presented into combined group boxes

3.2   Design Options for Multimodal UIs

In order to facilitate the development process of multimodal web applications we introduce a set of design options based on four parameters illustrated in Fig. 8. These design options take into consideration the ergonomic
criteria for the evaluation of human-computer interfaces presented in [1] and
adapt them for the development of MWUIs. For simplification, we consider
here only two interaction modalities, graphical and vocal, but other modalities can be taken into account later.

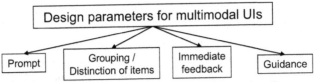

Figure 8. Design parameters for multimodal user interfaces

For each parameter, we provide a definition and we identify a list of possible values (e.g., corresponding to each value we refer to [14]), associating in the same time the corresponding CARE properties described in [6]:

1. *Prompting*: refers to the interaction channels available in order to lead the users to take specific actions whether it should be a data entry or other tasks. The possible values are: *Vocal* (assignment), *Graphical* (assignment), *Multimodal* (complementarity or redundancy).

2. *Grouping/Distinction of Items*: concerns the organization of information items in relation to one another. This criterion takes into account the topology (location) and some structural characteristics (format) in order to indicate the relationships between the various items rendered, to indicate whether or not they belong to a given class, or else to indicate differences between classes. This is further decomposed into:

   a. *Input*: any information input from the user to the system. The possible values are: *Vocal* (assignment), *Graphical* (assignment), *Multimodal* (equivalence or complementarity).

   b. *Output*: any information output from the system to the user. The possible values are: *Vocal* (assignment), *Graphical* (assignment), *Multimodal* (complementarity or redundancy).

3. *Immediate feedback*: concerns system responses to users' actions. These actions may be simple keyed entries or more complex actions such as stacked commands. In all cases computer responses must be provided, they should be fast, with appropriate and consistent timing for any transaction. The possible values are: *Vocal* (assignment), *Graphical* (assignment), *Multimodal* (complementarity or redundancy).

4. *Guidance*: refers to the means available to advise, orient, inform, instruct, and guide the users throughout their interactions with a computer (e.g., messages, alarms, labels). We offer a more precise level of detail corresponding to the two possible types of interaction considered in this section (i.e., graphical and vocal). Thus, the graphical guidance is sub-divided into *textual* and *iconic*, while the guidance for the vocal interaction can be *acoustic* or based on *speech*. The guidance parameter is further subdivided into two parameters:

   a. *Guidance for input*: any guidance offered to the user in order to guide him with the input. The possible values are: *Textual* (assignment), *Iconic* (assignment), *Acoustic* (assignment), *Speech* (assignment), or *Multimodal* (by combining the previous values in a complementary or redundant way).

b. *Guidance for immediate feedback*: any guidance offered to the user in order to guide him with the feedback. *Textual* (assignment), *Iconic* (assignment), *Acoustic* (assignment), *Speech* (assignment), or *Multimodal* (by combining the previous values in complementary or redundancy).

We exemplify the above design parameters with a possible design decision for a multimodal text entry where the user has to input his/her name (Fig. 9). Then value of the prompt parameter is multimodal as the system indicates in a redundant way the task to fulfill by using two modalities: graphical modality (the label Name) and vocal modality used by the systems to invite the user to input his name (1). The guidance for input is of type iconic and is composed of two elements (the microphone icon and the keyboard icon) indicating the available interaction modalities. User's input is of type multimodal as it can be provided in an equivalent manner by employing either the graphical modality (the user is typing his name in the text entry), either the vocal modality (the user is uttering his name using the microphone (2)).The guidance for feedback is of type iconic and is ensured by the loudspeaker icon, indicating the vocal feedback. The feedback of the system to the user's input is of type multimodal as it is expressed by means off two redundant modalities: graphical (the user's typing result) and vocal (the system is uttering the result of the input recognition (3)). Table 1 summarizes a subset of all possible combinations of input and feedback design options for a text entry (for the complete table, we refer to [14]). Only the graphical and vocal interactions are taken into account, but the proposition might be extended to other types of interaction.

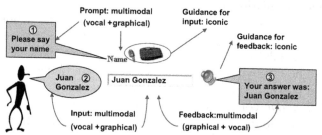

Figure 9. A possible design decision for a multimodal text entry

Table 1. Possible combinations of design options for input and feedback for text entry

Parameters	Rendering
Input= graphical Feedback= graphical and vocal	
Input= vocal Feedback= graphical and vocal	
Input= graphical or vocal Feedback= graphical	
Input= graphical or vocal Feedback= graphical and vocal	

4. TRANSFORMATIONS BASED ON DESIGN OPTIONS

One of the main advantages of the design space introduced in the previous section is given by the fact that each design option composing the space is independent of any existent method or tool, thus being useful for any developer of multimodal UIs. Under these circumstances, it would be useful to provide an explicit support of the introduced design options. In order to support the development of computer-aided design of MWUIs based on the design options defined in Section 3, we consider MultiXML, an assembly of five software modules. By using MultiXML, we want to address a reduced set of concerns by limiting the amount of design options, thus making the design space more manageable or tractable [7]. Our support involves a transformational approach detailed in [15]. The method consists of a forward engineering process composed of four transformational steps illustrated in Fig. 10. To ensure these steps, transformations are encoded as graph transformations performed on UsiXML models expressed in their graph equivalent. All design options correspond to a class in UsiXML meta-model (e.g., the *tabbed dialog box* value corresponds to *tabbedDialogBox* class, the *feedback* parameter corresponds to the vocalFeedback class).

The five software modules of *MultiXML* tool are (Fig. 10): *IdealXML* tool, *TransformiXML* tool, *GrafiXML* tool (automatically generates graphical UIs (XHTML) from the UsiXML Concrete UI Model), *CFB* (*Communication Flow Builder*) *Generator* tool (generates XML code corresponding to the Communication Flow Builder file format by applying XSL Transformations over the Concrete Vocal UI specification of UsiXML), *XHTML+Voice Generator* tool (generates XHTML+Voice code by applying XSL Transformation over the Vocal and Graphical specification of the CUI Model).

In the last step the final graphical UIs are obtained by interpreting the code of the previous step. In order to obtain the vocal and multimodal final UIs, we are not generating the code using our own tools, but we are employing a series of IBM tools. Thus, *NetFront*, the multimodal browser, interprets the XHTML+Voice code and generates the final multimodal UI. For the vocal UI, we are recovering the result produced by CFB Generator tool into *IBM Communication Flow Builder* graphical editor integrated in *IBM Voice Toolkit*. The produced VoiceXML specification is interpreted with *IBM VoiceXML browser*.

5. CASE STUDY

In order to exemplify the design options, an on-line car rental system is described. The main task is decomposed into three basic sub-tasks: determine rental preferences (the user has to select a series of information, such

as rental location, expected car features, type of insurance), determine car
(the system will launch the search of available cars depending on the preferences established in the previous sub-task. Based on the search results, the
user will select the car), provide payment information (the user provides a set
of personal information, such as name and card details; then the system
checks the validity of the card and finally, the user confirms the payment).

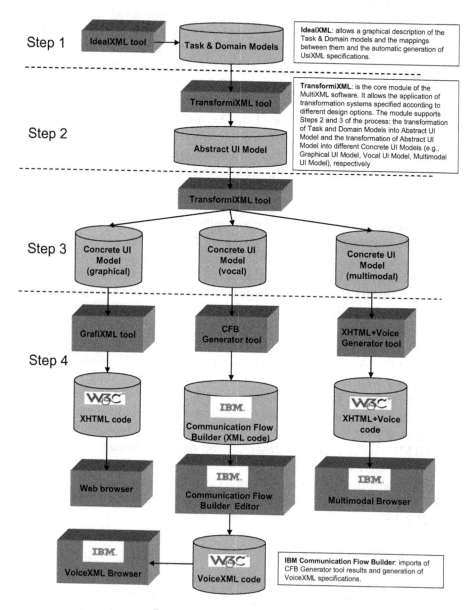

Figure 10. MultiXML software modules

Based on the design options detailed in Section 3.1 we will illustrate, using different graph transformation rules, their applicability for the car rental system. For final graphical UI (Fig. 14) we consider the parameter *sub-task presentation* and *sub-task navigation*. Fig. 11 illustrates the transformation rule applied in order to generate a UI where the presentation of the sub-tasks is *separated in three windows*. For each top-level abstract container, a graphical container of type window is created.

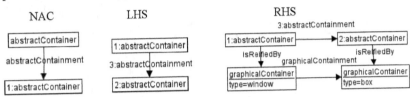

Figure 11. Create a window for each top-level abstract container

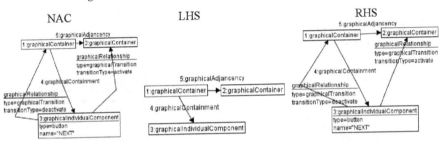

Figure 12. Endow the NEXT button with graphicalTransition features

The navigation between the windows is of type *sequential* and is concretized in a *global placement* of the (NEXT,PREV) buttons identified on each window. The navigation is assured only by these two logically grouped objects, so the value of the cardinality parameter is *simple*. The transformation rule that endows the NEXT button (similar for PREV button) with *activate* and *deactivate* features is presented in Fig. 12. For a multimodal UI (Fig. 15), a transformation rule generates a multimodal text input that accepts the name of the credit card holder (Fig. 13). We consider the following design options values: *prompt* (graphical and vocal), *input* (graphical or vocal), *feedback* (graphical and vocal), *guidance for input* (iconic with microphone and keyboard icons), or *guidance for feedback* (iconic with speaker icon).

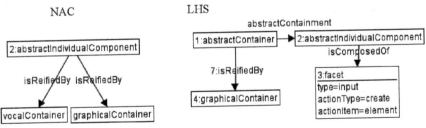

RHS

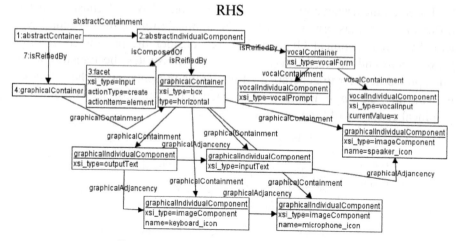

Figure 13. Generation of multimodal text input

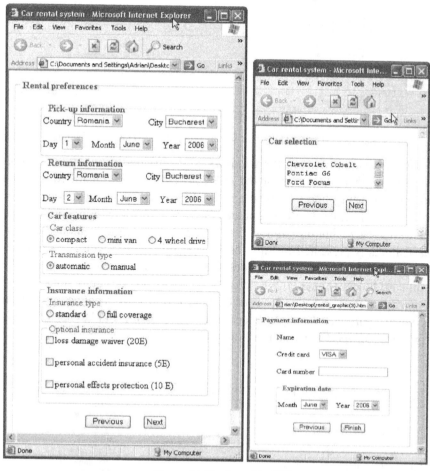

Figure 14. Final graphical UI

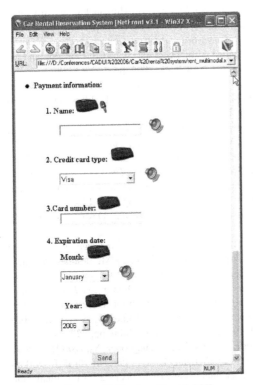

Figure 15. Final multimodal UI

6. CONCLUSION

We defined a design space for multimodal web applications based on design options having multiple design values which can be reused by any designer and developer in similar circumstances. Independently of that, these design options have been translated into parameters that govern design rules encoded as graph grammars. Each graph grammar is composed of graph transformation rules so as to perform each rule on the graph corresponding to the UsiXML specifications of the UI under study. A transformation engine could then process these rules. Multi-XML introduces a method for structuring the development of multimodal web applications whose results are recuperated in IBM Multimodal Toolkit, from which final UIs can be generated for graphical (XHTML) and multimodal (X+V) applications. For vocal UIs (VoiceXML), the recuperation is ensured by importing a CUI in the Communication Flow Builder format supported by IBM Voice Toolkit.

ACKNOWLEDGEMENTS

We gratefully acknowledge the support of the SIMILAR network of excellence (http://www. similar.cc), the European research task force creating human-machine interfaces similar to human-human communication of the European Sixth Framework Programme (FP6-2002-IST1-507609). This research is fully funded by SIMILAR. We also thank Didier Magotteaux and Vincent Wauters for the IBM Belgium grant received with the IBM Multimodal Toolkit™, Software Modeler™, and WebSphere™, with which this research is conducted.

REFERENCES

[1] Bastien, Ch., and Scapin, D.L., *Evaluating a User Interface with Ergonomic Criteria,* International Journal of Human-Computer Interaction, Vol. 7, 1995, pp. 105–121.

[2] Beaudouin-Lafon, M., *Instrumental Interaction: An Interaction Model for Designing*

Post-WIMP User Interfaces, in Proc. of the ACM Conf. on Human Factors in Comp. Systems CHI'2000 (The Hague, 1–6 April 2000), ACM Press, 2000, pp. 446–453.

[3]   Bouchet, J., and Nigay, L., *ICARE: A Component-Based Approach for the Design and Development of Multimodal Interfaces*, in Extended Abstracts of the ACM Conf. on Human Factors in Comp. Systems CHI'2004, ACM Press, New York, 2004, pp. 1325–1328.

[4]   Berti, S., and Paternò, F., *Migratory MultiModal Interfaces in MultiDevice Environments*, in Proc. of 7th Int. Conf. on Multimodal Interfaces ICMI'2005 (Trento, 4–6 October 2005), ACM Press, New York, 2005, pp. 92–99.

[5]   Chevassus, N., *SNOW – Service for Nomadic Workers, A Framework for Authoring and Exmpliting Multimodal Documentation*, W3C Seminar, 21 June 2005.

[6]   Coutaz, J., Nigay, L., Salber, D., Blandford, A., May, J., and Young, R., *Four Easy Pieces for Assessing the Usability of Multimodal Interaction: The CARE properties*, in Proc. of 5th IFIP TC 13 Int. Conf. on Human-Computer Interaction INTERACT'95 (Lillehammer, 27–29 June 1995), Chapman & Hall, London, 1995, pp. 115–120.

[7]   Hoover, S., and Rinderle, J., *Models and Abstractions in Design*, Design Studies, Vol. 12, No. 4, October, 1991.

[8]   Katsurada, K., Nakamura, Y., Yamada, H., and Nitta, T., *XISL: A Language for Describing Multimodal Interaction Scenarios*, in Proc. of 5th Int. Conf. on Multimodal Interfaces ICMI'2003 (Vancouver, 5–7 Nov. 2003), ACM Press, New York, 2003, pp. 281–284.

[9]   Limbourg, Q., Vanderdonckt, J., and Souchon, N., *The Task-Dialog and Task-Presentation Mapping Problem: Some Preliminary Results*, in Proc. of 7th Int. Workshop on Design, Specification, Verification of Int. Systems DSV-IS'2000 (Limerick, 5–6 June 2000), Lecture Notes in Comp. Science, Vol. 1946, Springer-Verlag, 2000, pp. 227–246.

[10] Limbourg, Q., Vanderdonckt, J., Michotte, B., Bouillon, L., and Lopez, V., *UsiXML: a Language Supporting Multi-Path Development of User Interfaces*, in Proc. of 9th IFIP Working Conf. on Engineering for Human-Computer Interaction EHCI-DSVIS'2004 (Hamburg, July 11–13, 2004), LNCS, Vol. 3425, Springer-Verlag, Berlin, 2005, pp. 200–220.

[11] MacLean, A., Young, R., and Moran, T., *Design Rationale: The Argument Behind the Artifact*, in Proc. of the Conf. on Human Aspects in Comp. Systems CHI'89, pp. 247–252.

[12] Mueller, W., Schaefer, R., and Bleul, S., *Interactive Multimodal User Interfaces for Mobile Devices*, in Proc. of 37th Hawaii Int. Conf. on System Sciences HICSS'2004, Track 9 (Hawai, 5–8 January 2004), IEEE Comp. Society Press, Los Alamitos, 2004.

[13] Rousseau, C., Bellik, Y., and Vernier, F., *Multimodal Output Specification/simulation Platform*, in Proc. of 7th Int. Conf. on Multimodal Interfaces ICMI'2005 (Trento, 4–6 October 2005), ACM Press, New York, 2005, pp. 84–91.

[14] Stanciulescu, A., *A Transformational Approach for Developing Multimodal Web User Interfaces*, DEA thesis, Univ. catholique de Louvain, Louvain-la-Neuve, 12 June 2006.

[15] Stanciulescu, A., Limbourg, Q., Vanderdonckt, J., Michotte, B., and Montero, F., *A Transformational Approach for Multimodal Web User Interfaces based on UsiXML*, in Proc. of 7th Int. Conf. on Multimodal Interfaces ICMI'2005 (Trento, 4–6 October 2005), ACM Press, New York, 2005, pp. 259–266.

[16] Vanderdonckt, J., Limbourg, Q., and Florins, M., *Deriving the Navigational Structure of a User Interface*, in Proc. of 9th IFIP TC 13 Int. Conf. on Human-Computer Interaction INTERACT'2003 (Zurich, 1–5 Sept. 2003), IOS Press, Amsterdam, 2003, pp.455–462.

[17] Ziegert, T., Lauff, M., and Heuser, L., *Device Independent Web Applications- The Author Once - Display Everywhere Approach*, in N. Koch, P. Fraternali, M. Wirsing (eds.), Proc. of 4th Int. Conf. on Web Engineering ICWE'04 (Munich, 28–30 July 2004), Lecture Notes in Computer Science, Vol. 3140, Springer-Verlag, Berlin, 2004, pp. 244–255.

Chapter 5

A GENERIC APPROACH FOR PEN-BASED USER INTERFACE DEVELOPMENT

Sébastien Macé and Éric Anquetil

IRISA - INSA, Campus Universitaire de Beaulieu, F-35042 Rennes Cedex (France)
E-Mail: {sebastien.mace, eric.anquetil}@irisa.fr – Web: www.irisa.fr/imadoc
Tel.: + 33 2 99 84 {7546, 7238} – Fax: +33 2 99 84 71 71

Abstract   Pen-based interaction is an intuitive way to realize hand drawn structured documents, but few applications take advantage of it. Indeed, the interpretation of the user hand drawn strokes in the context of document is a complex problem. In this paper, we propose a new generic approach to develop such systems based on three independent components. The first one is a set of graphical and editing functions adapted to pen interaction. The second one is a rule-based formalism that models structured document composition and the corresponding interpretation process. The last one is a hand drawn stroke analyzer that is able to interpret strokes progressively, directly while the user is drawing. We highlight in particular the human-computer interaction induced from this progressive interpretation process. Thanks to this generic approach, three pen-based system prototypes have already been developed, for musical score editing, for graph editing, and for UML class diagram editing

Keywords: Hand drawn symbol recognition, Pen-based interaction, Structured document interpretation, User interface development

1.   INTRODUCTION

As pen-based interfaces are in wide expansion, there is a lack of applications taking advantage of this intuitive and ergonomic way to draw structured documents, such as electronic figures, plans, musical scores, tables, diagrams, *etc.* Fig. 1 presents an example of a tablet PC with such an interaction: the user composes musical scores in a traditional way by drawing the symbols on the screen: the use of a pen and a touch screen reproduces the "pen-paper" metaphor. This editing application is an example of system developed thanks to the methodology we present in this paper.

G. Calvary et al. (eds.), Computer-Aided Design of User Interfaces V, 57–70.

Figure 1. Example of a tablet PC with a pen-based interface

This paper deals with the interpretation of hand drawn structured documents. The interpretation of the user *strokes*, which are the sequences of points captured by the touch screen between a pen-down and a pen-up, is called *on-line interpretation*. It is a complex problem of pattern recognition due to the variability of handwritten styles. This interpretation process is even more complicated in the context of structured document analysis, because these documents are constituted of many elements of various natures. Moreover, the same stroke can have different meanings according to the context in which it has been drawn, which must therefore be taken into account [1,9]. This justifies why few pen-based systems have been developed.

On-line interpretation can be either *lazy* [12] (*i.e.* occurring only when explicitly requested by the user) or *eager* [5] (*i.e.* occurring directly while the user is drawing). Lazy interpretation offers the advantage of not intruding into the user's creative phase during the document realization. Nevertheless, once the recognition process applied at once on all of his strokes, he has to examine the entire document to look for possible incorrect interpretations. Besides, it turns out that lazy systems are so far not robust enough and make too many mistakes, which reduces their usability. We believe that lazy recognition is a promising approach to offer unconstrained understanding of ink, but the difficulties to design automatic parsing coupled with a robust hand drawn shape recognition system show that it remains an open problem. Eager interpretation constitutes then another way to consider on-line structured document analysis. Every time the user draws a stroke, the system interprets it immediately; it then has to deal with documents in the process of realization and to make a decision as quickly as possible so that the user does not have to wait to continue his drawing. Moreover, it is possible to exploit the interaction with the user, who is aware of the system answers, and can then validate or reject them progressively. We believe that eager interpretation is a pertinent compromise, since these systems are often more robust and more efficient than lazy ones, which makes them more usable. The work we present in this paper is in the eager interpretation context: it aims at defining generic methods to interpret structured documents.

Most of the existing systems are adapted to analyze the elements of documents from a given domain, *i.e.* to only one kind of documents, and can not be generalized [3,6,13]. Some of them are based on existing libraries for pen-based applications [8], which aim at proposing generic graphical and pen-based editing functions in order to facilitate the development of such systems and to only focus on the analysis of the user strokes. Our goal is to go even further by formalizing the composition conventions of a document in order to eagerly analyze its elements. The idea is that from one pen-based system to another the needs are often the same, such as driving the recognition process and taking the relative positions of the document elements and the interaction with the user into account. Few generic systems for eager interpretation have been proposed [1,7,10]. Hammond *et al.* [7] present a hierarchical shape description language and Alvarado *et al.* [1] propose an approach based on the coupling of this formalism with dynamically constructed Bayesian networks, but, on the one hand, they only use local context of the shape to interpret it, and, on the other hand, they do not enable the representation of too complex elements such as symbols, drawings or text, which can be recognized by powerful hand drawn shape recognizers based, for instance, on neural networks [4] or hidden Markov models. We previously [9] presented an approach to design systems to eagerly interpret hand drawn structured documents using classical shape recognizers. We introduced a formalism which is an extension of the classical context-free grammars. In this paper, we present an evolution of this formalism, which makes it possible to model the interpretation of complex symbols in a more intuitive way. It is also easier to manipulate.

The main contribution of this paper is the specification of a system exploiting a generic approach to design pen-based systems with an eager interpretation process. To interpret the document elements, we use a *global vision* of these elements, to take their document context into account, and a *local vision*, to recognize their shape. This knowledge is coupled with the use of hand drawn shape recognition systems. We propose a formalism, based on *interpretation rules*, that allows modeling the composition conventions of documents of various domains, and by extension how the system must interpret the document elements and interact with the user. As this method is generic, it can be applied to various natures of structured documents, such as musical scores, graphs and class diagrams in the Unified Modeling Language (UML), which are the domains we present more in detail in this paper.

The following section introduces the architecture of the system we developed. Section 3 presents one particular component, a flexible rule-based formalism to model structured document interpretation. Section 4 highlights the consequence of the eager interpretation process on the human-computer interaction. Then, Section 5 describes three existing pen-based systems based on the approach. Finally, we summarize our future work.

2.   ARCHITECTURE OF THE SYSTEM

The system is illustrated by Fig. 2. It is based on a framework constituted of three main components:

1. A set of graphical functions and pen-based editing functions (1), which are domain-independent and can be exploited by any pen-based system.
2. A formalism to model on-line structured document interpretation (2), which defines document composition conventions in a given domain.
3. A hand drawn stroke analyzer (3), which exploits the knowledge modeled by a formalism to eagerly interpret handwritten structured documents.

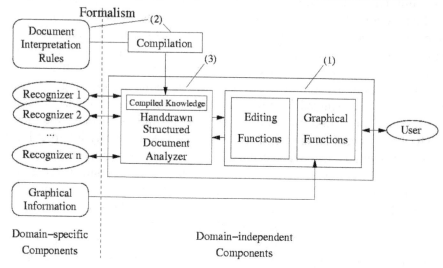

Figure 2. Architecture of the system

The graphical and pen-based editing functions and the hand drawn stroke analyzer are *domain-independent components*; they do not need to be rewritten for each pen-based system. The development of such systems with our approach only requires realizing the *domain-specific components*: writing the interpretation rules (embedded under a compiled form), designing the necessary hand drawn shape recognizers (which can be reused from one system to another) and specifying the graphical information (for instance visual aspect of the elements). The components of our system are well separated and can be modified and adapted independently of the others. We present these components more in detail in the next subsections.

2.1   A Set of Graphical and Pen-based Editing Functions

The first component of the system deals with the user interface and the display of the document. It exploits graphical information, such as images of the symbols, which are externalized because they are domain-dependent. This component also deals with pen-based interaction and editing: the user can draw *graphical gestures*, which are interpreted by the system as editing actions. He can for instance select graphical elements, move them to another part of the document, delete them, *etc.* It is also possible to undo the last element, zoom in or out, save or load a document. This offers an alternative to classical menu and button-based interaction. Some graphical gestures are presented in Subsection 4.4. Although we have developed our own graphical and pen-based editing functions, this component is not the main contribution of this paper, because other authors have proposed similar functions [8]. The originality of our work consists in the two following components.

2.2   A Formalism to Express Interpretation Rules

The second component of the system is a rule-based formalism that describes the structured document interpretation process. It models composition conventions (for instance chronological information: which element can or must be drawn before another one). It also represents physical information, such as the spatial structure of the document. Finally, it drives the use of hand drawn shape recognizers depending on the structural context of a stroke, *i.e.* depending on its location in relation to the other elements of the document, which is its main originality. The document interpretation rules for one domain are externalized from the system: they are easily modifiable, independently of the other components. It just needs to be transformed by the generic compiler of the system. This formalism is presented more in detail in Section 3.

2.3   A Stroke Analyzer

The last component of the system is a hand drawn stroke analyzer which is able to deal with documents during their realization. Thanks to the use of the knowledge modeled by the formalism, it analyzes the strokes directly while the user is drawing. It is able to call the pertinent hand drawn shape recognizers (for example, handwritten character recognizer, geometrical shape recognizer, *etc.*) depending on the structural context of the stroke, and then update the document contexts that will help recognizing the following strokes. This parser is generic which means it does not need to be adapted to each specific domain. In the next section, we focus on the modeling of the interpretation process and the exploitation of this knowledge by the analyzer.

3.   A FORMALISM FOR EAGER INTERPRETATION OF STRUCTURED DOCUMENT

We have seen that our approach is based on a formalism which aims at defining an eager interpretation of the elements of structured documents from various domains. The goal is then to propose a formalism which is as generic as possible. We previously [9] defined the four basic concepts that are, to our opinion, associated to the modeling of on-line structured document composition and eager interpretation: the *management of the chronological information*, the *representation of the document spatial structure*, the *driving of the recognition process by the document context analysis* and the *pen-based human-computer interaction*. The formalism we propose takes all these concepts into account. It is composed of interpretation rules which define the generating of the element which name they bear. Several rules can have the same name, which makes it possible to model different ways to compose the same element.

A rule takes a set of elements as parameters and returns a new one that can replace them; the parameters are the components of the new element. A parameter can be either a stroke or an already interpreted element, which allows a hierarchical shape description. The structure of a rule is composed of four blocks: a document context verification (*DCV*) block, a shape context verification (*SCV*) block, a shape recognition (*SR*) block and a document context creation (*DCC*) block, as follows:

> **SymbolName** *(Parameter 1 , ... , Parameter n)*
> *Document Context Verification (DCV) block.*
> *Shape Context Verification (SCV) block.*
> *Shape Recognition (SR) block.*
> *Document Context Creation (DCC) block.*

DCV and *DCC* blocks enable a global vision of the document in order to define in which document contexts an element must be situated. A *DCV* block specifies the document structural contexts that have to be verified by a rule to try it, whereas a *DCC* block indicates the contexts that are created due to the recognition of an element. The *SCV* and *SR* blocks enable, given a document context, a local vision of the element to recognize; it distributes the recognition process among local constraints, formalized in the *SCV* block, and recognizers, formalized in the *SR* block.

The analysis mechanism is illustrated by Fig. 3. When a new stroke, or more generally a new element, is analyzed, the goal is to find the rule to apply. Only the rules dealing with the new element are activated. An existing document is constituted, on the one hand, of the already interpreted elements it contains and, on the other hand, of its structural contexts. This knowledge defines a global vision of the document which must be exploited to analyze new elements. The analyzer identifies the elements of the document that can be associated to the new element to form a more complex one; this is modeled by the parameters of the rule. The analyzer also verifies the coherence of the new element with the structural context in which it is located; this is modeled by the *DCV* block. Only the rules that satisfy both of these criteria remain.

Once the analyzer has verified the coherence of the new element with the document context thanks to a global vision, it exploits a local vision to analyze the structural arrangement of the parameters of the rule; this is modeled by the *SCV* block. Then, if these constraints are satisfied, a shape recognition system can be used on the parameters of the rule in order to identify the corresponding new element. The rules that satisfy these blocks remain: they are applicable.

As more than one rule can be applicable, a *Rule Selection* component is exploited to make a decision. We give more information about the decision making process in Subsection 4.2.

Once interpreted, the new element is created; it replaces the parameters of the applied rule in the document. New structural contexts are created to help interpreting the following elements; this is modeled by the *DCC* block. Once a rule is applied, the current iteration of the analysis process is finished. Then, a new iteration begins, trying to eventually apply a rule on the new element, and so on until stability; as a consequence, a stroke can imply a sequence of transformations. If no rule can be applied on a stroke (*i.e.* if the first iteration does not succeed), it is rejected and disappears from the editing window.

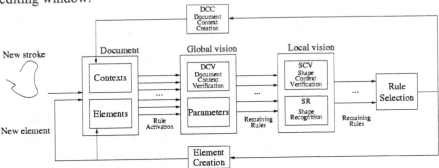

Figure 3. Illustration of the analysis mechanism

To illustrate the definition of each block, we present hereafter two examples of interpretation rules in the context of musical score editing: interpretation of quarter-notes (*QuarterNote* interpretation rule) and interpretation of sharps (*Sharp* interpretation rule). We also present on Fig. 4 some illustrations of these interpretation rules.

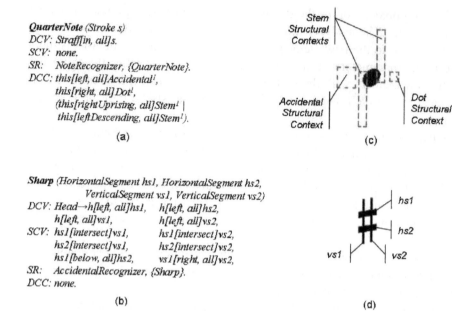

Figure 4. Two interpretation rules for quarter-note (a) and sharp (b) interpretation, the corresponding created document structural contexts (c) and sharp constituting elements (d)

A quarter-note is typically drawn with only one stroke, whereas a sharp is drawn with four of them, each one being a horizontal or a vertical segment. This explains the parameters of the corresponding interpretation rules. Moreover, as it can be seen in the rules, a block can be empty.

To understand the formalism, we present the syntax of each of the interpretation rule blocks. The *DCV block* is a list of structural contexts which have to be verified by the parameters of a rule; its syntax is as follows:

$$DCV: R_1[position_1, part_1]A_1, \dots, R_n[position_n, part_n]A_n.$$

This means that at the relative position *position$_i$* (e.g. on the left, above, etc.) of a reference R_i, the part *part$_i$* (e.g. one, all, the first, the highest points, etc.) of an analyzed element A_i exists. R_i and A_i do not have to be part of the parameters. For example, in the **Sharp** interpretation rule presented in Fig. 4, the *DCV* block specifies that the four segments constituting a sharp must be on the left of a same head. A saving operator, denoted "→", is used to associate an element to an identifier and reuse it afterwards.

The SCV block models local constraints about the rule parameters to recognize an element constituted of several sub-elements: it enables to identify which part of the new element corresponds to each parameter. The syntax is the same as in the *DCV* block, but this time A and B must be parameters. By default, there is no constraint on the drawing ordering of the elements; if necessary, a chronological operator can be used.

For example, in the **Sharp** interpretation rule, the *SCV* block specifies a spatial arrangement that the segments constituting a sharp must satisfy. In this rule, the structural context *[intersect]* is an alias for the context *[in,one]*. Fig. 4d illustrates how these elements must be located in relation to each other for the block to succeed. These local constraints are not necessarily enough to totally interpret the element. So we may want to exploit classical shape recognizers: this can be done with the *SR* block.

The SR block corresponds to the call to a hand drawn shape recognizer. As a consequence, only the relevant recognizers are invoked, depending on the context of an element. It is essential to increase the interpretation process robustness, since the less symbols a recognizer must interpret, the more efficient and the more reliable it is. The *SR* block syntax is:

SR: SymbolFamily, {AcceptedAnswers}.

This expression means that the recognizer of *SymbolFamily* is called, with the rule parameters as input; if its answer is included in *AcceptedAnswers* the recognition process is a success. Actually, the order of the elements presented to the recognizer is the order of the parameters in the declaration of the rule; so it is always the same. As a result, its work is relieved, because it has to interpret the elements always in the same order.

For example, in the **Sharp** interpretation rule, we exploit an accidental recognizer with as input the four segments the rule takes as parameters, always in this sequence; the expected recognizer answer is a sharp.

The DCC block is a list of document structural contexts that are created due to the recognition of an element. Its syntax is:

$$DCC: R_1[position_1, part_1]A_1^{m\_1}, \ldots, R_n[position_n, part_n]A_n^{m\_n}$$

This means that at the relative position *position_i* of an element R_i, the part *part_i* of an element A_i can exist. The current element is referenced as *"this"*. The number m_i indicates how many A_i can exist in this context and is * if there is no limit. For example, in the **QuarterNote** interpretation rule, the *DCC* block specifies that once a quarter-note exists, it is possible to draw an accidental on its left, a durational dot on its right, and a stem, either uprising or descending. A disjunction operator, denoted "|", is used to define an alternative between structural contexts.

Fig. 4c illustrates the position of the corresponding structural contexts in relation to the quarter-note. More information about the visualization of these structural contexts is given in Section 4.1. Aliases are defined in the **QuarterNote** and **Sharp** interpretation rules to specify that a head can be a whole-note, a half-note or a quarter-note, and that an accidental can be a flat, a sharp or a natural.

4.   EAGER INTERPRETATION AND USER INTERACTION

In this section, we present the human-computer interaction in the context of eager interpretation. The concepts are independent of the domain of the documents that are being drawn. We first explicit how the system can guide the user in the drawing process. Then, we highlight the importance of the interaction with the user within the interpretation process.

4.1   Drawing the Document Elements

To help the user to have reference marks, rectangles giving an indication of the document structural contexts that are generated in *DCC* blocks can be displayed. Whereas these rectangles are strict, structural contexts are not: the user does not have to draw the elements exactly in the rectangles. To lighten the editing area, a context is visible provided that it is not already filled with an element. Thus, as presented in Fig. 5, it is possible to switch between a *novice mode*, in which empty contexts are visible, and an *expert mode*, in which they are not. It is also possible to show only the boxes that are in the context of the pen, once again to lighten the editing area: it corresponds to a *contextual mode*. The experience shows that this last mode seems to be the most user-friendly, since it permits to only focus on potentially interesting structural contexts according to the pen position. We would like to note that the quarter-note structural contexts correspond to those declared in the *QuarterNote* interpretation rule defined in Fig. 4.

Figure 5. Three different visualization modes

4.2   Dealing with Ambiguities

Naturally, more than one rule can sometimes be applied at the same time to an element. In order to limit this, we firstly determine to which degree an element satisfies the contexts that are defined in an interpretation rule; it is then possible to make a decision between rules if the difference between their degrees is significant. We secondly use hand drawn shape recognizers with reject options, *i.e.* which do not give an answer unless their confidence is high enough [11]. The advantage is to filter possible interpretations, and to prevent from displaying an answer with a high probability of being wrong.

4.3   User Validation

As the recognition process is eager, the result of the analysis is displayed directly as the user is drawing. We can then exploit the human-computer interaction and integrate the user in the interpretation process, because he can validate or reject its results. Thus, if after the display of the answer, the user goes on with the drawing of the document, he implicitly accepts and validates it; on the contrary, if he does not agree, he can delete the new element with a deletion gesture and so explicitly reject it. The main consequence of this process is that it is not necessary for the analyzer to question a decision made beforehand, since it has been validated by the user. We believe that it is pertinent because it could be perturbing for the user to see the interpretation of an element changing after drawing another one. It is a major advantage of the eager interpretation process on the lazy one: indeed, the user limits the ambiguities, which makes the system more robust and more efficient, increasing its usability. The system is also faster, since it just has to interpret the last stroke.

4.4   Editing the Document

Every element of the document has a selection dot, which is a small red anchor point. In order to select an element, the user has to surround its selection dot. This way, it is not necessary to draw a stroke as big as the element. Several elements can be selected or other elements can be added to the selection in the same manner. When an element is selected, the document elements associated to it are also selected; they actually correspond to the elements which have been drawn in the different contexts it has created. Once selected, elements can be moved to another part of the document by pointing to one of them and moving the pen to the appropriate place. It is also possible to move an element directly by pointing at its selection dot and moving the pen (by drag and drop). To delete an element, the user can, for instance, move it outside the editing window. These mechanisms are illustrated by Fig. 6: on the left, the user draws a stroke around the selection dot of a half-note; in the middle, the note and its associated elements (*i.e.* its natural and its stem) are selected, and the user moves them with the pen; on the right, he raises the pen to drop the elements.

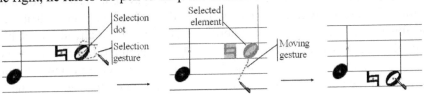

Figure 6. Selection and moving mechanisms: example on a half-note

5.   SYSTEMS DEVELOPED THANKS TO THE METHODOGY

Thanks to the generic method we present in this paper, we have already been able to develop three different prototypes, one for musical score editing, one for graph editing and one for UML class diagram editing. As mentioned in Section 2, we just needed to:

- Write the interpretation rules.
- Use existing recognition systems [2] or design new ones, here based on Radial Basis Function Networks (RBFN) classifiers [4,11].
- Specify the graphical aspects of the document elements.

We first developed a pen-based musical score editor, which is an evolution of the prototype introduced previously [9], with more available symbols. Fig. 1 presents this system, whereas Fig. 5 and Fig. 6 explicit some of the available symbols. Fig. 7 presents two screenshots of the system, on the left the interpreted symbols, and on the right the corresponding hand drawn strokes. In order to design a user-friendly system adapted to musician needs, it is developed in collaboration with professional musicians from the MIAC (Music and Image: Analysis and Creation) of the Rennes 2 University.

Figure 7. Screenshots of the pen-based musical score editor prototype

The second domain we developed is graph editing: it allows the drawing of nodes, represented by geometrical shapes (*e.g.* rectangles, triangles or circles), and of arcs. Each of these components can be drawn with one or several strokes. We then focused on one particular graph-based domain, which is UML class diagram editing. The corresponding system makes it possible to draw classes, represented by rectangles, and to write their name, attributes and functions. Aggregation and inheritance are one of the already available symbols. Fig. 8 shows screenshots of the graph editor (above) and of the UML class diagram editor (below). As in Fig. 7, interpreted symbols are on the left and the corresponding handwritten strokes are on the right. We have not yet associated our UML class diagram editor with a handwritten character recognizer: strokes corresponding to handwritten text are detected but not yet interpreted and so not changed. We would like to emphasize that although it is not visible on Fig. 7 and Fig. 8, the interpretation is eager: the user strokes are replaced with their corresponding symbols progressively.

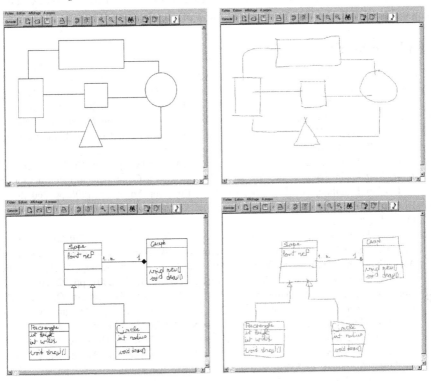

Figure 8. Screenshots of the graph and UML class diagram editor prototypes

6.   CONCLUSION

In this paper, we presented a new approach for pen-based system development. The aim is to interpret hand drawn structured documents eagerly, *i.e.* directly while the user is drawing. We emphasized the separation of the various components of our system, which can therefore be modified independently from the others. In particular, a major component is a rule-based formalism that models structured document interpretation; it can be adapted to various domains, such as musical score editing, graph editing and UML class diagram editing. We exploit human-computer interaction to integrate the user in the recognition process: he can validate or reject an answer given by the system. Future work will aim at defining test protocols at a larger scale in order to go on with improving the interaction with the user. The aim is to design pen-based systems that are as usable and intuitive as possible. In order to validate the genericity, we believe that the next challenge will be to apply this methodology to a new complex domain: electric diagram editing.

ACKNOWLEDGEMENT

Authors would like to thank Guy Lorette from the IMADOC team and Bruno Bossis from the MIAC team for their contribution to this work. This project benefits from the financial support of the Brittany Region.

REFERENCES

[1]   Alvarado, C., and Davis, R., *SketchREAD: A Multi-domain Sketch Recognition Engine*, in Proc. of the 17th Annual ACM Symposium on User Interface Software and Technology UIST'2004 (Santa Fe, 24–27 October 2004), ACM Press, New York, 2004, pp. 23–32.

[2]   Anquetil, É., and Bouchereau, H., *Integration of an On-line Handwriting Recognition System in a Smart Phone Device*, in Proc. of the 16th IAPR Int. Conf. on Pattern Recognition ICPR'2002 (Quebec, 11–15 August 2002), 2002, pp. 192–195.

[3]   Anstice, J., Bell, T., Cockburn, A., and Setchell, M., *The Design of a Pen-Based Musical Input System*, in Proc. of the 6th Australian Conf. on Computer-Human Interaction OZCHI'96 (Hamilton, 24–27 November 1996), IEEE Comp. Soc. Press, 1996, pp. 260–267.

[4]   Bishop, C.M., *Neural Networks for Pattern Recognition*, Oxford University Press, Oxford, 1995.

[5]   Blostein, D., Lank, A., Rose, A., and Zanibbi, R., *User Interfaces for On-Line Diagram Recognition*, in Proc. of the 4th IAPR International Workshop on Graphics Recognition Algorithms and Applications GREC'2001 (Kingston, 7–8 September 2001), Lecture Notes in Computer Science, Vol. 2390, Springer-Verlag, Berlin, 2001, pp. 92–103.

[6]   Donaldson, A.F., and Williamson, A., *Pen-based Input of UML Activity Diagrams for Business Process Modelling*, in Proc. of the 1st Workshop on Improving and Assessing Pen-Based Input Techniques (Edinburgh, 5 September 2005), 2005, pp. 31–38.

[7]   Hammond, T., and Davis, R., *LADDER: A Language to Describe Drawing, Display, and Editing in Sketch Recognition*, in Proc. of the 18th Int. J. Conf. on Artificial Intelligence IJCAI'03 (Acapulco, 9–15 Aug. 2003), M. Kaufmann, San Francisco, 2003, pp. 461–467.

[8]   Lank, E.H., *A Retargetable Framework for Interactive Diagram Recognition*, in Proc. of the 7th Int. Conf. on Document Analysis and Recognition ICDAR'2003 (Edinburgh, August 2003), IEEE Computer Society Press, Los Alamitos, 2003, pp. 185–189.

[9]   Macé, S., Anquetil, É., and Coüasnon, B., *A Generic Method to Design Pen-Based Systems for Structured Document Composition: Development of a Musical Score Editor*, in Proc. of the 1st Workshop on Improving and Assessing Pen-Based Input Techniques (Edinburgh, 5 September 2005), 2005, pp. 15–22.

[10] Mas, J., Sanchez, G., and Llados, J., *An Incremental Parser to Recognize Diagram Symbols and Gestures represented by Adjacency Grammars*, in Proc. of the 6th IAPR Int. Workshop on Graphics Recognition GREC'2005, 2005, pp. 229–237.

[11] Mouchère, H., Anquetil, É., and Ragot, N., *Étude et gestion des types de rejet pour l'optimisation de classifieurs*, in Actes du 15ème Congrès francophone Reconnaissance des Formes et Intelligence Artificielle RFIA'2006 (Tours, January 2006), 2006.

[12] Nakagawa, M., Machii, K., Kato, N., and Souya, T., *Lazy Recognition as a Principle of Pen Interfaces*, in Proc. of the ACM Conf. Companion on Human Factors in Computing Systems INTERCHI'93 (Amsterdam, 24–28 April 1993), ACM Press, 1993, pp. 89–90.

[13] Toyozumi, K., Mori, K., Suenaga, Y., and Suzuki, T., *A System for Real-time Recognition of Handwritten Mathematical Formulas*, in Proc. of the 6th Int. Conf. on Document Analysis and Recognition ICDAR'2001 (Seattle, 10–13 September 2001), pp. 1059–1064.

Chapter 6

PARTICIPATORY DESIGN MEETS MIXED REALITY DESIGN MODELS
Implementation Based on a Formal Instrumentation of an Informal Design Approach

Emmanuel Dubois[1], Guillaume Gauffre[1], Cédric Bach[2], and Pascal Salembier[3]

[1]*Computing Science Research Institute of Toulouse (IRIT) – LIIHS*
118 route de Narbonne – F-31062 Toulouse Cedex 9 (France)
E-mail: {Emmanuel.Dubois;Gauffre}@irit.fr – Web: http://liihs.irit.fr/{dubois, gauffre}
Tel.: +33 5 61 55 74 05 – Fax: +33 5 61 55 88 98
[2]*Metapages, 29, grande rue Nazareth, F-31000 Toulouse (France)*
E-mail: cedric@metapages.com
Tel. : +33 5 61 52 56 21 – Fax : +33 5 61 52 54 97
[3]*Computing Science Research Institute of Toulouse (IRIT) – GRIC*
118 route de Narbonne – F-31062 Toulouse Cedex 9 (France)
E-mail: p.salembier@tiscali.fr
Tel.: +33 5 61 55 74 05

Abstract   Participatory design and model-based approaches are two major HCI design approaches. Traditionally opposed, the first ones promote user's creativity while the second ones support a more systematic approach of the design space. In Mixed Reality domain, combining these two aspects is especially crucial in order to support the design and to help the users to take into account the wide variety of emerging technologies. We introduce in this paper a solution to bring these two approaches together. In addition, we illustrate how the outcomes of this combination of formal and informal approaches serve as input for the implementation of the designed solution

Keywords: Design method, Focus group, Mixed reality, Software modeling, User interface modeling

1.   INTRODUCTION

As illustrated in [4], the term Mixed System has been defined to denote every kind of interactive systems that combine physical and digital worlds: Tangible User Interface (TUI), Augmented Reality, Mixed Reality, etc.

G. Calvary et al. (eds.), Computer-Aided Design of User Interfaces V, 71–84.
© 2007 Springer.

Initially confined to specific applications domains such as military, surgery and maintenance, more and more areas try to adopt this interaction mode: games, museum, education, tourism, etc. In order to face this rapid expansion, prototype based development approaches are no longer sufficient and there is a crucial need to define design processes.

Traditionally, two forms of design approaches can be met in the field of interactive systems. The first one focuses on human-centered approaches and aims at understanding user's needs in a comprehensive way. The second one is more formal: it aims at structuring the design space and generating conceptual models in order to facilitate the transition between the requirements analysis phase and the development phase. It mainly relates to software engineering considerations.

Most of the time, these two approaches are used in a concurrent manner, by experts of different domains. In this paper we present an articulation of an informal design method, the focus-group, with a formal design model for mixed systems, the ASUR model. We show how the formal representation tool can be used as a resource for guiding the management of the Focus-Group, and how the outcome is directly reusable and beneficial in further steps of a development process. Before motivating the need for participatory design and modeling to connect rather than to compete, we introduce existing design approaches of both domains.

1.1　　Participatory Design Approaches

Participatory Design approach is a particular form of the more generic Human-Centered Design process. The main originality of Participatory Design is that it relies on an iterative approach. In addition, it relies on methods that involve the participation of users and are only a subset of the usability methods supporting Human-Centered Design [11]. Concretely, a splitting of the Participatory Design process into four steps, as described in [15], has been adopted and each of these steps is instrumented with several methods: 1) "user's observations" in situ with probes or in vitro within labs, 2) "ideas generations" with brainstorming or focus group, 3) "prototyping" with paper, video or mock-ups, and 4) "Evaluation" with user's test or speak aloud.

In comparison with other kinds of human-centered design approaches, Participatory Design specificity is the systematic use of creativity methods involving the active participation of users to generate ideas. The purpose is to identify interactive solutions for specific needs. Creativity methods are considered as informal or projective techniques for revealing in concrete terms the shapes of future systems whished by users. In other terms, these methods have a strong revealing power and constitute a way to generate useful and usable shapes of prototypes, good candidates to resolve requirements defined during observations steps of the Participatory Design. Creativity methods are sometimes considered to have an uncertain efficiency, to introduce biases and also to be used for marketing rather than scientific motives. But in our opinion one questionable assumption of Participatory Design is that it holds the point of view that detailed descriptions of the interactive components of the system as superfluous in the early phases of the design process [2]. The data collected during the creativity phases are then represented in a non formal way (for example, drawings, collages, role lists).

1.2   Mixed System Design Approaches

To overcome the development of multiple prototypes that mainly aims at proving the technical feasibility to combine new technologies, different design approaches has been explored in the field of mixed systems.

A first set of approaches aims at supporting the development of mixed systems. Many ready-to-use libraries have been developed to support specific features such as video-based marker tracking [12], gesture recognition [9], physical data sensing, etc. More than a support to the integration of various technologies, development environments have been worked out. For instance, AMIRE [7] and DWARF [1] offer a set of predefined components, patterns and connection facilities. Extension mechanisms are not clearly stated but such approaches provide the developers with a structured view of the application. Finally, additional works aim at connecting these advances with existing standardized tools (Director), or format (SVG).

A second set of approaches aims at better understanding and exploring the mixed system design solution. The TAC paradigm [17] and MCPrd [10] architecture describe the elements required in Tangible User Interfaces: one focuses on the description of physical elements while the second focuses on the software structure of TUI. Trevisan [18], ASUR [4] and IRVO [3] are models that aim at supporting the exploration of the design space: they are based on the identification of models, entities, characteristics and tools relevant for a mixed system. Finally, more recent works try to link mixed systems design and implementation steps. [3,16] propose two different solutions to project scenarios on two different software architecture models while [8] combine Petri Nets and DWARF components. High level of abstraction, component based approach, tools interoperability and implementation support constitutes the main challenges of today's mixed system design.

1.3   Interlacing rather than Comparing

As mentioned above, Participatory Design approaches support the elicitation of user's requirements by promoting the role and implication of the user during the design process: user may express a requirement, take part in the elaboration of design solution, test the solutions and identify new requirements. So far, existing Mixed Systems Design approaches adopts either a model-based approach or a technology-driven development process. In order to take advantage of the user's participation and outcomes of design models and software tools, combining these two approaches seems unavoidable.

But between these somewhat informal expression and collect of user's requirements and, the traditionally more formal design and implementation considerations, translation happens to be quite hectic. One of the main reason that creativity and user's implication are greatly supported by informal approaches, while formal HCI models and tools constitute a solid framework to describe and constrain design solutions. Combining the rigor of formal approaches with the revealing capabilities of informal approaches constitutes a critical challenge.

Participative simulation [6] has been proven to install and inject dynamism into a creative space. Similarly, in the context of mixed system design, we assume that joining together formal and informal approaches will facilitate the identification of design solutions and widened the exploration area. Indeed, in order to generate many ideas, informal techniques, such as the focus-group, usually rely on a set of points of interest to consider during the ideas elicitation phase [14]. But in the context of mixed systems, the points of interest must cover all the specificities and richness of possible mixed interaction situations. In order to systematize the exploration of all the different aspects, a formal approach will be helpful to present these multiple characteristics. In addition, there is a growing up interest in mixed systems, but every design participant is still not very familiar with them. Providing the participants with a formal presentation of what a mixed system is, will help them identify new possibilities, thus widening the explored design space.

We thus introduce in Section 3 the instrumentation of a focus-group method with the ASUR model, a formal description of user's interaction with a mixed system briefly presented in Section 2. Section 4 illustrates how to build upon the results of this articulation in further steps of the development process. Finally, we present some perspectives that constitute research avenues directly related to the work presented here.

2. ASUR MODEL

ASUR supports the description of the physical and digital entities that make up a mixed system and the boundaries among them. ASUR components include adapters (A_{in}, A_{out}) bridging the gap between both digital and physical worlds, digital tools (S_{tool}) or concepts (S_{info}, S_{obj}), user (U) and physical tools (R_{tool}) or task objects (R_{obj}). Arrows are used to express the physical and informational boundaries among the components. On the basis of previous works in the domain, design-significant aspects have been identified: ASUR characteristics improve the specification of components (*perception/action sense*, location, etc.) and relationships (*type of language, point of view, dimension, etc.*). A detailed list of components and relationships characteristics is presented in the ASUR-Metamodel [5].

Let us illustrate ASUR with a scenario. The user, User_0, handles and moves a physical object (R_{tool}-Cup) that is localized by a camera (A_{in} – Camera, *action sense* = physical action). The camera produces a picture (S_{info} – Video) and the cup position that will cause a deformation on the 3D object of the task (S_{obj} – 3D object), of which the cup is a physical representation.

If the user press the other adaptor (A_{in} – touch sensor, *action sense* = physical action) data that modifies the interaction mode (S_{tool} – Mode) is generated: its value set the deformation (rot., trans. or scaling) to apply on the 3D object. Video, 3D object and interaction mode are carried out by the output adaptor (A_{out} – Screen, *perception sense* = visual). Fig. 1 shows the resulting ASUR model, within GUIDE-ME (http://liihs.irit.fr/guideme).

In addition to manipulation tools, GUIDE-ME offers features dedicated to ASUR (patterns manipulation) and mixed system (ergonomic properties checking/definition). The model presented above corresponds to an existing mixed system; Section 3 shows how to insert ASUR in a Focus-Group to generate design solutions.

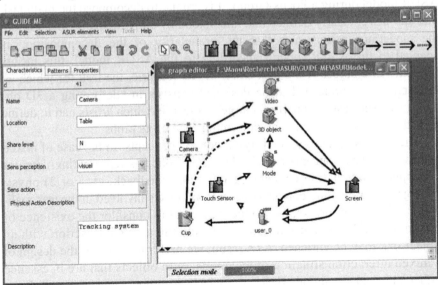

Figure 1. ASUR model of the scenario, designed in GUIDE-ME

3.   ASUR-BASED FOCUS-GROUP

Using the ASUR model as a support to guide and stimulate participants of a Focus-Group is made of ten steps. The five first steps are completely independent of the ASUR model and are similar to the first steps of a traditional HCI process: definition of task, domain and dialog models. The five others are specific to Mixed Systems: due to the presence of two worlds (physical and digital) identifying roles of the different objects and forms of exchange of data is very important. Moreover the amount of possibilities is very high and justifies the need of specific design steps to refine them. In this work, the remaining steps of the process are related to ASUR but might be linked to other models. We detail and illustrate these ten steps in the following paragraphs, on the basis of the previous scenario.

The **first step** aims at introducing the context of the session. The context is made of a design model and the application domain for which a mixed interaction techniques has to be designed. Moderator of the session must introduce both of them using illustrated examples (e.g., Section 2), storyboards to expose the application. In addition, a representation of the ASUR meta-model [5], including all entities and characteristics must be provided to the participants as a support for the following steps.

The **second step** is common to all HCI method: participants have to clearly analyze the user's task. Indeed, an ASUR model is helpful to describe user's interaction during one task. In order to take advantage of the ASUR model during a Focus-Group, it is crucial to decompose the main task into sub-tasks, clearly defined and understood by all participants. In addition, the moderator makes sure that the granularity of the decomposition is adapted to the ASUR model: according to the ASUR model, this means that only one object of the task exist. In our scenario, the task for which an interaction technique had to be designed consists in "deforming a 3D object". This sub-task was part of a larger project, in which artists had to define a posture to a digital puppet by deforming each of its limbs.

The **third step** aims at identifying domain concepts. In the case of mixed systems, domain concepts may be 1) digital concepts representing domains concepts or interaction concepts (navigation, feedback, etc.) or 2) physical objects representing domains concepts or objects involved in the task realization (table, pen, bricks, etc.). One may want to consider the existence of mixed object, but in our opinion, it is solely the user's interaction with an object that may be enriched. As a result, we prefer to consider the design of a mixed interaction situation or technique, with objects that are in essence either physical or digital. Based on a task decomposition to a granularity compatible with the ASUR model and produced in step 2, the moderator highlights the concepts and participants may precise the definition. In our scenario, relevant concepts are the 3D object and the interaction mode depicting the deformation to apply (rotation, translation, scaling). Other concepts may appear in the next steps of the process: for example, depending on the interaction techniques used to apply the deformation, an interaction feedback might be required, such as the video feedback of the proposed solution (cf. section 2). This illustrates the ability of our process to be used iteratively.

The **fourth step** aims at identifying the data that must be made perceivable in the physical world during the realization of the task. Only the data flows must be identified. The moderator has to avoid any discussion related to the data representation (sound, text, color, etc.) and ensure that every domain concept identified in step 3 is made perceivable at least one time. In our scenario, the interaction mode and the limb (3D object) have to be transferred to the physical world.

The **fifth step** is symmetrical to the previous one: it consists in identifying data flows aimed at the computer system. Without discussing the language used to transfer data, the moderator must ensure that every data provided by a user (position, data-capture) or the physical world (environmental data, physical object) is listed. In our scenario, required data flows carry the interaction mode and the deformation to apply.

The next steps correspond to the traditional definition of the interaction model, the correspondence between domain concepts (step 3) and interaction objects (e.g., GUI, speech). With mixed systems, the amount of possible interaction objects is very large: discussions within a focus-group are thus hard to control and to get focused. Linking the "formal" ASUR model within the next steps aims at supporting systematic exploration of design solutions.

The **sixth step** focuses on the digital concepts identified in step 3 and aims at attributing to each of them one of the 3 possible kinds of ASUR digital component (S component). They can be: 1) **Digital object** of the task (S_{obj}), such as the 3D object in our scenario; 2) **Digital information** (S_{info}) depicting a decor, help, data or feedback; in the initial version of our scenario, no such digital component is present. 3) **Digital tool** (S_{tool}): its state influences other digital components, such as the interaction mode in our scenario that has an effect on the deformation to apply to the 3D object.

The **seventh step** aims at identifying output and input ASUR adapters (A_{out} and A_{in}) required for supporting the data transfers identified respectively in steps 4 and 5. A first iteration basically conduces to the elicitation of one adapter for each data transfer identified. The role of the moderator is to help the participants identifying data transfers that might be managed by the same adapter: such decisions reduce the range of the design solutions. In our scenario, one output adapter is sufficient to transfer the interaction mode and the 3D object to the physical world. But the participants preferred to separate the input adapters carrying the mode and size of the deformation.

The **eighth step** aims at characterizing the data transfer to the physical world, i.e. the ASUR relationships originating from a component A_{out}. This consists in setting up a language to spread the data and it corresponds to the definition of one value for each ASUR characteristics of ASUR entities (components or relationships) involved in the data-transfer. For example in our scenario, the perception sense of the A_{out} and the type of language of the relationship between the A_{out} and the User must be defined. In order to explore all the possible solutions, the role of the moderator is to encourage the participants to go through the different ASUR characteristics. The moderator has to ensure that a systematic exploration of the characteristics is done. Of course, major adapter characteristics constrain some characteristics of other components and relationships: the "visual" *perception sense* is incompatible with the speech *type of language* of relationship. For each value associated to a major characteristic (e.g., *perception sense* = visual), a formatted table is proposed to the participants to collect possible solutions under this constraint. The table contains possible values of every other characteristic (*type of language* = text, picture, video, graphic, etc.), comments of the participants, illustration and reason of acceptance or rejection. Combinations of lines of a table represent design solutions for the considered adapter. Such combinations constitute ASUR patterns in Guide-Me.

The **ninth step** is symmetrical to the previous step: it aims at characterizing the data transfer to the digital world, i.e. the ASUR relationships aimed at a component A_{in}. Here, we could identify gesture, speech or keyboarding as type of language to transfer interaction mode and deformation to the computer system. The same formatted tables are used to collect the outcomes.

The **tenth step** aims at "breaking" relationships connected to A_{in} and A_{out} by inserting new entities. For example, instead of conveying the deformation by way of gesture as suggested in step 9, our final design solution rely on the spatial position a physical cup (R_{tool}).

The articulation we propose of ASUR and a Focus-Group covers the main models traditionally considered in HCI design: task and domain models (Step 2 and 3), presentation and dialog models (steps 4–9). But the ASUR model is limited to the description of one task: in order to fully cover a mixed interaction situation, several iterations of this process have to be conduced. Further work will focus on possible optimization of the process, especially concerning the order in which ASUR characteristics has to be considered. Using this process results in a combination of

- The participant's spontaneous implication.
- A support to the exploration of a very wide domain that makes it easier to the participants to consider different solutions.
- A structured support to collect the outcomes, i.e. the design solutions envisioned by the design team.

This structured support to collect the outcomes makes it easier for designer to integrate these results in the development process. Indeed, we illustrate in the following section how the ASUR-based expression of the outcomes is directly reusable for the implementation of the designed solutions.

4.   ASUR-BASED SOFTWARE DESIGN

So far, the ASUR model appears to be a good support for the elicitation of design solutions, through the exploration of a set of predefined characteristics. However, its high level of description does not provide any information for software development. In order to increase the power of the ASUR model with regard to the development process, we are developing an extension of the ASUR model: ASUR Implementation Layer (ASUR-IL). For each interactive task modeled in ASUR, a corresponding ASUR-IL diagram identifies software components required to implement this specific task:

- **ASUR-IL Adapters** (Fig. 2a): they correspond to the ASUR adapters (step 7, Section 3) and fulfill the same role. They represent input and output devices used to perform the task and enclose platform, drivers and libraries. This decomposition facilitates the evaluation of the system portability and highlights the data types provided by the libraries.
- **Entities**: they correspond to the digital objects involved in the interaction between a user and a mixed system (step 3, Section 3). Input/Output in this context correspond to bridges among physical and digital worlds. Rather controversial in traditional UI, the Input/Output separation appears to be technologically and/or spatially present in mixed interaction. As a result, we chose to adopt the terms of the MVC pattern [13] to decompose the ASUR-IL entities:
  - The *Model* of an entity contains data and rules specific to the application and may communicate with other component of the application kernel not directly related to the interaction. It represents a part of the functional core of the system (Fig. 2b-middle).
  - *Views* of an entity define the model representation that will be perceived by users (Fig. 2b-right). Depending on the chosen representation, additional elements might be required such as containers for example: their identification and definition is left to the system designer.
  - *Controllers* of an entity (Fig. 2b-left) are in charge of the data input to the entity. They are in charge of collecting and adapting data emitted by ASUR-IL adapters or entities.
- **Data exchanges**: communication between internal elements of an interactive system must not interfere with the user's interaction. Therefore, ASUR-IL data exchanges are asynchronous. The use of events constitutes a solution to implement this communication and ensure the components independence.

Building an ASUR-IL diagram from an ASUR modeling of a design solution, is based on the transformation of ASUR adapters, S components and relationships into ASUR-IL adapters, entities and data-exchanges.

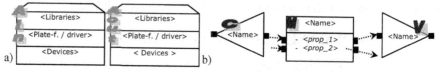

Figure 2. ASUR-IL elements

ASUR adapter transformation results into an ASUR-IL adapter. It leads to the definition of the triplet *<device, platform, library>* and it is constrained by the ASUR adapter characteristics *action sense* (physical action or language) and *perception sense* (view, audio, tactile, etc.). Once the triplet is identified, required or generated data is known. In the design solution of our scenario presented in Fig. 1, using a webcam with the ARToolkit enables the detection of physical motion of the cup, as required by the ASUR model (A_{in}-Camera, *action sense*=physical action). Similarly phidget sensors (www.phidgets.com) and API satisfy the second A_{in} that appears in the ASUR model. In output, we choose to translate the ASUR adaptor (A_{out}, perception sense = visual) into a screen, a windowing system and the Java SWING API. In addition, a window that contains graphical data is required (Fig. 3 left and right bottom).

ASUR S component transformation results into an ASUR-IL entity. It is constrained by the type of the component: S_{obj}, S_{tool} or S_{info}. A *component S_{obj}* (3D object) is transformed into one model with a number of connection ports equal to the number of data manipulated by the model. One or several views and controllers may be connected to the identified ports. In our scenario, we choose to represent position and state of the 3D object in a common 2D graphical view (Fig. 3, middle). A *component Stool* (interaction mode) is not linked to the functional core of the application. Its ASUR-IL Transformation is thus only composed of a controller and a view (Fig. 3, bottom center). A *component S_{info}* transformation depends of its role:

- Feedback: the MVC decomposition is no longer required since it just consists in translating a data-flow from one form to another. This is for example the case of the video feedback provided by the ARToolkit.
- Data or help: one model and one or more views and controllers are used.
- Decors: one model and one or more views are used. One controller may be useful to capture a query but it is not always required.

ASUR relationships "data exchanges" between ASUR adapters and S components are transformed into an ASUR-IL data-exchange between the corresponding ASUR-IL adaptors and entities. For example, the ASUR relationship between the Mode and the 3D object (Fig. 1) has been transformed into the data exchange between the Controller of the Mode and the Controller of the 3D Object (Fig. 3).

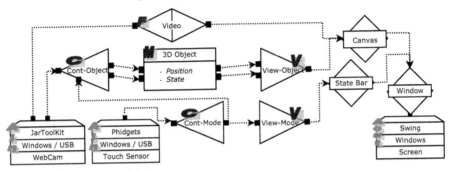

Figure 3. ASUR-IL diagram built from the ASUR diagram of Fig. 1

Other ASUR relationships are not present in ASUR-IL diagrams, because they implies physical parameters (constraints, data-exchange) that are out of the ASUR-IL scope. But, "representation links" (dashed arrow) may have an influence on the design option selected to implement views and controller. More generally, values of ASUR relationships characteristics (*point of view, dimension, language type*) have an impact on views and controllers. For example, if the type of language specified for the ASUR relationship carrying information to the user about the interaction mode is textual, a 2D graphic should not be the implemented solution. ASUR-IL does not support the precise description of the content and behavior of controllers and views: such constraints must be taken into consideration by the developer with respect to the ASUR characteristics expressed in the model.

Following the ASUR-IL decomposition, the role of the developer is to implement or reuse one software component for each ASUR-IL element and to assemble them. Changing one characteristic (or more) in the initial ASUR modeling directly impacts on the ASUR-IL diagram. Since each element of this diagram correspond to a single software component, the modified areas of an ASUR-IL diagram clearly identify which part of the system implementation has to be modified. Component to remove or introduce are thus easily identified and the implemented mixed system can rapidly evolve. Fig. 4 illustrates the assembly of software components corresponding to the ASUR-IL diagram presented in Fig. 3. This assembly has been composed within the "WComp Assistant" (http://rainbow.essi.fr/wcomp/web/), a component-based platform for wearable computing rapid prototyping. Each software component implemented follows the WComp specification which uses JavaBeans and Java events as interfaces. Using the introspection mechanism, it becomes easy to identify component interfaces and then to create the assembly specified by ASUR-IL.

Further work will focus on data-exchange characteristics (e.g., synchronism, parameter, etc.) and conditions of use of several views and controllers onto a single model. Finally, to facilitate the use of ASUR-IL, the integration of this notation into GUIDE-ME is unavoidable.

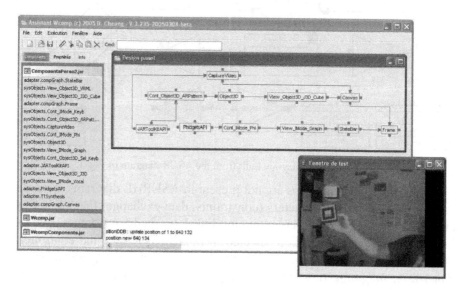

Figure 4. ASUR-IL identified components implemented and running in WComp platform

5.   CONCLUSION AND PERSPECTIVES

We have presented in this paper how the use of a formal representation tool, (ASUR model), can complement and support a traditional method of Participatory Design, (Focus-Group). By interlacing them, we keep advantages of both and tend to address some limits: guiding the generation of ideas, supporting the structuring of the outcomes of the Focus-Group, providing the experts of the design team with a common and easy access to a formal model. Beyond the crucial interlacing of user centered and model based approaches, we also have presented and illustrated how outcomes of this combination are integrated in the rest of the development process. Firstly using GUIDE-Me patterns leads to the modeling of the whole system. Secondly, the ASUR-IL notation supports the identification of software components required to implement the ASUR designed solution. Transformation rules from ASUR models to ASUR-IL diagrams have been developed and ensure a tight link between early design phases and implementation steps as demonstrated by the implementation of our ASUR-IL description with the WComp platform.

Further work is required at two levels. At a first level, the use of ASUR-Focus Group articulation in concrete design situations has shown that it supports ideas generation. But additional evaluations are required in order to quantify these benefits and identify additional tools required to instrument these sessions. At a second level, the description of ASUR-IL elements connection must be refined in order to express specific requirements such as synchronism, data-flow format and communication type, but also to include considerations related to the combination of several views and controllers on a unique model. There is also a need to investigate the combination of several tasks onto ASUR models and ASUR-IL diagrams fusion. Eventually additional translations rules have to be developed in order to take into account all the existing ASUR characteristics. To this end, we believe that transformation mechanisms of Model-Driven Engineering will be helpful.

Finally, articulating design specific methods seems to be required to assist the development process of mixed system. We believe that similar articulations are required to include other aspects of traditional HCI methods such as task model and dialogue model. Exploring MDE and in particular the weaving dimensions constitutes a promising way we are now exploring.

REFERENCES

[1] Bauer, M., Bruegge, B., Klinker, G., MacWilliams, A., Reicher, T., Riß, S., Sandor, C., and Wagner, M., *Design of a Component-Based Augmented Reality Framework*, in Proc. of ISAR'2001, IEEE Computer Society Press, Los Alamitos, 2001, pp. 45–54.

[2] Bodker, K., Kensing, F., and Simonsen, J., *Participatory IT design - Designing for business and workplaces realities*, The MIT Press, Cambridge, 2004.

[3] Delotte, O., David, B., and Chalon, R., *Task Modelling for Capillary Collaborative Systems based on Scenarios*, in Ph. Palanque, P. Slavik, M. Winckler (eds.), Proc. of 3rd Int. Workshop on Task Models and Diagrams for user interface design TAMODIA'2004 (Prague, November 15–16, 2004), ACM Press, New York, 2004, pp. 25–31.

[4] Dubois, E., Gray, P.D., and Nigay, L., *ASUR++: A Design Notation for Mobile Mixed Systems*, Interacting with computers, Vol. 15, No. 2003, pp. 497–520.

[5] Dupuy-Chessa, S., and Dubois, E., *Requirements & Impacts of Model Driven Engineering on Mixed Systems Design*, in Proc. of Ingénierie Dirigée par les Modèles IDM'2005 (Paris, 2005), pp. 43–54.

[6] Guyot, P., Drogoul, A., and Lemaître, C., *Using Emergence in Participatory Simulations to Design Multi-Agent Systems*, in Proc. of AAMAS'2005, 2005, pp. 199–203.

[7] Haller, M., Zauner, J., Hartmann, W., and Luckeneder, T., *A Generic Framework for a Training Application Based on Mixed Reality*, Technical report, Upper Austria University of Applied Sciences, Vienna, 2003.

[8] Hilliges, O., Sandor, C., and Klinker, G., *Interaction Management for Ubiquitous Augmented Reality User Interfaces*, in Proc. of 10th ACM Int. Conf. on Intelligent User Interfaces IUI'2006 (Sydney, 29 January-1 February 2006), ACM Press, New York, 2006, pp. 285–287.

[9] Hong, I.J., and Landay, J.A., *SATIN: A Toolkit for Informal Ink-based Applications*, in Proc. of ACM Symposium on User Interface Software and Technology UIST'2000, ACM Press, New York, 2000, pp. 63–72.

[10] Ishii, H., and Ullmer, B., *Emerging Frameworks for Tangible User Interfaces*, IBM Systems Journal, Vol. 39, Nos. 3–4, 2000, pp. 915–931.

[11] ISO/TS 16982, *Ergonomics of Human-System Interaction – Usability Methods Supporting Human-Centred Design*, International Standard Organization, Geneva, 2000.

[12] Kato, H., and Billinghurst, M., *Marker Tracking and HMD Calibration for a Video-Based Augmented Reality Conferencing System*, in Proc. of IWAR'99, San Francisco, p. 85.

[13] Krasner, G.E., and Pope, T., *A Cookbook for Using the Model-View-Controller User Interface Paradigm in Smalltalk-80*, Journal of Object Oriented Programming, Vol. 8, 1988, pp. 26–49.

[14] Krueger, R.A., and Casey, M.A., *Focus Groups: A Practical Guide for Applied Research*, Sage Publication Publisher, 2000.

[15] Mackay, W.E., Ratzer, A., and Janecek, P., *Video Artifacts for Design: Bridging the Gap Between Abstraction and Detail*, in Proc. of ACM Conf. on Designing Interactive Systems DIS'2000, ACM Press, New York, 2000, pp. 72–82.

[16] Renevier, P., *Systèmes Mixtes Collaboratifs sur Supports Mobiles : Conception et Réalisation*, Ph.D. thesis, Université Joseph Fourier, Grenoble 1, France, 2004.

[17] Shaer, O., Leland, N., Calvillo-Gamez E.H., and Jacob R.J.K., *The TAC Paradigm: Specifying Tangible User Interfaces*, Personal and Ubiquitous Computing, Vol. 8, No. 5, September 2004, pp. 359–369.

[18] Trevisan, D.G., Vanderdonckt, J., and Macq, B., *Conceptualising Mixed Spaces of Interaction for Designing Continuous Interaction*, Virtual Reality, Vol. 8, 2004, pp. 83–95.

Chapter 7

A METHOD FOR DEVELOPING 3D USER INTERFACES OF INFORMATION SYSTEMS

Juan Manuel González Calleros[1], Jean Vanderdonckt[1], and Jaime Muñoz Arteaga[2]

[1] *School of Management (IAG), Université catholique de Louvain*
Place des Doyens, 1 – B-1348 Louvain-la-Neuve (Belgium)
E-mail: {gonzalez, vanderdonckt}@isys.ucl.ac.be – Web: http://www.isys.ucl.ac.be/bchi
Tel: +32 10 47{8349, 8525} – Fax: +32 10 478324
[2]*Universidad Autonóma de Aguascalientes, Dpto. de Sistemas de Información*
Av. Universidad # 940 – C.P. 20100 Aguascalientes (México).
E-Mail: jmunozar@correo.uaa.mx – Web: http://148.211.40.92:8080/jaime/index.htm

Abstract   A transformational method for developing tri-dimensional user interfaces of interactive information systems is presented that starts from a task model and a domain model to progressively derive a final user interface. This method consists of three steps: deriving one or many abstract user interfaces from a task model and a domain model, deriving one or many concrete user interfaces from each abstract interface, and producing the code of the final user interfaces corresponding to each concrete interface. To ensure the two first steps, transformations are encoded as graph transformations performed on the involved models expressed in their graph equivalent. In addition, a graph grammar gathers relevant graph transformations for accomplishing the sub-steps involved in each step. Once a concrete user interface is resulting from these two first steps, it is converted in a development environment for 3D user interfaces where it can be edited for fine tuning and personalization. From this environment, the user interface code is automatically generated. The method is defined by its steps, input/output, and exemplified on a case study. By expressing the steps of the method through transformations between models, the method adheres to Model-Driven Engineering paradigm where models and transformations are explicitly defined and used

Keywords: 3D user interfaces, Model driven engineering, Scene model, Transformational approach, Virtual reality, World model

G. Calvary et al. (eds.), Computer-Aided Design of User Interfaces V, 85–100.

1. INTRODUCTION

Today, the development life cycle of 3D User Interfaces (UIs) mostly remains an art more than a principled-based approach. Several methods [1,3,7,8,9,10,11,15,17,18,19] have been introduced to decompose this life cycle into steps and sub-steps, but these methods rarely provide the design knowledge that should be typically used for achieving each step. In addition, the development life cycle is more focusing directly on the programming issues than on the design and analysis phases. This is sometimes reinforced by the fact that available tools for 3D UIs are toolkits, interface builders, rendering engines, etc. When there is such a development life cycle defined, it is typically structured into the following set of activities:

1. The **conceptual phase** is characterized by the identification of the content and interaction requests. The meta-author discusses with the interface designer to take advantage of the current interaction technology. The interface designer receives information about the content. The result of this phase is the production of UI schemes (e.g., written sentences, visual schemes on paper) for defining classes of interactive experiences (e.g., class Guided tour). Conceptual schemes are produced both for the final users and the authors. The meta-author has a deep knowledge of the content domain and didactic skills too. He/she communicates with the final user too, in order to focus on didactic aspects of interaction.
2. In the **implementation phase**, the UI designer builds the final user interface and the author interface on the basis of the UI schemes. The results of this phase are available as tools for the authors, which can be manipulated without a deep knowledge of computer science world. It is important to note that this implementation phase can be a personalization or a subsetting of existing tools, rather than a development from scratch.
3. In the **content development phase**, authors choose among the available classes of interactive experiences and instantiate the one that fits their particular needs (e.g., a guided tour, paths). They take advantage of a number of complementary subjects: editors (e.g., writer, 2D graphic artist), 3D modeler, and world builder.
4. In the **final user interaction phase**, the final user interacts with the contents of the 3D world, composed by the author, through the interface implemented by the interface designer. The final user interaction is monitored in order to improve both the usability of the interface and the effectiveness of content communication.

As opposed to a content-centric approach, some other authors advocate a user-centered approach; hence, involvement of users in the requirements analysis and evaluation are essential for achieving a usable product. They also argue for separating the conceptual part from the rest of the life cycle to identify and manage the Computing-Independent Models (CIM as defined in the Model-Driven Engineering –MDE) from the Computing-Dependent part. This part is in turn typically decomposed into issues that are relevant only to one particular development environment (Platform-Specific Models –PSM) as opposed to those issues which remain independent from any underlying software (Platform-Independent Models–PIM). In the MDE paradigm promoted by the Object Management Group (www.omg.org), it is expected that any development method is able to apply this principle of separation of concerns, is able to capture various aspects of the problem through models, and is capable of progressing moving from the abstract models (CIM and PIM) to the more concrete models (PSM and final code). The goal of this paper is to demonstrate the feasibility of a MDE-compliant method that is user-centered as opposed to contents-centric for developing 3D UIs.

The remainder of this paper is structured as follows: Section 2 summarizes related work, Section 3 outlines the general method and progressively explains all steps of the method based on models. Section 4 concludes the paper and presents some avenue for future work.

2.   RELATED WORK

Different categories of software exist to support the rendering of 3D UIs ranging from the physical level to the logical level. At the lowest level are located APIs such as OpenGL, Direct3D, Glide, and QuickDraw3D, which provide the primitives for producing 3D objects and behaviors. They offer a set of powerful primitives for creating, manipulating 3D objects, but these primitives are located at a level that does not allow any straightforward use for rendering higher level widgets. Several 3D desktop replacements for Microsoft Windows XP exist such as Microsoft Task Gallery (http://research. microsoft.com/adapt/TaskGallery/), the Infinite3D Cube (http://www.infinite -3d.com/), SphereXP (http://www.hamar.sk/sphere/) which is taking the known concept of three-dimensional desktops to its own level. It offers a new way to organize objects on the desktop such as icons and applications. SphereXP, like other similar environments, are usually limited to presenting existing interactive applications and their UIs in a flat 2D way, even if they are working in a 3D world (Fig. 1). Similarly, SUN has initiated the Looking Glass Project (http://wwws.sun.com/software/looking_glass/index.html) as a 3D desktop environment for Linux workstations. These environments are very powerful for their manipulation of windows in 3D, but they are not intended to render 2D UIs with 3D effects. Beyond existing 3D desktop environments is Metisse [4]. It consists of an X-based window system for two purposes: it should facilitate the development of innovative window management techniques and it should conform to existing standards and be robust and efficient enough to be used on a daily basis. Metisse is not focused on a particular kind of interaction (e.g., 3D), it should be considered rather a tool for creating new desktops, including 3D. On the other hand, it is actually possible to directly implement 3D UIs on top of 3D development toolkits such as Contigra, Croquet (http://croquetproject.org/). The advantage of these environments is that true 3D widgets (e.g., a ring menu could be implemented with an appropriate presentation and behavior). However, this assumes that we have to redevelop all widgets traditionally found in 2D UIs (e.g., a list box, a drop-down list) in these environments and that 3D containers are required to gather them, as windows play the role of containers for 2D widgets. RealPlaces (http://www-3.ibm.com/ibm/easy/eou_ext.nsf/publish/84) is a particular case where all office 3D widgets are already predefined with their behavior, but they cannot be changed or they do not necessarily correspond to their 2D counterpart.

Another series of approaches is often referred to as a model-based one [15] as they exploit specifications of the widgets, of the UI or of the complete scene to automatically generate VRML97 or X3D code of these UIs. The underlying model is frequently expressed in a XML-compliant language as the syntax of such a language is nowadays very widespread. Typical examples of such approaches include InTml (http://www.cs.ualberta.ca/~pfiguero/InTml/Introduction.html), VRIXML [6], and Flatland (based on 3dml, see http://mr.3dml.free.fr/).

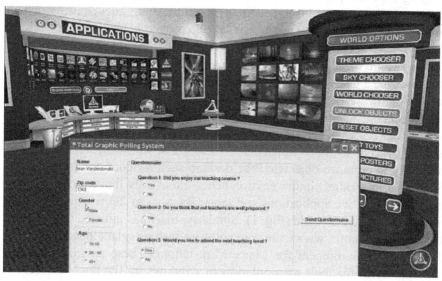

Figure 1. Flat rendering of a 2D window in a 3D world (Source: Windows 3DNA environment)

From these existing environments, we can observe that most of them are more oriented towards facilitating the life of the developer, but do not necessarily address the concerns of the designer and often forget the user requirements. It is not their purpose to provide designers and analysts with a complete environment that support them throughout the development life cycle. Therefore, such environments could be considered as software that could be complemented by design tools supporting more the conceptual phase than the development phase. In addition, they do not offer many choices in exploring design options and design alternatives during the design phase. These environments are usually restricted to one programming or markup language and do not allow easy porting code from one platform to another.

3.   METHOD OUTLINE

To address the aforementioned shortcomings, a method is now introduced that structures the development life cycle for 3DUIs from the conceptual phase to the final user interaction phase by incorporating explicitly user's requirements from the beginning. Since the method should be compliant with MDE and its principle of separation of concerns, the method (Fig. 2) is itself decomposed into a sequence of four steps. Each following subsection is dedicated to the definition, the discussion, and the exemplification of these steps on a running example: a virtual polling system for which different versions will be obtained.

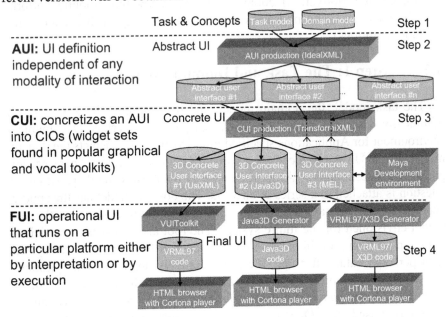

Figure 2. Outline of the method for developing 3D user interfaces

3.1   Reference Framework for Multi-target UIs

Prior to defining the concepts on which the rest of this paper will rely, we assume to rely on the Cameleon framework [2], which structures the development life cycle of multi-target UIs according to four layers: (i) the Final UI (FUI) is the operational UI, i.e. any UI running on a particular computing platform either by interpretation (e.g., through a Web browser) or by execution (e.g., after the compilation of code in an interactive development environment); (ii) the Concrete UI (CUI) expresses any FUI independently of any term related to a peculiar rendering engine, that is independently of any markup or programming language; (iii) the Abstract UI (UI) expresses any CUI independently of any interaction modality (e.g., graphical, vocal, tactile); and (iv) the Task & Concept level, which describes the various interactive tasks to be carried out by the end user and the domain objects that are manipulated by these tasks. We refer to [3] for more details and to [12] for its translation into models uniformly expressed in the same User Interface Description Language (UIDL), which is selected to be UsiXML, which stands for User Interface eXtensible Markup Language (http://www.usixml. org). Any other UIDL could be used equally provided that the used concepts are also supported. The Context of use describes all the entities that may influence how the user's task is carrying out with the future UI. It takes into account three relevant aspects, each aspect having its own associated attributes contained in a separate model: user type (e.g., system experience, task experience, task motivation), computing platform type (e.g., mobile platform vs. stationary one), and physical environment type (e.g., office conditions, outdoor conditions).

3.2   Step 1: The Task and Domain Models

The task model, the domain model, and the mappings between, are all graphically described using IdealXML tool [14], an Interface Development Environment for Applications specified in UsiXML. Fig. 3 depicts the domain model of our UI as produced by a software engineer. A participant participates to a questionnaire. A questionnaire is made of several questions. A question is attached to a series of answers. The domain model has the appearance of a class diagram. Fig. 3 illustrates a CTT representation of the task model envisioned for the future system. The root task consists of participating to an opinion poll. In order to do this, the user has to provide the system with personal data. After that, the user iteratively answers some questions. Answering a question is composed of a system task showing the title of the question and of an interactive task consisting in selecting one answer among several proposed ones. Once the questions are answered, the questionnaire is sent back to its initiator. All temporal relationships are enabling which means that the source task has to terminate before the target task can be initiated.

The dashed arrows between the two models in Fig. 3 depict the model mappings, such as manipulates relationships between the task and the domain model as dashed arrows. Provide Personal Data is mapped onto Participant class. Show Question is mapped onto the attribute title of class Question. The task Select Answer is mapped onto the attribute title of the class Answer. Finally, the task Send Questionnaire is mapped onto the method sendQuestionnaire of the class Questionnaire. The initial task may be considered as not precise enough to perform transformations. Indeed, the task Provide Personal Data is an interactive task consisting in creating instances of Participant. In reality, this task will consist in providing a value for each attribute of Participant. This could mean that the task model is not detailed up to the required level of decomposition.

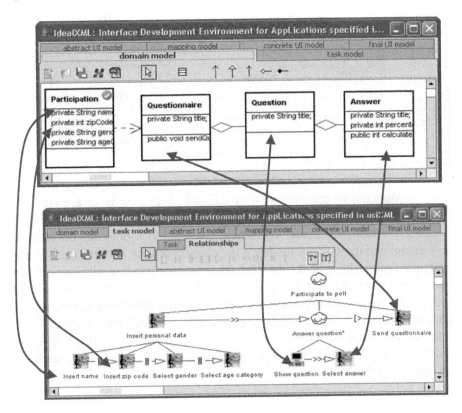

Figure 3. Process to create 3D user interfaces

Rule 1 is applied to the task and domain models. The Left-Hand Side (LHS) contains an **interactive** task (1) where the user action required to perform the task is of type **create**. This task manipulates a class from the domain model (2), which is composed, of an attribute that takes the value of a variable **x**. The Negative Application Condition (NAC) specifies that a task manipulates an attribute (3) whose name is stored in the same variable **x**. The Right Hand Side (RHS) specifies the decomposition of the task described in LHS (1) into an interactive task (2), which requires a user action of type **create**. Note the way they are named using a post-condition on their **name** attribute. The mappings between nodes and between edges belonging to the three components of a rule (i.e. NAC, LHS, and RHS) are specified by attached numbers. The application of this rule on the task and domain model represented in the form of a graph G is the following: when the LHS matches into G and the NAC does not match into G, the LHS is replaced by the RHS, resulting a transformed graph G'. Therefore, Rule 1 decomposes the task Provide Personal Data into four new sub-tasks, each of them manipulating an attribute of class Participant.

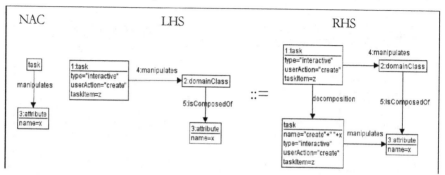

Rule 1. Consolidation of the task model

Consequently, to the execution of this rule, four new tasks are created: create name, create zipCode, create ageCategory and create gender. Fig. 3 contains the mapping model containing the mappings between the refined task model and the domain model of the opinion polling system. Each of the four new sub-tasks will be mapped on the corresponding attribute of the class Participant, the rest of the mappings remaining the same. Due to the fact that "create" is a very general action type and that both ageCategory and gender attributes hold an enumerated domain, "create" can be specialized into "select". Rule 2 is applied in order to achieve this goal. Rule 3 provides a default temporal relationship (set to enabling) when two sister tasks have no temporal relationship.

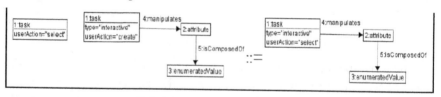

Rule 2. Specializing a user action

3.3   Step 2: From Task and Domain Models to Abstract Model

The second transformation step involves a transformation system that contains rules applied to transition from the task and domain model to the abstract model. Those rules create an abstract container (AC) for task that has task children, i.e. participate poll, insert personal data, and answer question for this example. Following the same mechanism of rule transformation, an abstract individual component (AIC) is created for every leaf task found the task model: insert name, insert zip code, select gender, select age category, show question, select answer and send questionnaire. Each AIC can be equipped with facets describing its main purpose/functionality. These facets are derived from the combination of task model, domain model and the mappings between them. Task definitions have information that is relevant for the mappings, such as: userAction, which could be: create, delete, modify, among others. According to these mappings it can be derived that AICs create name and create zipCode are equipped with an input facet of type "create attribute value". The generated abstract user interface is shown in Fig. 4, detailed description of the mapping rules applied are found in [16].

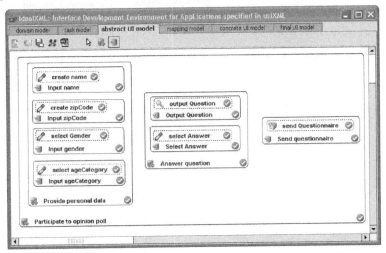

Figure 4. IdealXML Mapping from Task and Domain model to Abstract Model

3.4   Step 3: From Abstract Model to Final User Interface

The third step implies a transformational system that is composed of necessary rules for realizing the transition from AUI to CUIs. For this purpose, other design rules could be encoded in UsiXML so as to transform the AUI into different CUI depending the options decided. Since the AUI model is a

CIM, it is supposed to remain independent of any implementation. However, when it comes to transform this AUI into a corresponding CUI or several variants of it, platform concerns come into consideration. For this purpose, several design rules exist that transform the AUI into CUIs with different design options that will then be turned into final code when generated. We need to encode components that correspond to the meta-model of 3DUI in UsiXML. All information manipulated by all sub-tasks are all gathered in one container. In the 3D space we could imagine an infinity set of objects that could be used as containers. The virtual space is the basic container for all the concrete interface objects (CIO), i.e. entities that users can perceive and/or manipulate. So we could have **2D renders** such as *Polygons*, irregular or regular, n-sized; **3D renders** such as: polyhedrons, which involves prisms, parallelepipeds, pyramids, cones, spheres; also we consider the fact that any combination of surfaces and shape could be created and function as a container. See in Fig. 5 the meta-model corresponding to the definition of the environmental model, which is responsible for describing the world in which any 3D UI could be rendered.

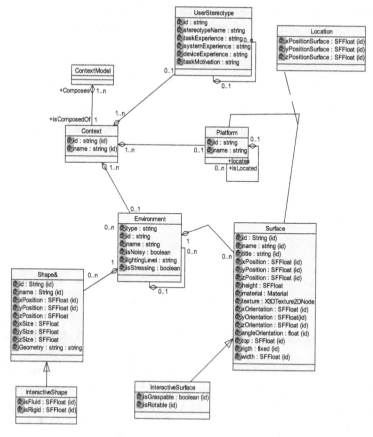

Figure 5. Environmental Model

To adhere to the principle of separation of concerns, the model is itself decomposed into parts gathering attributes of the same area of interest. The mapping rules applied to transform the AUI specification to CUIs. In this case, CUI specifications result from the application of design rules in TransformiXML. In Fig. 6, the screenshot reproduces the two worlds generated for a Java3D environment, where each AC (provision personal data and answer question) is mapped onto one scene at a time. All AICs belonging to each AC are then mapped recursively onto Java3D widgets depending on their data type. In this particular case, the designer selected also the graphical representation if any, along with the textual representing.

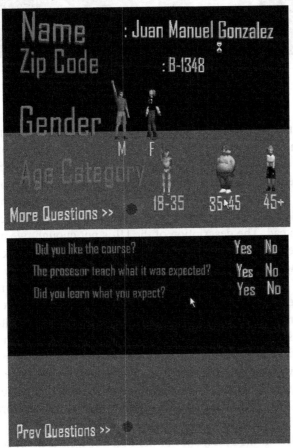

Figure 6. Java 3D representation of the polling system

In this visualization, we propose another way to represent the category selection. Instead of using a comboBox, or the traditional view of icons attached to radio button, we proposed the use of 3D personages instead of icons. This 3D graphic representation of the option could reinforce the understanding, notice that we keep the text below the personages.

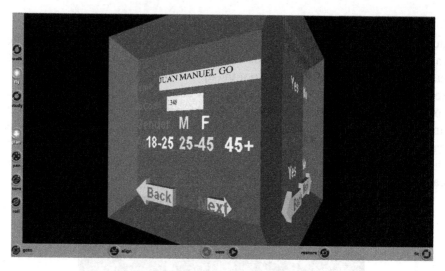

Figure 7. Polling system rendered in VRML

In Fig. 7, the decomposition of ACs is more fine-grained than in the previous cases: the information related to the person are first acquired in a rotating cube (which was selected as the container), then each pair of questions is presented at a time with the facilities of going forward or backward like a wizard. Since only 3 questions and one set of person information are considered, a cube is selected to present each part. If for any reason, more questions were defined, let us say 5, a regular volume with 6 faces would be generated instead. The description of the UI is not enough; we need an editor to manipulate the 3D objects easily with an automatic feedback of the modifications done by the user. We use for this purpose Maya, by specifying a Maya ASCII file as a result of the Abstract specification of the 3DUI. The files is opened in the Maya editor (Fig. 8) and finally exported in a target markup or programming language for virtual reality. Maya plug-ins offers, among others exporters, RawKee (http://rawkee.sourceforge.net/), an open source (LGPL) X3D plug-in, that exports Maya's 3D data as an X3D or VRML file with support for scripting. Fig. 9 reproduces some snapshots of the 3DUI rendered in VRML (Virtual Reality Markup Language).

The UsiXML specifications at the CUI could also be interpreted in VUI-Toolkit, a rendering engine for 3D UIs specified in UsiXML in VRML97/X3D. In the screenshot of the Fig. 10, we show the result of using the Toolkit that generates the 3D rendering of how our polling system could look in a 2D user interface. The 2D components have been enriched with volumes. One can discuss that the components are rendered as 3D widgets in a way that remains similar to the "Look & Feel" of 2D widgets, except that the "Feel" is a genuine 3D behavior. According to this view, this kind of FUI can be interpreted only as a 3D rendering of 2D UIs, even if their specifications are toolkit-independent [13]. This approach provides an option to the use of Java applets UIs to manipulate virtual applications in the Web, instead, the use of the VUIToolkit would not disrupt the 3D "look".

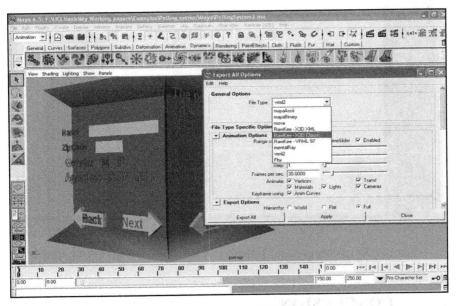

Figure 8. Edition of the 3DUI in Maya

Figure 9. Rendering of the 3DUI interface for the polling system in VRML

Figure 10. 3D rendering of the 2D interface for the polling system in VUIToolkit

4.   CONCLUSION

A method has been presented that decomposed the 3D UI development life cycle into four steps ranging from the most abstract (CIM) to the most concretes (PIM, then PSM) according to the principles of Model-Driven Engineering. The first step is intended to capture user requirements through a task model manipulating information contained in a domain model. The second step transforms this task model into an abstract UI model that is computing-independent. The third step supports in our case three transformations so as to obtain three types of final rendering: interpretation of the CUI UsiXML specifications in VUIToolkit (a 3D rendering engine that has been developed for this purpose), in Java3D and in VRML97/X3D.

The feasibility of the approach is much depending on the amount and the quality of the design rules that are also encoded in UsiXML. If a reasonably extensive set of rules is used, the generated results are usable. If this is not the case, the model resulting from the transformation could be considered as underspecified. It is then required to manually edit within a XML-compliant editor. Future work will therefore be dedicated to exploring more design options and encode them in UsiXML so as to serve better transformations. This does not mean that a generated 3D UI is as usable or more usable than a manually-produced one, but at least it could be obtained in a very fast way. Moreover, the exploration of alternative design options could be facilitated since they are operated at a higher level of abstraction than the code level.

ACKNOWLEDGEMENTS

We gratefully thank the support from the SIMILAR network of excellence (The European research taskforce creating human-machine interfaces SIMILAR to human-human communication), supported by the 6th Framework Program of the European Commission, under contract FP6-IST1-2003-507609 (http://www.similar.cc), the Alban program (www.programalban.org) supported by European Commission, and the CONACYT (www.conacyt.mx) program supported by the Mexican government. All information regarding UsiXML is accessible through http://www.usixml.org.

REFERENCES

[1] Bowman, D.A., Kruijff, E., LaViola, J., and Poupyrev, I., *3D User Interfaces: Theory and Practice*, Addison Wesley, Boston, July 2004.

[2] Calvary, G., Coutaz, J., Thevenin, D., Limbourg, Q., Bouillon, L., and Vanderdonckt, J., *A Unifying Reference Framework for Multi-Target User Interfaces*, Interacting with Computers, Vol. 15, No. 3, 2003, pp. 289–308.

[3] Celentano, A., and Pittarello, F., *A Content Centered Methodology for Authoring 3D Interactive Worlds for Cultural Heritage*, in D. Bearman, F. Garzotto (eds.), Proc. of Int. Cultural Heritage Informatics Meeting ICHIM'2001 (Milan, 3–7 September 2001), "Cultural Heritage and Technologies in the Third Millennium", Vol. 2, 2001, pp. 315–324.

[4] Chapuis, O., and Roussel, N., *Metisse is not a 3D Desktop*, in Proc. of ACM Symposium on User Interface Software and Technology UIST'2005 (Seattle, 23–26 October 2005), ACM Press, New York, 2005, pp. 13–22.

[5] Conner, D.B., Snibbe, S.S., Herndon, K.P., Robbins, D.C., Zeleznik, R.C., and van Dam, A., *Three-Dimensional Widgets*, in Proc. of the 1992 Symposium on Interactive 3D Graphics, Special Issue of Computer Graphics, ACM Press, New York, pp. 183–188.

[6] Cuppens, E., Raymaekers, Ch., and Coninx, K., *VRIXML: A User Interface Description Language for Virtual Environments*, in Proc. of the 1st ACM AVI'2004 Workshop "Developing User Interfaces with XML: Advances on User Interface Description Languages" UIXML'2004 (Gallipoli, May 25, 2004), LUC-EDM, 2004, pp. 111–118.

[7] Fencott, C., and Isdale, J., *Design Issues for Virtual Environments*, in Proc. of Int. Workshop on Structured Design of Virtual Environments and 3D-Components at the Web3D'2001 Conference (Paderborn, 19 February 2001).

[8] Fencott, C., *Towards a Design Methodology for Virtual Environments*, in Proc. of User Centered Design and Implementation of Virtual Environments UCDIVE'99 Workshop (York, 30 September 1999).

[9] Geiger, C., Paelke, V., Reimann, C., and Rosenbach, W., *Structured Design of Interactive Virtual and Augmented Reality Content*, in Proc. of Int. Workshop on Structured Design of Virtual Environments and 3D-Components at the Web3D'2001 Conference (Paderborn, 19 February 2001).

[10] Katsurada, K., Nakamura, Y., Yamada, H., and Nitta, T., *XISL: A Language for Describing Multimodal Interaction Scenarios*, in Proc. of 5th Int. Conf. on Multimodal Interfaces ICMI'2003 (Vancouver, 5–7 Nov. 2003), ACM Press, New York, 2003, pp. 281–284.

[11] Larimer, D., and Bowman, D., *VEWL: A Framework for Building a Windowing Interface in a Virtual Environment*, in Proc. of IFIP TC13 Int. Conf. on Human-Computer Interaction Interact'2003 (Zürich, 1–5 September 2003), IOS Press, Amsterdam, 2003, pp. 809–812.

[12] Limbourg, Q., Vanderdonckt, J., Michotte, B., Bouillon, L., and Lopez-Jaquero, V., *UsiXML: A Language Supporting Multi-Path Development of User Interfaces*, in Proc. of 9th IFIP Working Conf. on Engineering for Human-Computer Interaction jointly with 11th Int. Workshop on Design, Specification, and Verification of Interactive Systems EHCI-DSVIS'2004 (Hamburg, 11–13 July 2004), Lecture Notes in Computer Science, Vol. 3425, Springer-Verlag, Berlin, 2005, pp. 207–228.

[13] Molina, J.P., Vanderdonckt, J., Montero, F., and González, P., *Towards Virtualization of User Interfaces based on UsiXML*, in Proc. of the 10th Int. Conf. on 3D Web Technology Web3D'2005 (Bangor, 29 March–1 April 2005), ACM Press, New York, 2005, pp. 169–178.

[14] Montero, F., López-Jaquero, V., Vanderdonckt, J., Gonzalez, P., and Lozano, M.D., *Solving the Mapping Problem in User Interface Design by Seamless Integration in IdealXML*, in Proc. of 12th Int. Workshop on Design, Specification, and Verification of Interactive Systems DSVIS'2005 (Newcastle upon Tyne, 13–15 July 2005), Lecture Notes in Computer Science, Vol. 3941, Springer-Verlag, Berlin, 2005.

[15] Neale, H., and Nichols, S., *Designing and Developing Virtual Environments: Methods and Applications*, in Proc. of Visualization and Virtual Environments Community Club VVECC'2001 Workshop, Designing of Virtual Environments, 2001.

[16] Stanciulescu, A., Limbourg, Q., Vanderdonckt, J., Michotte, B., and Montero, F., *A Transformational Approach for Multimodal Web User Interfaces based on UsiXML*, in Proc. of 7th Int. Conf. on Multimodal Interfaces ICMI'2005 (Trento, 4–6 October 2005), ACM Press, New York, 2005, pp. 259–266.

[17] Sutcliffe, A., *Multimedia and Virtual Reality: Designing Multisensory User Interfaces*, Lawrence Erlbaum Associates, Mahwah, 2003.

[18] Waterworth, J.A., and Serra, L., *VR Management Tools: Beyond Spatial Presence*, in Proc. of ACM Conf. on Human Aspects in Computing Systems INTERCHI'93 (Amsterdam, 24–29 April 1993), Addison-Wesley, Reading, 1993, pp. 319–320.

[19] Zakiul, S., *Week 15 report on Project 6*, accessible at http://www.public.asu.edu/~zakiul/vrml/week15/week15.htm

Chapter 8

GESTACTION3D: A PLATFORM FOR STUDYING DISPLACEMENTS AND DEFORMATIONS OF 3D OBJECTS USING HANDS

Diane Lingrand[1,3], Philippe Renevier[3], Anne-Marie Pinna-Déry[1,3], Xavier Cremaschi[1], Stevens Lion[1], Jean-Guilhem Rouel[1], David Jeanne[2], Philippe Cuisinaud[1], and Julien Soula[1,*]

[1]*Polytech'Sophia, Département Sciences Informatiques, Univ. Nice-Sophia Antipolis, 930, route des Colles - B.P. 145 - F-06903 Sophia Antipolis Cédex (France)*
E-mail: lingrand@polytech.unice.fr – Web: http://www.i3s.unice.fr/~lingrand/
Tel.: +33 4 92 96 50 65 – Fax: +33 4 92 96 51 55
[2]*Univ. Nice - Sophia Antipolis, Ergonomy Dept*
[3]*Rainbow Team, Laboratoire I3S – UMR 6070 UNSA/CNRS, Univ. Nice-Sophia Antipolis, 930, route des Colles - B.P. 145 – F-06903 Sophia Antipolis Cédex (France)*
E-mail: Diane.Lingrand@unice.fr, {lingrand, renevier, pinna}@essi.fr
Tel.: +33 4 92 94 {5055, 5167, 5162} – Fax: +33 4 92 965 055
*: now at CSTB Sophia Antipolis

Abstract   We present a low-cost hand-based device coupled with a 3D motion recovery engine and 3D visualization. This platform aims at studying ergonomic 3D interactions in order to manipulate and deform 3D models by interacting with hands on 3D meshes. Deformations are done using different modes of interaction that we will detail in the paper. Finger extremities are attached to vertices, edges or facets. Switching from one mode to another or changing the point of view is done using gestures. The determination of the more adequate gestures is part of the work

Keywords: Abstract user interface models, Model-based design, Task modeling

1.   INTRODUCTION

In the early 80's, mice and graphic screens led to a revolution in computer interfaces and quickly became the by far most common 2D devices. Today, a growing number of 3D displays appear on the market: active or

G. Calvary et al. (eds.), Computer-Aided Design of User Interfaces V, 101–110.
© 2007 *Springer.*

passive 3D glasses, 3D Head Mounted Displays and now 3D LCD monitors. However, 3D devices such as pointers, 3D mice and gloves are not widely used, due to the high cost, a lack of applications and most importantly the low Ergonomy making their usage difficult. Our motivations come from two main applications. The first one is about Computer Graphics and 3D builders such as the well known Blender, 3DS Max or Maya. Building 3D worlds and 3D objects is commonly done using 2D devices (such as mouse and keyboard) and visualized on a 2D monitor. Designers of 3D worlds and 3D objects use 3 orthogonal planes in order to imagine the 3D world. Some 3D operations are made difficult and counter-intuitive by the limitations induced. Our 3D device enables intuitive manipulation in 3D space by capturing the user's 3D motion. To provide visual feedback to the user in this context, 3D vision is also mandatory.

The second application comes from the medical field where the images are often in 3D. Segmenting anatomical structures are done using different segmentation methods that may be automatic in some particular cases but often need user intervention for algorithm initialization, during convergence for local minimum avoidance or at the end, for refinement. This is the case when the physician needs very precise result, for example in brain anatomy labeling for spectroscopy. The human interaction with the model is actually tedious and physiologists are not as familiar with 3D projections as computer graphic experts: there is a need for an intuitive and 3D interface.

All the children are able to simply create and modify 3D models using their fingers on plasticine. Our idea is based on using the hands and, specially the fingers extremities in order to deform 3D meshes. However, how many hands and fingers to use and how to use them needs to be more precisely studied. Thus, Gestaction3D aims at building a platform for 3D interaction testing. The system is based on Computer Vision reconstruction and built with very cheap components in order to easily modify it and produce several prototypes at low cost.

2.   RELATED WORK

The dexterity of human hands allows us to execute tasks precise tasks at high speed. If necessary, the hands can easily be trained. Hand motion alone or with instruments have been employed with the aid of Computer Vision in HCI since several years [1,2,3,5,9,10,11,13,17].

Some systems use detection in 2D such as in the Magic Table [1] where colored tokens are detected on a table in order to interact both with real and virtual planar objects. Some others use 3D detection such as the GestureVR [13] or the VisionWand [3].

GestureVR [13] allows spatial interactions using 2 cameras with the recognition of 3 hand gestures. Two fingers and their orientations are detected. It permits also 3D drawing, robot arm manipulation and 3D scene navigation. The VisionWand [3] is a passive wand with colored extremities that is use for interactions with 2D objects and menus selection. The system allows the recognition of 9 different gestures. The motivations of the different works are manipulation of objects [1,3,14], pointing to objects or menus [11], gesture recognition for gesture command [15] or American Sign Language detection[6].

Moeslund and colleagues [11] have developed a system for pointing task using computer vision and a magnetic tracker mounted on the stereo glasses. Smith and colleagues [14] have explicited constraints that allow the manipulation of 3D objects using 2D devices. They apply their system for objects manipulation in a room (e.g., chairs, tables). Computer Vision based approaches using free hands for gesture recognition are still in a stage of research [5,10] even if some results are promising [17].

Limiting the known motions to a small set of gestures is mandatory both for the user (more gestures imply more learning) and the recognition system. In this work, we need to study how to interact with 3D objects in order to deform them according to different modes of interaction we will detail later in the paper. We also need to move our point of observation during the interaction. We want to be able to use our system both in an immersive room (dark) and in an usual office or in classroom. We want to use a passive system and decided to use colored and comfortable gloves. We focus also to increase the space of interaction that is really to much limited in systems such as the P5 gloves from *Essential Reality*.

3.   PLATFORM DESCRIPTION

Gloves are hand made from thin silk black gloves with 5 different colors located at each finger, switches and batteries. The stereo acquisition is done using two webcams Philips Fun II aligned in order to use the simplification of epipolar geometry in the case of standard geometry (Fig. 1). Thus, the depth is easily recovered: depth of fingers is inversely proportional to the 2D disparity between the 2 projections [8].

It is well known in Computer Vision that the extraction of points of interest and matching between two views is a difficult problem and that mistakes at this step may lead to the failure of the entire 3D reconstruction process. In our case, colored LEDs are easily segmented and 2D localized using the HSV color system in order to allow different lighting conditions.

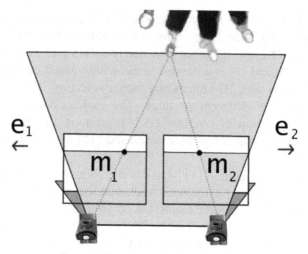

Figure 1. Standard geometry of cameras

The colors avoid the difficult matching points step [18]. Calibration is done in order to exploit the whole field of view with respect to the amplitude of displacements in the scene. Then, depth is directly recovered from 2D disparity. The platform is composed by a server and a client. The server is responsible of the acquisition of the 3D positions of the fingers and of the gesture recognition (Figs. 2 and 3).We will detail this part in the next paragraph (4). The client is responsible for the rendering process and for applying the displacement and deformations to the scene. Communication between the acquisition computer and the rendering machine is done with the VRPN library [16] in order to make its integration with Virtual Reality Systems possible. Among the different models of deformable objects [12], we chose the CGAL [7] implementation which manages useful operations such as mesh refinement. The 3D scene is then managed using OpenSG and displayed using stereo rendering to enable visual feedback to the user. On a desktop computer, the system uses VRex stereo glasses on a CRT monitor to enable visual feedback to the user. In an immersive room, the local stereo rendering is used.

4.   OBJECTS MODELLING AND DEFORMING

As a feedback to the user, detected positions of fingers extremities are rendered using small colored spheres (Fig. 3 bottom right). At the very beginning of our study, we observed that it is mandatory to have a 3D display in order to know if fingers are in front of or back to the objects we want to deform. We also observed that smoothing the mesh enables an interaction closer to the plasticine. In order to interact with a 3D mesh, several fingers extremities are followed.

Figure 2. User in front of the system. On the left computer, the VRPN server and the two webcam widgets with the coloured LEDs detected.
On the right computer, the VRPN client with the 3D rendering

A vertex is attached to a finger when the finger is detected in the 3D neighbourhood of the vertex. It is detached when the finger moves rapidly away from the vertex. When a vertex is attached to a finger, it moves according to 3D displacement of the finger. Depending on user's ability to move separately different fingers, different fingers can simultaneously be attached to different vertices, permitting to deform a 3D object as it were in deformable plasticine. We developed different modes of interaction:

- **Vertex mode**: the vertex is moving according to the corresponding finger motion. One vertex or several vertices can move simultaneously.
- **Facet mode**: one finger is attached to a facet which translates along its normal according to the translation component on this axis of the finger displacement.
- **Edge deletion**: edges that are selected are deleted.
- **Extrusion**: an edge is selected by its two vertices and it is extruded using vertices displacements.
- **Facet division**: when 2 vertices are selected, the corresponding facet is divided into two parts, adding a new edge.

The different modes can simply be activated using the keyboard. However, it is probably not satisfying to switch from natural displacements to keyboard, even if a second user is attached to the keyboard and can react to vocal command. We wanted to evaluate this point using different gestures to switch from a mode to another. Actually, these are simple gestures, mostly planar and should be improved later, for example using more sophisticated gesture recognition such as [17,4] (learning of the gesture structure).

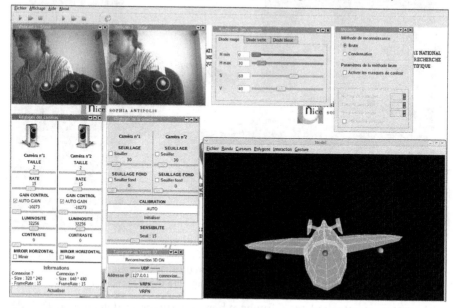

Figure 3. Focus on the application. On top left, the two acquired images with the detection of fingers extremities. On bottom left, the parameters of the cameras. Bottom right, the fingers in 3D (balls centered on the 3D reconstructed points)

5.   GESTURES INTERVIEWS

A first user-centered design was performed in order to establish gestures for the scene management according to the "3D interactions in a virtual environment" taxonomy of Bowman [2]:

- **Camera displacements**: translation and rotation relative to the camera centre (user point of view);
- **Single object displacements**: translation and rotation relative to the object gravity centre;
- **Object selection**: single selection or multiple selection;
- **Gesture on/off**: enabling or disabling the gesture recognition in order to ensure that the user really intends to issue a gestural command.

The final users are students in computer science. The design method is classic in the Human-Computer Interaction field. First, we ask to the users, thanks to a web form, some information especially about: (i) their customs, (ii) how they could accept a new input device for 3D interactions and

(iii) whether they thought using one or two hands during 3D interactions, etc. The form was also opened to non-student people, their answers consolidating students' ones. Once answers analyzed, we interview ten potential users (3 women and 7 men) in order to find the most intuitive gestures for the scene management.

Our final users are essentially (80%) male and young. They are familiar with 3D virtual environment (3D games, 3D conception). They are also aware of the difficulties of interacting in 3D environment with the 2D mouse and the keyboard (this requires to know many keyboard shortcuts to be efficient). Interviews are made in front of slides video-projected on screen. Slides sequentially illustrate the initial state of the 3D scene and the final state of the scene after each action (camera displacements, single object displacement and object selection). At the end of the interview, we discuss the gestures with the user. Each interview is filmed. After the interview analysis, we met four interviewed students (other could not come) in a participative design session. The result of this process is a first collection of gesture (shown on the movie). In many situations, users prefer a two-handed interaction.

Figure 4. Selection gesture: users agree for the same gesture!

For some actions, like selecting (Fig. 4) or taking an object, there is a consensus on "intuitive" gesture. But, for the other actions, like orienting the camera (Fig. 5), there are many gesture propositions. Consequently we decide to follow the consensus, when existed, and otherwise to impose one or two gestures for a command. One recurrent remark is about the non-dominant hand and a third modality. In front of a small screen, users prefer to use the keyboard rather than the second hand, but in front of a large screen (as it was the case during interviews), functionalities are expected to be attached to the second hand. A suggestion is also to use a carpet (or any device on the floor) for moving in the virtual scene, and also to try vocal recognition to limit the number of gestures.

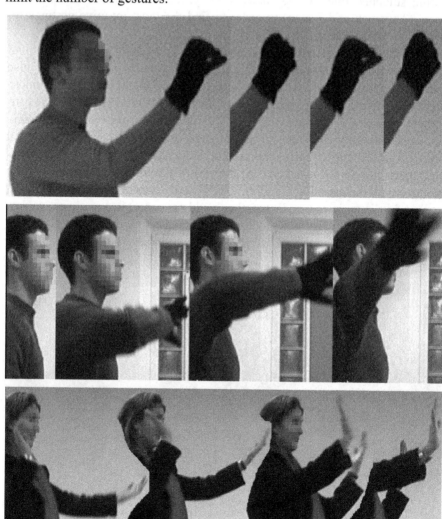

Figure 5. Gesture for rotation: different users mean different gestures!

6. CONCLUSION AND PERSPECTIVES

The platform described in this paper allows users to build and deform 3D objects using a low-cost passive glove. A first study has been done using users interviews in order to determine gestures associated to several commands: camera and objects displacements and selection. We now need to evaluate these gestures on the prototype and also to evaluate the most appropriate commands for interaction modes switching. This platform enable us to make further studies on gestures recognition with more elaborate models such as those described in [5,10]. We are now ready for further studies improving the interactions with 3D worlds.

ACKNOWLEDGMENTS

Authors would like to thank all people how have encouraged this work at the engineering school Polytech'Nice-Sophia and at the CSTB Sophia Antipolis where this platform has been tested.

REFERENCES

[1] Bérard, F., *The Magic Table: Computer-Vision Based Augmentation of a Whiteboard for Creative Meetings*, in Proc. of IEEE Workshop on Projector-Camera Systems PRO-CAM'2003, in conj. with 9th Int. Conf. on Computer Vision, Nice, 11–17 October 2003, accessible at http://iihm.imag.fr/publs/2003/PROCAM03_MagicTable_Berard.pdf.

[2] Bowman, D.A., Kruijff, E., LaViola, J.J., and Poupyrev, I., *3D User Interfaces: Theory and Practice*, Addison-Wesley, Reading, 2004.

[3] Cao, X., and Balakrishnan, R., *VisionWand: Interaction Techniques for Large Displays Using a Passive Wand Tracked in 3D*, in Proc. of 16th ACM Symposium on User Interface Software and Technology UIST'2003 (Vancouver, 2–5 November 2003), ACM Press, New York, 2003, pp. 173–182.

[4] Corso, J.J., Ye, G., and Hager, G.D., *Analysis of Multi-Modal Gestures with a Coherent Probabilistic Graphical Model*, Virtual Reality, Vol. 8, No. 4, Dec. 2005, pp. 242–252.

[5] Derpanis, K.G., *A Review of Vision-Based Hand Gestures*, Internal report, Centre for Vision Research, York University, Canada, 2004.

[6] Derpanis, K.G., Wildes, R.P., and Tsotsos, J.K., *Hand Gesture Recognition within a Linguistics-Based Framework*, in T. Pajdla, J. Matas (eds.), Proc. European Conference on Computer Vision (Prague, May 2004), Lecture Notes in Computer Science, Vol. 3021, Springer-Verlag, Berlin, 2004, pp. 282–296.

[7] Fabri, A., Giezeman, G.-J., Kettner, L., Schirra, S., and Schöonherr, S., *On the Design of CGAL a Computational Geometry Algorithms Library*, Software Practice and Experience, Vol. 11, No. 30, 2000, pp. 1167–1202.

[8] Faugeras, O., *Three-Dimensional Computer Vision: a Geometric Viewpoint*, The MIT Press, Cambridge, 1993.

[9] Jaimes, A., and Sebe, N., *Multimodal Human Computer Interaction: A Survey*, in Proc. of IEEE Int. Workshop on Human Computer Interaction, in conjunction with 9th Int. Conf. on Computer Vision, Nice, 11–17 October 2003.

[10] Moeslund, T.B., and Nørgaard, L., *A Brief Overview of Hand Gestures used in Wearable Human Computer Interfaces*, Technical Report CVMT 03-02, Laboratory of Computer Vision and Media Technology, Aalborg (Denmark), 2003.

[11] Moeslund, T.B., Störring, M., and Granum, E., *A Natural Interface to a Virtual Environment through Computer Vision-estimated Pointing Gestures*, in Proc. of Int. Workshop on Gesture and Sign Language based Human-Computer Interaction GW'2001 (London, 18–20 April 2001), Lecture Notes in Computer Science, Vol. 2298, Springer-Verlag, Berin, 2001, pp. 59–63.

[12] Montagnat, J., and Delingette, H., *A Review of Deformable Surfaces: Topology, Geometry, and Deformation*, Image and Vision Computer, Vol. 19, No. 14, Dec. 2001, pp. 1023–1040.

[13] Segen, J., and Kumar, S., *Gesture VR: Vision-Based 3D Hand Interface for Spatial Interaction*, in Proc. of ACM Int. Conf. on Multimedia Multimedia'98 (Bristol, 13–16 September 1998), ACM Press, New York, 1998, pp. 455–464.

[14] Smith, G., Salzman, T., and Stürzlinger, W., *3D Scene Manipulation with 2D Devices and Constraints*, in Proc. of Graphics Interface'2001 (Ottawa, 7–9 June 2001), Canadian Information Processing Society, Toronto, 2001, pp. 135–142.

[15] Starner, T., Leibe, B., Minnen, D., Westyn, T., Hurst, A., and Weeks, J., *The Perceptive Workbench: Computer-Vision-Based Gesture Tracking, Object Tracking, and 3D Reconstruction for Augmented Desks*, Machine Vision and Applications, Vol. 14, No. 1, April 2003, pp. 59–71.

[16] Taylor, R.M., Hudson, T., Seeger, A., Weber, H., Juliano, J., and Helser, A., *VRPN: A Device-Independent, Network-Transparent VR Peripheral System*, in Proc. of ACM Symposium on Virtual Reality Software & Technology VRST'2001 (Banff, 15–17 November 2001), ACM Press, New York, 2001, pp. 55–61.

[17] Ye, G., Corso, J.J., and Hager, G.D., *Gesture Recognition Using 3D Appearance and Motion Features*, in Proc. of IEEE Workshop on Real-Time Vision for Human-Computer Interaction (Washington, June 2004), in conj. with Conf. on Computer Vision and Pattern Recognition Workshop CVPRW'04, Vol. 10, 2004, p. 160.

[18] Zhang, Z., Deriche, R., Faugeras, O., and Luong, Q.-T., *A Robust Technique for Matching Two Uncalibrated Images through the Recovery of the Unknown Epipolar Geometry*, Artificial Intelligence Journal, Vol. 78, Nos. 1–2, 1994, pp. 87–119. Appeared also as INRIA Research Report No. 2273, May 1994.

Chapter 9

DESIGNING AND DEVELOPING MULTI-USER, MULTI-DEVICE WEB INTERFACES

Fabio Paternò and Ines Santos

ISTI-CNR, Via G.Moruzzi 1,56124 Pisa (Italy)
E-mail: fabio.paterno@isti.cnr.it – Web: http://giove.cnuce.cnr.it/~fabio/
Tel.: + 39 050 3153066 – Fax: + 39 050 3138091

Abstract   The need for support of multi-user interaction is growing in several application domains, including the Web. However, there is a lack of tools able to support designers and developers of multi-user, multi-device interactive applications. In this paper we present a proposal for this purpose describing how it can provide support at both design and run-time. The design and development process can start with task model descriptions and such logical information is used to generate interfaces adapted to the target platforms and mechanisms for their coordination at run-time

Keywords: Authoring environments, Model-based design, Multi-Device User Interfaces, Multi-User, Software architectures

1.   INTRODUCTION

The Web is the most common user interface. In this area there is an increasing number of applications that can be accessed through both desktop and mobile devices. Given the progress made in network technology and access, we have reached a stage in which team-work is widely supported even in Web applications (see for example [2]). Unfortunately, in most systems data is organized and published on the Web using "Web oriented database systems". This type of application permits only asynchronous work. Some support for cooperative applications is provided by workflow systems, which are able to coordinate the tasks performed by various users (see for example [11]) but they are not able to support synchronous work (multi-user applications that allow cooperation between several users in real-time). The few existing

G. Calvary et al. (eds.), Computer-Aided Design of User Interfaces V, 111–122.
© 2007 *Springer.*

authoring environments for synchronous work applications do not take into account that users can access them though different types of devices.

The goal of this paper is to present an environment supporting the design and generation of Web synchronous applications (same time, different place) and an associated architecture able to support them at run-time. Our environment allows developers of collaborative applications to focus on the tasks that users wish to accomplish. The importance of such task-oriented approach for cooperative application has been shown in several works, see for example [7,8]. To this end, it allows them to identify, implement and iterate over the main aspects of the cooperative applications. Since tasks in some applications must be performed by a user before another user can begin a different task, the desired order of task performance must be preserved in the resulting cooperative system. Thus, the run-time architecture must have knowledge of the task model and how it is mapped onto the user interface implementation in order to make them consistent in terms of the possible dynamic evolution. While tools supporting model-based approaches to user interface design and development exist, see for example [1,6,10], none of them has addressed the possibility of supporting generation and run-time support of multi-user, multi-device synchronous applications.

In the following, we first discuss background and related work. Then, we show how cooperative multi-user applications can be designed and how the corresponding user interface implementations adapted to different platforms are obtained. Then, we present the corresponding software architecture, including mechanisms for synchronous cooperation. We also briefly describe an example application. Lastly, we draw some conclusions and provide indications for future work.

2.   BACKGROUND AND RELATED WORK

The new environment presented in this paper has been obtained by extensively redesigning a previous tool called TERESA [6]. TERESA is a multi-device, single-user interface authoring environment that was developed to allow designers to start with a task model in order to obtain different user interfaces for different target platforms. By platform we mean a set of devices that share similar interaction resources (such as the graphical desktop, the graphical mobile device, the vocal device). In the development process, logical descriptions of the user interface are used as well: the abstract interface description is a modality-independent description and the concrete interface description is a modality-dependent refinement of the abstract one; both are implementation-language independent. Thus, for example at the abstract level we can say that we need a selection object without any indication of how the selection can be performed: it could be a graphical selection or a vocal command or a gesture. At the concrete level, we assume a modality and we indicate an interaction techniques supported by such a modality. In the case of a graphical desktop platform, we can indicate a list or a radio-button or a pull-down menu to perform a selection. In the logical user interface descriptions there are logical interactors (such as edit, select, activator, description) and logical composition operators indicating how they should be put together (such as grouping, hierarchy, ordering). Thus, depending on the target platform, when designers move from the abstract to the concrete level, different sets of possible interaction techniques are considered, which are then implemented according to the target implementation language (that can be, for example, XHTML, Java, C++). However, TERESA supported only single user interfaces. Our new tool extends its functionality in many respects in order to support the design and development of Web applications involving cooperation among multiple users performing different tasks through different devices.

Some environments for development of multi-user interfaces already exist: for example, GroupKit [8,9] is a toolkit that simplifies the development of groupware applications to support distance-separated collaborative work. However, it does not address the issue of supporting interaction among multiple users interacting through different device types. WebSplitter [5] aims at supporting collaborative Web browsing by creating personalized partial views of the same Web page depending on the user and the device. To this end, developers have to specify the Web content in XML and define a policy file indicating the tags content that can be presented depending on the user and the device. In addition, they have to define XSL modules in order to transform the XML content into HTML or WML. At run-time a proxy-server generates the Web pages for multiple users, which provide each user with a presentation depending on his/her privilege and device. This approach has several drawbacks. Developers have to manage a plethora of low-level details to specify XML content, policy files, and XSL transformations.

We have similar goals but have adopted a different solution using logical descriptions of interactive systems. They are still specified using XML-based languages but developers can work directly on the logical representations without having to learn the many possible implementation languages. As Greenberg has indicated [3], we aim to remove low-level implementation burdens and supply appropriate building blocks in order to give people a language to think about their user interface and allow them to concentrate on creative design. In addition, we are able to support the design of collaborative applications, in which the results of the actions of one user can change the interface of another.

Other work in this area is the thin-client groupware [4]. It focuses on the use of server-side software components to obtain low-resource collaborative client solutions (e.g., chat, email) through some basic mechanisms provided for this purpose. Our solution differs in that it is based on the use of logical descriptions that provide designers with easier to manage representations of the underlying implementation.

3.   THE AUTHORING OF MULTI-USER INTERFACES

Our environment allows designers to develop multi-user, multi-device interfaces starting with the task model of the application. It can be graphically specified in the ConcurTaskTrees notation, a hierarchical notation providing the possibility of specifying temporal relations among tasks as well as the objects they manipulate and a number of their attributes. The task model of a cooperative application is developed in such a way that the task model of each role involved can be specified separately. In addition, designers can specify the cooperative part. The purpose of this part is to indicate temporal and semantic relations among tasks performed by different users. Thus, it indicates high-level cooperative tasks, which are activities that are decomposed into subtasks performed by different users, and specifies their refinement, down to the corresponding basic tasks performed by each user, along with their temporal constraints. Then, the tool is able to firstly transform the task model into a logical user interface description and then into a user interface implementation. Before starting such transformations designers have to indicate the target platform for the user interface of each role. Thus, the tool supports iterative refinement and generation of interfaces structured according to the task model structure and selects the implementation techniques depending on the interaction resources available in the target platform. For example, a high cardinality selection can be implemented with a list in the desktop and with a pull-down menu on a mobile device in order to consume less screen space.

Fig. 1 shows the authoring environment when the logical interface is obtained from the task model. The logical user interface is structured into presentations listed in the top-left area. In the top-right part, the abstract description of the selected presentation is highlighted, whereas the bottom-right displays the possible refinement of the currently selected element in the abstract part for the current target platform.

Another addition in this new environment is the possibility of generating interaction techniques supporting communication among users. Thus, for example, while in the single user environment it is possible to associate the activator interactor with calls to content-server or local functions, in this new version it is also possible to include a type of activator interaction, which sends information to the user interface of another user. In this case, the designer should also indicate the user role and the interactor identifier in the corresponding interface that is to receive the transmitted information.

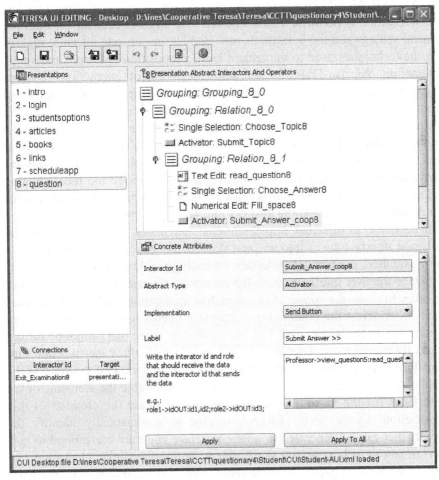

Figure 1. The Cooperative TERESA authoring environment

For example in Fig. 1, the lower section of the part associated with the concrete attributes provides a text box where the designer specifies that the information corresponding to the value of the view question5 interactor should be sent to the Professor when this button is selected and should also be associated to the value of the read_question8 interactor of the corresponding user interface. More in general, it is possible to indicate the value of one or multiple interactors of the current user interface and specify one or multiple interactors in the user interfaces of the target roles that should receive such values.

For each role, once the corresponding concrete interface has been defined with the support of our authoring environment, then the system generates the corresponding user interface for the indicated platform. For example, Cooperative Teresa generates XHTML implementations for desktop platforms and XHTML Mobile Profile implementations for mobile platforms. This last transformation is performed in a modular way so as to account for both the general settings and the indications provided by the concrete interface regarding the techniques used to implement both composition operators and single interaction objects. Thus, for the implementation of interaction elements grouping, for example, the concrete graphical desktop interface can choose from among field sets, bullets, the same background color or positioning the elements nearby vertically or horizontally. As a further example, it can choose to implement a navigator interactor through a graphical or a textual link or a button. When an interaction technique is selected then the associated attributes are enabled so that designers can specify the most suitable values. Thus, the concrete interface has a role of connecting high-level descriptions (the task model and the abstract interface) and implementations, which can be made in different implementation languages. This means that the concrete interface takes into account the features of the corresponding platform and there is a concrete interface for each possible platform.

Once the user interfaces (one for each potential user role) are generated, in order to make the cooperative interactive application work the developers have to associate the potential user interface events with the corresponding basic tasks in the task model. The basic tasks are those that cannot be further logically decomposed. Creating this association will allow the run-time support for the cooperative interface to have an updated view of the state of the application and use the task model to enable and disable the elements of the interfaces for the various users accordingly. To ease the creation of this association, Cooperative TERESA is able to automatically identify the events that can be generated in a user interface and may correspond to task performance, such as selection of images, buttons, or links, change of text fields and loading pages. Thus, it automatically lists, on one side, the basic tasks supported by the interface considered and, on the other side, the list of the potential events so that the designer only has to indicate their correspondences. Two different events may happen to correspond to one basic task (for example, when the selection of two different links has the same effect).

4.   RUN-TIME SOFTWARE ARCHITECTURE

In our runtime software architecture for multi-device, multi-user Web applications we have one groupware server and various clients, which can be executed in different platforms (Fig. 2). At the implementation level the groupware server is obtained by adding some servlets and JSP pages in an Apache/Tomcat server, which also contains the application. For each client, in addition to the application we have a JavaScript and an applet. The JavaScript has to:

- Capture the events that occur on the Web application and communicate them externally.
- Disable interface elements that correspond to basic tasks logically disabled according to the task model.
- Change the state of some interface elements in order to present information generated by other users.

The types of events that can be captured by the JavaScripts are clicks on images and elements of a form, changes in form elements, and the loading of Web pages. The communication between the JavaScripts and the external world is performed through an applet, which communicates with a servlet in the groupware server. The references to the applet and Javascript are automatically added to the Web page upon its generation.

The groupware server is mainly composed of three components: the synchronizer manager, the interactive simulator and the event-task association table. The synchronizer manager is implemented as a Java Servlet, which can be called by the client applets and communicates with the content server. It can also provide the client applets with some information. The event-task associations table indicates which events should occur in order to perform each basic task. It plays an important role because it allows the environment to link the actual user behavior with the semantic information contained in the task model. The interactive simulator is software that contains the task model of the cooperative application and is able to list the basic tasks enabled according to the temporal relations specified in the task model. When it receives notification that a basic task has been performed then its state is updated so that it can provide an updated list of enabled and disabled tasks.

At run-time, in order to coordinate the actions of users belonging to different roles while interacting with an application developed with Cooperative TERESA, it is necessary to capture the actions that each user performs. For this purpose each Web applications contains a script, which collects all the events performed by the users and sends them to the applet. The most important features sent to the servlet are the events performed by the user and the role that the user is playing. The groupware server of Cooperative TERESA is responsible for the coordination between the roles. For this purpose it needs to know the basic tasks performed by the user. This is obtained by exploiting the association table created at design-time. After receiving information on the event performed, the Synchronizer Manager in the groupware server uses these associations to retrieve the corresponding task.

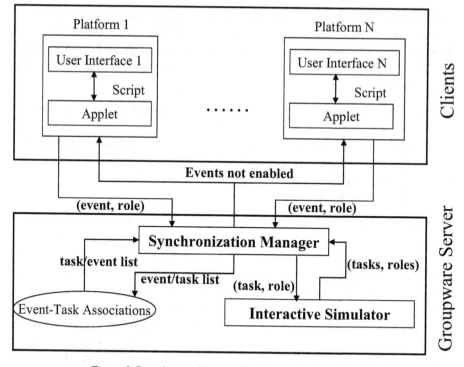

Figure 2. Run-time architecture for Cooperative TERESA

If the corresponding task exists then it communicates it, along with the associated role, to the interactive simulator. If it does not exist, then the event does not correspond to any task and is ignored. The interactive simulator updates its state by performing the indicated basic task and identifying the updated list of enabled tasks. This information is passed on to the synchronizer manager, which identifies the list of disabled basic tasks and the corresponding interface events with the support of the event-task association table. Then, it sends the list of user interface events not enabled according to the task model to each client. In particular, this information is sent to the applet, which, in turn, communicates it to the script, which disables the corresponding interface elements that are not enabled at that time.

The run-time support is also able to manage the exchange of information among various users so that if one user sends information to another one, such information will appear in the user interface of the other user according to the indications given at design-time. Indeed, there are interface elements that allow the user to send information, not to the content server, but to another user through the groupware server. In practice, Cooperative TERESA is able to associate specific attributes to buttons used to send information to other users. The JavaScript is able to recognize these attributes so that when the corresponding buttons are selected then the information to transmit externally is sent to the groupware server through the applet, with indications on the user who should receive it and to which interactor of the corresponding interface such information should be associated. Then, the server communicates with the applet of the target interface, which uses the local script to update the page content of the target interface, thus implementing our push mechanism.

5.   EXAMPLE APPLICATION

Web-based learning applications offer flexibility and saving costs. Online courses can be taken in synchronous sessions. Taking into account this new learning trend, the example chosen to demonstrate Cooperative TERESA concerns an application that supports the cooperation and communication between professors and students. Thus, the roles involved are:

- **Student** – After inserting personal data, the student has a number of options available, such as scheduling an appointment with the teacher, answering to questions on a number of topics, and entering the books and articles has read.
- **Professor** – The professor has various options available: such as consulting appointments, after viewing all the details of the appointment s/he can send a confirmation or refuse the appointment, explaining the reason to the student; visualizing the student's answers, verifying them and submitting a comment to the student.

In the example implemented, the student role uses a desktop environment and the professor role a PDA because we assume that the teachers want to be able to accomplish their tasks from any location. For example, the student can choose a question from five different topics (see Fig. 3, desktop interface). Upon the choice of the topic, a question and a set of four possible answers appear.

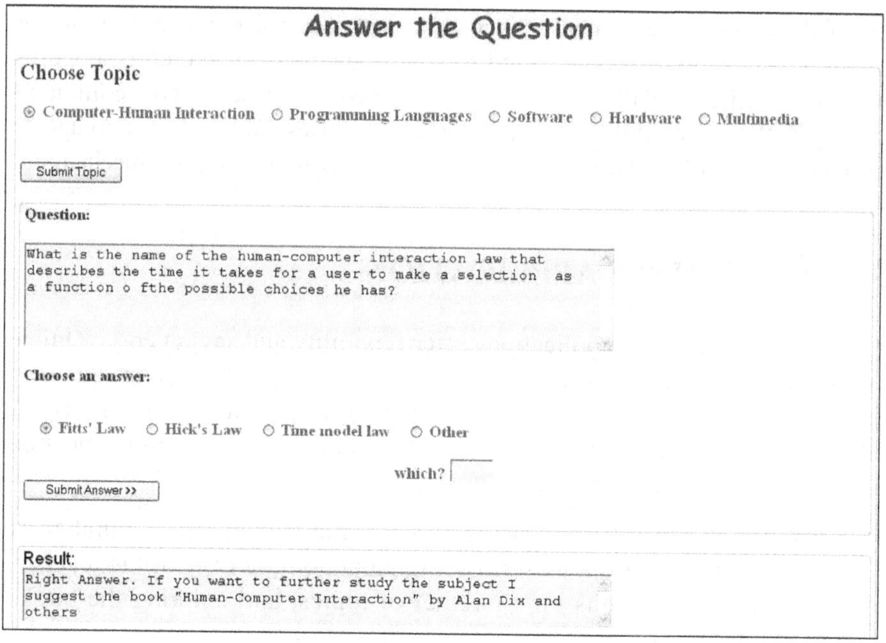

Figure 3. Example generated with Cooperative TERESA for desktop student interface

After selecting one of the answers the student must press a button to send it. This action disables all the previous actions, changing the fields to a grey color, and sends the student's selected question and answer to the professor. Upon the submission of the answer by the student, the professor is now able to access the "Student's Performance" link. In the Web page that appears, in the top part the professor can analyze information about the student (sent by the student upon the log in), the question and the answer, and in the bottom part indicate to the student if the answer is correct or incorrect, including a comment (Fig. 3). Then, the student can immediately visualize the professor's comment.

Another possibility of interaction between professor and student is the scheduling of an appointment with the professor. The student can schedule an appointment by sending the date, the hour and the motive of the appointment. After visualizing the appointment information, the professor can choose if he/she is available. If not available, the professor writes the reason and submits it to the student. If available, the professor simply sends the date and time back to the student as confirmation. After, the student can see if the professor will be at the appointment, and if not, why. The example chosen covers the communication and cooperation aspects of multi-user applications.

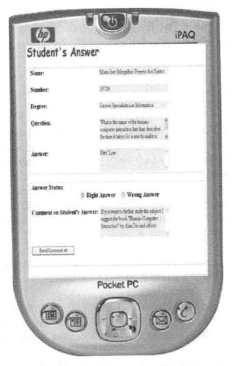

Figure 4. Example generated with Cooperative TERESA for PDA teacher interface

6.   CONCLUSION AND FUTURE WORK

We have presented an environment able to support design, development and run-time support for multi-user, multi-device Web applications. Our prototype has been validated with the development of an application for e-learning supporting cooperation between students and teachers. This has shown the feasibility of the approach and its possible advantages: the environment actually allows designers to focus on the tasks to support, the relations among tasks performed by different users, and the logical structure of the corresponding user interface without having to manage a plethora of low-level implementation details. Then, a specific run-time architecture is able to support even synchronous communication among users interacting through different types of devices. Thus, the Web interface of one user can be dynamically modified to present information generated by other users.

Future work will be dedicated to extending the set of possible platforms for the user interfaces involved in the multi-user application, also considering various modalities, such as vocal, gestural and graphical modality, and different ways to combine them. This means integrating into Cooperative

Teresa the already existing transformations: from abstract TERESA XML first to the concrete descriptions of the corresponding platforms and then to the final interfaces in implementation languages able to support such modalities.

REFERENCES

[1]   Abrams, M., Phanouriou, C., Batongbacal, A., Williams, S., and Shuster, J., *UIML: An Appliance-Independent XML User Interface Language*, in Proc. of the 8th WWW conference WWW8 (Toronto, 11–14 May 1999), Elsevier, Amsterdam, 1999.

[2]   Girgensohn, A., and Lee, A., *Developing Collaborative Applications on the World Wide Web*, in Proc. of ACM Conf. Summary on Human Factors in Computing Systems CHI'98 (Los Angeles, 18–23 April 1998), ACM Press, New York, 1998, pp. 141–142.

[3]   Greenberg, S., *Toolkits and Interface Creativity*, Special Issue on Groupware, Journal Multimedia Tools and Applications, Kluwer, 2004.

[4]   Grundy, J., Wang X., and Hosking, J., *Building Multi-device, Component-based, Thin-client Groupware: Issues and Experiences*, in Proc. of 3rd Australasian Conf. on User Interfaces CRPITS'2002, Vol. 7, Australian Computer Society, Inc., January 2002, pp. 71–80.

[5]   Han, R., Perret, V., and Naghshineh, M., *WebSplitter: Orchestrating Multiple Devices for Collaborative Web Browsing*, in Proc. of ACM Conf. on Computer Supported Cooperative Work CSCW'2000 (Philadelphia, 2-6 December 2000), ACM Press, New York, 2000, pp. 221–230.

[6]   Mori, G., Paternò, F., and Santoro, C., *Design and Development of Multi-Device User Interfaces through Multiple Logical Descriptions*, IEEE Transactions on Software Engineering, Vol. 30, No. 8, August 2004, pp. 507–520.

[7]   Paternò, F., *Model-based Design and Evaluation of Interactive Applications*, Springer-Verlag, Berlin, 1999.

[8]   Pinelle, D., Gutwin, C., and Greenberg, S., *Task Analysis for Groupware Usability Evaluation: Modeling Shared-Workspace Tasks with the Mechanics of Collaboration*, ACM Transactions on Computer-Human Interaction, Vol. 10, No. 4, December 2003, pp. 281–311.

[9]   Roseman, M., and Greenberg, S., *Building Real Time Groupware with GroupKit, A Groupware Toolkit*, ACM Transactions on Computer-Human Interaction, Vol. 3, No. 1, March 1996, pp. 66–106.

[10] Stanciulescu, A., Limbourg, Q., Vanderdonckt, J., Michotte, B., and Montero, F., *A Transformational Approach for Multimodal Web User Interfaces based on UsiXML*, in Proc. of 7th Int. Conf. on Multimodal Interfaces ICMI'2005 (Trento, 4–6 October 2005), ACM Press, New York, 2005, pp. 259–266.

[11] Trætteberg, H., *Modeling Work: Workflow and Task Modeling*, in J. Vanderdonckt, A.R. Puerta (eds.), Proc. of 3rd Conf. on Computer-Aided Design of User Interfaces CADUI'99 (Louvain-la-Neuve, 21–23 October 1999), Kluwer Academics, Dordrecht, 1999, pp. 275–280.

Chapter 10

A SYSTEM TO SUPPORT PUBLISHING, EDITING, AND CREATING WEB CONTENT FOR VARIOUS DEVICES

Márcio Maia Silva and Elizabeth Furtado

University of Fortaleza, Av. Washington Soares, 1321 - Fortaleza, CE 60.811-905 (Brazil)
E-mail: {marcioms, elizabet}@unifor.br – Web: ead.unifor.br/luqs
Tel.: +55 85-34773079 – Fax: +55 85-34773055

Abstract   One of the main goals of the Internet is to disseminate information, which grows fast and the need to maintain it up-to-date is fundamental. The advent of mobile devices and the growth of resources for these devices, as a way to access the Internet, are re-directing software companies to design multi-device user interfaces to disseminate information. There is a challenge in this situation: how to update information on the Internet in an easy and fast manner, and also that can be accessed through various devices? This research consists in developing a system to support the publication and edition of content for the web, which includes a flow of activities that makes it possible to create this content to various devices

Keywords: Content Management, Design Patterns, User Interface Design

1.   INTRODUCTION

Various institutions, trying to offer better services on the web for their visitors, have already noticed the problem of updating information in a fast manner; therefore, they have acquired tools for content management. Such tools allow the publication of various contents on the web, without requiring programming technical knowledge, thus, allowing content managers to speed up the creation and maintenance process of web pages. The content manager is an expert in a certain domain, who is responsible for creating the information that will be available on web pages. Many of these tools offer search services, notification, sending and printing of content; numbering pages and ordering of contents; and document preview before its effective

G. Calvary et al. (eds.), Computer-Aided Design of User Interfaces V, 123–136.
© 2007 *Springer.*

publication. However, in order to allow more flexibility for more experienced content managers while creating web pages, these tools should support activities of user interface design, such as, planning the navigability of pages and defining interactive objects (e.g., menus, buttons), thus, allowing them to think about the site structure and navigation as a whole, before focusing only on the content.

Institutions also face another problem, which is to use existing technological resources to provide more flexibility and agility to visitors while they perform their activities. Because of that, they try not only to make updated information available, but also accessible in various devices (such as: palmtop, digital television, kiosks, mobile phones). This work involves studies to integrate the following subjects: i) content management, which involves updating and publishing content of web pages; and ii) user interface design for various devices, which includes planning the navigability, creating user interfaces, and generating these user interfaces for various devices.

This work presents a computational system to support creating and publishing web contents, and also supporting user interface design for various devices. The user of this system follows a flow of activities to edit and update the web content and to design the user interfaces of these contents. During user interface design, patterns of user interface components are made available in order to allow the mapping between user interface objects of different devices. The user of this system is the content manager, but it can also be used by the designer to support the user interface design process.

This article is organized as follows: in the first section, we describe the problems and motivations, which defined the starting point and the encountered challenges; then, we describe related works that were useful as theoretical basis; finally, before the discussion and conclusion, we describe the proposal of this work.

2.   PROBLEMATIC AND MOTIVATION

In order to contextualize the problematic of this work, we will initially present the tool that we have developed to support professors (content managers) in creating didactic materials of the electricity course made available in a distance learning environment on the web. This tool, called FEMDI (Tool to Elaborate Didactic Material) [12], was developed to solve the problem of encountered difficulties when updating the content of didactic materials for web pages. They needed a reasonable team of programmers to include the content in HTML code, thus, generating extra costs for the courses.

In FEMDI, the professor creates the didactic material without the need to have programming skills, and publishes the material on the web. This tool offers fixed page templates, which help in creating web pages and in including the content in these pages. A page template is a web page in which there are tags (markers) that indicate the exact place where the content will be inserted. When creating a page, the content manager selects a page template, among the ones in FEMDI, and then, informs the name of the page (e.g., capillarity.jsp), a brief description of the page, as well as its content. Fig. 1 shows the screen for the creation of web pages and inclusion of content, using a page template. For the tag of simple text [TXTSMP01], content mangers include the subject title "Capillarity", and for the tag of hypermedia text [TXTHPM01], they can use a series of hypermedia resources to include in the text. Currently, this tool is being widely used by professors and it decreases the difficulties of maintaining didactic contents updated, editing and publishing them efficiently. However, new requirements have emerged, such as, users (students) wanting to access the courses using other devices, and content managers requiring more freedom to structure their own site (course), in this case, to create their own page templates.

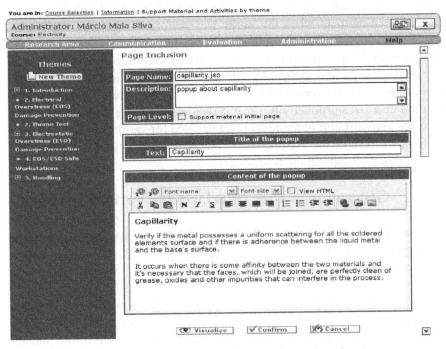

Figure 1. Screen for the creation of pages and inclusion of content

3.   RELATED WORK

In order to attend these requirements, we have researched and studied tools for content management and scientific works related to user interface design for various devices.

3.1   Tools for Content Management

In the content management scenario, various tools emerged with catego-
rizations according to their objective: content management for portals, blogs,
electronic business, discussion forums, distance learning, among others. Further information can be found in the OpensourceCMS web site [15]. Particularly, we point out the tools Notitia [6], KBX [6], and Content [8], which
were developed aiming at supporting the edition and publication of content
on the web. These tools have the following positive characteristics: they do
not require programming skills and they offer visual support for the creation
of web pages. However, all of the pages are pre-defined by fixed page templates and there is no support to structure the navigability among pages.
Tools that support the definition of this navigability can be classified as prototyping tools, such as Denim [14] and Demais [3], which focus on the user
interface design process. They do not include the entire development lifecycle of a web site until the publication of pages with its edited content.

Up to the moment when this study was performed, the previously mentioned content management tools still do not provide any strategy to make
content available in various devices; they offer the edition and publication of
web contents only in desktops. In order to make it possible, the content manager needs to specify the content in a different manner for each device. This
solution decreases productivity since it requires doubling information and it
becomes very difficult to maintain them updated for various devices.

In order to show the existing techniques and products in this problematic,
we will describe them in the next section.

3.2   Generation of User Interfaces for Various Devices

Researches related to the creation of models, tools, and languages aim at
helping the development of Multiple User Interfaces (MUI), which compre-
hends an interactive system that [17], for instance provides multiple visions
of the same information in these different platforms.

ArtSTudio [7] supports a reification process based on the definition of
user interfaces in abstraction levels: an Abstract User Interface (AUI) [7] is a
representation of domain concepts and functions independent of the interactions evaluated for the application goal [4]. A Concrete User Interface (CUI)
[7] is still a prototype that is only executed in the development environment.
A Final User Interface (FUI) is expressed in the source-code, such as Java
and HTML. The advantage of this proposal is that for one AUI, it is possible
to obtain various CUIs (one CUI for each specific device), thus, guaranteeing the independence between what must exist in the user interface (necessary content) and how it must exist (content handled by the user interface).

Other research works have proposed solutions to improve the productivity in the development of interactive systems for various devices through the reuse of Human-Computer Interaction (HCI) patterns. We can define HCI patterns as a tested solution for a usability problem (such as lack of orientation, difficulty in finding information) that happens in a certain context (e.g., search, visualization). In Javahery [10], we noticed how HCI patterns can facilitate the user interface migration process between different platforms by encapsulating high level design options, thus, allowing designers to operate with a higher level of abstraction.

Appleton [2] describes two proposals for the migration of UIs existing in a certain platform for other platforms, which we focus on the redesign proposal. Redesign performs a direct transformation between patterns, for instance, from a set of HCI patterns for desktops for a set of HCI patterns for palmtops.

Concerning languages for the development of MUI, we point out XML-based languages, such as XIML [16], UIML [1], and UsiXML (USer Interface eXtensible Markup Language, a User Interface Description Language accessible at http://www.usixml.org) [20]. They allow the separation of user interface description from the content, thus, providing a manner to specify how user interface components must interact and a way to decipher rules that define standards of interaction behavior. The disadvantage of this solution is that languages require programming skills to specify CUI. SketchiXML [9] is a sketching tool which generates user interface specifications written in UsiXML [20]. Even though there are some tools that offer visual support to design user interfaces for various devices, such as ARTStudio [7], Teresa [13], and Damask [11], we have faced the following challenge: how can we edit, update, and publish content also?

As a consequence of this study, we have decided to implement new functionality to support designing user interfaces and integrate them to the functionality in FEMDI, thus, generating the tool called SAPEC-WEB, in order to make it possible to migrate the edited content to various devices.

4.   CHARACTERISTICS AND WORKFLOW OF SAPEC-WEB

The basic architecture of SAPEC-WEB was designed based on the concepts of the Model-View-Control (MVC) architecture pattern [5]. Aiming at having portability, we decided to develop SAPEC-WEB using the Java technology. In [18], the implementation details are described. We prioritize in this article, the characteristics and procedures to use the tool.

4.1   Characteristics of SAPEC-WEB

The characteristics included in the proposed tool were the following:

a) **Generation of user interface and visual support to structure the site based on the navigation model** – we proposed a new navigation model and implemented new graphical functionality to support editing this model. The navigation model is composed of workspaces, which are working areas that will be transformed into web pages through the application of the process. We have defined two kinds of workspaces:

- *Simple Workspace* (SW), which represents a working area reserved for the execution of activities by users.
- *Complex Workspace* (CW), which represents a structure of two or more areas, similar to a frame, in which each area will be occupied by one or more simple workspaces.

The workspaces have properties, which are: name, type (simple or complex), and description; the complex workspaces have some specific properties: quantity of areas, form of division of the areas (in lines or columns); width/height of each area; and the simple workspace that will initially occupy each area. The possibilities of relationships between the workspaces are defined through the following navigation patterns:

- *Sequential navigation pattern*: it is a simple navigation between workspaces, where each workspace points to another workspace or to other workspaces, in a sequential manner.
- *Multidirectional navigation pattern*: in this pattern, various simple workspaces are inter-related, which have *n-to-n* associations, that is; each SW calls the other SWs.
- *Frame navigation pattern*: it defines a structure composed of two or more areas. It is used to represent a frame structure, where, in most of the cases, one of the areas is fixed, occupied by a page composed of navigation items, and in the other areas, there are pages that are presented according to the selection of the navigation items mentioned previously.

b) **Use of the concept of user interfaces in various levels of abstraction** – we added the concept of CUI before the generation of the FUI. We did not adopt the concept of AUI because we use the notion of prototyping based on Architecture-Centric characteristic [19], where prototypes help to define the development platform (including programming language, and interaction device) from the beginning of the process. The platform decision directly affects the number of objects in a workspace and the kind of navigation among workspaces, which change depending on the size of objects and spaces of the selected device. Initially the CUI is composed of user interface objects (such as: link, image, video, flash animation, simple text, hypermedia text), then, these objects will be instantiated to generate pages with the edited content. A CUI defines the interior (objects) of the created workspaces. When generating CUIs, we select the style file (.css) that will define the visual of the page. This file defines colors, types of fonts, size of fonts, among other characteristics.

c) **Use of HCI patterns** – we adopted the use of CUI design patterns, such as: key-word search, bread crumbs, and information portal [10], to reuse user interface specifications and to map specifications for different devices. In this work, not all of the CUI objects are patterns, but all of them have properties. For instance: the user interface object "link" has class style, destination page, name, among other properties; the pattern "left lateral menu" also has properties, such as, quantity of items and ordering of these items. Contrarily to the user interface objects, the patterns are created to solve an HCI problem for a certain context. Fig. 2b illustrates the FUI in a palmtop, for the example of the FUI in the desktop shown in Fig. 2a. We can see that the pattern "fixed left lateral menu" was mapped to the pattern "fixed superior menu" and all of the other user interface objects and contents were kept.

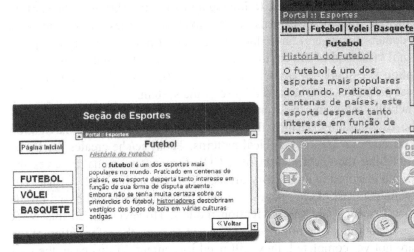

Figure 2a. FUI for desktops   *Figure 2b.* FUI for palmtops

d) **Use of transformation rules** – we adopted the redesign strategy, which performs direct transformation between patterns for different devices. To perform redesign, transformation rules are used to consider various technical and usability characteristics. Transformation rules can be of three types: usability rules, restrictive rules, and ergonomic rules. Usability rules aim at guaranteeing the usability of user interfaces generated for various devices. Therefore, there are specific usability rules for each device. For instance, a usability rule can define that a page in a mobile phone must contain no more than 500 characters. That is, a page with 100 characters in a desktop will be divided in two pages in a mobile phone. Restrictive rules define some restrictions concerning the use of resources that are used for desktops, but that are not appropriate for other devices. For instance, a rule can restrict the use of a frame in a palmtop. Ergonomic rules define some user interface characteristics that must be followed to guarantee that the user interface is appropriate for the device. For instance, an ergonomic rule for the Digital TeleVision (DTV) can define that the size of the font must be the minimum of 16.

4.2   Workflow of SAPEC-WEB

SAPEC-WEB proposes a workflow that describes its functionality in two phases: i) User interface design phase, to support the user (user interface designer and content manager) when creating navigation models and concrete user interfaces; ii) Content management phase, to support the content manager when editing, publishing, and creating the final user interfaces.

In each one of these phases, we perform activities that generate artifacts that are used in other activities, following a process (workflow). The starting point of our approach happens after stakeholders (designers, engineers and/or content managers) have done a clear description of the user requirements and tasks and of the environment where the system will be used. This description is essential in deriving and constructing models to represent the universal properties of users and the use of the system.

Generally, following the workflow, the use of the system is the following: the user initially designs the site navigation, creating the navigation model through navigation graphical patterns. Then, he/she creates the CUIs. After finishing the specification of a CUI, the content manager saves the CUI, which is stored in a directory of SAPEC-WEB in the XML format. The FUIs, which consist of web pages, are automatically generated based on the CUI specifications and the navigation models. However, since this work involves the activity of editing content, in some cases, the information of the CUIs are not yet completed; they still need its content. In this case, the user requires the generation of the page template that will be used to create pages that contain the edited and managed content. We have decided, first, to generate web pages for desktops, and then, based on them, generate pages for other devices. We decided that because many people are used with the user interface web standard for desktops. In this article, we will show the generation of CUIs for the electricity course, using the implemented functionality of the SAPEC-WEB, which are integrated to a distance learning environment.

Then we will describe the process aiming at migrating the edited content to various devices.

4.2.1   Generation of concrete user interfaces

In order to content managers have more freedom to structure their own site (course), and some support to reuse specifications of the organization of pages, without compromising their creativity and without requiring programming skills, they use our tool to generate CUIs. During the generation of CUIs, the content manager inserts patterns of user interface components and user interface objects, selecting them and filling out their attributes.

Fig. 3 illustrates the SAPEC-WEB screen used by the user to generate the CUI for a topic of the electricity course. This screen is divided in two parts. In the left side, there is the hierarchy of course topics. In the middle part, there is a space for the edition of the CUI. This CUI was associated to the style sheet represented in the file called "style-desktop-pattern.css". The user inserted the pattern "Fixed Superior Menu" and a button. The resulting CUI that we see in the middle of the screen is composed of four elements: Fixed Superior Menu, a simple text, a hypermedia text, and a button. In the right side, the user can associate this CUI with the workspaces that have already been created.

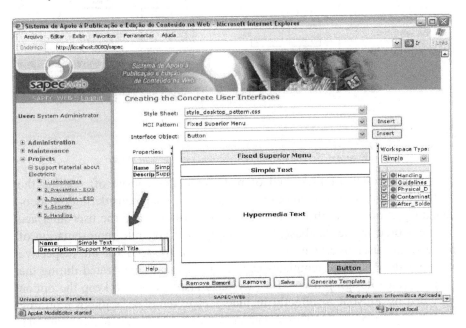

Figure 3. Screen for the generation of concrete user interfaces

We suggest to the content managers specify one navigation model to each course topic. Fig. 4 illustrates the screen of the module that supports the visual construction of the navigation model associated to the generic topic "electricity". The model was specified using the frame navigation pattern, where each area represents one specific topic.

Concerning to the content management phase, as previously mentioned, there are user interface objects that when inserted in the CUI are already instantiated. For instance, when inserting an object of the type "Button", the content manager informs its label. The same thing happens with objects of the type "items of a menu". In the specific case of object for "Hypermedia Text", the edition of its contents is made afterwards, using the graphical editor of the FEMDI system, shown in Fig. 1. In this case, the content manager clicks on the button "generate template", located in Fig. 3, to require the generation of the page template that will be used to edit the page contents.

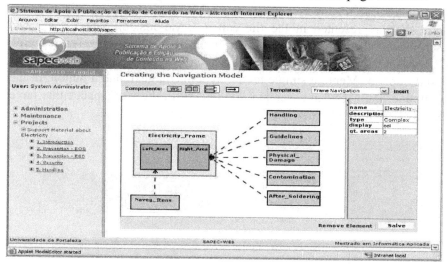

Figure 4. Screen for the generation of navigation model

The generation of FUIs and of page templates consist of: reading the XML file with the specifications of the generated CUI, considering the associated style; obtaining the source code of the patterns and the user interface objects stored in the database; and changing the concrete representation of patterns and user interface objects contained in the CUI for the respective source-code. The page templates can be automatically generated during the user interface design process. But, we have also decided to keep the option provided by FEMDI to directly include a page template, without requiring the generation of CUIs. This decision makes SAPEC-WEB more flexible, also, allowing its use only for content management, not necessarily for user interface design. But, on the other hand, it does not allow the automatic generation of pages for other devices, since the system uses the definitions of CUIs and of navigation models to map the patterns and generate the pages for other devices.

4.2.2   Generation of pages for other devices

Our proposal consists in generating FUIs for various devices based on CUIs and on navigation models created for desktops. From the CUIs, the system obtains the patterns and user interface objects. From the navigation models, the system obtains the pages (workspaces), and from the FUIs, the system obtains the content. Up to the moment, as we have not implemented all functionalities, we only describe in the next paragraphs this migration process specification. Concerning the obtained information, the process to generate pages for various devices consists of three actions: inclusion and removal of user interface objects; mapping of patterns, and division of pages.

In the first action, the process consists of verifying if all of the user interface objects in the CUI for desktops are supported in the destination device, removing the ones that are not supported. In this moment, the system consults a base of restrictions for the selected device. The FUIs for desktops offer, for the designer, more resources, since they have more processing power, and more possibilities of navigation than any other device. Desktop screens are bigger and accept a variety of user interface objects. For instance, animation files in shockwave flash are not supported in mobile phones. In this case, the call for this file would be replaced by a warning message in order to allow the intervention of the designer to adjust the generation of the user interface.

In the second action, the process proposes the transformation of user interface objects and patterns, which consists in transforming patterns and user interface objects from the CUI into patterns and objects appropriate for the destination device. In SAPEC-WEB, the definition of mapping between patterns is performed by HCI experts, who are supported by programmers, who create the source-code of the patterns. As well as for the patterns, the programmers also create the source-code of the user interface objects for each device.

The final stage of the process for the generation of user interfaces for other devices consists in dividing a desktop page in two or more screens of another device, when necessary. It depends on the following features: size of the content of a page, navigation patterns, among others. To do that, the process uses some transformation rules, which allow the identification of the need to include user interface objects, to divide the pages, and to remove resources. For instance, it is identified that the frame navigation pattern for desktop is not appropriate for the DTV. So, a web page, containing one area occupied by navigation items, and the other area occupied by pages associated to each selected navigation item, will be divided. The first DTV screen will show only the navigation items. After an item is chosen, a new DTV screen will show its content. If the size of the content is big, many TV screens can be used. The division of pages also includes handling the navigation among them. Shortcut keys to navigate to home or end can be included. In the DTV screen, these options should be on the bottom bar composed of colored buttons as depicted in any DTV remote control.

5.   DISCUSSION

The following is a discussion of the systems (SAPEC-WEB and FEMDI) being used by two professors and two designers, during the construction of the electricity course. While the users interacted with the systems, we noticed that the SAPEC-WEB was serving the purpose of supporting the user interface design process in a usable and efficient manner. The professors organized their ideas during the creation of navigation models, with no difficulty. They talked us, it was better to design the desktop version of a user interface and that they were not able to design it for a mobile version, for instance. Then they created the CUIs to generate the page templates, and, at last, they edited the content to generate web pages for desktops. It is important to observe that, if there is not the creation of CUIs and navigation models, it is not be possible to generate pages for other devices automatically.

Using FEMDI, new page templates were requested and there was the need to allocate programmers to create more page templates. Using SAPEC-WEB, the reuse of patterns brought productivity to the process, thus, facilitating the creation of page templates. So far, they required us to implement HCI patterns specific to the learning domain (such as revision patterns, exercise patterns). All of the activities using SAPEC-WEB did not require the users to program. However they were not free to modify or to create a pattern. It requires an effort of programming to include the pattern source-code.

6.   FUTURE WORK

For future work, SAPEC-WEB will be used to edit and publish the content for the WEB as well as for the DTV. For this, it is necessary to create and implement usability patterns for the DTV in SAPEC-WEB, and to define three types of rules: ergonomic; usability; and restrictive. There is also the need to create an application for the DTV that will be accessible from the Access Portal for users to navigate through content (such as news, distance learning courses).

We think that the edition of content for the DTV must be done semi-automatically by TV broadcasters and content producers, that is, based on the edited WEB content, SAPEC-WEB must apply specific usability patterns for the DTV to generate a XML document for the DTV. The content producer will obtain this document and will make the desired arrangements.

Concerning the publication of content in the DTV, broadcasters and content producers will transmit, via broadcast, the XML document with the content generated by SAPEC-WEB, as well as all of the other desired information (such as a programming guide) to be read by the Access Portal application. Therefore, the user interface elements will be dynamically placed in the DTV screen.

7.   CONCLUSION

This work has presented a system that has an original characteristic to support the creation of content starting from user interface design. Through its implemented functionality and offered artifacts (such as navigation model, patterns), the system allows content managers to create the site and generate user interfaces for web. They do this with more freedom and in an easy way, through various visual supports. The system encourages the reuse of user interface specifications and could decrease the time and effort spent on future projects. An important characteristic in this system is its extensibility. The system, through the creation of restrictions for devices, mapping between patterns for user interface components, and the use of transformation rules, makes its use practical for the generation of content for various devices for the dissemination of information.

REFERENCES

[1]   Ali, M.F., Perez-Quiñones, M.A., and Abrams, M., *Building Multi-Platform User Interfaces with UIML*, in A. Seffah, H. Javahery (eds.), « Multiple User Interfaces - Cross-Platform Applications and Context-Aware Interfaces », John Wiley & Sons, New York, November 2003, pp. 95–118.

[2]   Appleton, B., *Patterns and Software: Essential Concepts and Terminology*, 2000, accessible at http://www.cmcrossroads.com/bradapp/docs/patterns-intro.html.

[3]   Bailey, B.P., and Konstan, J.A., *Are Informal Tools Better? Comparing DEMAIS, Pencil and Paper, and Authorware for Early Multimedia Design*, in Proc. of the ACM Conf. on Human Factors in Computing Systems CHI'2003 (Ft. Lauderdale, 5–10 April 2003), ACM Press, New York, 2003, pp. 313–320.

[4] Bass, L., Little, R., Pellegrino, R., Reed, S., Seacord, R., Sheppard, S., and Szczur, M.R., *The Arch model: Seeheim revisited (version 1.0): The UIMS Developers Workshop (April 1991)*, SIGCHI Bulletin, Vol. 24, No. 1, 1992.

[5] Buschmann, F., Meunier, R., Rohnert, H., Sommerlad, P., and Stal, M., *Pattern-Oriented Software Architecture: A System of Patterns*, John Wiley & Sons Ltd., 1998.

[6] Calandra Soluções, 2005, accessible at http://www.calandra.com.br.

[7] Calvary, G., Coutaz, J., Thevenin, D., Limbourg, Q., Bouillon, L., and Vanderdonckt, J., *A Unifying Reference Framework for Multi-Target User Interfaces*, Interacting with Computers, Vol. 15, No. 3, 2003, pp. 289–308.

[8] Content – Gerência de Conteúdo, 2005, accessible at http://www.content.com.br/index-content.asp.

[9] Coyette, A., and Vanderdonckt, J., *A Sketching Tool for Designing Anyuser, Anyplatform, Anywhere User Interfaces*, in Proc. of 10th IFIP TC 13 Int. Conf. on Human-Computer Interaction INTERACT'2005 (Rome, 12–16 September 2005), Lecture Notes in Computer Science, Vol. 3585, Springer-Verlag, Berlin, 2005, pp. 550–564.

[10] Javahery, H., Seffah, A., Engelberg, D., and Sinnig, D., *Migrating User Interfaces Across Platforms Using HCI Patterns*, in A. Seffah, H. Javahery (eds.), « Multiple User Interfaces - Cross-Platform Applications and Context-Aware Interfaces », John Wiley & Sons, New York, November 2003, pp. 241–259.

[11] Lin, J., and Landay, J., *Damask: A Tool for Early-Stage Design and Prototyping of Multi-Device User Interfaces*, in Proc. of the 8th Int. Conf. on Distributed Multimedia Systems VC'2002 (San Francisco, 26–28 September 2002), 2002, pp. 573–580.

[12] Mattos, F., Maia, M., and Furtado, E., *Formação Docente em Processos Colaborativos Online: Em Direção a Novos "Círculos de Cultura"?*, in Proc. of IX WIE - Workshop de Informática na Escola SBC'2003, 2003.

[13] Mori, G., Paternò, F., and Santoro, C., *Tool Support for Designing Nomadic Applications*, in Proc. of ACM Conf. on Intelligent User Interfaces IUI'2003 (Miami, 12–15 January 2003), ACM Press, New York, 2003, pp. 141–148.

[14] Newman, M.W., Lin, J., Hong, J.I., and Landay, J.A., *DENIM: An Informal Web Site Design Tool Inspired by Observations of Practice*, Human-Computer Interaction, Vol. 18, No. 3, 2003, pp. 259–324.

[15] OpensourceCMS, 2005, accessible at http://www.opensourcecms.com.

[16] Puerta, A.R., and Eisenstein, J., *XIML: A Multiple User Interface Representation Framework for Industry*, in A. Seffah, H. Javahery (eds.), « Multiple User Interfaces - Cross-Platform Applications and Context-Aware Interfaces », John Wiley & Sons, New York, November 2003, pp. 119–148.

[17] Seffah, A., Radhakrishnan, T., and Canals, G., *Multiple User Interfaces over the Internet: Engineering and Applications Trends*, in Proc. of the IHM-HCI'2001 Workshop: French/British Conf. on Human Computer Interaction, Lille, 10–14 September 2001.

[18] Silva, M.M., *Sistema de Apoio à Publicação e Edição de Conteúdo Web para Diversos Dispositivos Utilizando Padrões*, Dissertação defendida no MIA, Universidade de Fortaleza, Fortaleza, 2005.

[19] Sousa, K., Mendonça, H., and Furtado, E., *UPi – A Software Development Process Aiming at Usability, Productivity and Integration*, in Proc. of the 2005 Latin American Conf. on Human-computer interaction CLIHC'2005 (Cuernavaca, 23–26 October 2005), ACM Int. Conf. Proceeding Series, Vol. 124, ACM Press, New York, 2005, pp. 76–87.

[20] Vanderdonckt, J., *A MDA-Compliant Environment for Developing User Interfaces of Information Systems*, in O. Pastor, J. Falcão e Cunha (eds.), Proc. of 17th Conf. on Advanced Information Systems Engineering CAiSE'05 (Porto, 13–17 June 2005), Lecture Notes in Computer Science, Vol. 3520, Springer-Verlag, Berlin, 2005, pp. 16–31.

Chapter 11

TRANSFORMATIONAL CONSISTENCY

Kai Richter
Computer Graphics Center (ZGDV)
Fraunhoferstraße 5 – D- 64283 Darmstadt (Germany)
E-Mail: kai.richter@zgdv.de – Web: http://www.ksrichter.de/Mambo/
Tel: +49-6151-155-609 – Fax: +49-6151-155-451

Abstract   This article describes how the development of user interfaces for different devices can be improved and accelerated by integrating design support methods into the interactive design process that are based on a transformational consistency measure

Keywords: Consistency, Metrics, Multiple user interfaces, User interface design

1.   INTRODUCTION

Applications that can adapt to user, device, and context of use help to reduce development costs and to improve usability in a time where diversity of computing devices and the range of their potential usage is constantly growing. Methods to improve the development of such applications are necessary to reduce development effort and to optimize the design of such systems.

With the availability of entire new classes of devices and services, developers of interactive systems have been confronted with the multi-dimensional space of platform-, user-, and application-specific requirements [24]. Each combination of contextual parameters can possibly occur and has to be addressed by the system design, resulting in different instances of one and the same system. At the same time, these cross-device applications have to maintain a certain cross-device experience and integrity that requires the coordination and integration of the different development paths.

Seffah and Javahery [22] have coined the expression of Multiple User Interfaces (MUI) to give a name to the undeterminable nature of these systems. MUI represent an integration of different aspects of adaptive and adaptable

G. Calvary et al. (eds.), Computer-Aided Design of User Interfaces V, 137–150.
© 2007 *Springer.*

user interfaces, such as multi-modality, user adaptation, device- and platform independence and so forth. As a result of this multiplicity many aspects of human-computer interaction have to be reconsidered and revalidated with respect to the dimensions involved [3,21]. What does that mean for the design of such systems?

1.1   Abstraction vs. Compatibility

Current approaches of MUI are based on the definition of an abstract specification of task, application, or context, which then are iteratively reified into concrete presentations. Generally, existing solutions differ in the level of abstraction, the number of intermediate reification steps, and in the complexity of the abstract specification involved according to the CAMELEON reference model [3]. Technically this has been realized by two major approaches that slowly seem to converge: (model-based) user interface management systems (UIMS) [23] and cross-platform user interface toolkits (UITK) such as Sun Java, Microsoft .Net, and Trolltech Qt.

1.1.1   UIMS

The most fundamental advantage of *model-based methods* is the possibility to model any aspect of an application on a high level of abstraction. This leads to many degrees of freedom concerning the possible adaptation routines. Further, the generated user interfaces are inherently guaranteed to follow general design rules, are therefore consistent over platforms and contribute to a coherent user experience amongst different instances of a user interface [26]. At the same time, this obvious advantage has been argued to be the main disadvantage with respect to the establishment of model-based development processes in industrial application. As Trætteberg [25] argues, a manufacturer's decision to move to a model-based UIMS means to abort existing processes and expertise, to fully adapt the complex and non-standard methods, and to run into the danger of requiring features not yet supported by the UIMS. This step obviously intimidates most decision-makers.

1.1.2   UITK

Toolkit-based methods are the most common way how user interfaces are developed today. Methods and tools for graphically designing and modifying user interfaces are at hand and widely spread. Toolkit-based approaches have been proven to be at the same time efficient and flexible enough to meet industrial needs. So it is no wonder that manufacturers are making large efforts to address the challenge of MUI based on toolkits and well-know components and programming interfaces. However, toolkits support for cross-device applications still is at an early stage. Further, the employment of component-level specifications clearly limits the possibility to abstract and adapt presentation and interaction. Yet, the availability of a declarative user interface description language for the next generation of *Microsoft Windows* indicates the plans for the future of the most widespread operating system: i.e., promoting the separation of presentation and application logic.

To trade-off the potential of abstraction against the compatibility with existing processes will be a challenge for the development of MUI systems. Recent developments have indeed revealed the tendency towards convergence, such as the visual design of model-based user interfaces in the GRAFIXML tool [5], the encapsulation of abstract specifications in toolkits [16], or the integration of meta-information in component-based approaches like W3C XFORMS (http://www.w3.org/MarkUp/Forms/).

1.2   Automation vs. Design

Any abstracted specification of a user interface employed in MUI systems has to be reified into a presentation the user finally interacts with. A core aspect of MUI systems is the automation of the reification process by means of general rules that map abstract levels into more concrete. As mentioned above, by following such rules a coherent and consistent presentation spanning multiple platforms can be reached [26]. Depending on the level of abstraction this reification can be sequenced into several steps. Whereas automatic reification is expected to speed up the development process, automatically generated presentations have turned out to be problematic compared to manual design concerning design quality and the possibility of detail modifications. This automation vs. design trade-off can be broken down into three closely inter-related problems:

- **Mapping problem** – The more abstract the initial specification for the application to be designed the more mapping steps have to be made from abstraction to generation. Each step requires generalized rules to be applied to a specific problem, holding the danger of erroneous of sub-optimal adaptations [14].
- **Round-trip problem** – While abstract descriptions allow a comprehensive perspective on an application it requires a high mental effort for the designer to anticipate results of changes he made in the final design. Therefore modifications in the final design are necessary for designers to keep in control. How can these changes in the final design now be reflected into the abstract specification [2]?
- **Optimization problem** – Cross-device design is a trade-off between general presentation rules and individual optimizations. The result of

general presentation rules is often of a quality that is not acceptable for commercial applications [14]. Optimizing a presentation to a certain device results in an exception to the generalization. How can an application be optimized to a certain device while reducing loss of cross-device consistency [1]?

Again, the convergence between flexible and customizable toolkits and economic and general model-based methods seems to be needed. To give designers of MUI the possibility to seamlessly switch between *top-down* reification processes, *bottom-up* abstractions, also as *lateral* translations, in other words *multi-path development* [3,9,24], will be necessary to resolve the above mentioned conflicts.

2.   CROSS-PLATFORM OPTIMIZATION

As we have argued above, one of the core problems in MUI development is the trade-off between generalized automatic design and specific manual optimization. Either we optimize the design to the specific requirements reducing usability and consistency or we cling to a consistent but aesthetically unpleasant design. How can this be conflict be resolved?

As a general approach, we suggest to include quality criteria (quantitative interface metrics) into the MUI design process. In the past, such criteria have been used to support the design of user interfaces for a specific target. Examples are layout appropriateness [20] or aesthetics [11]. Such criteria should reflect qualitative design-, functional-, or usability-related aspects of a user interface. Such criteria then could be used to control the design process by evaluating the results of either manual or automatic reification, translation or refinement processes.

- **Algorithmic optimization** – quality criteria can be included into the user interface generation process as part of an optimization algorithm (e.g., SUPPLE [7]).
- **Methods for design guidance** – quality criteria can be implemented as part of a visual design environment providing the designer with dynamic guidelines and visualizations to achieve optimal design.

In the following, we will discuss an example of a criterion capturing the *consistency* of a user interface. We have chosen consistency as it is generally assumed to be one of the most important usability criteria. In the context of MUI consistency is considered as an important means to improve the transfer of knowledge among different applications [13]. Consistency across different instances of an application will help to improve cross-device usability [6,19].

2.1   Consistency Metrics

Only few approaches have been developed to assess consistency of a user interface. Different aspects of consistency appear in some of the above mentioned metrics (such as consistency with the task in the layout appropriateness measure of Sears) but are not explicitly assigned to that.

Mahajan and Shneiderman [10] have presented SHERLOCK, a family of tools that generate a consistency-report across all dialogs of a application summarizing aspect such as: density, aspect ratio, area used by components, griddedness, balance, consistency of typefaces and colors. Further the homogeneity of terminology (are the same words used), and of button position (do buttons have the same size, aspect ratio, labels) and position button groups are evaluated. While SHERLOCK has proven to contribute to more consistent design it is dedicated to assess consistency within an application for a single platform. In SHERLOCK consistency is operationalized in terms of similarity. Similar or equal items are grouped and deviant items are considered as inconsistent. Similarity, however, is no suitable measure for cross device consistency. It is not able to account for the different device-specific requirements and adaptations. If we take for instance the same application on desktop and palmtop PC. How could layout be consistent in terms of similarity between those two given the enormous difference in screen real estate [17]?

2.2   Transformational Consistency

Consistency is assumed to support the transfer of cognitive skill between different tasks or systems [13]. Singley and Anderson [23] have found empirical evidence supporting the hypothesis that this transfer is based on re-use of learned behavior or rules. The more rules are applicable to a new situation, the easier the transfer. Consistency allows detecting similarities between situations. This means that similarity and consistency are not identical. What is exactly the relation between consistency and similarity?

It can be stated that similarity includes consistency, but consistency does not require similarity in terms of having a related set of properties. The transformational consistency approach [18] focuses on the relation between two instances of a system. It assumes that consistence is no fixed system property but reflects the relation between the language of the designer, expressed through his design and the language of the user as recipient [15].

Transformational consistency means that two systems do not have to be similar to be perceived as consistent, but that the relation between two systems has to be regular. If a certain property of the one system can be mapped into the corresponding property of the other system by a regular transformation a user will perceive this transformation and use it for anticipation. He will therefore perceive the systems as consistent. In other words, the user has to be able to understand how a system is related to the other system in order to perceive the regularity of transformation and further the consistency of their relation.

2.2.1   Definition

Formally, transformational consistency can be defined as follows. Let P_A be the property on the one system and P_B the corresponding property on the other system. The transformational consistency approach now states that the relation between A and B is consistent as long as the transformation T describes the mapping of each occurrence of P_A into P_B:

$$\forall P_{A1...An}, P_{B1...Bn} : T(P_A) \rightarrow P'_A = P_B$$

Transformation strategies can be a single transformation or a combination of basic transformations, as for instance for a presentational property could be rotation, translation, scaling, etc. [18].

2.2.2   Example

Two instances of an application on a palmtop and a desktop PC may serve as an example with respect to control position. On a desktop Windows PC the application has a toolbar with a number of symbols representing functions. This toolbar is located on the top of the application window just below the menu bar. On the *Microsoft* palmtop operating system *Windows Mobile* these toolbars are normally located at the bottom line just above the menu bar. The menu on these devices is located at the bottom of the screen. To describe the transformation between the two instances of the application we could say that the interface has been flipped along the horizontal middle axis. According to the transformational approach, this is consistent if it is applied to all occurrences of toolbars in the application.

2.2.3   Calculation

The transformational consistency measure can be assessed for any element in the dialog with respect to any property, including nominal-, ordinal-, and interval-scaled property measures. The calculation follows a straightforward algorithm that can be described in four steps:
- **Grouping of elements**: elements in the user interface on one system are grouped with respect to their similarity in the property assessed (e.g., all *OK* buttons, all buttons with a certain position, etc.).

- **Calculation of transformation**: for each element in a group and for all groups the transformation vector is calculated (e.g., the translation in pixels).
- **Calculation of consistency**: consistency is calculated as homogeneity of the transformation, this can be the *conditional probability* ($p(B \mid A)$) or the *variance* ($\sigma^2(|A - B|)$).
- **Analysis**: the *cumulative* analysis gives a consistency measure over all elements and therefore can be used as *post-hoc* evaluation of an interface. The *detailed* analysis examines the single groups and elements and can be used as feedback during the design process.

2.2.4 Background

The transformational approach has been applied in the TACTICS [8] UIMS to derive consistent variants and refinements of a user interface. Transformation rules can be applied to single controls or entire designs to allow more control for the designer.

In the UsiXML (http://www.usixml.org) environment transformation forms a core process in the reification also as in the translation of models [9]. Stored transformations here allow the generation consistent variants of a source model.

To explore the psychological basis of the transformational approach, we have conducted a number of empirical studies to explore the impact of transformations on the perception of cross-device applications. As a first step, we have focused on the layout of graphical interfaces, but, as we will argue later-on, we assume this approach to be also applicable to other dimensions of a user interface.

- **Mental representation** – As the transformational states that the user can profit from consistent transformations by anticipating such transformations in the analogical information processing system, known effects of analogical information processing such as the mental rotation effect [4] should affect the perception of transformed user interfaces. In fact, it has been shown that the time a participant took to repeated an input sequence on a rotated variant of an interface was depending on the rotation angle ($t(0°) < (t(90°) = t(270°)) < t(270°)$).
- **Consistency measure** – A first laboratory study where 17 users first had to use an application on a desktop PC and were then asked to continue on a PocketPC revealed a pattern supporting the validity of the consistency metrics. The consistency of the transformation between instances for both devices was designed to be maximum (*REG*; position and type of control was almost equal on both devices), medium (*MED*) and highly inconsistent (*HIG*; position and type of controls was varied in half / all of the

interfaces leading to measures of 0.2 and 0.5). The fourth condition was a highly consistent but mirrored interface (*MIR*) where all elements were consistently flipped along the horizontal axis. The results revealed a pattern indicating that the interface with high transformational consistency could be used faster (summed duration in msec, see Fig. 11) and was rated as more usable (using the SUS) than the low consistent ones. No difference between mirrored and regular transformations could be observed as expected. Due to large variance between users in the given setting the results failed to reach statistical significance (Duration: *F(16)=0.8336*).

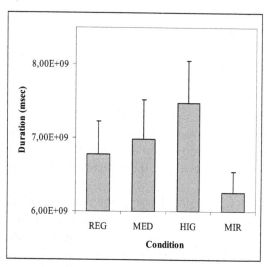

Figure 1. Mean summed durations for the four consistency conditions

These first results support the assumption that transformational consistency might be used to improve usability of cross-platform user interfaces. However, further research will be needed to get deeper insights into the phenomenon and to determine cross-effects, like for instance what happens if a system has been used for a while, will the consistency effect fade? What properties of a user interface are more important to be kept consistent than others, we currently have only observed position?

3.   GUIDANCE FOR CONSISTENT DESIGN

Above, we have argued for the integration of quantitative metrics into the design process. We have further shown that the consistency metrics is a valid qualitative criterion that can serve to asses certain aspects of inter-device usability. Methods that support the design of consistent MUI have to integrate into the design process and give *immediate feedback* and advice during interaction. Further, development support should not require the designer to edit additional data, beyond what is relevant for design; therefore required metadata should be extracted *dynamically* by the support system. The potential integration of the support system in today's *graphical user interface designers* is necessary, to allow the designer to maintain existing workflow and expertise.

The major aspect of the methods presented here, is the *application-wide perspective* inherent to the transformational approach. While visual design tools focus on single dialogs supporting alignment and similar sizing of elements in the same dialog, consistent design requires observing all elements in an application. In other words, if we compare one button to all other elements in a dialog, we want to be able to assess the position of all similar buttons in all dialogs.

3.1   Consistency Ghosts

Common graphic tools and visual designers provide dynamic rulers and grids that guide alignment and size of new elements. This well-established, simple and intuitive support method can help to quickly align elements and control them for equal proportions. Consistency ghosts follow this approach and provide dynamic lines and ghost-images indicating the alignment and size of similar elements in other dialogs of the same application (in intra-device settings). In cross-device design, consistency ghosts can be used to show, how similar elements have be transformed with respect to properties like position, size, alignment, etc. Fig. 2 gives an example for consistency ghosts that appear while translating the *Open*-button. The lines show the main left alignment rulers for other element on other dialogs. We therefore could choose one alignment to achieve a better griddedness over the application's dialogs.

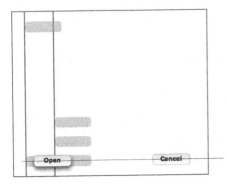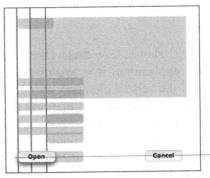

Figure 2. Consistency Ghosts guiding the designer while positioning a new button

The grey silhouettes are the ghost images of other elements in other dialogs that are located nearby. To make position consistent the designer can choose to place the new button on a place that has been used for other similar buttons. To reduce the distracting information, different filtering methods could be applied. One possibility would be to show only controls of same type, with positions nearby, or which share other properties with the current control. A levelled shading concept could also be applied that shows those elements more clearly, which are closer to the current element.

The rules give direct and intuitive feedback on the consistency of the positioning of different elements over the different screens. If several rules are located very closely (as in the right figure above) it is likely that the interface could profit from laying them out together. In addition to the movement of single elements, this method can be used to move entire sets of elements on different dialogs at once. By moving a vertical rule we could move all elements that are oriented to this rule and thus reduce the number of rules.

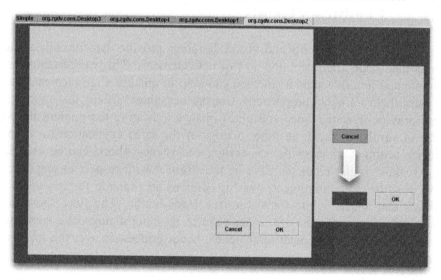

Figure 3. A ghost image in inter-device design, here the displacement of a button on the mobile device is shown

Fig. 3 shows, how these ghost images have been applied in an example design application. It is assumed that in the design of cross-device applications the related elements on both platforms can be identified (i.e., how element *A* is displayed of platform *P1* and *P2*). If so, we can easily calculate the transformation applied on *A* to adapt it from *P1* to *P2* with respect to a defined criterion, which could be for instance the position of a control.

This transformation now can be compared to the transformations applied to other similar elements, as for instance, other *Cancel*-buttons, or other buttons on the same position, etc. If all other buttons have been translated to another position (indicated by the grey ghost image) we would suggest the designer to move the new button there too. It is important to note that the designer is free to follow the advice. If design aspects require another position he can do so. But he is informed that this leads to less consistent design. Thus, he is able to trade-off consistency vs. optimal design.

3.2   Dynamic Templates

Templates are prototypes for layouts that can be used for new content to be display in a consistent way. In general, a number of templates is defined in an initial stage of design. During design, new dialog are assigned to templates and the layout is adapted (e.g., *Macromedia Dreamweaver* templates for HTML). Nichols *et al.* [12] have introduced so-called *smart templates* that allow the definition of different levels of quality in layouts for different devices. The problem is that templates often have to be extended and modified during design as not all requirement can be foreseen resulting in changes and inconsistencies between different generations of instances.

Fig. 4 outlines the principle of dynamic templates for consistent design. Templates are derived at design time from existing dialogs, i.e., every dialog can serve as template. A template now can be re-used in two ways: either the underlying *layout grid* (i.e., the alignment rules of the elements) are used to guide alignment in new interfaces, or all the *elements* used in the template are newly instantiated and made available in the new dialog (this can be exploited by sub classing the dialogs, so that changes in the class are reflected into the instances).

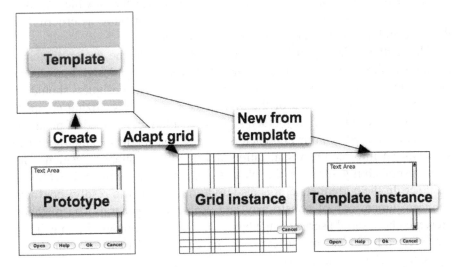

Figure 4. With dynamic templates the designer can dynamically derive instances of designs for new dialogs

How does this apply to cross-device consistency? First, intra-device consistency, as supported by dynamic templates is a pre-condition for cross-device consistency (see above). The more consistent the application is the more reliable is the calculation of groups for the consistency measure. Second, if uniform templates have been used, transformations can be generalized to all instances of a template leading to consistency in the manual design.

Template-based development does integrate very well into existing toolkit-based development processes and visual interface builders as it requires minimal metadata (when applied to layout properties such as position and size) and follows common object oriented methods.

4.   CONCLUSION

In this article we have motivated the development of *methods for design guidance* that can be used support the optimized design of MUI. This can be used to overcome the trade-off between device optimization and cross device consistency. This is applicable to both model-based and toolkit-based methods and this therefore contributes to the convergence of both methods.

By providing immediate feedback to the designer individual changes and optimizations can always be evaluated against external quality criteria. This allows the designer to interactively change a generated design in a visual environment without running into the danger of causing inconsistencies with respect to other instances of the interface. As an example for such a quality criterion we have introduced a psychologically funded consistency measure based on the transformational approach. This measure can be applied to various aspects of a user interface and is therefore very flexible. As one application of this metrics we have shown how it can serve as criterion in dynamic and interactive methods of design guidance.

The methods described here are complementary to the design methods mentioned above. They are neither indented to substitute design knowledge nor are they an alternative to model-based methods. The designers should be supported in the perception of the system as a whole, visualizing complex relations between the single elements of a user interface. Instead of planning for intelligent methods this approach is targeted to support the intelligent designer in an information visualization and interaction support fashion. The final responsibility—this is the clear statement here—will stay with the designer. In the current state, it is also up to the designer to resolve conflicts between dimensions of consistency and usability in general. The methods presented here should serve as incubator for tools that support him in gaining the information necessary to evaluate the design and to make a qualified decision on changes necessary.

Another core concept presented here is the introduction of the *application-wide* perspective during design. While visual design tools generally have a perspective limited to the current dialog, application-wide perspective detects inconsistencies and breaks in an application's user interface. Consistency ghosts allow to visualize this and to easily correct inconsistencies in a graphical manner.

Currently, the metrics have been applied to visual properties such as position and colour. Other dimensions and also other modalities will have to be addressed in future. The empirical validation of the consistency measure still is very preliminary. Even though first results support the idea more detailed experiments will have to be run to gather more evidence. Further, it will be necessary to gain more insights how transformational consistency interacts with other usability criteria and how conflicts can be visualized or resolved. While the transformational consistency measure is a simple and straight-forward metrics it requires the valid operationalization of the target criteria, which can be categorical of probabilistic. In fact, other calculi are possible than the mean probability used above and further evaluation will be needed to explore the most powerful predictor on usability measures like completion times, task load, and usability.

REFERENCES

[1] Ali, M.F., Perez-Quinones, M.A., and Abrams, M., *Building Multi-platform User Interfaces with UIML*, in [22], pp. 11–25.

[2] Bergman, L., Banavar, L., Soroker, D., and Sussman, J., *Combining Handcrafting and Automatic Generation of User-Interfaces for Pervasive Devices*, in Proc. of the 4th Int. Conf. on Computer-Aided Design of User Interfaces CADUI'2002 (Valenciennes, 15–17 May 2002), Kluwer Academic Publishers, Dordrecht, 2002, pp. 155–166.

[3] Calvary, G., Coutaz, J., Thevenin, D., Limbourg, Q., Bouillon, L., and Vanderdonckt, J., *A Unifying Reference Framework for Multi-Target User Interfaces*, Interacting with Computers, Vol. 15, No. 3, June 2003, pp. 289–308.

[4] Cooper, L.A., and Shepard, R.N., *Chronometric Studies on the Rotation of Mental Images*, in W.G. Chase (ed.), "Visual information processing", Academic Press, New York, 1973, pp. 75–176.

[5] Coyette, A., and Vanderdonckt, J., *A Sketching Tool for Designing Anyuser, Anyplatform, Anywhere User Interfaces*, in Proc. of 10th IFIP TC 13 Int. Conf. on Human-Computer Interaction INTERACT'2005 (Rome, 12–16 September 2005), Lecture Notes in Computer Science, Vol. 3585, Springer-Verlag, Berlin, 2005, pp. 550–564.

[6] Denis, Ch., and Karsenty, L., *Inter-usability of Multi-device Systems - A Conceptual Framework*, in [22], pp. 374–385.

[7] Gajos, K., and Weld, D.S., SUPPLE: *Automatically Generating User Interfaces*, in Proc. of the ACM Int. Conf. on Intelligent User Interfaces IUI'2004 (Funchal, 13–16 January 2004), ACM Press, New York, 2004, pp. 93–100.

[8] Kovacevic, S., TACTICS – *A Model-Based Framework for Multimodal Interaction*, in Proc. of the AAAI Spring Symposium on Intelligent Multi-Media Multi-Modal Systems, 1994.

[9] Limbourg, Q., and Vanderdonckt, J., *Addressing the Mapping Problem in User Interface Design with UsiXML*, in Proc. of 3rd Int. Workshop on Task Models and Diagrams for user interface design TAMODIA'2004 (Prague, November 2004), ACM Press, New York, 2004, pp. 155–163.

[10] Mahajan, R., and Shneiderman, B., *Visual and Textual Consistency Checking Tools for Graphical User Interfaces*, IEEE Transactions on Software Engineering, Vol. 23, No. 11, November 1997, pp. 722–735.

[11] Ngo, D.C.L., Samsudin, A., and Abdullah, R., *Aesthetic Measures for Assessing Graphic Screens*, J. of Information Science and Engineering, Vol. 16, No. 1, 2000, pp. 97–116.

[12] Nichols, J, Myers, B.A., and Litwack, K., *Improving Automatic Interface Generation with Smart Templates*, in Proc. of 9th ACM Conf. on Intelligent User Interfaces IUI'2004 (Funchal, 13–16 January 2004), ACM Press, New York, 2004, pp. 286–288.

[13] Nielsen, J., *Coordinating User Interfaces for Consistency*, The Morgan Kaufmann Series in Interactive Technologies. Morgan Kaufmann Publishers, San Francisco, 1989.

[14] Puerta, A., and Eisenstein, J., *Towards a General Computational Framework for Model-Based Interface Development Systems*, Knowledge-Based Systems, Vol. 12, 1999, pp. 433–442.

[15] Reisner, P., *What is consistency?*, in Proc. of IFIP TC 13 Third Int. Conf. on Human-Computer Interaction INTERACT'90 (Cambridge, August 1990), North-Holland, Amsterdam, 1990, pp. 175–181.

[16] Richter, K., and Enge, M., *Multi-Modal Framework to Support Users with Special Needs in Interaction with Public Information Systems*, in Proc. of 5th Int. Symposium on Human Computer Interaction with Mobile Devices and Services MobileHCI'2003 (Udine, 8–11 September 2003), L. Chittaro (ed.), Lecture Notes in Computer Science, Vol. 2795, Springer-Verlag, Berlin, 2003, pp. 286–301.

[17] Richter, K., *A Transformation Strategy for Multi-device Menus and Toolbars*, in Proc. of the ACM Conf. on Human Factors in Computing Systems CHI'2005 (Portland, 3–7 April 2005), ACM Press, New York, 2005, pp. 1741–1744.

[18] Richter, K., *A Transformational Approach to Multi-Device Interfaces*, in Proc. of the ACM Conf. on Human Factors in Computing Systems CHI'2005 (Portland, 3–7 April 2005), ACM Press, New York, 2005, pp. 1126–1127.

[19] Richter, K., Nichols, J., Gajos, K., and Seffah, A., *The Many Faces of Consistency in Cross-Platform Design*, in Proc. of ACM Conf. on Human Factors in Computing Systems CHI'2006 (Montreal, 22–23 April 2006), ACM Press, New York, 2006.

[20] Sears, A., *AIDE: A Step Toward Metric-Based Interface Development Tools*, in Proc. of the 8th ACM Symposium on User Interface Software and Technology UIST'95 (Pittsburgh, 15–17 November 1995), ACM Press, New York, 1995, pp. 101–110.

[21] Seffah, A., and Javahery, H., *Executive summary and book overview*, in [22], pp. 1–9.

[22] Seffah, A., and Javahery, H., *Multiple User Interfaces: Cross-platform and context-aware interfaces*, John Wiley & Sons, West Sussex, 2004.

[23] Singley, M.K., and Anderson, J.R., *The Transfer of Cognitive Skill*, Cognitive Science Series, Harvard University Press, Cambridge, 1989.

[24] Thevenin, D., Coutaz, J., and Calvary, J., *A Reference Framework for the Development of Plastic User Interfaces*, in [22], pp. 29–51.

[25] Traetteberg, H., *Integrating Dialog Modelling and Application Development*, in Proc. of the First International Workshop on Making Model-based User Interface Design Practical MBUI'2004 (Funchal, January 13, 2004), CEUR Workshop Proceedings, Vol. 103, 2004.

[26] Wiecha, Ch., Bennett, W., Boies, S., Gould, J., and Greene, S., *ITS: A Tool for Rapidly Developping Interactive Applications*, ACM Transactions on Information Systems, Vol. 8, No. 3, July 1990, pp. 204–236.

Chapter 12

RAPID PROTOTYPING OF DISTRIBUTED USER INTERFACES

José Pascual Molina Massó[1,2], Jean Vanderdonckt[1], Pascual González López[2], Antonio Fernández-Caballero[2], and María Dolores Lozano Pérez[2]

[1] School of Management (IAG), Université catholique de Louvain
Place des Doyens, 1 – B-1348 Louvain-la-Neuve (Belgium)
E-mail: {molina, vanderdonckt}@isys.ucl.ac.be
Tel: +32 10/478525 – Fax: +32 10/478324 – Web: http://www.isys.ucl.ac.be/bchi
[2] Lab. of User Interaction & Software Engineering
Inst. de Investigación en Informática de Albacete (I3A), Universidad de Castilla-La Mancha
Campus universitario s/n – S-02071 Albacete (Spain)
E-mail: {jpmolina, pgonzalez, caballer, mlozano}@dsi.uclm.es
Tel: +34 967/599200 – Fax: +34 967/599224 – Web: http://www.i3a.uclm.es

Abstract   This paper introduces a software tool for rapid prototyping of interactive systems whose user interfaces could be distributed according to four axes defined in a design space: type of computing platform, amount of interaction surfaces, type of interaction surface, and type of user interface. This software is based on a virtual toolkit for rendering the user interfaces in a virtual world depicting the real world in which the distribution occurs. The virtual toolkit consists of a layer for rendering a concrete user interface specified in a user interface description language. This paper presents its extension to modeling the external environment in terms of the design space so as to render the context of use in which the user interfaces are distributed. For each axis, a pair of functions enables exploring the axis in decreasing and increasing order so as to explore various situations of distribution, axis by axis, or in a combined way. As the interfaces resulting from this rendering are truly executable ones, this system provides designers with an acceptable means for generating ideas about how a user interface can be distributed in a context of use, and helps to evaluate the quality of a solution at an early design stage. Four representative situations located on the design space are implemented and discussed: distribution in a multi-platform context, distribution of the workplace, ubiquitous computing, and ambient intelligence, thus proving the coverage of the design space and the capabilities of the whole system

Keywords: Ambient intelligence, Context-aware computing, Distributed computing, Distributed interfaces, Pervasive computing, Ubiquitous computing, User interface extensible markup language, Workplace distribution

G. Calvary et al. (eds.), Computer-Aided Design of User Interfaces V, 151–166.

1.   INTRODUCTION

Distributed User Interfaces (DUIs) [1,6,14] apply the notion of distributing parts or whole of a user interface (UI) across several places or locations like Distributed Systems [12] do for general software. In studying DUIs, we have identified two main classes of problems: an ontological confusion about the various concepts and associated definitions expressing how and according to what to distribute a given UI; a practical problem of experimenting a DUI at early design time before developing it completely.

The first class of problems is motivated by observing that the several recent advances in DUIs (among them are [4,7,9,12,14,17,18,19,20]) do not necessarily rely on the same concepts of distribution and, when it is the case, the definition and/or the axes according to which the distribution may take place largely vary from one research to another. Although significant efforts exist to shed some light in this area and to structure DUI design issues, mainly in [1,6], the relationship between these design issues and their corresponding physical configurations are not always straightforward to establish.

The second class of problems poses even more challenges because developing DUIs eminently require a sophisticated architecture, and due to that level of sophistication it not surprising that DUIs are slow to obtain, expensive to produce, and probably equally complex to use.

The aforementioned observations show that designing a DUI remains a complex problem which may prevent designers from exploring design issues because of their associated cost. If the development cost of several DUIs is too high with respect to the benefit of exploring different design issues and physical configurations for distribution, it is likely that this exploration will be abandoned soon due to lack of flexibility. In addition, the usability issues raised by distributing a UI across one or several dimensions [10,21] are serious and could be hard to uncover before a really usable solution is found.

Therefore, we argue that rapid prototyping of DUIs [10,19] turns to be an important issue: not only rapid prototyping could be used as a vehicle for developing and demonstrating visions of innovative DUIs, but also they could help showing various distribution configurations before going to full implementation [2]. However, rapid prototyping is also a challenging problem, as the design space of DUIs covers a wide range of different possibilities. In order to tackle this complexity, the approach presented in this paper is to develop a software tool which supports rapid prototyping of DUIs based on a limited, but significant, set of four design dimensions.

The remainder of this paper is sequenced as follows: the four design dimensions for DUIs will be defined in a design space in Section 2, namely based on an environment model. This design space will be then exploited to compare related work in consistent terms in Section 3. Section 4 will exemplify four frequently found situations where UIs are distributed across one dimension of the design space considered at a time, while showing that combination is allowed. Each subsection is devoted to each design dimension. Section 5 will sum up the benefits of the rapid prototyping approach.

2.   DESIGN SPACE FOR DISTRIBUTED USER INTERFACES

The design space described in this paper relies on an environmental model and four axes or dimensions which are explained in terms such as "digitization" or "dematerialization", to cite just a couple of them. But, prior to defining these concepts on which the rest of this paper will rely, there are others that also support this work and so they must be explained before continuing. These are the UI development framework used, and the notion of context of use and interaction surface.

2.1   Foundation

In this paper, it is assumed that the development of user interfaces relies on the CAMELEON framework [3], which structures the development life cycle of multi-target UIs according to four layers (Fig. 1):

1. The *Final UI* (FUI) is the operational UI, i.e. any UI running on a particular computing platform either by interpretation (e.g., through a Web browser) or by execution (e.g., after the compilation of code in an interactive development environment).
2. The *Concrete UI* (CUI) expresses any FUI independently of any term related to a peculiar rendering engine, that is, independently of any markup or programming language.
3. The *Abstract UI* (UI) expresses any CUI independently of any interaction modality (e.g., graphical, vocal, or tactile).
4. The *Task & Concept* level, which describes the various interactive tasks to be carried out by the end user and the manipulated domain objects.

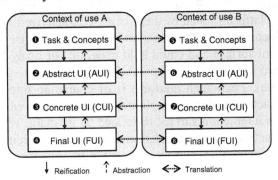

Figure 1. The Cameleon user interface reference framework

We refer to [3] for more details and to [13] for its translation into models uniformly expressed in the same User Interface Description Language (UIDL). The selected language for this work is UsiXML [13], which stands for User Interface eXtensible Markup Language (http://www.usixml.org). Any other UIDL could be used equally provided that the used concepts are also supported.

The *Context of use* describes all the entities that may influence how the user's task is carrying out with the future UI. It takes into account three relevant aspects, each aspect having its own associated attributes contained in a separate model: *user type* (e.g., system experience, task experience, task motivation), *computing platform* type (e.g., mobile platform vs. stationary one), and *physical environment* type (e.g., office conditions, outdoor conditions).

Finally, we define the concept of *interaction surface*, which was introduced by [5], as any physical surface which can be "acted on or observed" so as to support user interaction with a system, whether visible or embedded. For instance, an interaction surface could be a screen, a monitor, a wall display, a table equipped with camera tracking techniques, or a pad with projection. See [5] for a complete definition of physical (e.g., weight, size, material, shape, solidity/fluidity/nebulosity) and modality attributes.

2.2 Environment Model

For the purpose of this work, a richer environment model has expanded UsiXML's existing physical environment model with the concept of interaction surface. The physical environment (Fig. 2) is expanded with a characterization of its physical space, described as a scene which is in turn decomposed in surfaces, to be connected together or not through position and orientation. This characterization is deeply inspired by world modeling which is traditional to VRML97/X3D 3D worlds [16]. Each surface composing the physical space (e.g., the walls, the table, or the doors of a room) could be declared as an interaction surface which can be acted on or observed, depending on input/output.

A second addition is that each environment could comprise one or several computing platforms, each of them being characterized with a series of attributes. Each computing platform could be located precisely with respect to an environment surface and could hold none, one or many hardware platforms, which are declared as a general form of output (e.g., a display, a monitor, a screen). Each such platform is of course an interaction surface which could be acted on (by using pointers) and/or observed (by looking at the screen). Each interaction surface is defined by its shape, which is the area sensible to interaction. Hardware platforms are therefore considered as rectangular-shaped interaction surfaces. One could imagine probably other shapes like a circle or an oval, but in our implementation, only convex surfaces are subject to the FUI rendering.

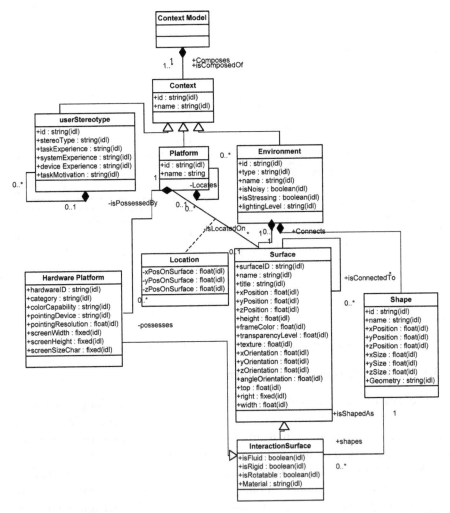

Figure 2. The expanded environment model, based on the notion of interaction surface [5]

2.3 Definition of the Design Space

The proposed DUI design space is decomposed into four design axes or dimensions (Fig. 3): type of computing platform, amount of interaction surfaces, type of interaction surface, and type of user interface. They are respectively explained in more detail in the following subsections. Lyytinen and Yoo [15] have studied how conventional systems may evolve in the future towards ubiquitous computing through two dimensions: the level of system integration within the ambient environment and the degree of mobility. These two dimensions correspond to type of interaction surface and type of computing platform respectively in the design space of Fig. 3.

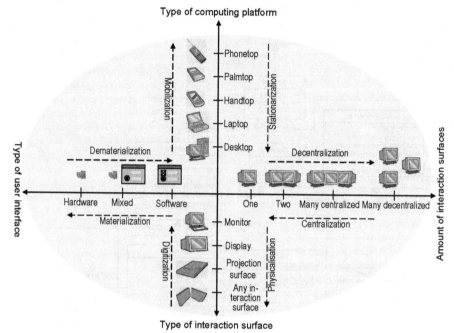

Figure 3. The four design dimensions of the DUI design space

2.3.1   Type of computing platform

The *type of computing platform* represents the first axis along which a UI may be distributed, meaning here that parts or whole of an existing UI may transit from one computing platform to another. On this axis, the computing platforms are ranked by decreasing order of mobility:

- "Stationarization" is the process consisting of rendering a FUI on a target platform which is more stationary than the source platform. Each progressive graduation on this axis could be achieved by performing an abstraction from CUI to AUI, followed by reification from AUI to CUI, and then restricted by a selection to more stationary platforms [3]. A simple translation from CUI to CUI may also work.
- "Mobilization" is the inverse process. To support moving along this axis, various operations are diversely supported in the literature such as direct transfer (simple translation without any modification), migration, copying, or duplication [1].

2.3.2   Amount of interaction surfaces

The *amount of interaction surfaces* denotes how many interaction surfaces are used to render the DUI. Typical cases are: a single monitor per computing platform, two dual monitors [10], three to five monitor display wall (e.g., www.panoramtech.com, www.go-1.com), and many displays which could be centralized per computing platform or decentralized, thus posing the problem of multiple foci of interest for one task [21]. These are the terms that characterize this axis:

- "Decentralization" is the process consisting of rendering a FUI on more interaction surfaces than previously, the displays being connected to the same computing platform or not. Each progressive graduation on this axis could be achieved by performing a decomposition of the source UI (e.g., by graceful degradation [8], by fragmentation [20], by semantic re-design [18]) which are then rendered on the various interaction surfaces.
- "Centralization" is the inverse process. To support it, various operations like union, merging, re-composition may occur before re-rendering the gathered pieces on less interaction surfaces.

2.3.3   Type of interaction surface

The *type of interaction surface* depicts the level of physicality of the interaction surface used to render the UI. A computer monitor or a public display are considered as *digital* interaction surfaces, as opposed to projection surfaces which are considered as *physical* ones since the UI is rendered by projection from a projector and user's events are tracked by camera recognition techniques borrowed from signal processing domain. Consequently:

- "Physicalization" is the process of rendering a FUI on a target interaction surface that is more physical than the source one. For this purpose, different rendering functions should be implemented depending on the type of interaction surface used. Whether the surface resolution changes, re-purposing functions could be called to reshuffle the UI components.
- "Digitization" is the inverse process (to digitize = to convert data such as an image to a digital form – source: Merriam Webster On-line).

2.3.4   Type of user interface

The *type of user interface* expresses the physicality level of the FUI components. A DUI is said to be *software* when all its components are traditional software widgets, *hardware* when all its components are physical objects like switches, buttons, and *mixed* when components could either be software or hardware simultaneously. Therefore:

- "Materialization" is the process consisting of changing the distribution of the FUI towards more physical components (to materialize = to cause to appear in bodily form – source: Merriam Webster On-line). Each progressive graduation on this axis could be achieved by performing a decomposition of a source FUI into smaller pieces and re-assigning dedicated pieces to physical objects instead of software objects. This obviously touches the area of tangible UIs.

- "Dematerialization" is the inverse process (to dematerialize = to cause to become or appear immaterial – source: Merriam Webster On-line). To support it, a FUI is decomposed into fragments, some of them being re-assigned to digital objects (e.g., widgets). When a digital object is transformed to a physical one, its CUI definition is abstracted [3] into an AUI counterpart, followed by a reification from AUI to CUI, and then restricted by a selection to only those objects belonging to the physical world. In this way, it is possible to find out an object in the physical world with an equivalent behavior, the presentation of which does not matter [22].

2.4   Software Tool for Rapid Prototyping

To support the various operations involved in the design space defined in Fig. 3, VUITOOLKIT [17] has been developed above UsiXML and expanded with the environment model of Fig. 2 so as to render a CUI as a FUI in a virtual world. First, the environment model gives rise to a virtual world composed on surfaces, some of them being interactive. In particular, computing platforms could be located on some of these surfaces or considered as an interaction surface per se. Second, the toolkit abstracts objects [23] from Web3D languages (e.g., VRML, VRML97, X3D which are typically used in modeling virtual reality worlds and scenes). To bridge the gap between a UsiXML specification and its counterpart in virtual reality, and to render it properly in the virtual world, several cases could occur (Table 1):

1. *Direct mapping between a CUI and a Web3D primitive.* This mapping could be one-to-one (bijection) or one-to-many (composition of objects). It is not always possible to set a one-to-one mapping as those Web3D languages define basic elements such as shapes and sensors that must be used together to create interactive elements, e.g., 3D widgets. The new standard X3D does not change this status, even though it includes new 2D geometry nodes that make easier to draw 2D interfaces in a 3D world. Therefore, some basic widgets (e.g., a window) were redeveloped from scratch by assembling shapes together with their behavior.

2. *New mapping between a CUI and a Web3D counterpart.* Sometimes, no object exists natively in the Web3D language to ensure the mapping. In this case, there is a need to fill this gap by introducing a new widget in the Web3D world by appropriate implementation. This is what happens with the CUI used as a starting point for the toolkit, for each of them there is an element in the toolkit that can be used for their representation in the FUI. For this purpose, all widget classes defined in a UsiXML-compliant CUI have been sub-classed into their equivalent objects in virtual reality. Typical examples of these objects include check box, radio button, list box,

combo box, slider, and cursor. This correspondence remains incomplete: some CUI attributes are not subject to any rendering in the virtual world, some other attributes missing in the CUI definition are added because they are necessary to render their presentation and their behavior [16,17], such as those properties for the position and the dimensions of the widget.

3. *No possible mapping.* Despite the efforts to establish a mapping between any CUI and its counterpart, the UsiXML concept of box (the layout is decomposed into a hierarchy of vertical and horizontal boxes) is transformed into a system where coordinates of objects are computed from constraints imposed on them, instead of solving the constraints at rendering time. In case of rendering on a surface which is not a computing platform screen (e.g., a wall), surface attributes are exploited.

Table 1. Possible mappings between 2D and 3D

CUI level (UsiXML)	VUIToolkit (VRML97 / X3D)
$\exists$ individual CIO c	$\exists$ widget w such as $f(c)=w$ (direct mapping)
	$\exists$ widget w such as $\forall\ c_i \in c,\ \exists\ f_i\ \|\ f_i(c)=w_i$ (new mapping between properties)
	$\nexists$ widget w such as $f(c)=w$ (no possible mapping)

3. RELATED WORK

Several advanced researches could be classified according to the design space depicted in Fig. 3. Due to limited space, we only discuss those considered as the closest ones to this work.

MODIE [14] and DYNAMO-AID [4] provide a distribution manager which distributes the sub-task of a task model to various computing platforms in the same environment. This system completely supports mobilization and stationarization as the UIs could be distributed to any platform, but only one interaction surface is used at a time as a platform screen with digital objects. Therefore, the three other dimensions are not covered. This process is task based since the task model initiates the distribution of the UI fragments corresponding to the sub-tasks. Conversely, in our approach, no task model is used: each UI is first designed in an interface builder (e.g., GrafiXML – http://www.usixml.org) or imported from an external format in this editor. Each CUI resulting from this editing is then assigned to one or several interaction surface, whether it is a computer screen or not. Then, each CUI could be manipulated in direct manipulation [17] to support operations like transfer, copy, clone, duplicating, or migration.

In the MIGRATION project [1,18], partial and full migrations are supported, thus covering centralization and decentralization on top of the rest. In Everywhere [20], physicalization and digitization are added since UIs could be rendered on various interaction surfaces such as large screens, white-board, wall displays as well as personal surfaces. Only digital interfaces are considered as opposed to 3DSim [19], where only hardware interfaces are supported because it is the tool's goal to prototype physical interfaces in an environment, thus also providing some sort of rapid prototyping. The material development of the physical UI is conducted after the prototype is validated. The situation is similar for [9]. XIN [12] consists of a XML-compliant language for expressing interactive systems which are distributed across various locations, with some workflow support between them. However, it does not detail much the UI structure and presentation and the world is not modeled.

In this paper, the environment model is produced as a virtual reality scene, thus allowing the rendering of both software (e.g., widgets) and hardware (e.g., physical buttons) objects, but this is achieved for rapid prototyping purposes only. It is obvious that it cannot produce a physical UI, but the corresponding UsiXML specifications could be passed to the team in charge of the development. The tool provides basic operations such as copy a CUI from one surface to another one, whether they belong to a computing platform or not, duplicate, migrate. Composition and decomposition algorithms are beyond the scope of this paper and could be found in the literature [1]. Here, they are done by graphically selecting the portions subject to (de)composition. In the next section, we exemplify the use of the design space and the tool with four representative situations where a UI is distributed.

4. FOUR SITUATIONS OF DISTRIBUTED USER INTERFACES

4.1 Across Multiple Computing Platforms

Multi-platform computing could be considered as a distribution case where a software UI is distributed successively from one platform to another one. Fig. 4 graphically depicts an example of mobilization, where a UI rendered on a monitor of a stationary PC is migrated to the screen of a highly portable platform, which can be carried by everyone. This operation is represented on the design space by laptop (top axis), one screen at a time (right axis), platform (bottom axis), and digital UI (left axis).

In order to trigger the migration, each window is augmented by an additional button freezing the UI state and allowing the user to move the window to another target, before releasing it [17]. Once migrated, the user can continue her task by manipulating the window objects. In case of migrating only a portion of it, the user can graphically select the objects subject to transfer.

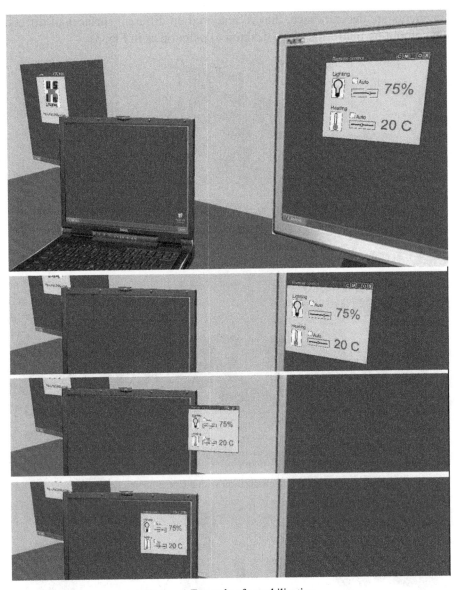

Figure 4. Example of a mobilization

4.2   Across Multiple Interaction Surfaces

Workspace analysis could be considered as a distribution case where a software UI is distributed across multiple interaction surfaces. Workspace analysis is typically interested in investigating how information and related functions could or should be located so as to optimize the workflow, to minimize movements between locations, while allowing several persons working together. Fig. 5 graphically depicts an example where various UI fragments are decentralized, that is, rendered on different surfaces of different computing platforms (from desktop to palmtop as in Fig. 3).

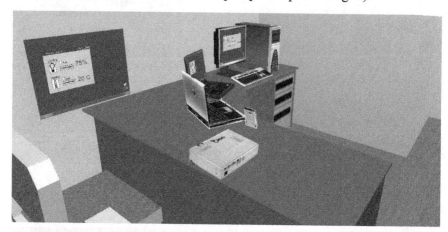

Figure 5. Example of a decentralization with different interaction surfaces

Figure 6. A software UI projected onto a wall

4.3   Across Different Types of Interaction Surfaces

Ubiquitous or pervasive computing could be considered as a distribution case where a software/hardware UI is distributed across multiple interaction surfaces of different types. The right part of Fig. 5 demonstrates how a software UI could be distributed simultaneously on different monitors as well as an image projected onto a wall (Fig. 6 for the detailed view).

Physicalization is supported in our tool simply by moving the concerned UI from a digital interaction surface onto a physical one. The migration button is used again for this purpose, but the UI could only be released when it flies over a physical surface. Digitization is supported similarly in the inverse way. In the target interaction surface is comparable, respectively more limited in real estate than the source surface, the UI could remain unchanged, respectively be submitted to a graceful degradation process. In the case of Fig. 6, the UI remains software, thus keeping the UI definition unchanged. However, when it comes to make a UI material (through a materialization process), the UI should accommodate some changes explained in the next subsection.

4.4   Multiple Types of User Interfaces

Ambient intelligence [8,11,14,19] could be considered as a distribution case where the UI consists of software and/or hardware parts distributed in the environment. Fig. 7 exemplifies a situation where a software UI distributed across several computer screens co-exists with a physical UI embedded in the wall. In this case, the lighting and heating controls are no longer software objects, but built-in physical objects. When a software UI is submitted to materialization, the system attempts to discover a physical object which is equivalent enough in behavior to be used as a physical object. To this end, a CIO is abstracted into its corresponding Abstract Individual Component (AIC in UsiXML) at the AUI level. At this level, possible reifications of this AIC are identified and examined. If a reification corresponds directly to the initial CIO, this reified CIO is selected. Otherwise, the closest possible reification is preferred.

For instance in Fig. 7, the label displaying "75%" is transformed into a LED object displaying the same information, the heating toggle button in the software UI becomes a physical switch in the hardware UI, the "Auto" check boxes become another physical two-state switches, and the sliders become physical cursors. Ultimately, the physical objects of Fig. 7 and the software objects of Fig. 6 should be considered similar at the AUI level since they correspond to the same definition of abstract containers and individual components. Only the objects type changed. Also note that the layout changed since the initially horizontal software controls (embedded in a horizontal box) now become vertical after performing a reshuffle of the presentation ensure by the rendering engine of the VUItoolkit.

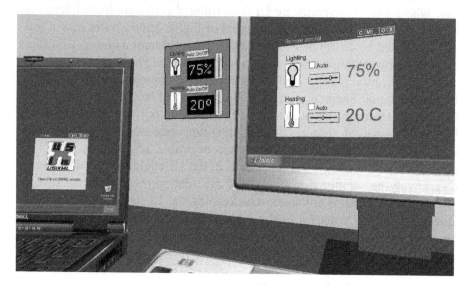

Figure 7. A co-habitation of a software UI rendered on a screen and a physical UI rendered on a wall considered as an interaction surface

5.   CONCLUSION

In this paper, we introduced a design space for distributed user interfaces consisting of four dimensions which are supported in a tool for rapid prototyping them by direct manipulation. In addition, a pair of functions was defined for each axis to denote the progression or regression along each axis. These functions are ensured thanks to the rendering capabilities of VUI-Toolkit, a virtual toolkit for rendering a concrete UI specified in UsiXML. A richer environment model has been defined so as to represent the world in which the distribution may occur, thus providing a direct feedback of the configuration under study.

The various operations provided by the toolkit enable designers to explore various distributions and keeping the one which is finally found adequate to the final goals. In the future, we plan to extend this work with multiple rooms and multiple users' characterizations. "The reality of this situation (provided by this virtual representation manipulation), when you do not believe in it, refuses to disappear" (Peter Viereck).

ACKNOWLEDGEMENTS

We gratefully acknowledge the support of the SIMILAR network of excellence (http://www. similar.cc), the European research task force creating human-machine interfaces similar to human-human communication of the European Sixth Framework Programme (FP6-2002-IST1-507609). This research is fully funded by SIMILAR. The authors would like also to thank the reviewers for their comments and Gaëlle Calvary for her feedback on an early version of this manuscript.

REFERENCES

[1] Berti, S., Paternò, F., and Santoro, C., *A Taxonomy for Migratory User Interfaces*, in Proc. of 12th Int. Workshop on Design, Specification, and Verification of Interactive Systems DSV-IS'2005 (Newcastle upon Tyne, 13–15 July 2005), M. Harrison (ed.), Lecture Notes in Computer Science, Vol. 3941, Springer-Verlag, Berlin, 2005.

[2] Bischofberger, W.R., and Pomberger, G., *Prototyping-Oriented Software Development–Concepts and Tools*, Springer-Verlag, Berlin, 1992.

[3] Calvary, G., Coutaz, J., Thevenin, D., Limbourg, Q., Bouillon, L., and Vanderdonckt, J., *A Unifying Reference Framework for Multi-Target User Interfaces*, Interacting with Computers, Vol. 15, No. 3, June 2003, pp. 289–308.

[4] Clerckx, T., Vandervelpen, Ch., Luyten, K., and Coninx, K., *A Task Driven User Interface Architecture for Ambient Intelligent Environments*, in Proc. of 10th ACM Int. Conf. on Intelligent User Interfaces IUI'2006 (Sydney, 29 January-1 February 2006), ACM Press, New York, 2006, pp. 309–311.

[5] Coutaz, J., Lachenal, Ch., and Dupuy-Chessa, S., *Ontology for Multi-surface Interaction*, in Proc. of 9th IFIP TC 13 Int. Conf. on Human-Computer Interaction INTERACT'2003 (Zurich, 1–5 September 2003), IOS Press, Amsterdam, 2003, pp. 447–454.

[6] Demeure, A., Calvary, G., Sottet, J.-B., Ganneau, V., and Vanderdonckt, J., *A Reference Model for Distributed User Interfaces*, in Proc. of 4th Int. Workshop on Task Models and Diagrams for user interface design TAMODIA'2005 (Gdansk, 26–27 September 2005), ACM Press, New York, 2005, pp. 79–86.

[7] Dey, A.K., Salber, D., and Abowd, G.D., *A Conceptual Framework and a Toolkit for Supporting the Rapid Prototyping of Context-Aware Applications*, Human-Computer Interaction Journal, Vol. 16, Nos. 2–4, 2001, pp. 97–166.

[8] Florins, M., Simarro, F.M., Vanderdonckt, J., and Michotte, B., *Splitting Rules for Graceful Degradation of User Interfaces*, in Proc. of 10th ACM Int. Conf. on Intelligent User Interfaces IUI'2006 (Sydney, 29 January-1 February 2006), ACM Press, New York, 2006, pp. 264–266.

[9] Gea, M., Garrido, J.L., López-Cózar, R., Haya, P.A., Montoro, G., and Alamán, X., *Task Modelling for Ambient Intelligence*, in Proc. of 12th Int. Workshop on Design, Specification, and Verification of Interactive Systems DSV-IS'2005 (Newcastle upon Tyne, 13–15 July 2005), Lecture Notes in Comp. Science, Vol. 3941, Springer-Verlag, Berlin, 2005.

[10] Grudin, J., *Partitioning Digital Worlds: Focal and Peripheral Awareness in Multiple Monitor Use*, in Proc. of ACM Conf. on Human Aspects in Computing Systems CHI'2001 (Seattle, 31 March-5 April 2001), ACM Press, New York, 2001, pp. 458–465.

[11] Gu, T., Pung, H.-K., and Qing Zhang, D., *Toward an OSGi-Based Infrastructure for Context-Aware Applications*, Pervasive Computing, October–December 2004, pp. 66–74.

[12] Li, B., Tsai, W.-T., and Zhang, L.-J., *A Semantic Framework for Distributed Applications*, Proc. of the 5th Int. Conf. on Enterprise Information Systems ICEIS'2003 (Angers, 22–26 April 2003), Volume IV - Software Agents and Internet Computing, pp. 34–41.

[13] Limbourg, Q., Vanderdonckt, J., Michotte, B., Bouillon, L., and Lopez, V., *UsiXML: a Language Supporting Multi-Path Development of User Interfaces*, in Proc. of 9th IFIP Working Conference on Engineering for Human-Computer Interaction jointly with 11th Int. Workshop on Design, Specification, and Verification of Interactive Systems EHCI-DSVIS'2004 (Hamburg, July 11–13, 2004). Lecture Notes in Computer Science, Vol. 3425, Springer-Verlag, Berlin, 2005, pp. 200–220.

[14] Luyten, K., Vandervelpen, Ch., and Coninx, K., *Task Modeling for Ambient Intelligent Environments: Design Support for Situated Task Executions*, Proc. of 4th Int. Workshop on Task Models and Diagrams for user interface design TAMODIA'2005 (Gdansk, 26–27 September 2005), ACM Press, New York, 2005, pp. 87–94.

[15] Lyytinen,K., and Yoo, Y., *Issues and Challenges in Ubiquitous Computing*, Communications of the ACM, Vol. 45, No. 12, 2002, pp. 62–65.

[16] Molina, J.P., Vanderdonckt, J., Montero, F., and Gonzalez, P., *Towards Virtualization of User Interfaces based on UsiXML*, in Proc. of 10th ACM Int. Conf. on 3D Web Technology Web3D'2005 (Bangor, 29 March-1 April 2005), ACM Press, New York, 2005, pp. 169–178.

[17] Molina, J.P., Vanderdonckt, J., and González, P., *Direct manipulation of User Interfaces for Migration*, in Proc. of 10th ACM Int. Conf. on Intelligent User Interfaces IUI'2006 (Sydney, 29 January-1 February 2006), ACM Press, New York, 2006, pp. 140–147.

[18] Mori, G., and Paternò, F., *Automatic Semantic Platform-dependent Redesign*, in Proc. of Joint sOc-EUSAI'2005 (Grenoble, October 2005), pp. 177–182.

[19] Nazari Shirehjini, A.A., Klar, F., and Kirste, T., *3DSim: Rapid Prototyping Ambient Intelligence*, in Proc. of the 2005 Joint Conf. on Smart objects and ambient intelligence: innovative context-aware services: usages and technologies sOc-EUSAI'2005 (Grenoble, October 2005), ACM Int. Conf. Proc. Series, Vol. 121, 2005, pp. 303–307.

[20] Pinhanez, C., *The Everywhere Displays Projector: A Device to Create Ubiquitous Graphical Interfaces*, in Proc. of the 3rd Int. Conf. on Ubiquitous Computing Ubi-Comp'2001 (Atlanta, 30 September- 2 October 2001), Lecture Notes in Computer Science, Vol. 2201, Springer-Verlag, Berlin, pp. 315–331.

[21] Tan, D.S., and Czerwinski, M., *Effects of Visual Separation and Physical Discontinuities when Distributing Information across Multiple Displays*, in M. Rauterberg, M. Menozzi, J. Wesson (eds.), Proc. of 9th IFIP TC 13 Int. Conf. on Human-Computer Interaction INTERACT'2003 (Zurich, 1–5 September 2003), IOS Press, Amsterdam, 2003, pp. 9–16.

[22] Vanderdonckt, J., Bouillon, L., Chieu, C.K., and Trevisan, D., *Model-based Design, Generation, and Evaluation of Virtual User Interfaces*, in Proc. of 9th ACM Int. Conf. on 3D Web Technology Web3D'2004 (Monterey, April 5–8, 2004), ACM Press, New York, 2004, pp. 51–60.

[23] Vanderdonckt, J., and Bodart, F., *Encapsulating Knowledge for Intelligent Automatic Interaction Objects Selection*, in Proc. of the ACM Conf. on Human Factors in Computing Systems INTERCHI'93 (Amsterdam, 24–29 April 1993), ACM Press, New York, 1993, pp. 424–429.

Chapter 13

THE COMETS INSPECTOR
Manipulating Multiple User Interface Representations
Simultaneously

Alexandre Demeure, Gaëlle Calvary, Joëlle Coutaz, and Jean Vanderdonckt
CLIPS-IMAG, BP 53, F-38041 Grenoble Cedex 9 (France)
E-mail: {Alexandre.Demeure, Gaelle.Calvary, Joelle.Coutaz, jeanvdd}@imag.fr
URL: http://www-clips.imag.fr/iihm
Tel.: +33 4 76 51 48 54 – Fax: +33 4 76 44 66 75

Abstract   Three types of representation are typically produced during the User Interface (UI) development life cycle: a conceptual representation holding the models used for elaborating a UI, an internal representation concerning the code of the UI, and an external representation expressing the look and feel of the UI. While the end user typically manipulates the external representation only, the designer and the developer respectively focus on the conceptual and internal representations. The Comets Inspector gathers all three representations into a single environment, thus providing the user (actually, the designer and the developer; in the future, the end-user) with multiple views of a same UI simultaneously. Each representation is made observable and modifiable through one or many "mini-UIs". Consistency is ensured through mappings between these representations. From a methodological point of view, the benefit is the integration of three stakeholders' perspectives in a consensual and consistent way, enabling the exploration and manipulation of design alternatives at run time. In particular, when the context of use will be changing, the end-user will be able to inspect the UI capabilities and control its adaptation, thus sustaining explicit plasticity

Keywords: Abstract user interface model, Comet, Conceptual representation, External representation, Internal representation, Model-based design, Plasticity of user interfaces

1.   INTRODUCTION

Ubiquitous computing has led to new requirements in Human-Computer Interaction (HCI), in particular the need for interactive systems to adapt or

167

G. Calvary et al. (eds.), Computer-Aided Design of User Interfaces V, 167–174.

be adapted to their contexts of use while preserving usability. This *plasticity* property [5] has been studied for many years, mostly focusing on design time. In reality, neither the context of use nor the adaptation can always be envisioned at design time. As a result, part of plasticity has to be computed at run time. This paper presents an early prototype called the Comets Inspector that overcomes the plasticity issue. It favours the exploration of design alternatives both at design time and run time by embedding the all development life cycle of a User Interface (UI) in a single tool. It integrates three representations that traditionally need difficult conciliations between their stakeholders: the designer, developer and end-user. Fig. 1 elicits the three representations (inspired from [3,13]):

1. The *Conceptual Representation* models a UI using a given syntax and semantics according to consistent stylistics, which can be textual, graphical or both. This representation includes multiple models depending on the design method: typically task, domain, user, platform, environment, abstract and concrete UIs, etc. This representation is intended for the designer to capture UI requirements and information that will be turned into design options later on.
2. The *Internal Representation* consists of pieces of code programmed in an appropriate language (e.g., C, Tcl/Tk, Flash) for implementing a particular UI. This representation is typically the developer's one, where the UI code should reflect the design options decided by the designer.
3. The *External Representation* refers to the UI rendering which is visible and manipulable by the end-user. This rendering could be achieved through interpreters and/or code generators. This representation is the common view that is made visible to the end-user. The other representations are not usually.

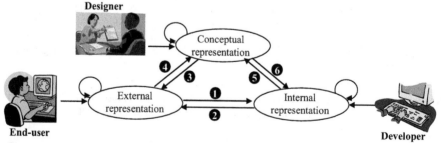

❶ : Generation of the UI code from its appearance (see UIMSs, toolkits, interface builders).
❷ : Elaboration of the rendering from parts of the application/UI code.
❸/❻ : Generation of the UI appearance/code from the application's syntax and semantics (see MB-IDE).
❹/❺ : Recovering of design time models from the UI appearance/code (see reverse engineering).

Figure 1. The three representations of a UI making explicit six possible development paths

Fig. 1 makes explicit six possible development paths (1 to 6). Actually, these paths mainly suffer from five major shortcomings: 1) only one representation is available at a time; 2) most representations are limited to design time; 3) the mappings between all representations are not always ensured; 4) the manipulation of each representation is somewhat tedious; and 5) this manipulation is usually built-in. These five shortcomings are discussed in Section 2 with regard to the state of the art. They are turned into requirements that motivate both the Comet concept and the Comets Inspector described in Section 3. Section 4 discusses perspectives to the work.

2.   RELATED WORK

FormsVBT [1] is probably the first manifestation of an environment combining more than one of the aforementioned representations at least: at design-time, the designer is able to manipulate T_eX specifications describing the look and feel of a graphical dialog box. This conceptual representation is directly mapped onto an external representation, a genuine UI which can be tested by the user for acceptance. The system also works the other way: when the external representation is affected, the conceptual representation is updated accordingly, thus maintaining a bijective mapping.

Teallach [2] supports the more general problem of maintaining mappings between representations [8] in a more sophisticated way: a conceptual representation is established based on a task and a domain models from which an external representation could be produced. The task or the domain models could be used separately or together. If an external representation is built manually, it is then possible to link it to the task and domain afterwards.

In [6], a methodology is developed that systematically produces a UI through a sequence of steps: task modelling, derivation of a dialog graph from the task model, and production of a final UI. Again, an external and an internal representation could be produced from a conceptual representation. The system does not work the other way: if the final UI is modified, these modifications are lost for the next re-generation. This problem is often referred to as the *round-trip engineering*. The situation is similar in [9].

An interesting idea introduced in [10] is to simultaneously provide the user with both the conceptual and external representations to the user so as to establish a more direct correspondence between the two views. This combination of views is maintained even at run-time. In [12], a forward engineering method is adopted to derive the internal and external representations from a conceptual representation that progressively goes from the task model to abstract presentations.

By examining these representative cases of the related work and other similar cases, we define five requirements to overcome the shortcomings elicited in Section 2:

- **Requirement n°1: all representations should be available simultaneously**, as opposed to one representation at a time or moving from one representation to another one as in FormsVBT [1] and Teallach [2].
- **Requirement n°2: all representations should be manipulated at runtime**, as opposed to design-time only. This is very relevant for propagating changes at run-time such as adaptations in case of plastic UIs. For instance, a UsiXML (http://www.usixml.org) specification could be conveyed and interpreted at run-time, including its adaptation rules that are embedded in the conceptual representation. But this is so far not supported in tools such as InterpiXML, the Java interpreter for UsiXML.
- **Requirement n°3: all representations should be coordinated in a consistent way**, as opposed to ensuring partial mapping or no mapping at all. Therefore in theory, six sets of mappings should be maintained (see Section 1). In practice, the requirement could be alleviated to be compliant with requirement number 2 that calls for an acceptable latency.
- **Requirement n°4: each representation should be manipulable via a dedicated "mini-UI"**, as opposed to other related works where the operations attached to each representation were not always salient. Various interaction styles could be relevant to take into account the different syntactic and semantic skills [7] of the stakeholders.
- **Requirement n°5: each "mini-UI" should be autonomous**, as opposed to tied up with the rest of the application and the environment.

The following section shows how the Comets inspector fully or partially addresses the five above requirements.

3. THE COMETS INSPECTOR

The notion of *Comet* has been fashioned from a software engineering perspective as *plastic interactors*, i.e. interactors capable of adapting or being adapted to the context of use while preserving usability [4,5]. A comet is "a self descriptive interactor that publishes the quality in use it guarantees for a set of contexts of use. It is able to either self-adapt to the current context of use, or be adapted by a tier-component. It can be dynamically discarded, respectively recruited, when it is unable, respectively able, to cover the current context of use" [5]. As opposed to Abstract Interaction Objects [14] and plastic widgets [11], a Comet is more powerful in that it embeds the alternate presentations depending on the context of use, the mechanisms to switch between them, and an underlying software architecture for controlling its behavior. A Comet comes with three facets [4,5]: Presentation, Abstraction, and Control). Presentation and Abstraction are logical facets in charge of selecting the physical presentation/abstraction appropriate in the current context of use (Fig. 2).

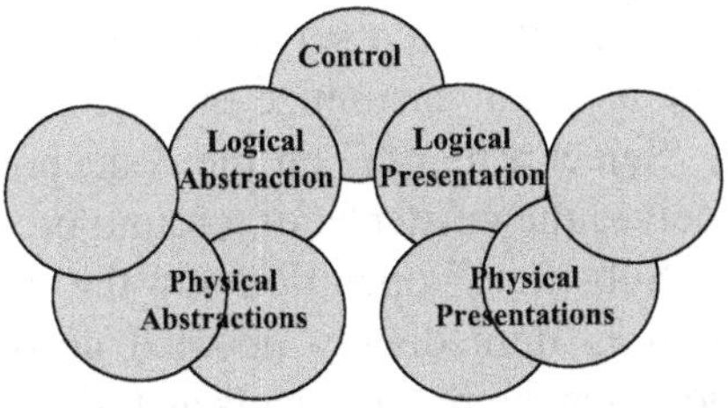

Figure 2. A comet, a software architecture construct made of a control, a logical abstraction and a logical presentation in charge of dealing with their potentially multiple physical abstractions and/or presentations. This "polymorphism" may be useful for adapting to the context of use

To address the five requirements introduced in Section 2, a Comets inspector has been designed and fully developed on top of the Tcl/Tk environment. Fig. 3 reproduces a screen shot of the inspector opened with a comet-based running example: the Home Heating Control System (HHCS).

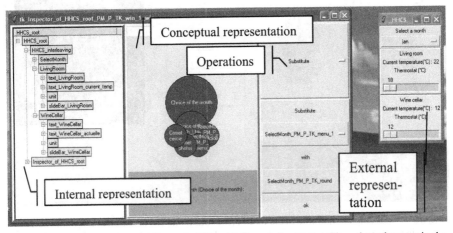

Figure 3. The three representations of a UI in the Comets Inspector. The selected comet in the conceptual representation is "Select a month"

HHCS (see the external representation on the right window in Fig. 3) is intended to help the user in managing the temperature at home. The user selects the month, browses the rooms and, if necessary, sets the thermostats of the rooms. The inspector makes observable the conceptual, internal, and external representations of HHCS. The conceptual representation (middle part of the left window in Fig. 3) depicts HHCS in terms of comets: both the control and the current/available logical and physical presentations are displayed (the abstractions have not been considered in this early version). The facets of the comets are depicted as circles according to Fig. 2. The internal representation (left part of the left window in Fig. 3) materializes the hierarchy of Abstract Containers and Abstract Individual Components of the UI. The external representation consists of the direct rendering of the UI as perceived by the end-user. Thanks to a set of operations (right part of the left window in Fig. 3), the user can customize the UI. Let us suppose that when browsing the comet "Select a month" on the conceptual representation (see Fig. 3), the user perceives the existence of a round presentation. He/she simply selects both the "Substitute" operation and the round presentation. The external representation is immediately updated accordingly (Fig. 4). The Comets inspector addresses the requirements as follows:

- **Requirement n°1**: the three representations are available at any time as explained above.
- **Requirements n°2 & 3**: all three representations are manipulable at any time, whether it is at design- or at run-time. Consistency is ensured as illustrated on the "Substitute" operation (Figs. 3 and 4).

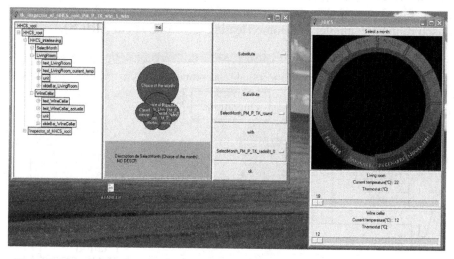

Figure 4. Choosing an alternate presentation (the round one for the "Select a month" comet) in the conceptual representation. The external representation is updated accordingly

Substitution can be performed between panels and windows. This is an easy way to implement detachable/(re)attachable UIs. For instance, in Fig. 5, a window-based presentation has been preferred for the comet "Set temperature of the living room". The UI has been detached accordingly in the external representation.

- **Requirements n°4 & 5**: As depicted in Fig. 3, each representation has its graphical autonomous mini-UI. However, they need further work to be usable by an end-user. It is also possible to manipulate each representation with Tcl/Tk commands, for instance for adding a comet to the hierarchy.

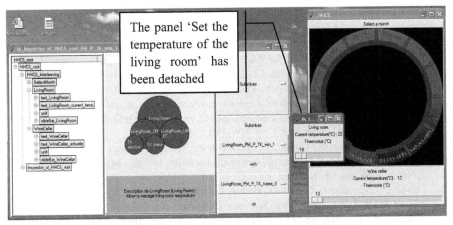

The panel 'Set the temperature of the living room' has been detached

Figure 5. The Comets Inspector supports detachable UIs

4. CONCLUSION

Until now, the effort has been set on software architecture for both integrating the three stakeholders' perspectives, and supporting the polymorphism of comets. In the near future, the effort will be set on the conceptual representation so that comets could tell their tasks, concepts, structures and requirements in terms of context of use. After that, the focus will be set on UI in order to surpass the rapid prototyping tool and provide the end-user with a powerful tool for customizing his/her UI. Then, some evaluation will be conducted before providing a library of comets.

ACKNOWLEDGEMENTS

We gratefully acknowledge the support of the SIMILAR network of excellence (http://www.similar.cc), the European research task force creating human-machine interfaces SIMILAR to human-human communication (FP6-2002-IST1-507609). Jean Vanderdonckt would like to thank University Joseph Fourier which supported his position as invited professor for two months from May 2006.

REFERENCES

[1] Avrahami, G., Brooks, K.P., and Brown, M.H., *A Two-view Approach to Constructing User Interfaces*, in Proc. of the 16th Annual Conference on Computer graphics

and interactive techniques SIGGRAPH'89 (Boston, 31 July-4 August 1989), Computer Graphics, Vol. 23, No. 3, July 1989, pp. 137–146.

[2] Barclay, P.J., Griffiths, T., McKirdy, J., Paton, N.W., Cooper, R., and Kennedy, J., *The Teallach Tool: Using Models for Flexible User Interface Design*, in A. Puerta, J. Vanderdonckt (eds.), Proc. of 3rd Int. Conf. on CADUI'99 (Louvain-la-Neuve, 21–23 October 1999), Kluwer Academics Pub., Dordrecht, 1999, pp. 139–157.

[3] Barthet, M.-F., *The DIANE Method and its Connection with MERISE Method*, in Proc. of World Confererence "Ergonomic design, interfaces, products, Information" IEA'95 (Rio de Janeiro, 16–20 October 1995), pp. 106–110.

[4] Calvary, G., Dâassi, O., Coutaz, J., and Demeure, A., *Des Widgets aux Comets pour la Plasticité des Systèmes Interactifs*, Revue d'Interaction Homme-Machine, Europia, Vol. 6, No. 1, 2005, pp. 33–53.

[5] Calvary, G., Coutaz, J., Dâassi, O., Balme, L., and Demeure, A., *Towards a new Generation of Widgets for Supporting Software Plasticity: the "Comet"*, Proc. of 9th IFIP Working Conference on EHCI jointly with 11th Int. DSVIS Workshop, EHCI-DSVIS'2004 (Hamburg, July 11–13, 2004). Lecture Notes in Computer Science, Vol. 3425, Springer-Verlag, Berlin, 2005, pp. 306–324.

[6] Dittmar, A., and Forbrig, P., *Methodological and Tool Support for a Task-Oriented Development of Interactive Systems*, in A. Puerta, J. Vanderdonckt (eds.), Proc. of 3rd Int. Conf. on Computer-Aided Design of User Interfaces CADUI'99 (Louvain-la-Neuve, 21–23 October 1999), Kluwer Academics Pub., Dordrecht, 1999, pp. 271–274.

[7] Jarke, M., and Vassiliou, Y., *A Framework for Choosing a Database Query Language*, ACM Computing Surveys, Vol. 17, No. 3, September 1985, pp. 313–370.

[8] Limbourg, Q., Vanderdonckt, J., and Souchon, N., *The Task-Dialog and Task-Presentation Mapping Problem: Some Preliminary Results*, in F. Paternò, Ph. Palanque (eds.), Proc. of 7th Int. Workshop on Design, Specification, Verification of Interactive Systems DSV-IS'2000 (Limerick, 5–6 June 2000), Lecture Notes in Computer Science, Vol. 1946, Springer-Verlag, Berlin, 2000, pp. 227–246.

[9] Luyten, K., Clerckx, T., Coninx, K., and Vanderdonckt, J., *Derivation of a Dialog Model from a Task Model by Activity Chain Extraction*, in J. Jorge, N.J. Nunes, J. Falcão e Cunha (eds.), Proc. of 10th Int. Workshop on Design, Specification, and Verification of Interactive Systems DSV-IS'2003 (Madeira, 4–6 June 2003), Lecture Notes in Computer Science, Vol. 2844, Springer-Verlag, Berlin, 2003, pp. 203–217.

[10] Navarre, D., Palanque, P., Paternò, F., Santoro, C., and Bastide, R., *A Tool Suite for Integrating Task and System Models through Scenarios*, in C. Johnson (ed.), Proc. of 8th Int. Workshop on DSV-IS'2001 (Glasgow, 13–15 June 2001), Lecture Notes in Computer Science, Vol. 2220, Springer-Vrlag, Berlin, pp. 88–113.

[11] Nylander, S., Bylund, M., and Waern, A., *The Ubiquitous Interactor – Device Independent Access to Mobile Services*, in R. Jacob, Q. Limbourg, J. Vanderdonckt (eds.), Proc. of 5th Int. Conf. of Computer-Aided Design of User Interfaces CADUI'2004 (Funchal, 13–16 January 2004), Kluwer Academics, Dordrecht, 2005, pp. 269–280.

[12] Paternò, F., and Santoro, C., *One Model, Many Interfaces*, in Ch. Kolski, J. Vanderdonckt (eds.), Proc. of 4th Int. Conf. on Computer-Aided Design of User Interfaces (Valenciennes, 15–17 May 2002), Kluwer Academics Publications, Dordrecht, 2002, pp. 143–154.

[13] Tarby, J.-C., *Gestion Automatique du Dialogue Homme-Machine à partir de Spécifications Conceptuelles*, Ph.D. thesis, Univ. of Toulouse I, Toulouse, 20 September 1993.

[14] Vanderdonckt, J., and Bodart, F., *Encapsulating Knowledge for Intelligent Automatic Interaction Objects Selection*, in Proc. of the ACM Conf. on Human Factors in Computing Systems INTERCHI'93 (Amsterdam, 24–29 April 1993), ACM Press, New York, 1993, pp. 424–429.

Chapter 14

A GENERIC APPROACH FOR MULTI-DEVICE USER INTERFACE RENDERING WITH UIML

Kris Luyten, Kristof Thys, Jo Vermeulen, and Karin Coninx
Expertise Centre for Digital Media – IBBT
Hasselt University – transnationale Universiteit Limburg
Wetenschapspark, 2 – B-3590 Diepenbeek (Belgium)
E-mail: {Kris.Luyten,Kristof.Thys,Jo.Vermeulen,Karin.Coninx}@uhasselt.be
Tel.: +32 11 268411 - URL: http://www.edm.uhasselt.be

Abstract   We present a rendering engine for displaying graphical user interfaces on multiple devices. The renderer interprets a standardized XML-based user interface description language: the User Interface Markup Language (UIML). A generic architecture for the renderer is defined so that deployment of the engine on different devices implies only little effort. We show that our rendering engine can be used on iDTV set-top boxes, mobile phones, PDAs and desktop PCs, and smoothly integrates with both local and remote application logic. As a test bed for the UIML specification we also explore support for extensions to UIML that enable the user interface designer to maximize accessibility and target multiple devices and different types of users at once

Keywords: Abstract user interface models, Model-based design, User Interface Description Language

1.   INTRODUCTION

There is a real need for User Interface (UI) design tools to support multi-device UI creation, even though there are many different existing solutions for this purpose. Most solutions are limited however since they specifically target a predefined range of platforms, e.g., a browser environment like Mozilla XUL (http://developer.mozilla.org/en/docs/MDC:About), specific programming languages (e.g., bound to Java like Jaxx – see http://www.jaxx framework.org - or jXUL3 – see http://jxul.sourceforge.net/) or a limited set

G. Calvary et al. (eds.), Computer-Aided Design of User Interfaces V, 175–182.

of interaction modalities (mostly graphical UIs). In contrast, UIML (http://www.uiml.org) is a *metalanguage* that can be used to specify the four different aspects of a UI (structure, style, content and behavior) independently [2]. None of these parts contain information that is related to a specific platform, programming language or modality. Although the language is syntactically generic, it allows some semantic constructs that imply a dependency on a certain platform, programming language or modality. In this paper we show how these limitations can be overcome and we discuss the foundations of the UIML rendering engine we provide to the community.

To our knowledge, only little has been published about the actual architecture of similar rendering engines. Roughly, there are two approaches for XML-based UI specification languages: the language can target a generic but limited set of widgets or the language is very close to the final widget set and thus specific for a certain type of platform. The former is often used for multi-device UI description languages (e.g., [3] and [7]), while the latter often relies on a certain rendering platform such as a browser. Most implementations that are publicly or commercially available are also limited to use with one particular programming language (or, in many cases, one virtual machine) and widget set.

Section 2 provides an introduction to UIML and explains the basic structure and constructs of this XML-based language. Section 3 gives a short introduction and overview of the UIML rendering engine architecture. Next, Sections 4 and 5 discuss the extensions we created to enhance support for multiple devices and multiple users. Finally, Section 6 provides a conclusion.

2. THE USER INTERFACE MARKUP LANGUAGE (UIML)

UIML [1] is a high-level markup language to describe the structure, style, content and behavior of a UI. For a thorough discussion of the UIML language we refer to the specification [1]: we will limit the UIML overview in this paper to the essential constructs. UIML offers a clear separation of concerns which is reflected in the four different aspects of a UI that can be specified in this metalanguage. Fig. 1 shows a skeleton of a UIML document at the top of the figure. In the past there were attempts to create a generic vocabulary by Abrams *et al.* [3]. In our approach we try to support a generic set of interactors that can be used across vocabularies, but also allow to use vocabulary specific interactors. If the designer wants to differentiate the interface for a platform because of the availability of certain widgets, she or he can do so with our implementation. The multi-vocabulary approach that our implementation supports is described in [4].

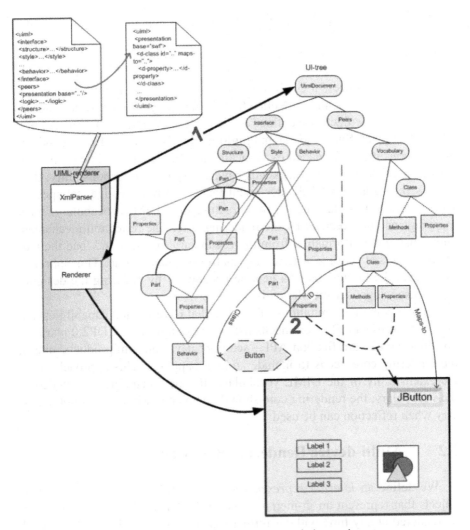

Figure 1. An overview of the UIML rendering engine

3. UIML-RENDERER ARCHITECTURE

3.1 Multi-device Architecture

A prerequisite for the renderer to work is the availability of a .Net or Java Virtual Machine on the target device. Most mobile and even embedded devices support one of these two virtual machines. Our implementation is built in such a way that there are no further dependencies on exactly which version or type of virtual machine, it simply relies on the virtual machine as a dynamic execution environment that allows loading new functionality on demand while running the UI. This enables us to support multiple mapping vocabularies on-the-fly.

Our UIML renderer consists of one rendering core and multiple rendering backends that contain code that is only used by a specific vocabulary. A rendering core can process a UIML document and builds an internal representation of the UIML document. Notice that the mappings from abstract interactors to concrete widgets are defined in the peers section (the vocabulary) of a UIML document. Since the mapping information is provided from outside of the renderer, it can be loaded dynamically and applied at runtime to the rendering core. The rendering backends have a very limited responsibility: they process the parts of a UIML document that can rely on widget-set specific knowledge. Notice that due to the structure of a UIML vocabulary, most mappings can be executed by the rendering core. The reflection mechanism allows using the information from the vocabulary to detect and load the required widgets at runtime without any platform-specific code. This approach overcomes the limitations of a generic vocabulary by allowing the designer to also use widget-set specific parts.

To overcome the limitations of devices that have limited capabilities and no means to use a reflection mechanism (for example the MIDP2.0 platform does not include a reflection API – see http://java.sun.com/products/midp/), the rendering core needs to include ad-hoc mappings. This approach limits the extensibility of the UIML vocabulary: if a new mapping is included in the vocabulary, the rendering core should be updated while this is not necessary when reflection can be used.

3.2   Multi-device Rendering Behavior

We define an *internal representation* of a UIML document as a set of objects that represent an in-memory tree of the UIML document which can be rendered at any time without further transformations. This reflects step 1 in Fig. 1. We define a *concrete instantiation* of a UIML document as a set of objects that represent an in-memory tree of the UIML document where each object that represents a UIML part has a reference to a final widget on the target platform. This reflects step 2 in Fig. 1. Fig. 1 shows the overall behavior of a UIML-renderer. The renderer uses several stages, where each stage processes a certain aspect of the UIML document. We identified three different stages of processing that are required for a flexible rendering engine:

- **Pre-processing**: during this stage a UIML document can be transformed into another UIML document. Section 4 gives some examples of transformations that require a pre-processing stage.

- **Main processing**: during this stage a UIML document will be interpreted and a concrete instantiation of the document using the UI toolkits that are available on the target platform will be generated.
- **Post-processing**: during this stage the runtime behavior strategies of UI will be selected.

The main processing stage is more specifically composed out of the following steps, illustrated in Fig. 1:

1. The UIML-renderer takes an UIML document as input, and looks up the rendering backend library that is referred to in the UIML document.
2. An internal representation of the UIML document is built. Every part element of the document is processed to create a tree of abstract interface elements.
3. For every part element, its corresponding style is applied.
4. For every part element, the corresponding behaviour is attached and the required libraries to execute this behaviour will be loaded just-in-time.
5. The generated tree is handed over to the rendering module: for every part tag, a corresponding concrete widget is loaded according to the mappings defined in the vocabulary and linked with the internal representation. For the generated concrete widget, the related style properties are retrieved, mapped by the vocabulary to concrete widget properties and applied on the concrete widget.

This section focused on the main processing stage of the rendering engine. The next sections will discuss the pre-processing and post-processing stages. Both are important not only to support multiple devices, but also to be able to transform the UIML document according to some parameters before rendering and to support a smooth integration with the target environment.

4. THE PRE-PROCESSING STAGE

In the pre-processing stage the renderer will apply transformations on the UIML document before creating a concrete instantiation of the UI. The transformations will be applied on this input document: this results in an intermediate document version that can be pre-processed by other predefined transformations.

In this section we discuss two different pre-processing stages that are supported by the UIML.net rendering engine: applying user profiles for more accessible UIs and applying layout constraints to maximize UIML document portability across platforms.

The support for more accessible user interfaces is accomplished by using a MPEG-21 description profile of the usage environment (a separate part of the MPEG-21 part 7 specification). The usage environment can describe the accessibility characteristics that the UI needs to take into account for a particular user. A user agent reads the characteristics from the MPEG-21 file and transforms the values found in the properties of the internal representation of the UIML document so that they convey to the required characteristics. For example; a MPEG-21 profile can define the colour vision deficiency for the user and provide required values for foreground and background colours. The user agent will transform the matching properties that are found in the internal representation into values that make sure the colours that cause the colour vision deficiency are not used. A full description of this approach can be found in [5].

For the layout management preprocessor to act as a pre-processing stage like described in this section, we consider the specification of the layout constraints to be a part of the UIML specification [1]. We allow the designer to use spatial layout constraints to specify the layout of the UI. The layout management preprocessor will generate a platform specific layout using absolute positioning that is consistent with the predefined set of constraints. The usage of spatial layout constraints makes a UIML document even more portable across platforms and adds a certain degree of plasticity to it. In the past, the layout specification in a UIML document was embedded in the structure and style descriptions and relied on platform specific constructs (e.g., the availability of the Java GridBagLayout class). A full description of this approach can be found in [6].

5.   THE POST-PROCESSING STAGE

Once a concrete instantiation is created by the rendering engine, it can still be further manipulated. The primary function of the postprocessing stage is to bind the UI with the application logic. Our renderer allows the application logic to subscribe to events from the UIML user interface. This is realized through reflection and aspect oriented programming techniques. Arbitrary object instances can be connected to the UIML document after the main processing stage, and it is possible to tag their methods with information declaring interest in specific events from certain parts of the user interface. Upon connection, the renderer inspects the connected object to check whether any of its methods are interested in user interface events, and if so, a hook between that particular event and the object's method will be dynamically created, similar to a callback function. Furthermore, a method can state that it wants to receive the internal representation of a part element, when the event gets fired. The properties of this part element can be queried or manipulated, and the application logic can even act upon the concrete widget instantiation. This mechanism allows for interesting applications. For instance; suppose we have a UIML login form, which connects to a database. When the authentication mechanism changes, the developer can just replace the existing authentication library. Due to the dynamic nature of this binding, nor the user interface, nor the renderer has to be changed.

As an extension module we added support for adaptive navigation through the UI. In implementing UIML renderers on resource-constrained devices for different types of users, navigation through the UI should be carefully defined. On devices with limited navigation input possibilities, e.g., arrow-buttons only as found on the remote control of a television, UI designers want to specify how users can navigate between different interface elements. The post-processing stage to support adaptable navigation uses a separate navigation specification that can be applied on the final UI. Since the internal representation is still available during the post-processing stage, this information can still be used. For example, the hierarchy of parts from the UIML document indicates which concrete widget is a container for other ones.

The navigation specification defines how the focus is handled, using *init* and *focus-transition* rules similar to the working of a state transition network. The *init* rule specifies the element that gets the focus when the parent container is entered. A *focus-transition* specifies the element that gets the focus when a navigation event is generated (e.g., left button pressed). The UIML-renderer applies these rules by capturing the events generated by the UI and checks whether the event is a navigation event and can be processed. One of the benefits of this approach is that navigation through the generated UI can be optimized for on the screen sizes or user preferences.

6. CONCLUSION

Our demonstrator shows a functional UIML renderer on multiple devices that is capable of generating personalized and platform-specific user interfaces from a high-level user interface description. The renderer will be demonstrated on a mobile phone, PDA, desktop PC and for a set-top box. We provide a UIML renderer that processes the UIML document on the client device. This approach results in greater flexibility and better support for just-in-time render- and runtime adaptations of the UI.

The .Net version of the UIML renderer presented in this paper is available as free software at http://research.edm.uhasselt.be/uiml.net. As far as we know it is the only free (as in freedom) implementation of the UIML 3.0 standard that is available. It has been used and tested in several projects, and we want to encourage everyone to use the rendering software and contribute in any possible way. Although the renderer runs on Java virtual machines as well as .Net virtual machines, only the latter is publicly available.

ACKNOWLEDGMENTS

Part of the research at EDM is funded by the European Fund for Regional Development, the Interdisciplinary Institute for Broadband Technology (IBBT) and the Flemish Government.

REFERENCES

[1] Abrams, M., and Helms, J., *User Interface Markup Language (UIML) Specification version 3.1*, Technical report, Oasis UIML Technical Committee, 2004.

[2] Abrams, M., Phanouriou, C., Batongbacal, A.L., Williams, S.M., and Shuster, J.E., *UIML: An Appliance-Independent XML User Interface Language*, in Proc. of 8th World-Wide Web Conf. WWW'8 (Toronto, May 11–14, 1999), Computer Networks, 1999.

[3] Farooq Ali, M., Pérez-Quiñones, M.A., Abrams, M., and Shell, E., *Building Multi-Platform User Interfaces with UIML*, in Ch. Kolski, J. Vanderdonckt (eds.), Proc. of 4th Int. Conf. of Computer-Aided Design of User Interfaces CADUI'2002 (Valenciennes, 15–17 May 2002), Information Systems Series, Kluwer Academics, Dordrecht, 2002, pp. 255–266.

[4] Luyten, K., and Coninx, K., *UIML.NET: an Open UIML Renderer for the .Net Framework*, in R. Jacob, Q. Limbourg, J. Vanderdonckt (eds.), Proc. of 5th Int. Conf. of Computer-Aided Design of User Interfaces CADUI'2004 (Funchal, 13–16 January 2004), Information Systems Series, Kluwer Academics, Dordrecht, 2005, pp. 259–270.

[5] Luyten, K., Thys, K., and Coninx, K., *Profile-Aware Multi-Device Interfaces: An MPEG-21-Based Approach for Accessible User Interfaces*, in Proc. of Accessible Design in the Digital World, 2005.

[6] Luyten, K., Vermeulen, J., and Coninx, K., *Constraint Adaptability for Multi-Device User Interfaces*, in Proc. of ACM CHI'2006 Workshop on The Many Faces on Consistency, ACM, Montreal, 2006.

[7] Merrick, R.A., Wood, B., and Krebs, W., *Abstract User Interface Markup Language*, in K. Luyten, M. Abrams, Q. Limbourg, J. Vanderdonckt (eds.), Proc. of the ACM AVI'2004 Workshop "Developing User Interfaces with XML: Advances on User Interface Description Languages" UIXML'04 (Gallipoli, May 25, 2004), Gallipoli, 2004, pp. 39–46.

Chapter 15

DEVICE INDEPENDENT LAYOUT AND STYLE EDITING USING MULTI-LEVEL STYLE SHEETS

Walter Dees

Philips Research Laboratories
High Tech Campus 31 – NL-5656 AE Eindhoven (The Netherlands)
E-Mail: walter.dees@philips.com – Tel.: +31 40 2745438

Abstract   This paper describes a layout and styling framework that is based on the multi-level style sheets approach. It shows some of the techniques that can be used to add layout and style information to a UI in a device-independent manner, and how to reuse the layout and style information to create user interfaces for different devices

Keywords: Adaptation, Concrete user interface, Device independent authoring, Layout, Multi-platform user interfaces, User interface generation, Style, Multi-level style sheets

1.   INTRODUCTION

Traditionally, UI designers had the luxury of using WYSIWYG tools to create user interfaces with pixel-precise accuracy. With the growing need for device independent user interfaces and context-awareness, this luxury will have to be given up [1]. UIs will need to be adapted at run-time to the UI device and the context at hand. To enable this, the majority of solutions for device independent and context-aware UIs in literature, focus on automatic generation of user interfaces from abstract models. However, automatic generation of UIs has a number of issues:

1. It means a significant change in the role and skill-set of a UI designer.
2. It is still not clear whether creating UIs by specifying a potentially complex abstract model and transforming that abstract model into concrete UIs will actually be less time consuming than creating UIs by hand for each different device/context under consideration.

G. Calvary et al. (eds.), Computer-Aided Design of User Interfaces V, 183–190.
© *2007 Springer.*

3. Automatic generation of user interfaces may result in UIs that are unattractive and hard to use, since a UI designer typically has less control over the look & feel of the UI. This is illustrated in Fig. 1. On the left it shows a UI that is automatically generated from an abstract UI model, and on the right is a UI as it might have been created by a UI designer. For example, the UI on the right has application specific widgets for buttons Play, Prev, Next, and Stop and for the volume control, that are more appropriate in case of playing music. It also has a better layout, since all three lists are made to fit next to each other, and a better look & feel, since it uses UI specific decorations and color schemes.

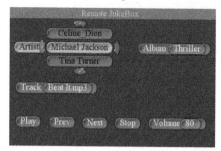 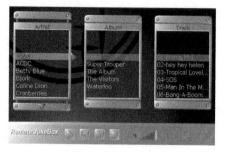

Figure 1. Automatically generated UI (left) vs. hand-crafted UI (right)

In order to overcome some of these problems, and to alleviate the transition for UI designers from single device UI design towards (semi-) automatic generation of UIs, the multi-level style sheets approach has been developed [2]. It allows the UI designer to focus on creating UIs for just a small set of key devices, whilst at the same time enabling reuse for other devices. This paper describes the work that has been done on a layout and styling framework that is based on this multi-level style sheets approach.

2. KEY ASPECTS OF THE LAYOUT AND STYLING FRAMEWORK

The key aspects of the device-independent layout and styling framework described in this document are:

- Independence from UI toolkits and widget sets that exist for different devices/contexts. Current UI style and layout editors typically focus on only one toolkit and one widget set.
- Ability to automatically extract and reuse layout and style information for different devices. Current UI style and layout editors typically don't re-use this information across different devices.
- Allowing for editing steps that are as WYSIWYG as possible, to give the author sufficient control over the resulting UI.

These key aspects are discussed in the following sections.

2.1 Widget Database

In order to make the layout and styling framework independent from the UI toolkit and widget sets, we make use of meta-descriptions of widgets.

```
<widget id="button" name="Swing Button" version="1.0">
    <widgettype purpose="generic"> push-button </widgettype>
    <uitoolkit> Java Swing </uitoolkit>
    <inputmodality> pointer </inputmodality>
    <datatype> none </datatype> <!-- the type of data associated with the widget -->
    <attribute type="resource" name="label" default=""> xsd:string </attribute>
    <attribute type="style" name="width" default="50px"> styletype:width </attribute>
    <attribute type="style" name="bgcolor" default="#aaaaaa"> styletype:color </attribute>
    <screenshot>
        <name> jbutton.png </name>
        <contentarea resizehorizontal="true" resourceref="label" minsize="label.width">
            <upperleft> (2px, 2px) </upperleft>
            <upperright> (button.width - 2px, 2px) </upperright>
            <lowerleft> (2px, button.height - 2px) </lowerleft>
        </contentarea>
        <!-- non-resizable areas for the button's top, left, right and bottom border -->
        <nonresizablearea>
            <upperleft> (0, 0) </upperleft>
            <upperright> (button.width, 0) </upperright>
            <lowerleft> (0, 2px) </lowerleft>
        </nonresizablearea>
        ...
    </screenshot>
</widget>
```

Figure 2. Example of a Widget Description

Fig. 2 shows an example of such a widget description. It contains some meta-data about the widget, such as which UI toolkit it belongs to, which input-modality the widget can be used with, the data type that is associated with the widget, and the style and resource attributes that are relevant for this widget. In addition, it contains a screenshot of the widget. This meta-information is useful for selecting the appropriate widget from the database [8], and for manipulating the widget's style attributes, resources, etc. in a layout and styling framework.

In order to be able to manipulate the widget screenshots in a WYSI-WYG-like manner inside a device-independent layout and styling frame-work, we provide a number of extensions on top of the nine-part tiling technique as described in [5,6]. For example, we define which regions of the widget are related to its content (i.e., resources/data that populates the wid-get), and which regions of the widget are non-resizable. By doing so, we can resize the widget in the UI without creating distortions to important areas, such as surrounding borders (Fig. 3).

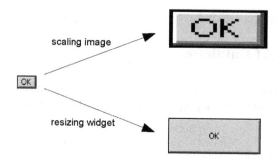

Figure 3. Scaling the image of a button vs. resizing using non-resizable areas

In order to deal with multiple non-resizable areas in a single widget, we created a technique called "banding", in which a widget's screenshot is split up in rows and columns that cannot be resized. Simply resizing the resizable areas of a widget screenshot could lead to gaps and/or overlaps in the widget preview. Therefore, the complete row in which the non-resizable area is located is considered non-resizable in vertical direction. The same holds for the column in horizontal direction. Fig. 4 illustrates this technique.

By using meta-descriptions of widgets and widget previews, we can abstract away from the UI toolkits and widget sets that could be used within the framework. There is no need to implement all the widgets inside the editor. The disadvantage is of course that the editor can not be fully WYSIWYG. The technique of using screenshots provides only a semi-WYSIWYG representation of the UI. However, as long as it is easy to generate a preview of the final rendered UI, using an underlying code generator and/or device simulator, this might be acceptable to a UI designer. As part of our future work we need to investigate if that assumption is true, and look at ways to improve the WYSIWYG experience, e.g. for vector graphics based widgets, you could use the Artistic Resizing technique [3].

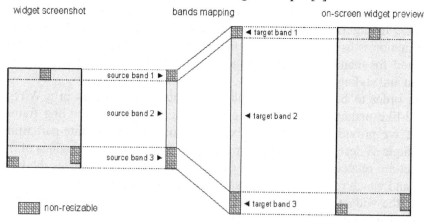

Figure 4. Resizing an image (in vertical direction) using non-resizable bands

2.2   Multi-level Style Sheets

One of the important aspects of the device-independent layout and styling framework, is to store the layout information in a multi-level style sheet. To define the layout we could use automatic layout generation techniques, such as [4,7], or by simply putting all UI elements in a grid-layout. But, as we argued before, the result may be undesirable, and the designer may want to provide his own pixel precise layout for some devices. Multi-level style sheets enable that, whilst at the same time enabling re-use of this information, even if he provided this information for only one device.

We analyzed which layout primitives designers currently use in various UI toolkits to create pixel-precise layouts, and selected the following set to define the layout (keeping in mind the re-use aspect for different devices):

- XY-layout with a virtual coordinate system that has been defined in terms of per mills of the surrounding screen or area.
- Areas that can be placed on top of a screen using the XY-layout of the screen. Areas have their own XY-layout, and can therefore be reused as building blocks for screens with different dimensions.
- Inside an area, widgets, other UI assets, and other areas can be placed by using absolute positioning with respect to the area, or by aligning them according to guides, or the area itself. Guides are lines that can be drawn inside an area to which widgets and UI assets can be glued. The order in which these UI elements are glued to a guide, provides information on how to order these UI elements on screens with different dimensions.

We want store this layout information inside the multi-level style sheet to enable re-use across devices. However, most updating strategies as defined previously in [2] require some form of equality. This is a problem because layout is more about similarity than about equality (i.e., not many devices have exactly the same layout). Therefore, we added a new strategy for updating multi-level style sheets called the average-updating strategy.

According to this strategy, a style attribute in a node of the multi-level style sheet tree will be given the average value of the values defined by its child nodes for that attribute, with the additional rule that child nodes for which no value is specified are assumed to have the average value. For numeric style-information, such as size, color, and position, it is clear what this means. For example: assume that the size of an element is defined to be 125 by 20 per mille of a 640x480 screen. If for a 800x600 screen it will be defined as 100 by 15 per mille, the parent node (e.g. all devices with a 4x3 aspect ratio) will be given the average of 112.5 by 17.5 per mille. This process is repeated for its parent, grandparent etc, until the whole device hierarchy is updated with new average values for this attribute. The question is now: what does it mean to have an average value for screen layouts?

Fig. 5 shows two different layouts (as a tree structure). On the left, the UI has a single screen. On the right, the UI has two screens, whereby screen 1 contains area 1 and 2, and screen 2 contains area 3 (without UI element 5) together with an additional area 4. Note: the layout tree structure should not be confused with the device-abstraction tree structure inside a multi-level style sheet. A layout tree would be the value for a single layout attribute inside a single node of a multi-level style sheet. Note 2: the term "screen" is used to represent the contents of the most outward logical window. Screens are navigable, i.e., if a link is followed, the contents of the logical window are completely replaced with new content. We consider how the UI is split up over several screens, also part of the layout.

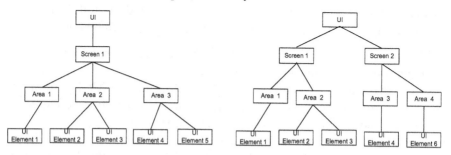

Figure 5. Example of two different layouts

To determine the average layout, we analyze for every UI the number of occurrences of every child-parent relationship. The most occurring parent for a child is considered to be the average parent for that child, and that relationship gets added to the average layout. If two different child-parent relationships have equal occurrence, both get added to the average layout. In that case, if a node in the multi-level sheet inherits from such average layout it can arbitrarily choose one of these relationships for its UI. Fig. 6 shows the average layout for the two layouts given in Fig. 5.

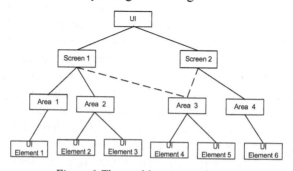

Figure 6. The resulting average layout

The average-strategy has the benefit that values will always be lifted inside the multi-level style sheet, and hence it promotes re-use. And, in the case of layout information, the lifted information always constitutes a complete UI, i.e., without any dangling screens, areas or UI elements.

2.3   Generating User Interfaces

To demonstrate the techniques described in the previous sections, we developed an editor (Fig. 7). It features an editing canvas on which UI elements (such as widgets from the widget database) can be added, sized and positioned in a WYSIWYG-like manner. This canvas is related to one of the screens that has been defined for a UI (see bottom of Fig. 7). The lower left of Fig. 7 shows a panel for changing the style attributes of the selected widget. On the top-left, next to the task-list tab, is a pull-down box to select the device for which the UI is being developed (in this case "test PC"). It is very easy to switch between the UI for different devices.

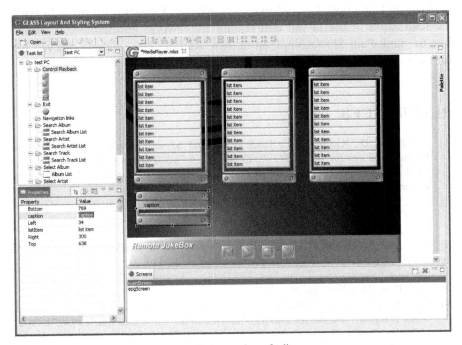

Figure 7. Screenshot of editor

In addition, the editor features a means to generate the final UI for one or more devices, as well as a means to edit the underlying XML data of e.g. the multi-level style sheets. Note that this editor is part of a bigger UI adaptation framework, which uses for example task models as input to select widgets from the widget database. Hence, the task list which is shown at the top-left of Fig. 7.

3.   CONCLUSION

This paper describes some techniques that can be used to create a device-independent layout and styling framework. Multi-level style sheets play a key role in this framework, and allow reuse of layout and style information to create user interfaces for different devices. As part of our future work on a more elaborate UI adaptation framework, we plan to make use of the information within a task/dialog model (such as groupings and sequences of subtasks) as input to automatically generate some default layouts and to split the UI over several screens. Furthermore, we plan to improve the WYSIWYG experience, and field-test the framework with UI designers, to see whether they appreciate working with it.

ACKNOWLEDGEMENTS

First and foremost I would like to thank Bart Golsteijn for his help with the realization of the layout and styling framework. Furthermore, I would like to thank Paul Shrubsole, Paul de Bra, Reinder Haakma and Jan van Ee for their input and interesting discussions on this topic.

REFERENCES

[1] Bergman, L.D., Kichkaylo, T., Banavar, G., and Sussman, J, *Pervasive Application Development and the WYSIWYG Pitfall*, in Proc. of 8th IFIP Int. Conf. on Engineering for Human-Computer Interaction EHCI'2001 (Toronto, 11–13 May 2001), Lecture Notes in Computer Science, Vol. 2254, Springer-Verlag, Berlin, 2001, pp. 157–172.

[2] Dees, W., *Handling Device Diversity through Multi-level Style Sheets*, in Proc. of the 8th ACM Int. Conf. on Intelligent User Interfaces IUI'2004 (Funchal, 13–16 January 2004), ACM Press, New York, 2004, pp. 229–231.

[3] Dragicevic, P., Chatty, S., Thevenin, D., and Vinot, J.L., *Artistic Resizing: A Technique for Rich Scale-Sensitive Vector Graphics*, in Proc. of the 18th ACM Symposium on User Interface Software and Technology UIST'2005 (Washington, 23–26 October 2005), ACM Press, New York, pp. 201–210.

[4] Gajos K., Christianson, D.B., Hoffmann, R., Shaked, T., Henning, K., Long, J.J., and Weld, D.S., *Fast and Robust Interface Generation for Ubiquitous Application*, in Proc. of 7th Int. Conf. on Ubiquitous Computing UbiComp'2005 (Tokyo, 11–14 Sept. 2005), Lecture Notes in Comp. Science, Vol. 3660, Springer-Verlag, Berlin, 2005, pp. 37–55.

[5] Hudson, S., and Smith, I., *Supporting Dynamic Downloadable Appearances in an Extensible User Interface Toolkit,* in Proc. of the ACM Symp. on UI Software and Technology UIST'1997 (Banff, 14–17 October 1997), ACM Press, New York, 1997, pp. 159–168.

[6] Hudson, S., and Tanaka, K., *Providing Visually Rich Resizable Images for User Interface Components,* in Proc. of the ACM Symposium on User Interface Software and Technology UIST'2000 (San Diego, 5–8 November), ACM Press, New York, 2000, pp. 227–235.

[7] Lok, S., Feiner, S., and Ngai, G., *Evaluation of Visual Balance for Automated Layout*, in Proc. of the 8th ACM Int. Conf. on Intelligent User Interfaces IUI'2004 (Funchal, 13–16 January 2004), ACM Press, New York, 2004, pp. 101–108.

[8] Vanderdonckt, J., and Bodart, F., *Encapsulating Knowledge for Intelligent Automatic Interaction Objects Selection*, in Proc. of the ACM Conf. on Human Factors in Computing Systems INTERCHI'93 (Amsterdam, 24–29 April 1993), ACM Press, New York, 1993, pp. 424–429.

Chapter 16

AUTOMATIC INTERFACE GENERATION THROUGH INTERACTION, USERS, AND DEVICES MODELING

Enrico Bertini[1], Giuseppe Santucci[1], and Andrea Calì[2]

[1]*Dipartimento di Informatica e Sistemistica, Università di Roma "La Sapienza"*
via Salaria 113 – I-00198 Roma (Italy)
E-Mail: {bertini, santucci}@dis.uniroma1.it
Web: http://www.dis.uniroma1.it/{~bertini, ~santucci}
Tel.: +39 06 49918484, +39 06 3280210373 – Fax: +39 06 85300849
[2]*Faculty of Computer Science, Free University of Bozen-Bolzano*
Piazza Domenicani 3 – I-39100 Bolzano (Italy)
E-mail: cali@inf.unibz.it, ac@andreacali.com – Web: http://www.inf.unibz.it/~cali/
Tel.: +39 0471 016222 - Fax: +39 0471 016009

Abstract   We present a system for designing Internet based applications that automatically adapt to different devices. We define a model that describes the user interaction in terms of elementary input/output actions. Then, we model devices to implements the user interaction in a multi-device context. Finally, we model users, to further adapt the interface

Keywords: Adaptive interfaces, Internet based applications, User modeling

1.   INTRODUCTION

The system presented in this paper allows for automatically generating user interfaces for Internet based applications, adapting the interaction to different mobile devices and user preferences. It models the user interaction in terms of input output activities, implementing the interface on different devices; the availability of end user preferences makes this process more smooth. The system is thought to deal with simple Internet based applications/services, like reserving a hotel room or finding a restaurant; it is out of the scope of our approach to redesign generic web sites making them accessible through different devices or implementing complex web applications.

G. Calvary et al. (eds.), Computer-Aided Design of User Interfaces V, 191–200.

The rest of this chapter is structured as follows: Section 2 describes related proposals, Section 3 describes the system architecture, Section 4 introduces the model that supports the design of adaptive applications, Section 5 describes how we model users, Section 6 deals with the metrics we use in the generation process, Section 7 provides a real example, and, finally, in Section 8, some conclusion and open issues are discussed.

2. RELATED WORK

Our proposal presents strong connections with *model-based* user interface design [11]. Puerta and Eisenstein in [4] propose a design framework that consists of a *platform model*, a *presentation model*, and a *task model*. The designer builds the user interface by means of Abstract Interaction Objects (AIOs) [12] that are platform-neutral widgets he can assemble to design the interface in an abstract manner.

The TERESA system [10] is based on task modelling and allows, through a very structured process to design multi-device applications. In [6] the interface adaptation is driven both by device and user preferences. The system formalizes the interface specification, the device model, and the user model and generates the interface solving an optimization problem. Other proposals come from research on data-intensive web design [5], that stems from past research on model-based hyper-media design, like, e.g., RMM [7], having major focus on data modeling. This approach suggests a process in which the designer starts from a data model (e.g., an entity-relationship schema) and on top of it creates a hypertext model that defines the connection points between the web pages (links).

Our system performs *matchmaking* to drive the interface generation. There are several known matchmaking systems [1,8,9]; our system adopts a novel, flexible approach for modeling and reasoning about profiles that are incomplete and/or inconsistent. Most proposals use a task model to build the interface; our system is based on a different specification that models input and output data and state transitions, allowing to design *in one step* simple services, and this is one of the main contribution of our work.

In addition, we use a UML Activity Diagram, resulting in a more natural introduction of our method in existing software development groups. Finally, our adaptations mechanism is based on both device and user preferences, while most of the literature is focused only on device adaptation.

3. THE SYSTEM ARCHITECTURE

The system architecture (Fig. 1) relies on few loosely coupled functional modules, to reduce the exchange of data and allowing for a parallel development of the two main functionalities: (i) service modeling and web page generation (left) and (ii) device and user modeling (right). In the upper part we can see two editors. The *Service Editor*, whose goal is to allow a service designer to describe, through a UML activity Diagram, a service behavior. The designer describes the service graphically accessing Application Data to select the data used within the application. The *Profile Editor*, whose goal is to model both users and devices. Users and devices characteristics are stored in a suitable format (User Profile Data and Device Profile Data). The Interface Generator is in charge of producing on the fly the HTML pages, implementing the service for the actual device and user.

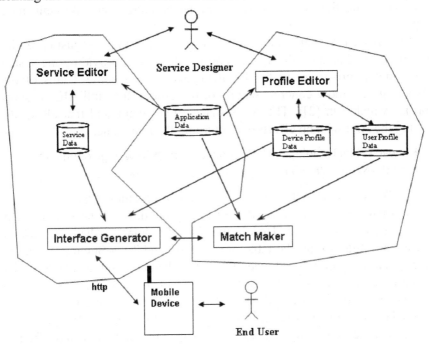

Figure 1. The system architecture

4. MODELING THE INTERACTION

Our proposal relies on a model describing the information that is exchanged between the user and the system foreseeing different ways of presenting the same information exchange on different physical devices. The model consists of two main parts: (i) a set of Abstract Interaction Units (AIUs) to be used as building blocks for abstract interface definition and (ii) the UML *Activity Diagram* as formalism to connect the AIUs that compose the interface. Using this approach the designer can specify the information content of each interaction and the connection between the various parts, designing the behavior of the application. The set of AIUs has been produced analyzing the user interfaces that are actually used to model standard web applications. Starting from specific interaction elements, we have grouped them into higher level units based on functional similarity. Such units express the key interactive features the specific elements of each group have in common. The UML *Activity Diagram* is basically a state chart diagram in which each state represents an activity and each transition is triggered by the end of this activity. The model, as can be argued, seems to be quite appropriate to describe the elements we are dealing with. How the *Activity Diagram* can be used to glue together the AIUs will be explained in Section 7, through an example.

We foresee two main interaction activities: browsing, i.e., just observing something produced by the system and inputting, i.e., providing the system with some information. In the following we discuss some details of two AIUs to give a more concrete feeling of our approach (a full AIUs description is available in [2]). The AIUs share a Quit command that allows for leaving the AIU with no effects and returning the null value.

BrowseTable(TableId, TableDescription,ListOfBrowsingCommands, Mode) :{NULL, elemOfListOfBrowsingCommands}

The BrowseTable AIU allows for browsing a relational table; usual facilities of panning are provided, if possible, by the device. The table description is a two value record: [TableName, TableSummary], where TableName is used as a title during the table presentation and TableSummary is a text description that can be used when the video channel is not available or disturbed or as an alternative when the device capability of displaying a large table is very poor. The ListOfBrowsingCommands is a set of server side table manipulation commands (e.g., moving quickly to a tuple). The null value signals that the user terminated the AIU through the Quit command. The parameter Mode has two values: (i) *Full*: the table is presented to the user without any omission; (ii) *Automatic*: based on the user profile the table is reduced (server side, through selection and projection operations).

USAGE: the purpose of this AIU is to allow the user to digest some pieces of information presented in a tabular way.

InteractTable(TableId, TableDescription, ListOfBrowsingCommands, Mode):{NULL, elemOfListOfBrowsingCommands, tableTuple)

The InteractTable AIU is quite similar to the BrowseTable AIU. The main difference is that the user can leave the AIU by selecting a tuple (that is returned by the AIU).

USAGE: the purpose of this AIU is to allow the user to provide the system with some input, input that is produced through the interaction with a table, i.e., the user selects a tuple.

5.   MODELING USERS PREFERENCES

We model services and users using a logic-based formalism, so that the system is able to match user profiles (demand profiles) and service profiles (supply profiles) by using techniques based on logic foundations. While a service is modeled by providing the description of the service itself, a user is modeled by describing the *class* of services he/she may be interested in.

We adopt a special Description Logic, tailored for our needs: such formalism is able to (i) represent also quantitative information; (ii) deal with conflicting and incomplete information with suitable reasoning services. Due to lack of space, we refer the reader to [3] for the details about syntax and semantics of this particular language. When matching a demand profile and a supply profile, the system returns as a result a *penalty* value, which is a real number; the greater the penalty, the less the two profiles fit each other. Penalties are described by means of *penalty functions* defined by domain experts and are use to rank the matched objects, allowing for further adapting the interface.

6.   DEVICES AND AIUS METRICS

In order to implement the AIUs on physical devices, we need some figures about their capabilities. Moreover, we need to investigate the AIUs as well because of the size of the parameters they handle heavily affects their implementation (e.g., the way in which the user interacts with a relational table may differ depending on the number of tuples and attributes). A full description of the metrics used for characterizing devices and AIUs is out the scope of this paper; for reference purpose we provide just few examples of them.

6.1   Devices Oriented Metrics

Concerning devices we use, among the others, the following functions:
- int RN(dev) (Row Number), returning the number of rows the device is able to display;

- boolean CVS(dev) (Continuous Vertical Scrolling), returning the availability of a continuous (i.e., pixel based) vertical scrolling;
- boolean JE(dev) (Java Enabled), true if the device is Java enabled;

6.2   AIUs Oriented Metrics

Concerning the AIUs, we shows some metrics about the text based AIUs, distinguishing between table and pure text oriented AIUs:

- int N(table), (Row Number) returning the number of rows the AIU needs to display;
- int CN(table), (Column Number) number of columns the AIU needs to display;
- int CHN(text), (CHaracter Number) number of characters the AIU needs to display.

6.3   Issues on AIUs Implementation

A systematic analysis of the AIUs implementation is out of the scope of this paper. Here we discuss, as a working example, the implementation on the device d of the AIU a, InteractTable, whose purpose is to display a table containing a set of objects (one per row) allowing the selection of a specific object. Assume that the following figures hold:

- RN(a)= 40 (i.e., the tables contains 40 objects);
- CN(a)= 105 (i.e., each row needs 105 columns to be displayed);
- CN(d)= 30 (i.e., the device can handle 30 columns);
- RN(d)= 14 (i.e., the device can handle 14 rows);
- RVS(d)= true (i.e., the device allows for row based vertical scrolling);
- PVS(d)= true (i.e., the device allows for page based vertical scrolling);
- COHS(d)= false (i.e., no column based horizontal scrolling);
- PHS(d)= true (i.e., no page based horizontal scrolling).

Based on these figures, we can argue that the AIU can be easily displayed for what concerns the number of rows: it requires $\lceil 40/14 \rceil = 3$ page based vertical scrolling commands. On the other hand, handling 95 columns on a device that is able to display only 30 columns and does not allows for horizontal scrolling is not an easy task. The only way is to present the table to the user in a two steps interaction: (i) the user is presented with a table whose column occupation is less than 30 (the column selection and order is driven by the actual user model), (ii) an additional command allows for detailing a single row, simulating the horizontal scroll. Section 7 shows an application of this technique.

7.   A CASE STUDY

We provide an example, modeling a service that allows for choosing a tourist event and reserving a hotel room (Fig. 2). The user starts selecting a tourist event through an *InteractTable*; then s/he chooses the city and starts inputting data about room booking details (period, people, etc.). The hotel selection is modeled through an *InteractTable* AIU; once the hotel has been selected, the user can browse the hotel description and the hotel image; after that, through a *SelectChoice* AIU s/he can confirm the reservation.

(a)

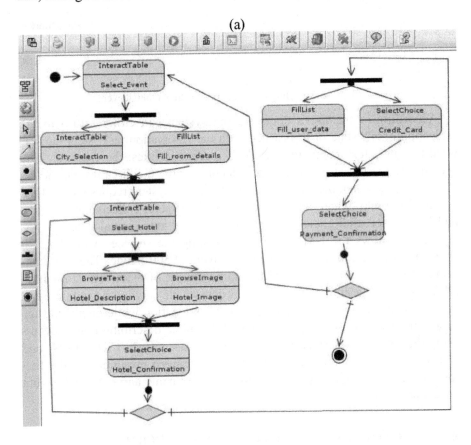

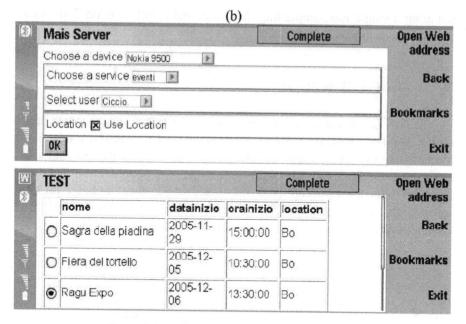

Figure 2. Modeling a service for selecting a tourist event

According to the user's decision, the system can either return to the "selecting hotel" state or to proceed with the reservation task, stepping forward to a new fork containing two concurrent activities: the customer data specification (*FillList* AIU) and the selection of the credit card type (*SelectChoice* AIU). When the user ends these tasks the system requests for a final confirmation and, when the user confirms, the system collects the data and makes the reservation; otherwise the user is routed to the initial state.

Fig. 2a shows the UML diagram modeling the service, while Fig. 2b shows the adaptation of the service on a Nokia 9500 phone. The user connects to the system and provides the minimum set of pieces of information needed to start the interaction: the used device, the service she is interested in, user name, and whether or not use her/his location while displaying the data. After that the user is presented with the table describing tourist events using the strategy described in Section 6. Because of user Ciccio likes food and does not care about money the table is arranged presenting in the first rows food events and as first columns the event name and other details but the event cost.

8. CONCLUSION AND FUTURE WORK

In this paper we presented a novel approach for implementing, on a variety of portable devices, simple Internet based applications. The main ideas supporting our proposal are: (i) a model characterizing the user interaction in terms of *input/output activities*, (ii) the embedding of such a model within the standard UML activity diagram, and (iii) the modeling of users and devices. A preliminary set of tests produced encouraging results and we are currently setting up a comprehensive set of experiments, whose results will be available in a very short time. Finally, some aspects of our approach deserve more analysis: we are currently working on defining a complete set of AIUs and devices metrics (mainly covering multimedia issues, e.g., annotated video streaming).

REFERENCES

[1] Basu, C., Hirsh, H., and Cohen, W., *Recommendation as Classification: Using Social and Content-based Information in Recommendation*, in Proc. of 15th National/10th Conf. on Artificial Intelligence/Innovative applications of Artificial Intelligence AAAI'98 (Madison, 26–30 July 1998), American Association for Artificial Intelligence, Menlo Park, 1998, pp. 714–720.

[2] Bertini, E., and Santucci, G., *Modelling User-system Data Exchange to Design Adaptive Interfaces*, in G. Calvary, G. Santucci (eds.), Proc. of Int. Workshop on Plastic Services for Mobile Devices PSMD'2005 (Rome, 12 September 2005), 2005, accessible at http://www.dis.uniroma1 .it/~psmd05/ papers/007.pdf.

[3] Calì, A., Calvanese, D., Colucci, S., Di Noia, T., and Donini, F.M., *A Logic-based Approach for Matching User Profiles*, in Proc. of 8th Int. Conf. on Knowledge-Based Intelligent Information & Engineering Systems KES'2004 (Wellington, 22–24 September 2004), Part III, Lecture Notes in Computer Science, Vol. 3215, Springer-Verlag, Berlin, 2004, pp. 187–195.

[4] Eisenstein, J., Vanderdonckt, J., and Puerta, A., *Applying Model-Based Techniques to the Development of User Interfaces for Mobile Computers*, in Proc. of the 6th Int. Conf. on Intelligent User Interfaces IUI'2001 (Santa Fe, 14–17 July 2001), ACM Press, New York, 2001, pp. 69–76.

[5] Fraternali, P., *Tools and Approaches for Developing Data-Intensive Web Applications: A Survey*, ACM Computing Surveys, Vol. 31, No. 3, 1999, pp. 227–263.

[6] Gajos, K., and Weld, D.S., Supple: Automatically Generating User Interfaces, in Proc. of the 9th Int. Conf. on Intelligent User Interfaces IUI'2004 (Funchal, 13–16 January 2004), ACM Press, New York, 2004, pp. 93–100.

[7] Isakowitz, T., Stohr, E.A., and Balasubramanian, P., *RMM: a Methodology for Structured Hypermedia Design*, Commununications of the ACM, Vol. 38, No. 8, 1995, pp. 34–44.

[8] McDonald, D.W., and Ackermann, M.S., *Expertise Recommender: A Flexible Recommendation System and Architecture,* in Proc. of ACM Conf. on Computer-Supported Cooperative Work CSCW'2000 (Philadelphia, 2–6 December 2000), ACM Press, New York, 2000, pp. 231–240.

[9] Middleton, S.E., Shadbolt, N., and De Roure, D., *Ontological User Profiling in Recommender Systems*, ACM Transactions on Information Systems, Vol. 22, No. 1, 2004, pp. 54–88.

[10] Mori, G., Paternò, F., and Santoro, C. *Tool Support for Designing Nomadic Applications*,

in Proc. of the 8th ACM Int. Conf. on Intelligent User Interfaces IUI'2003 (Miami, 12–15 January 2003), ACM Press, New York, 2003, pp. 141–148.

[11] Puerta, A., and Eisenstein, J., Towards a General Computational Framework for Model-based Interface Development Systems, in Proc. of the 4th ACM Int. Conf. on Intelligent User Interfaces IUI'1999 (Los Angeles, 5–8 January 1999), ACM Press, New York, 1999, pp. 171–178.

[12] Vanderdonckt, J., and Bodart, F., *Encapsulating Knowledge for Intelligent Automatic Interaction Objects Selection*, in Proc. of the ACM Conf. on Human Factors in Computing Systems INTERCHI'93 (Amsterdam, 24–29 April 1993), ACM Press, New York, 1993, pp. 424–429.

Chapter 17

THE META SKETCH EDITOR
A Reflexive Modeling Editor

Leonel Nóbrega[1], Nuno Jardim Nunes[1] and Helder Coelho[2]
[1]Department of Mathematics and Engineering, University of Madeira,
Campus da Penteada, 9000-390 Funchal (Portugal)
Tel: +351 291 705150 – Fax: +351 291 705199
E-Mail: {lnobrega, njn}@uma.pt – Web: http://dme.uma.pt/njn/
[2]Department of Informatics, Faculty of Sciences, University of Lisbon,
Bloco C6, Piso 3, Campo Grande, 1749-016 Lisbon (Portugal)
Tel: +351 21 750 0122 – Fax: +351 21 750 0084
E-Mail: hcoelho@di.fc.ul.pt – Web: http://www.di.fc.ul.pt/~hcoelho/

Abstract   The Model Driven Development has its foundations on metamodeling and new tools are required in order to support users on the definition and customization of their modeling languages. The MetaSketch Editor takes advantage of the current OMG technology to provide the metamodeling mechanisms required to support the integration of some widely used human-computer interaction (HCI) notation into the UML, through precise and semantically sound meta-modeling extensions. With this integration, HCI field could contribute to leverage the model-driven development paradigm and support automatic generation of interactive applications

Keywords: Metamodeling, Model Driven Development, Modeling Tools, UML 2.0

1.   INTRODUCTION

The Object Management Group (OMG – an open-membership computer industry specification consortium) is currently preparing the final release of the formal editions of UML 2.0 specification, concluding the long standardization process of this major revision of the language. The results of this process were not only an improved language, with new constructs and better syntactic and semantic definitions, but also the bases for a paradigm shift, on the context of OMG technologies, which was made publicly notorious with the presentation of the Model Driven Architecture (MDA) [10] initiative. It is

201

G. Calvary et al. (eds.), Computer-Aided Design of User Interfaces V, 201–214.

now clear that UML 2.0 language was designed for the Model Driven Development (MDD) paradigm, providing support for modeling the different aspects of a system using different levels of abstraction as proposed in MDA (although it can be used in the traditional way).

Further, the architecture created to define the UML 2.0 language can be also used to define UML 2.0 dialects and even other modeling languages, in Cris Kobryn words [4]: *"We need to keep in mind that all living languages, both natural and synthetic, must evolve or perish. Consequently, we should look forward to natural selection taking its course in the marketplace, choosing among the various UML 2.0 dialects"*. This vision is far from what we might anticipate at the beginning of the UML 2.0 revision. OMG does not promote a unique modeling language but essentially a common infrastructure to define modeling languages. It is now envisioned that different UML 2.0 dialects will appear, tailoring the language for specific domains, or proposing new modeling constructs not present on the standard definition of the language.

The combination of the UML 2.0 infrastructure and enhanced extensibility mechanisms, with the clear emphasis on model driven development, creates a unique opportunity to bridge the gap between software engineering (SE) and human-computer interaction (HCI). For long, we have been arguing that the UML provides the basis for semantic bridging between the two disciplines [7]. However, the limitations of the 1.x versions of the language, and supporting tools, have always prevented effective co-generation and co-evolution of artifacts between usability and software development concerns.

With the advent of UML 2.0 the technology is in place to provide the flexible extension required to support the integration of HCI notations and techniques into the mainstream software engineering language. In [5], we already provided an example of such integration, providing semantic and syntactic integration of ConcurTaskTrees (CTT) into the UML 2.0. Nevertheless, this integration requires metamodeling support that is not present in existing tools. Here we describe how metamodeling support could be created through a reflexive Meta-Object Facility (MOF) 2.0 editor – the MetaSketch editor.

In the context of the OMG technology, a metamodel is an instance of the MOF 2.0 (the OMG core model that provides the foundation for defining modeling languages), meaning that a metamodel is a model that conforms to the MOF 2.0 (and not to the UML 2.0). Although, we can use UML modeling tools to create metamodels (the MOF 2.0 and the UML 2.0 share the same core constructs – the UML 2.0 Infrastructure) those tools are arguably adequate for metamodeling. Furthermore, a metamodel is not the final goal but the vehicle used to produce models, thus it is not reasonable to create a new modeling tool each time a new metamodel is required. Instead, we propose that the metamodel definition should be a parameter provided to the modeling tool, allowing the required edition support for the new languages being defined.

The MOF 2.0 profile mechanism reduces this problem but it is far from providing a complete solution, since we can only extend the metamodel (we cannot remove or modify any metamodel elements).

The idea behind the MetaSketch Editor was to support flexible metamodeling and overcome the limitations of existing tools. The MetaSketch Editor is able to edit any MOF 2.0 compliant model. OMG designed both the UML 2.0 and the MOF 2.0 models to be MOF 2.0 compliant. This reflexive nature of the MOF 2.0 enables the MetaSketch Editor to edit the metamodel and the model of MOF 2.0, as we describe in Section 3. We believe this is a first step towards integrating some widely used HCI notation into the UML through precise and semantically sound metamodeling extensions that could leverage the model-driven development paradigm and support automatic generation of interactive applications. Without this kind of enhanced extensibility mechanisms the HCI field could be prevented from contributing to the paradigm shift that will eventually dominate the SE arena in the near future.

This paper is structured in five sections, this introduction being the first. In Section 2, we briefly introduce the OMG support for metamodeling. A detailed description of the MetaSketch editor is presented in Section 3. Section 4 presents an example of how the MetaSketch editor could be used to extend the UML to integrate the widely used CTT notation. Finally, Section 5 presents our main conclusions and future work.

2. THE OMG METAMODELING SUPPORT

In 1999, the UML 1.3 RTF (Revision Task Force) recommended that the next RTF for UML 2.0 should pay special attention to extensibility, a requirement resulting from significant problems identified by users and tool vendors about the existing extensibility mechanisms [3]. In particular, the following improvements were recommended for consideration by the workgroup UML 2.0 RFP (Request for Proposals) draft:

- **Architecture**: Define a physical metamodel that is rigorously aligned with the MOF meta-metamodel using a strict metamodeling approach. Provide improved guidelines to determine what constructs should be defined in the kernel language and what constructs should be defined in UML profiles or standard model libraries.
- **Extensibility**: Provide a first-class extensibility mechanism consistent with a 4-layer metamodel architecture. Improve the rigor of profile specifications so that they can support increased user demands for language customization.

In fact, the existing recommendations reflect these requirements. The OMG designed the UML 2.0 and the MOF 2.0 models to be MOF compliant and instantiate from MOF 2.0. The compliance was achieved by defining a set of base classes that form the foundation for both models. The UML 2.0 infrastructure; being an instance of MOF, is a consequence of the strict metamodeling approach followed to define the UML 2.0. A simplified description of these dependencies is depicted in Fig. 1.

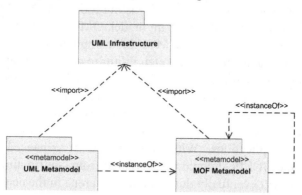

Figure 1. UML 2.0 and MOF 2.0 dependencies

As we can see in Fig. 1, not only the UML is an instance of MOF, but also the MOF can be expressed as an instance of itself (this reflexive property of MOF is explored in the MetaSketch tool in Section 3).

The Object Constraint Language (OCL) completes the metamodeling infrastructure provided by OMG. The language allows setting of pre- and post-conditions, invariants, and other surroundings required to a complete definition of metamodels. The use of OCL improves the overall semantic definition of metamodels - with a more precise characterization of the different constructs - and contributes to develop robust mechanisms to check and validate the user models.

The OMG introduced directly in MOF an extension mechanism based on the notion of profile: *"The intention of profiles is to give a straightforward mechanism for adapting an existing metamodel with constructs that are specific to a particular domain, platform, or method. (...) It is not possible to take away any of the constraints that apply to a metamodel such as UML using a profile, but it is possible to add new constraints that are specific to the profile."* [8]. Profiles are not a first-class extension mechanism since they only allow, to some sense, monotonous changes to a given metamodel, i.e., we can only introduce new constructs (stereotypes) with additional attributes (tag values) and new constraints, but we cannot remove or directly change any existing element in the metamodel. According to the OMG *"first-class extensibility is handled through MOF, where there are no restrictions on what you are allowed to do with a metamodel: you can add and remove metaclasses and relationships as you find necessary"* [11]. Consequently, a tool that only allows the definition of profiles does not realize all the potential that OMG technologies provide for metamodeling purposes. At this extensibility level only a MOF based tool can achieve such demand.

3. THE META SKETCH EDITOR

The MetaSketch editor was planned primarily to support the definition of UML extensions, in order to meet the necessities of our research agenda in terms of modeling tools. The decision of starting the development of this editor was made because we were facing several problems to use the available tools to attain our goals. The question was not only if we could specify the extensions, but how can we validate and use the extended metamodel. We assumed that the same principles that Model-Driven Development propose, for building software systems, should be applied to modeling tools, i.e., the metamodel definition must be the main artifact of a modeling language definition and the coding of the metamodel should not be required.

The architecture of the MetaSketch editor reflects these ideas: instead of having an editor compliant with the last UML language specification, we develop and editor that is meta-metalevel compliant with MOF 2.0, allowing the definition of user models for any modeling language that can be described in terms of MOF (i.e., which the metamodel is an instance of MOF). This approach was followed in the past by a consortium of CASE tool vendors through the CDIF standard, defined for supporting the interchange of models between different CASE tools, which most heavily influenced the architecture of the UML modeling framework [1].

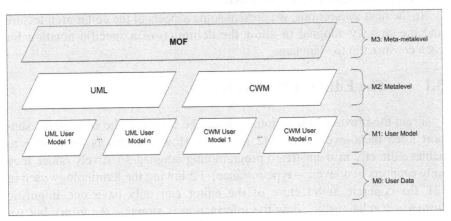

Figure 2. An instantiation of OMG four-layer architecture

As mentioned previously, the MOF was designed to be an instance of itself, meaning that MOF can be describes using itself. Consequently, the MetaSketch can edit any MOF model, in particular, the editor can edit the UML specification and any other MOF compliant metamodel. Fig. 3 presents this editor usage scenario. From the illustration we can see that the M2 level is occupied by the MOF specification and the M1 level we have the UML and CWM specifications (and any other modeling language that can be described using MOF, including MOF).

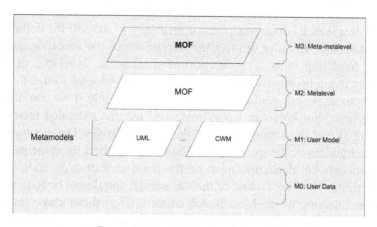

Figure 3. Using the MOF as metamodel

To ensure the practicability of this approach, we use the XMI format (version 2.1) to save both the model and metamodel (naturally, the content of the XMI depends on the modeling metamodel). We strictly adhere to this standard and avoid including any non-compliant extension or modifications, as a mean to maximize the interoperability with other tools (particularly relevant for the case of UML models).

In the next subsections, we present some aspects of the editor architecture and the strategy adopted to allow the definition of a specific notation for each construct in the language.

3.1   The Editor Architecture

From the previous discussion, it should be clear that the editor must support three meta-levels (M3, M2 and M1). However, this is impossible to achieve directly in mainstream programming languages natively (since they only supports two levels – type/instance). Following the terminology used in [2], the concrete architecture of the editor can only have one linguistic *instance-of* relationship (how the information is stored – *the form*), but we can have as many logic *instance-of* relationships as we need (what information is stored – *the content*).

The strategy used to support multiple modeling levels with just one instance level is known as Level Compaction [2]. In this strategy the *instance-of* relationships between some meta-levels are logic and not linguistic. In the case of MetaSketch editor, we compact the M2 and M1 level, assuming that *instance-of* relationships between the user model concepts and the metamodel concepts, are logic and established at runtime. Fig. 4 details these aspects of the architecture. The dependencies *instanceOf* are the linguistic and the *instantiate* are the logic relationships.

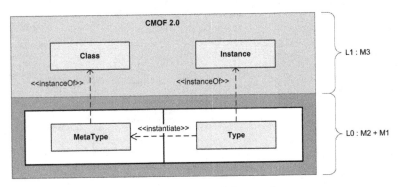

Figure 4. M2 + M1 Level Compaction

Having the types and meta-types at instance level (L0), allows runtime support, enhancing the flexibility in terms of modeling language extensibility support that was the ultimate requirement for the editor.

3.2 Modeling Language Notation

Certainly that one of the most important aspect of a modeling language is the notation. Without notation the models would be useless, since they would completely fail their ultimate goals of communicating concepts to and between humans. The MetaSketch is a graphical modeling editor and, therefore, a graphical representation should be provided for each construct of the underlying language. We have created an XML format to support these syntactical definitions. The representations are defined through the composition of simple shapes from a predefined set (similar of what can be found in other formats like SVG). We included in MetaSketch a geometry management mechanism based on the notion of *glue* that adjusts, at runtime, the spatial relationship between the different shapes composing the representations (it is similar of what we could found in many GUI Toolkits). Besides the geometry, the shapes have properties whose value is computed dynamically based on the slot values of the instance they represent (i.e., we could specify that the *Text* property of a *Label* shape is determined by the value of the slot *Name* of the instance represented).

Despite the flexible management mechanism, the results are identical to what can be found in the mainstream modeling editors, despite not using internally implemented representations which is an important requirement for a meta editor. A screenshot of the editor is presented in Fig. 5, where this mechanism is put into action through the editing of a class diagram.

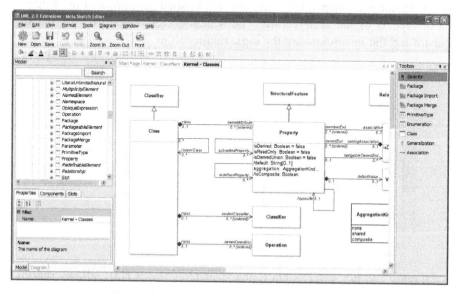

Figure 5. A screenshot of the MetaSketch editor

The edition of a model is always carried out in a context of a diagram: *what we see* and *what we can do* is determined by this context. From the perspective of the editor, a diagram is a drawing area, a set of graphics and a set of behaviors (or interactor, as we call them in the MetaSketch editor terminology).

An interactor represents a unit of interaction within a diagram: provides feedback to the user; collected and validate the required data; and handle the execution of associated commands. There are different types of interactors, depending on type of graphical representation (node or link) and interactors to support the drag & drop facilities.

Similarly to the representations, we have to specify each type of diagram that we can use for a particular modeling language, mainly corresponding to the definition of the diagram's interactors either to create or allowing the drag & drop of existing concepts.

Fig. 6 highlights the main concepts of the architecture (all concepts in Semantic block belong, naturally, to the MOF implementation).

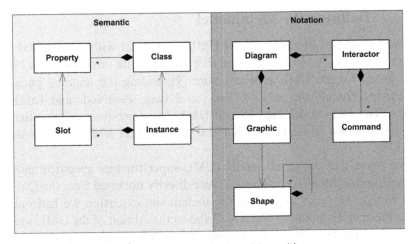

Figure 6. High-level description of the architecture

4. EXAMPLE: EXTENDING THE UML 2.0 TO SUPPORT CTT

In this section, we demonstrate the usage of the MetaSketch editor extending the UML 2.0 to integrate the ConcurTaskTree (CTT) [12] notation and semantics. A detailed description of this extension is provided in [4]. Here we concentrate on the impact of such integration at the meta-editing level in order to illustrate the advantage of MetaSketch in bridging SE and HCI. For the semantic details of this integration please refer to [4].

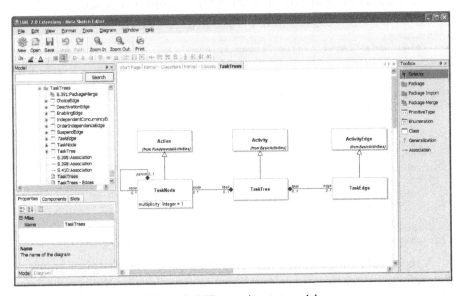

Figure 7. CTT extension metamodel

4.1   Defining the Metamodel

The first step is the extension of UML metamodel with the required concepts to model CTT. We start by editing the XMI file provided by U2 Partners' group for the UML superstructure [9], adding the required packages and classes, namely the package Tasks and Task, TaskNode and TaskEdge classes. The metamodel used to edit UML 2.0 superstructure specification was based on the ad/02-12-08 MOF 2.0 specification XMI file provided by OMG [8].

We stress that the initial model (UML superstructure specification) and the metamodel (MOF specification) were directly obtained from the OMG in XMI format. In order to support the metamodel extension we had only to create the specific notation file. Fig. 7 shows the edition of the UML specification for including the CTT concepts. The result of this process is a XMI file (named UMLCTT.xmi) containing the UML extended with new constructs like Task, TaskNode and TaskEdge.

4.2   Representations for CTT Constructs

The next step is the definition of representation for the new constructs. Since we are only extending the UML, we can include the representations on the XML file that we created for the UML notation. The next fragment of XML shows the definition of the TaskNode representation. We choose a rounded rectangle with a centered label to represent a Task node in a CTT. This structured can be identified on the XML starting at node tag.

```
<graphic name="TaskNodeRepresentation" concept="TaskNode">
  <slots>
    <slot name="label" value="semantic.name"/>
  </slots>
  <node width="120" height="40">
    <composed>
      <glue left="0" right="0" top="0" bottom="0"/>
        <rounded background="WhiteSmoke" radius="20"/>
        <glue left="4" right="4" top="4" bottom="4"/>
      <label value="@label" font-family="Arial"/>
    </composed>
  </node>
  <thumbnail width="64" height="64">
    <composed>
      <glue left="12" right="12" top="20" bottom="20"/>
      <rounded background="WhiteSmoke"/>
    </composed>
  </thumbnail>
</graphic>
```

A representation definition has three main parts. The first, is a group of slot definitions, where we can name some expressions (in the current case, we define that *label* denotes the expression *semantic.name*, which corresponds to the value of the attribute *name* of the instance associated with the representation). The next part it is the graphical definition of the representation. It can start by *node* (as in the showed XML), *link* or *callout*, depending on the type of graphic that we choose. Finally, in the third part, we can define an icon like version of the representation to use on toolbox and treeview controls. Here we only make a brief outlook of notation format; a full explanation is out of the scope of this paper.

4.3 Diagram Definition for CTT

To be able to create a CTT tree we have to introduce a new type of diagram – the CTT Diagram type. A diagram definition is essentially the definition of interactors that can be used. The interactor definition includes the sequence of commands that must be executed when the user completes the interaction. The Task Tree Diagram definition is partially illustrated in the following XML fragment. It shows that, in the case of a TaskNode, the interactor must execute four commands. The first command creates the instance of TaskNode concept. The next two commands establish association new TaskNode instance and the task tree instance. The last command creates the representation.

```xml
<diagram name="Task Tree Diagram" concept="Task">
   <interactors>
     <InteractorNode target="Task" name="Task Node">
       <CreateConcept concept="TaskNode" variable="newTask"
         owner="container.semantic" ownerType="Task"
         ownerProperty="node"/>
       <SetProperty concept="TaskNode" property="superTask"
         value="source.semantic"/>
       <SetProperty concept="TaskNode" property="subTask"
         value="semantic"/>
        <CreateNode graphic="TaskNode" semantic="newTask"/>
     </InteractorNode>
        ...
   </interactors>
</diagram>
```

4.4 Creating UML Task Trees diagrams

Combining the UML metamodel extension and the notation definitions for the new constructs, we can use the MetaSketch editor to create UML models with Task Tree specifications. Fig. 8 presents a Task Tree diagram using the MetaSketch editor. The toolbox on the right side lists the available interactors for the current diagram.

It shows that we can create task nodes or relate nodes with temporal operators. On the left side there is a tree representation of the model been edited and a property inspector.

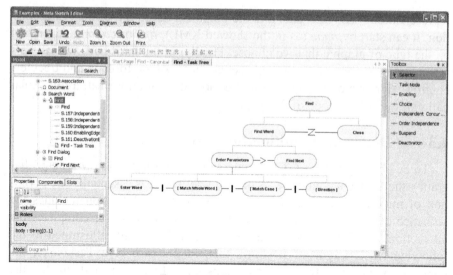

Figure 8. Task Tree diagram

The editor supports the usual facilities like multiple undo, zooming and layout arrangement. We should stress that the editor providing the screenshot in the previous figure is precisely the same editor that was used to extend the metamodel and introduce the CTT concepts in the first place.

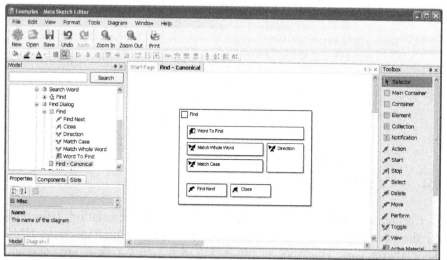

Figure 9. Canonical Prototype diagram

This reflexible characteristic of the MetaSketch editor provides seamless integration of new modeling constructs into the UML 2.0, for additional notations (for instance, Canonical Abstract Prototypes as described in [6] and shown in Fig. 9).

5. CONCLUSION

The object-oriented UML language is the mainstream technology in the software engineering field to represent, document and interchange software based artifacts. Any effort to integrate software engineering and human-computer interaction will require that HCI notations seamless fit with the OMG standards. This integration is increasingly important since the new UML 2.0 specification provides enhanced extensibility mechanisms and supports the model-driven development paradigm.

However, effective UML 2.0 extensions to integrate HCI concerns require metamodeling support, which is not feasible with existing tools. Here we present MetaSketch a reflexive editor that enables editing of any MOF 2.0 compliant model, including the UML 2.0. Taking advantage of this new tool we can integrate different HCI notations (such as CTT or CAPs) into the UML 2.0 providing semantically sound metamodeling extensions that could leverage the MDD paradigm.

So far we have successfully extended the UML 2.0 to support a widely used task and prototype notations. In [6], we presented an UML 2.0 compliant extension that supports CTTs and Canonical Abstract Prototypes, we even demonstrated how the two notations could be used together to simulate abstract representations of user-interfaces. However, these are not the only useful HCI notation required for modern interactive system development. MetaSketch can provide the metamodeling mechanisms required to support the integration of a widely number of different notations and ensure they are compliant with the SE mainstream language and related technologies that support model-driven development or tool interchange.

We believe this is the first step required to provide an effective bridge between HCI and SE. The longstanding mismatch between the two fields can now be crossed, through the inclusion of new UML dialects. Just as Kobryn predicted all living languages must evolve of perish, we believe that MetaSketch will give HCI an equal opportunity in the UML dialect arena.

REFERENCES

[1] Atkinson, C., and Kühne, T., *Rearchitecting the UML Infrastructure*, ACM Transactions on Modeling and Computer Simulation, Vol. 12, No. 4, October 2002, pp. 290–321.

[2] Atkinson, C., and Kühne, T., *Concepts for Comparing Modeling Tool Architectures*, in Proc. of 8th Int. Conf. on Model Driven Engineering Languages and Systems MoD-ELS'2005 (Montego Bay, 2–7 October 2005), Lecture Notes in Computer Science, Vol. 3713, Springer-Verlag, Berlin, 2005, pp. 398–413.

[3] Kobryn, C., *UML 2001: A Standardization Odyssey*, Communications of the ACM, Vol. 42, No. 10, October 1999, pp. 29–37.

[4] Kobryn, C., *UML 3.0 and the Future of Modeling*, Software and System Modeling, Vol. 3, No. 1, 2004, pp. 4–8.

[5]　Nóbrega, L., Nunes, N.J., and Coelho, H., *Mapping ConcurTaskTrees into UML 2.0*, in Proc. of 12th International Workshop on Design, Specification, and Verification of Interactive System DSV-IS'2005 (Newcastle upon Tyne, 13-15 July 2005), Lecture Notes in Computer Science, Vol. 3941, Springer-Verlag, Berlin, 2005.

[6]　Nóbrega, L., Nunes, N.J., and Coelho, H., *DialogSketch: Dynamics of the Canonical Prototypes*, in Proc. of 4th Int. Workshop on TAsk MOdels and DIAgrams for user interface design: For Work and Beyond TAMODIA'2005 (Gdansk, 26–27 September 2005), ACM Press, New York, 2005.

[7]　Nunes, N.J., and Falcão e Cunha, J., *Towards a UML profile for interaction design: the Wisdom approach*, in Proc. of 3rd Int. Conf. on The Unified Modeling Language, Advancing the Standard UML'2000 (York, 2–6 October 2000), Lecture Notes in Computer Science, Vol. 1939, Springer-Verlag, Berlin, 2000, pp. 101–116.

[8]　Object Management Group, *MOF2 XMI revised submission*, ad/02-12-08, 2002.

[9]　Object Management Group, *XMI for U2 Partners' UML 2.0: Superstructure*, 2nd revised submission (ad/03-01-02), 2003.

[10]　Object Management Group, *MDA-Guide*, v1.0.1, (omg/03-06-01), 2002.

[11]　Object Management Group, *Meta Object Facility (MOF) 2.0 XMI Mapping Specification*, v2.1 (formal/05-09-01), 2005.

[12]　Paternò, F., *Model-Based Design and Evaluation of Interactive Applications*, Springer Verlag, Berlin, 1999.

Chapter 18

A HYBRID TOOL FOR USER INTERFACE MODELING AND PROTOTYPING

Hallvard Trætteberg

Dept. of Computer and Information Sciences (IDI)
Norwegian University of Science and Technology (NTNU)
Sem Sælands v. 7-9, N-7491 Trondheim (Norway)
E-mail: hal@idi.ntnu.no – Web: http://www.idi.ntnu.no/~hal/
Tel.: +47 7359 3443 – Fax: +47 7359 4466

Abstract   Although many methods have been proposed, model-based development methods have only to some extent been adopted for UI design. In particular, they are not easy to combine with user-centered design methods. In this paper, we present a hybrid UI modeling and GUI prototyping tool, which is designed to fit better with IS development and UI design traditions. The tool includes a diagram editor for domain and UI models and an execution engine that integrates UI behavior, live UI components and sample data. Thus, both model-based user interface design and prototyping-based iterative design are supported

Keywords: Model-based user interface design, User interface prototyping

1.   INTRODUCTION

With the standardization of UML and specialized UML profiles, modeling of systems and software artifacts seems to be accepted in the engineering community. Model-driven architecture (MDA) and engineering (MDE) and service oriented architecture (SOA) all rely on models for representing the structure and functionality of software. For many, if not most, information systems (IS), models are crucial to managing the complexity of both the outside world and the computerized information system (CIS).

The field of model-based user interface design (MBUID) has a long tradition [8,10,14], but it has been noted that UI modeling is not very common [6]. One reason is that many actors and activities that are part of

G. Calvary et al. (eds.), Computer-Aided Design of User Interfaces V, 215–230.
© 2007 Springer.

user-centered, iterative design are not well supported by models, so alternative representations and means of communicating ideas must be used. E.g., most tools take a top-down approach to UI design by requiring task and dialog models before moving to concrete design, while iterative design methods often require support for bottom-up design.

In this paper we present our work on a hybrid UI modeling and GUI prototyping tool. First we give a brief overview of the "standard" model-based UI design approach and compare this to prototyping-oriented iterative design. The notion of complementing representations is used to motivate our hybrid modeling and prototyping tool, which is then presented. We finally compare our approach and the tool with others' work.

2. MODEL-BASED UID MEETS UI PROTOTYPING

Research in model-based UI design has resulted in many specific modeling languages methods. Although there is no UML of UI design, there seems to be a general agreement of three classes of models [10,12,14]. *Task* and *domain* models focus on the user's and designer's knowledge of the user, their goals and the tasks they need to perform. *Dialog* models focus on input and output of information, Abstract Interaction Object (AIO) [13] structure and dynamic behavior. Dialog models abstract away details of interaction style and client platform. Models of *concrete design* describe the structure and details of Concrete Interaction Objects (CIOs) [13] and is specific to interaction style and client platform. In the model-based approach, design progresses from task models, through dialog models to concrete interaction design, in a top-down process. Parts may be generated, based on logical dependencies, using formal systems like predicate logic, process algebra, Petri nets, state machines, etc. [8].

There is no *conflict* between model-based UI design and user-centered design, since modern model-based design has a strong focus on task, domain and user models. E.g., Mobile [9] claims to supports user-centered design by including all three classes of models. There is however, a *tension* between these approaches since their respective processes and techniques are different. User-centered design is by nature iterative, meaning that design is moved forward by cycling through UI (re)design, prototyping and evaluation. Testing by end-users is considered important and will in most case rule out using (only) abstract and formal prototypes.

Prototypes are one of many design representations that are used in a user-centered process, others are sketches, scenarios, storyboards and mock-ups. Common for all these are that they are concrete and informal, as creative processes are best supported by flexible representations, and formal representations are found to be constraining, as are their tools [4].

There are many important characteristics of models in general, that makes it desirable to combine model-based and user-centered approaches. A hybrid approach and tool should integrate complementing representations, rather then force designers to select one, to be less constraining and more useful. The tool should support moving between abstract and concrete representations, and change the level of completeness and formality according to the needs of the process.

The following sections will describe two complementary representations, CAP and DIAMODL, and a hybrid model-based prototyping tool, designed to improve support for the movements between informal and formal representations of abstract dialog and concrete interaction.

3.   THE CAP AND DIAMODL NOTATIONS

In this section, we present the two notations CAP and DIAMODL, that our tool supports.

3.1   Canonical Abstract Prototypes

Prototyping is a crucial part of iterative design and prototypes are used throughout the design process both alone, as a medium for evolving and communicating design ideas, and with end-user testing to resolve design issues. In [2], Constantine notes that prototypes can be placed along an "abstraction continuum" (Section 2, second paragraph).

To support "smooth progression from abstraction toward realization", he introduces his Canonical Abstract Prototypes (CAP). Simply stated, a CAP is a low-fidelity prototype consisting of nested rectangular regions representing user interface components, where the components' interactive function is indicated by an icon and a name. The icons are drawn from a standardized set, hence the term "canonical". Material components roughly correspond to output of information, while tool components correspond to input/editing and actions.

Fig. 1 shows a CAP example, with two components for viewing mailboxes and messages, labeled "view mailboxes" and "view messages", respectively. The interactive function is indicated by the icon and includes selection, i.e. input of an element, in addition to output of a set of elements. A third component labeled "view message", contains three sub-components labeled "from", "subject", and "content" and is used for viewing individual messages. As can be seen, the nesting and layout makes the diagram look fairly similar to a quickly assembled widget hierarchy in an interface builder.

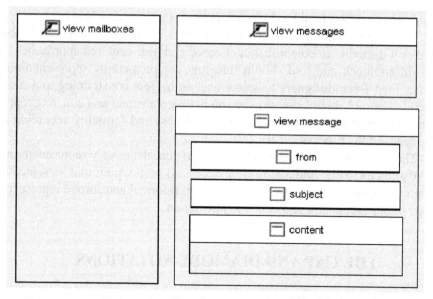

Figure 1. Canonical Abstract Prototype example

3.2   The DIAMODL Notation

The DIAMODL notation [11] is a diagram language for modeling abstract dialog, both information handling and activation logic, which is particularly suited for business applications. The *interactor* and *gate* concepts specify the input and output function of an AIO. The *variable, computation* and *connection* concepts are used for specifying how data is stored, transformed transported among interactors.

Fig. 2 shows a simple model where these five concepts are used. The upper left box is a variable and is used to store data. This particular one is limited to holding a String and currently contains "Hallvard". The two boxes with title bars to the right are interactors and the attached triangles are gates. As indicated by the gates, the upper interactor may output and input a String, while the lower one may output an Integer. The variable is connected to the output gate of the former interactor, while the input gate is connected to a computation, the output of which is further connected to the output gate of the latter interactor. The name and the input/output types suggest that the computation computes the length of the input String. Hence, this particular model specifies a UI through which the user may edit a String and see its length.

In addition to these five concepts, states (an interactor is also a state) and transitions are used for specifying the activation and deactivation of interactors, while UML class and object diagrams are used for data modeling.

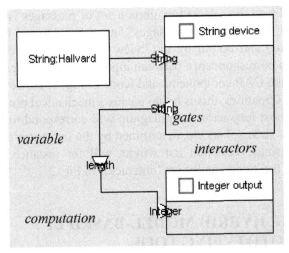

Figure 2. The variable, interactor, gate, computation and connection concepts

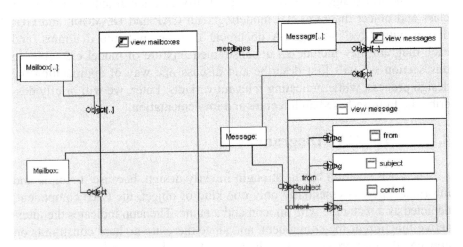

Figure 3. DIAMODL example

In Fig. 3, a DIAMODL example corresponding to the CAP example in Fig. 1 is shown. As above, interactors are shown as rectangles with gate triangles on their left side, either pointing into for user output or out for user input. Variables are labeled with class names and multiplicity. Computations are shown as free-floating triangles, and are labeled by attribute, association or operation names from the UML model (not shown). Connections are shown as edges and may optionally be labeled with attribute or association names, to indicate an embedded computation. This particular model is a formalization/explication of the corresponding CAP diagram, where the data types and input/output functions of the interactors are made explicit. The "view mailboxes" interactor outputs a set of mailboxes and lets the user select (input) one of them. From the selected mailbox a set of messages is computed and used as output by the "view messages" interactor. One of these messages may be selected and output by the "view message" interactor. As can be seen, there is a correspondence between input and output gates on interactors in Fig. 3 and the CAP components and icons in Fig. 1. However, since CAP has no formal semantics, this is by no means a mechanical process.

The innermost interactors in a diagram will correspond to CIOs like text fields, buttons, sliders, lists etc, determined by the interactor's input and output gates. A single selection list widget will for instance be capable of implementing the "view mailboxes" interactor in Fig. 3.

4.   THE HYBRID MODEL-BASED UI PROTOTYPING TOOL

Our hybrid diagram editor supports a mix of a small subset of UML's class and object diagrams, UI modeling with CAP and DIAMODL and GUI design with "live" widgets. A document may be split into diagrams, and each diagram may include an unconstrained mixture of model elements. In this section we will first describe and discuss one way of approaching the design process, while indicating relevant variants. Later, we will briefly describe the Eclipse-based architecture and implementation.

4.1   The CAP Diagram

The CAP notation has its strength in early design, because it simple and informal. There is essentially only one kind of object, the CAP component, depicted as a rectangle with an icon and a name. The icon indicates the interactive function of the component, and since there are no hard constraints on how components are composed, the icon may be changed at will.

The creation tool palette (left in Fig. 4) includes the most common kinds and the icon may later be changed to a more specialized one, by using the contextual menu. The component name typically indicates the kind of information a component handles, like "send message" or "view messages". If the name is recognized as a <verb> <noun> phrase with a CAP-specific vocabulary, the interactive function/icon will change automatically. E.g., changing the name of a component to "edit element", will change the icon correspondingly.

Although informal, CAP diagrams can provide important information about tasks, domain objects and actions. At some point, however, it will become important to be more explicit about what is left implicit in CAP.

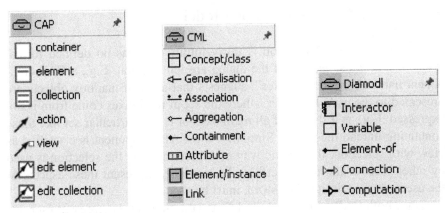

Figure 4. The CAP, domain and DIAMODL modeling tools

4.2 The Domain Model

A natural second step is to define the meaning of the terms used on the CAP diagram(s) in e.g., UML. In the editor we support the following object-oriented concepts (middle in Fig. 4): class, generalization, attribute, association (with roles) and aggregation/containment, element/instance and link.

Non-verb terms in a CAP diagram will typically show up in the domain model as names of classes, attributes, associations and roles. E.g., the terms "mailbox" and "message" give rise to two classes, the term "messages" refers to both a class and an association between the two classes, and terms "from", "subject" and "content" are attributes of "message". It is possible to define the classes, attributes and associations side-by-side the CAP components, and/or in a separate diagram.

One way of validating the domain model is to create sample data based on a user story or scenario, to ensure that the data are meaningful to the end-user. In the editor, instances of both classes and associations (objects and links in UML terminology) may be created as diagram elements, while attribute values are edited in a property sheet. Later in the process, the sample data will be used to populate a "live" user interface, so it's important to provide sensible data to avoid taking the focus away from the user interface structure and logic. To avoid constraining the designer, we support making the sample data first, and then create the class diagram. For instance, if ethnographic methods are used to collect field data from a workplace, these may be "transcribed" into objects and links in a diagram. The classes and association may be introduced when our understanding of the domain is more complete. There is currently no tool for doing this automatically, i.e. deriving a complete class diagram from a set of instances and links, but we hope to provide some support easing this process in the future.

4.3   The DIAMODL Dialog Model

Although the CAP notation is fairly intuitive, it has no defined formal semantics, so most aspects of the dialog are left implicit. E.g., a CAP component named "view mailboxes", suggests that a set of mailbox objects are presented to the user. However, where the set of mailboxes come from is not expressed. E.g., is it the set of all mailboxes or is it a particular set like those containing unread messages? Similarly, if a CAP component is classified as view with selection, there is no way of expressing how the selection is used by other parts of the user interface. To explicitly represent these aspects of the user interface design, DIAMODL must be used.

Since both CAP components and DIAMODL interactors represent user interface containers or components, the CAP component hierarchy usually corresponds to similar DIAMODL interactor hierarchy. After creating the CAP diagram, it may be *evolved* into a DIAMODL diagram, by adding gates, variables, connections, states and transitions. For instance, the "view mailboxes" component in the CAP diagram in Fig. 1, may be formalized as an interactor that outputs a set of mailboxes and lets the user input (select) one of them. This means that the interactor must have both output and input gates, and that their multiplicities are "unbounded" and 1, respectively, as shown in the DIAMODL diagram in Fig. 3. As mentioned, the CAP components are drawn from a standardized set, and a similar set of standard interactors has been added to the creation tools palette. Hence, gates may either be added manually, or the CAP components be replaced by their interactor counterpart.

Variables, computations and connections may also be added, by means of the DIAMODL specific tools palette (right in Fig. 4). In the example model in Fig. 3, we have added variables to hold both the output and input data for the "view mailboxes" interactor. The input data, i.e. selected mailbox, is connected through a computation to another variable, holding sets of messages. The computation is labeled "mailboxes" and refers to the association from the domain model. In this case the association is used as a function, and we can see that the variable types are correct, as the multiplicity of the association is 1-n, i.e. the "messages" function maps from a single mailbox instance to a set of messages. Both attribute and association names may be used as labels/functions on computations and connections.

Transitions between interactors and/or states are typically introduced last, to express when the various interactors are active and what triggers their activation or deactivation. The need for transitions and states depends on characteristics of both the style of interaction and client platform. E.g., speech interfaces are usually more sequential than forms based business applications, and interfaces for PDAs with small screens have more navigation than their desktop counterpart.

Table 1 summarizes the supported language constructs.

Table 1. Language constructs

Concept	Notation
class (of domain objects)	a box with name label and attribute compartment
association (between two classes)	a line with name label, decorations indicating aggregation or containment, and role name and multiplicity labels.
attribute (of a class)	a label with type and name
object/instance (of a class)	a box with underlined name label
Link (association instance)	a line
attribute (value in object)	entry in property sheet for object
interactor (abstract interaction object)	a box with name label and decomposition compartment
variable	a box with type and value label
computation (function)	a triangle point in flow direction, with name or function label
Gate (I/O for interactor)	a computation attached to the left side of an interactor
connection	rectilinear line with name or function label, that attaches to variable and computation/gate
CAP classification	icon left of interactor's label
widget	Itself, i.e. the widget is "live" inside the diagram editor
state (interactor without I/O)	rounded rectangle
Transition (between states)	line with arrow

4.4   Combining Interactors and Concrete Widgets in a Testable GUI Prototype

The dialog model describes the abstract logic, but says nothing about what the GUI will look or feel like. To be able to communicate with end-users it is important to give it a concrete visual representation, and to further evaluate the design by means of end-user testing, it is also necessary to make a testable prototype with real data and functionality. To support this, the editor lets the designer add "live" user interface components to the diagram, link the interface components to the inside of the corresponding interactors and execute the dialog model.

As mentioned in Section 3.2, the innermost (leaf) interactors of a dialog model correspond to or may be implemented by specific CIOs. E.g., the "view mailboxes" interactor in Fig. 3 may be implemented by a single selection list box. The editor includes a palette of tools for inserting standard widgets into interactors and means for defining how the logical gate model for output and input is mapped to the event and property model of the widgets. To make the widgets easier to combine with the interactors, the editor includes a palette of predefined interactors with embedded widgets, that may be added as replacements for the ones already present in the diagram.

The interactors model in Fig. 2 is shown left in Fig. 5, augmented by concrete widgets. A text field has been inserted in the "String device" interactor while a spinner has been chosen for the "Integer output" interactor, and both are connected to the gates of their respective interactors. Values are continuously propagated and as can be seen, the spinner has been updated to reflect the length of the current String value, as computed by the computation element.

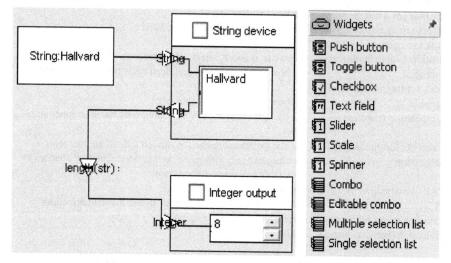

Figure 5. Concrete widgets from a palette (right) may be inserted into the interactors

In general, propagation of values through the network of connections is triggered whenever a value changes, either when the user interacts with a widgets or a variable changes, e.g., when the objects, links and attribute values specified as sample data are edited. If the widgets are correctly attached to the interactor gates, the UI will be functional and testable. In Fig. 6, a prototype for the larger example model from Fig. 3 is shown. The top left variable contains the two mailboxes defined as sample data and these are propagated into the list box inside the "view mailboxes" interactor. The user has selected the "Inbox" instance and its contained messages, as computed by the "messages" function, are shown in a list box inside the "view messages" interactor. Finally, the user has selected the first of these messages and its "from", "subject" and "content" attribute values are shown in respective text fields.

4.5   Top Down vs. Bottom Up Modeling

The process that has been outlined above starts with an informal CAP diagram, evolves it into a more formal domain and dialog model and adds live widgets to give a functional prototype that the end-user may interact with. Although the prototype does not have the look and feel of a high-fidelity prototype, it may still be used to validate the abstract logic of the UI.

A more bottom-up approach is also supported. Since the "raw" widgets are available in a dedicated widgets palette, as shown right in Fig. 5, they may initially be inserted without their interactor counterpart. With a decent layout, it can be made into a non-functioning horizontal GUI prototype, that may be validated as such. The widgets may even be operated, but to make such a prototype functional, the abstract logic must be added, by wrapping the widgets in the corresponding interactors, connecting the widgets to the gates, and adding other DIAMODL language elements.

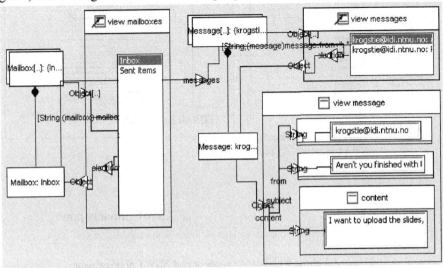

Figure 6. A testable GUI prototype for the example model

We have tried out both top-down and bottom-up processes in design workshops and in our experience both processes have their advantages and it is important to be able to vary between abstract and concrete representations of the same design. To better support this we are considering ways of quickly hiding different elements of the design, to leave only those that are relevant for the goal of the current design activity. In addition, we are working on ways of generating standalone UIs. Currently we are able to generate XSWT XML for the widget hierarchy that may be previewed using the XSWT plug-in for Eclipse. The XML may be edited to provide a reasonable layout and hence a more realistic prototype, as shown at the bottom of Fig. 7.

4.6   The Editor Architecture and Implementation

The editor is heavily based on the open-source Eclipse project. First, it is implemented as an Eclipse editor plugin and integrated with the Eclipse

Workbench framework, as shown in Fig. 7. Second, the Eclipse Modelling Framework (EMF) and Graphical Editor Framework (GEF) are used for implementing the diagram language model and editor, based on the MVC-based architecture, as outlined in [5]. Third, the Standard Widget Toolkit (SWT) is used for the "live" widgets inside the editor. Finally, the editor integrates with several third-party plugins for Eclipse.

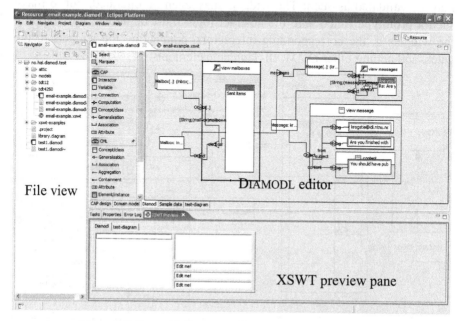

Figure 7. Eclipse with DIAMODL editor and XSWT preview pane

The overall architecture is shown in Fig. 8. The thick boxes represent so-called plugins and the thin boxes are packages within the plugin. Three kinds of arrows denote different kinds of dependencies: The thick arrows denote plugin extension, the thin arrows denote inheritance and the dashed arrows denote association in an object structure.

The design is conceptually split along two axes (light grey lines); *generic* vs. *specific* and *model*-oriented vs. *editor*-oriented. The *generic model* is implemented using EMF, and includes both the visual part of a diagram and a generic semantic part. The specific *diamodl model* extends the generic semantic model. The *generic editor* is based on GEF and provides direct manipulation of the diagram, The specific *diamodl editor* extends is with diamodl specific visual elements and semantics.

The use of EMF is vital, as it allows implementing the model with an efficient in-memory representation, change event service suitable for MVC and XMI-based persistence. The diamodl documents are XMI generated derived directly from the language model and EMF instances. Template documents containing all the basic symbols use the same XMI format, and cut & paste within the editor and across applications is implemented using XMI serialisation/deserialisation. EMF is also used in the diamodl runtime: Our editor's UML subset is mapped to EMF's meta-objects, and the instances and links from the domain model that are used during execution are actually EMF instances. To support custom functions in computations and connections, the pnuts scripting engine (Pnuts - http://www.pnuts.org/ - is a Java VM-based scripting language that was chosen over Rhino JavaScript and BeanShell because of its clean, elegant and extensible design. Support for the other scripting languages is easily added by means of plug-in extension) has been extended to support EMF. Advanced EMF-based services like validation and declarative constraints with OCL are in progress within the Eclipse EMFT project, and we believe EMF is a firm foundation to build modelling tools upon.

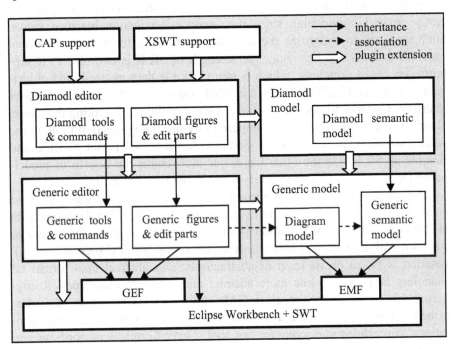

Figure 8. Overall architecture

5.   COMPARISON AND RELATED WORK

In order to provide a testable GUI prototype, our hybrid tool combines three elements: 1) user interface modeling, 2) domain modeling and 3) live user interface components and data. In this section, we compare our work with others' covering at least two of these elements.

UMLi/ARGOi [3] extends UML's activity diagram and the ArgoUML tool with support for interaction, hence covering both user interface and domain modeling. Their tool does not however support executing the model(s). The PetShop tool [7] uses an object-oriented variant of Petri Nets for specifying behavior of an application's UI and supports execution and linking to a real GUI designed in JBuilder. They build on a stronger formal theory, which covers both object and GUI behavior, so more of the total application logic may be specified. Compared to model-based tools like Pet-Shop, the strength of our tool is twofold: 1) Our interactors are combined with live widgets, so the abstract behavior in a sense becomes concrete, making it easier to validate specification based on the observed behavior, and 2) since DIAMODL is partly based on UML class, object and state diagrams, it should be easier to learn.

Sketching tools like SILK [4] support live user interface components, and partly cover UI modeling, since they support navigation between views. Such tools try to recognize the designer's intention, to provide additional semantic actions and behavior. The strength of SILK is twofold: 1) It supports pen-based sketching, which is more flexible than mouse-based object-manipulation and 2) What you see is what you use, i.e. the model is the user interface. Our tool tries to build on the second of these, by making the model "live". We also to some extent support 1) by providing creation tools in the palette which understand mouse gestures, but our tool is not as fluid and flexible as SILK. On the other hand, our tool retains the benefit of model-based tools, by being able to specify more of the UI's behavior.

In between tools based on formal models and sketching tools, we find CanonSketch [1], which combines quick sketching of CAP diagrams with HTML generation. The intention is much the same as ours, the ability to work on both abstract and concrete representations. Their choice of the CAP notation is based on its level of abstractness: less abstract than formal UI modeling languages, while more abstract than concrete prototypes. Recognizing this, we chose to integrate CAP into the DIAMODL notation as described in this paper, and CanonSketch's authors kindly provided implementations suggestions and icons for our tool. CanonSketch does not however, support modeling the domain and the deeper UI logic and behavior. The combined notation CAP and DIAMODL lets us provide added value: both the ability to specify and execute deeper UI behavior and support for populating the UI with sample data.

The most wide-spread tools covering two of the mentioned elements are data modeling and database tools with GUI support. E.g., Microsoft Access supports modeling and entering data and building form-based user interfaces. However, such tools have an implicit UI model that is not exposed to the designer, so it is impossible to edit the dialog structure or behavior, e.g., to add functionality or integrate custom user interface components. One of the few tools that support some level of user interface modeling is Genera's Genova tool (http://www.genera.no). However, their UI model focuses on choice of concrete user interface elements and layout and not on deeper structure or behavior.

6. CONCLUSION AND FURTHER WORK

Model-based user interface design and iterative design are rooted in different traditions. To take advantage of both, we need methods and tools that let the designer combine complementary representations in a flexible manner. Our hybrid tool for model-based UI design and prototyping supports diagram-based, executable user interface models integrated with live UI components, so functional GUI prototypes may be built. The feasibility of the approach has been tested in case studies, and its use in a master course has shown that the combination of CIOs and executable AIOs gives added value to both. We have yet to gain industrial experience with the tool, and further work is needed in two directions.

First, we need a better understanding of how model-based UI design and GUI prototyping may be integrated with current industrial practice. Although the model-based UI design notations are well aligned with IS models, it is not clear how system developers and user interface designers should align their processes. Similarly, although the tool supports both abstract modeling and concrete prototyping, it is not clear how engineers and interaction designers should utilize the tool in an integrated method.

Second, the Eclipse frameworks, sub-projects and third-party plug-ins provide many opportunities for integration. We have started to integrate our editor with the XSWT XML language for SWT UIs, to allow DIAMODL to control complete SWT UIs. We need to provide access to corporate data by means of XML and database supports, and are looking at the IBM DB2 plug-ins for Eclipse, and the IBM Integration plug-in for the open-source Derby database. On longer term, the Graphical Modeling Framework (GMF) project recently initiated by IBM and Borland for building EMF+GEF-based editors, may be provide a better platform than our own.

REFERENCES

[1] Campos, P.F., and Nunes, N.J., *CanonSketch: a User-Centered Tool for Canonical Abstract Prototyping*, in Proc. of 9th IFIP Working Conf. on Engineering for Human-Computer Interaction jointly with 11th Int. Workshop on Design, Specification, and

Verification of Interactive Systems EHCI-DSVIS'2004 (Hamburg, July 11–13, 2004). Lecture Notes in Computer Science, Vol. 3425, Springer-Verlag, Berlin, 2005, pp. 146–163.

[2]   Constantine, L., *Canonical Abstract Prototypes for abstract visual and interaction design*, in J. Jorge, N. Nunes, J. Falcão e Cunha (eds.), Proc. of 10th Int. Conf. on Design, Specification, and Verification of Interactive Systems DSV-IS'2003 (Madeira, 4–6 June 2003), J. Jorge, N.J. Nunes, J. Cunha (eds.), Lecture Notes in Computer Science, Vol. 2844, Springer-Verlag, Berlin, 2003, pp. 1–15.

[3]   da Silva, P.P., and Paton, N.W., *UMLi: The Unified Modeling Language for Interactive Applications*, in A. Evans, S. Kent, B. Selic (eds.), Proc. of Third Int. Conf. on Unified Modeling Language - The Unified Modeling Language, Advancing the Standard UML'2000 (York, 2–6 October 2000), Lecture Notes in Computer Science, Vol. 1939, Springer-Verlag, Berlin, 2000, pp. 117–132.

[4]   Landay, J.A., and Myers, B., *Sketching Interfaces: Towards More Human Interface Design*, IEEE Computer, Vol. 34, No. 3, March 2001, pp. 56–64.

[5]   Moore, W., Dean, D., Gerber, A., Wagenknecht, G., and Vanderheyden, Ph., *Eclipse Development using the Graphical Editing Framework and the Eclipse Modelling Framework*, IBM RedBooks, Vervante, 2004.

[6]   Myers, B., Hudson, S.E., and Pausch, R., *Past, Present and Future of User Interface Software Tools*, ACM Transactions on Computer-Human Interaction, Vol. 7, No. 1, March 2000, pp. 3–28.

[7]   Navarre, D., Palanque, P., Bastide, R., and Sy, O., *A Model-Based Tool for Interactive Prototyping of Highly Interactive Applications*, in Proc. of 12th IEEE Int. Workshop on Rapid System Prototyping RSP'2001 (Monterey, 25–27 June 2001), IEEE Computer Society Press, Los Alamitos, 2001, pp. 136–141.

[8]   Paternò, F., *Model-based Design and Evaluation of Interactive Applications*, Series of Applied Computing, Springer-Verlag, London, 2000.

[9]   Puerta, A.R., Cheng, E., Ou, T., and Min, J., *MOBILE: User-Centered Interface Building*, in Proc. of the ACM Conf. on Human Factors in Computing Systems CHI'99 (Pittsburgh, 15–20 May 1999), ACM Press, New York, 1999, pp. 426–433.

[10] Szekely, P., *Retrospective and Challenges for Model-Based Interface Development*, in J. Vanderdonckt (ed.), Proc. of 3rd Int. Workshop on Computer-Aided Design of User Interfaces CADUI'96 (Namur, 5–7 June 1996), Presses Universitaires de Namur, Namur, 1996, pp. xxi–xliv.

[11] Trætteberg, H., *Modelling Direct Manipulation Using Referent and Statecharts*, in P. Markopoulos, P. Johnson (eds.), Proc. of the Fifth Int. Eurographics Workshop on Design, Specification and Verification of Interactive Systems DSV-IS'98 (Abingdon, 3–5 June 1998), Springer-Verlag, Vienna, 1998, pp. 278–292.

[12] van der Veer, G.C., and van Welie, M., *Task Based Groupware Design: Putting Theory into Practice*, in Proc. of ACM Conf. on Designing Interactive Systems: Processes, Practices, Methods, Techniques DIS'2000 (New York, 17–19 August 2000), ACM Press, New York, 2000, pp. 326–337.

[13] Vanderdonckt, J., and Bodart, F., *Encapsulating Knowledge for Intelligent Automatic Interaction Objects Selection*, in Proc. of the ACM Conf. on Human Factors in Computing Systems INTERCHI'93 (Amsterdam, 24–29 April 1993), ACM Press, New York, 1993, pp. 424–429.

[14] Vanderdonckt, J., *A MDA-Compliant Environment for Developing User Interfaces of Information Systems*, in O. Pastor, J. Falcão e Cunha (eds.), Proc. of 17th Conf. on Advanced Information Systems Engineering CAiSE'05 (Porto, 13–17 June 2005), Lecture Notes in Computer Science, Vol. 3520, Springer-Verlag, Berlin, 2005, pp. 16–31.

Chapter 19

TOWARDS A SUPPORT OF USER INTERFACE DESIGN BY COMPOSITION RULES

Sophie Lepreux[1,2] and Jean Vanderdonckt[2]

[1]*Université de Valenciennes, LAMIH – RAIHM UMR CNRS 8530,*
Campus du Mont-Houy – F- 59313 Valenciennes Cedex 9(France)
E-mail: sophie.lepreux@univ-valenciennes.fr
[2]*School of Management, Université catholique de Louvain,*
Place des Doyens 1 – B-1348 Louvain-La-Neuve (Belgium)
E-mail: {lepreux, vanderdonckt}@isys.ucl.ac.be
URL: http://www.isys.ucl.ac.be/bchi/members/{sle,jva}
Tel.: +32 10 47 85 25 – Fax : +32 10 47 83 24

Abstract   The design of user interfaces is a step which takes a long time. The automatic generation of these interfaces induces shorter durations. With this automatic generation, the UIDLs have appeared. They allow specifying an interface using a Description Language. A step which also takes a long time is the redesigning of the user interface to take into accounts users remarks. We propose to use the operators of the tree algebra with a UIDL as UsiXML which is structured as a tree to improve this step of design. These operators help the designer to modify the interfaces and to reuse parts of interfaces. We have estimated the saving of time in two case studies

Keywords: Tree algebra, User interfaces engineering, User interface extensible mark-up language

1.   INTRODUCTION

In general, the User Interface (UI) design step takes a long time. Once the specifications have been validated, the designer creates the UI mock-up and the prototype. Later, the validation step is again challenged by the users of the UI. Sometimes, it must be remade; often, it must be improved. Many design processes are iterative so this part is realized at several times [8]. Often the users request simple modifications as "move this part of the interface in another screen" or "add a field here with this information" and so on. These requests, which are simple in theory, are expensive to implement if the

231

G. Calvary et al. (eds.), Computer-Aided Design of User Interfaces V, 231–244.
© 2007 Springer.

environment is not adapted to these needs [11]. We attempt to enrich the design environment by operators to simplify the redesign of the user interfaces. These operators are able to adjust the user interface after the deletion or the addition of an item. Consequently, they should bring a saving of time. The action analysis brings us a mean to estimate this saving of time [7]. Moreover, these operators allow the reuse of existing user interfaces. The operators are combined with an UIDL (User Interfaces Descriptor Language) to reuse parts or the whole of existing user interfaces. The proposed operators are used in this paper at the design time; however they can be used at the run time. For example, the Rainbow project [4] attempts to apply some operators as fusion by union or intersection at the run time in order to obtain a context-adapted user interface. They use the language SUNML which is a simple language, adapted to structural assembling of abstract widgets [12] and so of HCI components. As far as we are concerned, we hope to use the operators at the runtime, i.e., UIDL files interpretation should contain the results section issue of operator, as well as at the design time within the editor. This article is focused on the design time. Indeed, another problem emerges at the run time about the data contained in the widgets.

The second part presents the UIDL which is used in this research, named UsiXML. The third part introduces the operators used to design and redesign UI and which are implemented in the editor associated to UsiXML named GrafiXML. The operators are evaluated with the GOMS method upon two case studies. The first one aims at illustrating the help brought by the operators to designing a UI and the second one aims at validating the operators to the redesign of UI. The paper ends with a conclusion and future work.

2.   DESIGNING USER INTERFACES WITH USIXML

To allow high-level design operations on any GUI, we should rely on a high level description of the initial user interface. This description will be expressed in the UsiXML (User Interface eXtensible Markup Language – http://www.usixml.org [9]) UIDL. The principles set out below are, however, generally applicable to any UIDL such as UIML [1] or XIML [5]. UsiXML is structured according to the four abstraction levels of the CAMELEON reference framework [2] for multi-target UIs (Fig. 1). A *Final User Interface* (FUI) refers to an actual UI rendered either by interpretation (e.g., HTML) or by code compilation (e.g., Java). A *Concrete User Interface* (CUI) abstracts a FUI into a description independent of any programming or markup language in terms of Concrete Interaction Objects (CIO) [12], layout, navigation, and behavior. An *Abstract User Interface* (AUI) abstracts a CUI into a definition that is independent of any interaction modality [9].

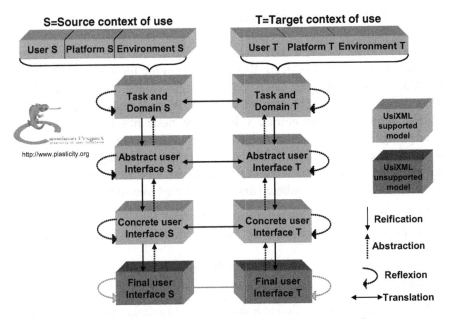

Figure 1. The four abstraction levels used in the framework

The Tasks & Concepts level describes the interactive system specifications in terms of the user tasks to be carried out and the domain objects of these tasks. As the operators used to compose the user interface will be defined, in the first time, to be specific to one modality (e.g., graphical, vocal), the CUI level is the best candidate for a formal definition.

3. USING OF THE OPERATORS FOR THE USER INTERFACES COMPOSITION

To improve the development step of user interfaces corresponding at the time where the user asks the designer to modify the user interface, we propose to use a set of operations such as the union, the intersection, the selection, which is developed in the next part. These operators can also be used to reuse existing user interfaces. In general, the same information can be found in several user interfaces within the same application or the same domain.

3.1 Defining of the Operators

The operators are first defined, based on the UsiXML concepts of a Concrete User Interface. Then, the implementation of the operators in an existing editor is described. For the most important operators, we provide a complete formal definition which is defined thanks to a tree algebra for XML [6].

3.1.1   XML document as a tree structure

Jagadish *et al.* define a data model [6]. A data tree is a rooted, ordered tree, such that each node carries data (its label) in the form of a set of attribute-value pairs. Each node has a special, single valued attribute called *tag* whose value indicates the type of element. A node may have a *content* attribute representing its atomic value. Each node has a virtual attribute called *pedigree* drawn from an ordered domain. The pedigree carries the history of "where it came from". Pedigree plays a central role in grouping, sorting and duplicate elimination. They define a pattern tree as a pair $P = (T, F)$, where $T = (V,E)$ is a node-labeled and edge-labeled tree such that:

- Each node in V has a distinct integer as its label ($i);
- Each edge is either labeled pc (for parent-child) or ad (for ancestor-descendant);
- F is a formula, i.e. a Boolean combination of predicates applicable to nodes.

This pattern is used to define a database and to define the predicate used in the operations. This notation is specific to the database. So we propose a variant which is adapted to documents specific to interface. Indeed, in the HCI case, the most important is the structure and not the content. For example, it is more important to know that the window has a box as sub-element than that the window have a height=300. So the attributes are stored with the tag. A node is a tag with these attributes and their content. The pattern tree keeps coherent with the variant definition. Another point specific to the database is that the data are in several data trees so the operators use a collection of data trees in input and output. In the HCI case, the input is one (for the unary operators) or two (for the binary operators) XML documents so one or two data trees. With this notation, the Selection, the Normal union and the Difference operators are formal defined here.

Selection. The selection is a unary operator. It takes a tree in input with a pattern tree and gives a tree in output. The definition brought by Jagadish *et al.* can be adapted. The output $\sigma(T, P)$ of the selection operator is a tree. The output is defined as follow. A node u in the input tree T belongs to the output iff u matches some pattern node in P, or u is a descendant of a node v in T which matches some pattern node w. Whenever nodes u, v belong to the output such that among the nodes retained in the output, u is the closest ancestor of v in the input, the output contains the edge (u,v). The relative order among nodes in the input is preserved in the output, i.e. for any two nodes u,v in the output, whenever u precedes v in the tree T, u precedes v in the tree of the output. For example, the selection operator applied with the pattern presented in Fig. 2b to the tree presented in Fig. 2a and is illustrated in Fig. 3.

a)   Window (id=window, name=window, width="300" height="200")

Box (type=« vertical »)

Output (Default value =« customer form »)

Box (type = horizontal)   Box (type = horizontal)   Box (type = horizontal)

Output   Input   Output   Input   Button   Button
(...)   (...)   (...)   (...)   (DefaultContent = Save)   (DefaultContent=Close)

b) $1

ad

$2

$2.tag = output

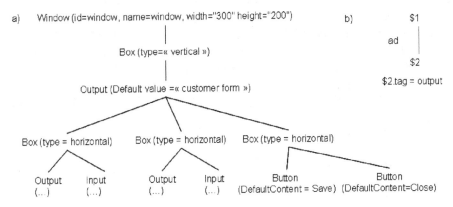

Figure 2. (a) A one-tree XML interface ; (b) a pattern tree

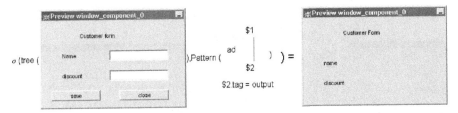

o (tree (   ),Pattern ($1   ad $2   )   ) = $2 tag = output

Figure 3. Selection of output in a user interface

Normal Union. The Union operator takes a pair of trees T1 and T2 as input and produces an output tree as follows.

Firstly, the root of the output tree T3 is created:
If (T1.$1.tag == T2.$1.tag ==window) then T3.$1.tag = window with
    If (horizontal Union) then content.width = T1.$1.content.width + T2.$1.content..width then (vertical) content width = max (T1.$1.width, T2.$1.width) and
    If (vertical Union) then content.height = T1.$1.content.height + T2.$1.content.height else (horizontal Union) content.height = max(T1.$1.content.heiht, T2.$1.content.height)
If (T1.$1.tag == window && T2.$1.tag == box) then T3.$1 = T1.$1.
If (T1.$1.tag == box && T2.$1.tag == window) then T3.$1=T2.$1.
Then
    To obtain a vertical Union: The child of the new root is added with tag = Box and type = "vertical". Their left child(s) are the children of the root of T1 and their right child(s) are the children of the root of T2.
    To obtain a horizontal Union: The child of the new root is added with tag = Box and type = "horizontal". Their left child(s) are the children of the root of T1 and their right child(s) are the children of the root of T2 (Fig. 4).
    Else T3.$1.tag = box with content.type = "horizontal" or "vertical"

according to type of the Union. Their left child(s) are the children of the root of T1 and their right child(s) are the children of the root of T2.

For each node in the left and right subtrees of the new root node, all attribute values are the same as the input trees.

The duplicates must be deleted (this part is not detailed here).

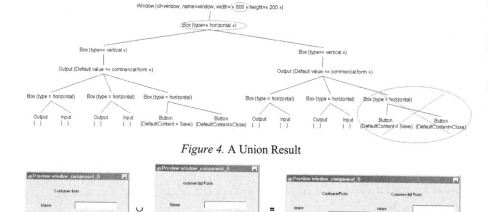

Figure 4. A Union Result

Figure 5. Union of two user interfaces

Difference. The difference operation takes a pair of trees T1 and T2 as input and produces an output tree. The tree T2 is presented as pattern tree to identify the nodes of the second input which are in the first input tree. Then the identified nodes can be deleted. This operator corresponds to the node Deletion defined by Jagadish *et al.* [6] and adapted to the HCI domain. The delete operator takes a Tree as input and a pattern tree P and a delete specification (DS) is a sequence of expressions of the form $i or $i*, where $i is one of the node labels appearing in P. It generates a tree as output, as follows. Every node in T that matches some pattern node labeled $i in P, under some embedding, is marked i. The output tree is a copy of the marked input tree. Whenever a node u in the output corresponds to an input node marked i and the pattern node labeled $i in P, then

- If DS contains the expression $i*, the node u is deleted with all its descendants.
- If DS contains the expression $i, then node u is deleted, and each of its children is made a direct child of u's parent. These children retain their relative order, and are inserted in the same position with respect to node u's siblings as node u used to be.

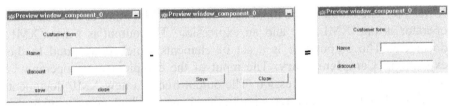

Figure 6. Difference between two interfaces

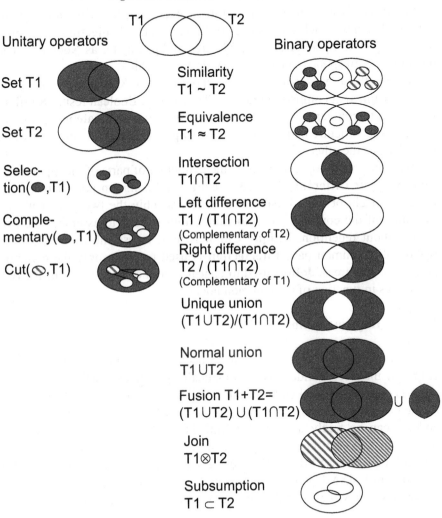

Figure 7. Illustration of composition/decomposition operators

Due to space limitations, the definition of the remaining operators will be limited in natural language as they can be obtained by analogy to the previous ones. The set of operators is presented in Fig. 7. Each UI is shown as a set. The operators are unitary as: **Set**: The input of the set operator is one

XML tree. The output is the input tree. **Selection**: The input of the Selection operator is one XML tree and an expression. The output is a new XML document. The output tree is a set of elements which correspond to the expression. **Complementary**: The input of the complementary operator is one XML tree and an expression. The output tree is a new XML document corresponding to the input tree without the elements which correspond to the expression. **Cut**: The input of the cut operator is one XML tree and a parameter as a Node. The new output tree corresponds to the input tree without the elements which correspond to the parameter. **Projection**: The input of the projection operator is one XML tree and parameter as Node (*N*). The output tree corresponds to the search node and its child.

Among the binary operators (the input is two XML trees) are some operators aimed at comparing two UIs. They have a Boolean result: **Similarity** is used to compare the structure and not the data. **Equivalence** is used to compare the structure and the data. **Subsumption** is used to verify that one is a subset of the other.

The other binary operators allow the extracting of parts of the input trees: **Left or Right Difference** is used to extract the common part of two trees from one (right or left). **Fusion** is used to assembly the two trees with the repetition of the common part. **Normal Union** is used to assembly the two trees without repetition. **Unique Union** is used to assembly the two trees without the common part. **Intersection** is used to select only the common part of the two trees. **Join** is used to concatenate the set of nodes of the two input trees in function of the common nodes.

3.1.2   Implementation

Some of the above operations have been implemented in GrafiXML, a graphical interface builder that automatically generates UsiXML specifications as opposed to final code for other builders. GrafiXML has been implemented in Java 5.0 and today consists of more than 100,000 lines of Java code. It can be freely downloaded from http://www.usixml.org as it is an open source project regulated by Apache 2.0 open licence and available on SourceForge. GrafiXML is able to automatically generate code of a UI specified in UsiXML into (X)HTML or Java. For the purpose of the examples below, we will rely on the Java automated code generation.

3.2   Evaluation of the Benefits brought by the Operators

In this part, two case studies of UI design are presented. The first case study, in the insurance domain, aims at showing how the operators can be used to reuse the parts of one or more user interfaces. The second case study aims at presenting how to use the operators to modify an existing user interface according to user's suggestions. The GOMS (Goals, Operations, Methods and Selection rules) model is used to evaluate the saving in time (Table 1 [3,10]). For example, to modify a title of a window, the user right click on the window which costs 0.3s, to move hand to point device, 0.075s to execute a mental step, 1.5s to use a mouse and 0.075 to execute a mental step. Then, the user hits the title which costs 0.28s by letter, 0.075 to execute the mental step. To finish the user clicks on "validate". It costs 1.5s to use mouse and 0.075 for the mental step. The using of an operator costs 1.5 to use the mouse, 0.075 to execute the mental step, 1.2 to choose among methods and 0.075 to execute the mental step, the result cost is 2.85s.

Table 1. Average times for computer interface actions

Physical Movements		
Enter one keystroke on a standard keyboard	.28 second	Ranges from .07 second for highly skilled typists doing transcription, to .2 second for an average 60-wpm typist, to over 1 second for a bad typist. Random sequences, formulas, and commands take longer than plain text.
Use mouse to point at object on screen	1.5 second	May be slightly lower – but still at least 1 second – for a small screen and a menu. Increases with larger screen, smaller objects.
Move hand to pointing device or function key	.3 second	Ranges from .21 second for cursor keys to .36 second for a mouse.
Mental actions		
Retrieve a simple item from a long-term memory	1.2 second	A typical item might be a command abbreviation ("dir"). Time is roughly halved if the same item needs to be retrieved again immediately.
Execute a mental "step"	.075 second	Ranges from .05 to .1 second, depending on what kind of mental step is being performed.
Choose among methods	1.2 second	Ranges from .06 to at least 1.8 seconds, depending on complexity of factors influencing the decision.

3.2.1   First case study: Operators for reusing user interface parts

We consider an information system in which the same information can be found in several interfaces, as for the insurance application. The needs of insurance companies is to manage the relation with customers (registration, movements, terminate), to manage damages (report, negotiate with another company, compensate the client) and so on. To design the user interfaces of such an application, the designer begins by specifying the items to place, places the items which compose the interface, and finishes positioning and putting them together. The designer makes the two first initial user interfaces corresponding to the Client registration and the Vehicle registration (Fig. 6). From these first interfaces, others interfaces can be partly designed using the operators. The forms "Client Modifying" and "Vehicle Modifying" (Fig. 7) made with operators induce a cost of 35.025 seconds and 76.17 seconds, while those made without operators induce a cost of 37.875 seconds and 101.82 seconds (Table 2). The use of operators leads a benefit about 6% and 25% for the two considered forms. The using of the operators is still significant with the design of the bill UI (Fig. 8). The benefit equals 92.72 % (Table 3).

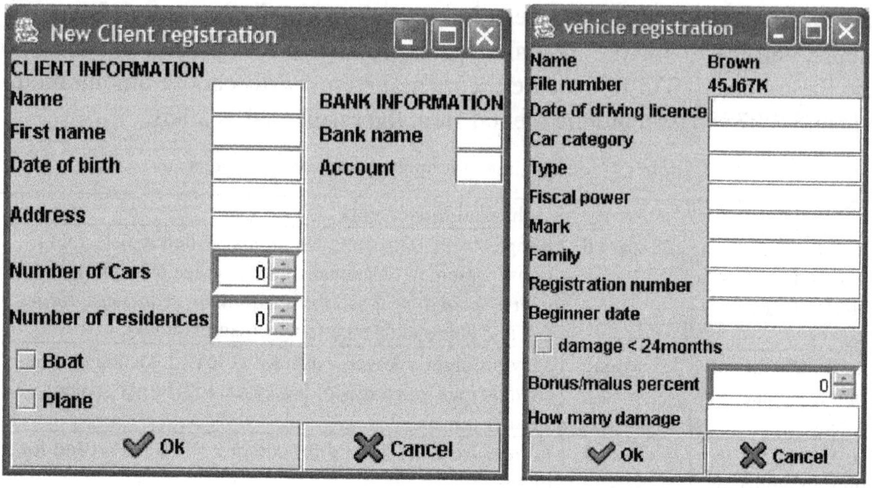

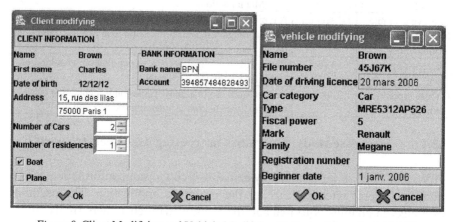

Figure 8. Initial User Interfaces for Client Registration and Vehicle Registration

Figure 9. Client Modifying and Vehicle Modifying UI Derived from the initial UI

Table 2. Time evaluation to design UI

Goal	Action	without operators	Time	with operators	Time
Create the Client Modifying	Modifying of the title	Right Click on the window Tape the new title	1.5+0.075+ 0.3+0.075+ 0.28*9+0.075+1	Right Click on the window	1.5+0.075+ 0.3+0.075+ 0.28*9+0.075

Goal	Action	without operators	Time	with opera-tors	Time
UI from the Client Registration UI		Validate	.5+0.075 =6.12	Tape the new title Validate	+1.5+0.075 =6.12
	Modifying of 3 items from input to output	Point the input Right Click with the mouse to delete Select output Place the Output Click Tape Validate	3*(1.5+0.075+1 .2+0.075+ 1.5+0.075+ 1.5+0.075+ 1.5+0.075+0.3+ 0.28*10+0.075+ 0.3+1.5+0.075) =**37.875**	Selection Difference Select output Place the Output Click Tape Validate	1.5+0.075+ 1.2+0.075+ 1.5+0.075+ 1.2+0.075+ 1.5+0.075+ 3*(1.5+0.075+ 1.5+0.075+ 1.5+0.075+0.3 +0.28*10+0.0 75+0.3+1.5+0. 075)=**35.025**
Create the Vehicle Modifying UI from the Vehicle Registration UI	Modifying of the title	Same as client	6.12	Same as Client	6.12
	Modifying of 6 items from input to output	The same as Client with 6 in place of 3	75.75	Selection Replace 3 by 6.	64.35
	Delete of 7 items	Point the input Right Click with the mouse to delete	7*(1.5+0.075+ 1.2+0.075) =19.95 =**101.82**	Selection and Difference	5.7 =**76.17**

Table 3. Time evaluation to design UIs

Design	without operators	Time	with operators	Time
Create the Bill UI from the Vehicle Modifying UI and Client Modifying UI	Modifying of the title Copy of 14 items from Client UI Copy of 14 items from Vehicle UI Copy of 14 items from Vehicle UI Place all the items	4.72 32.4 32.4 32.4 119.7 =**221.62**	Modifying of the title Select Select Union Union	4.72 2.85+ 2.85+ 2.85+ 2.85+ = **16.12**

3.2.2   Second case study: Operators for helping the designer during the user interface design process

This case study attempts to show the benefit in term of time induced by the using of the operators. Three cases are considered:

1. The user thinks that the user interface contains too much information. One solution is to place a set of information in a new interface. To illustrate with the insurance UIs, the user decides that the bank information

should be in another (a new) window. In this new window, the name of the client must appear.
2. It is the same case as the previous one, but the proposition is to place the information in another existing interface.
3. The UI of two interfaces are light so they could be gathered. For example, the "client registration" and the "vehicle registration" can be gathered in a new interface. The difference of time for each of the three cases is shown in Table 4. The times obtained without using operators are approximate because they depend on the number of items. In this case, the number of items is arbitrary fixed at 8 and the time to reorganize is fixed at 100s.

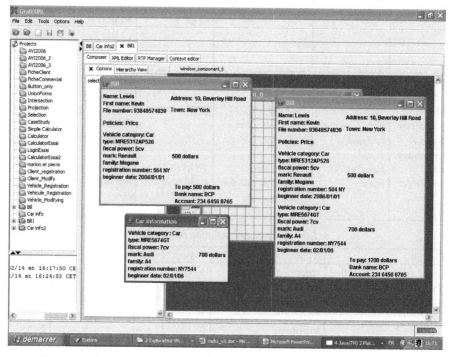

Figure 10. The design of the Bill UI with Union operator applied to mediate UIs

Table 4. Time evaluation to modify the UIs

Design	without operators	Time	with operators	Time
Case 1	Select and cut the items to extract	18.51s	Select items to extract (with Selection operator)	2.85s
	Create a new project	1.275s		
		1.575s	Difference	2.85s
	Paste the items in the new project	1.275s	Select items to duplicate (with Selection operator)	2.85s
	Select and copy the items to duplicate	18.51s	Union	2.85s
				=11.4s
	Paste the items	1.275		
	Reorganize the first interface	100s (arb)		

Design	without operators	Time	with operators	Time
	Reorganize the new interface	100s (arb) = **242.42s**		
Case 2	Select and Cut	18.51s	Select items to extract	2.85s
	Paste in another UI	1.275s	Difference	2.85s
	Reorganize the first one	100s(arb)	Union	2.85s
	Reorganize the second one	100s(arb) =**219.785**		=**8.55s**
Case 3	Select all the items of one UI	18.51s	Union	**2.85s**
	Paste in the other	1.275s		
	Reorganize the final UI	100 (arb) =**119.785**		

4.   CONCLUSION

This paper presented some composition operators coming from tree algebra which are interesting for the visual design of user interfaces. Moreover, at the design time, the work granularity is not only at the individual object level but also at a upper level of a coherent set of elements. These sets of elements correspond to tasks or sub-tasks, and often a leaf of the task tree. These operators have been coupled to the UIDL named UsiXML for two reasons: (1) UsiXML is a language adapted to the specification of user interfaces and (2) the operators are adapted to a tree structure which fits well the purpose of a XML-compliant language like UsiXML. The tree algebra is an advantage as it allows manipulating user interfaces structured as a set of elements. However we think that the operators could be divided into two groups. The first one is based on the set theory; the operators of this group manipulate the elements taken individually in interfaces. The second group is based on the tree algebra; the operators of this second group manipulate sets of elements and modify both the structure and the node of trees. Two case studies have presented the using of the operators for a simplified insurance application and the benefit of time has been evaluated with the GOMS method. The interest of the using of operators has been proved even if an evaluation with real designer in a real case is still to be done.

ACKNOWLEDGEMENTS

We gratefully thank the support from the SIMILAR network of excellence (The European research taskforce creating human-machine interfaces SIMILAR to human-human communication), supported by the 6th Framework Program of the European Commission, under contract FP6-IST1-2003-507609 (http://www.similar.cc). The authors thank also the Nord-Pas de Calais regional authority (Projects MIAOU and EUCUE) and the FEDER

(Fonds Européen de Développement Régional, European Fund for Regional Development) for supporting a part of this work.

REFERENCES

[1] Ali M.F., Pérez-Quiñones, M.A., and Abrams, M., *Building Multi-Platform User Interfaces with UIML*, in A. Seffah, H. Javahery (eds.), "Multiple User Interfaces: Engineering and Application Framework", John Wiley, Chichester, 2004, pp. 95–118.

[2] Calvary, G., Coutaz, J., Thevenin, D., Limbourg, Q., Bouillon, L., and Vanderdonckt, J., *A Unifying Reference Framework for Multi-Target User Interfaces*, Interacting with Computers, Vol. 15, No. 3, June 2003, pp. 289–308.

[3] Lewis, C., and Rieman, J., *Task-Centered User Interface Design, a Practical Introduction*, 1993, accessible at http://hcibib.org/tcuid/.

[4] Dery-Pinna, A.-M., and Fierstone, J., *Construction d'interfaces utilisateurs par fusion de composants d'IHM : un atout pour la mobilité*, in Proc. of Mobilité & Ubiquité'2004 (Nice, 1–3 June 2004), ACM Press, New York, 2004, pp. 60–65.

[5] Eisenstein, J., Vanderdonckt, J., and Puerta, A., *Model-Based User-Interface Development Techniques for Mobile Computing*, in Proc. of 5th ACM Int. Conf. on Intelligent User Interfaces IUI'2001 (Santa Fe, January 14–17, 2001), ACM Press, New York, 2001, pp. 69–76.

[6] Jagadish, H.V., Lakshmanan, L.V.S., Srivastava, D., and Thompson, K., *TAX : A Tree Algebra for XML*, in G. Ghelli, G. Grahne (eds.), Proc. of 8th Int. Workshop on Database Programming Language DBPL'2001 (Frascati, 8–10 September 2001), Lecture Notes in Computer Science, Vol. 2397, Springer-Verlag, Berlin, 2001, pp. 149–164.

[7] Kieras, D.E., *Towards a Practical GOMS Model Methodology for User Interface Design*, in M. Helander (ed.), "Handbook of Human-Computer Interaction", Elsevier Science, Amsterdam, 1988.

[8] Lepreux, S., Abed, M., and Kolski, C., *A Human-Centred Methodology Applied to Decision Support System Design and Evaluation in a Railway Network Context*, Cognition Technology and Work, Vol. 5, 2003, pp. 248–271.

[9] Limbourg, Q., Vanderdonckt, J., Michotte, B., Bouillon, L., and Lopez, V., *UsiXML: a Language Supporting Multi-Path Development of User Interfaces*, in Proc. of 9th IFIP Working Conf. on Engineering for Human-Computer Interaction jointly with 11th Int. Workshop on Design, Specification, and Verification of Interactive Systems EHCI-DSV-IS'2004 (Hamburg, 11–13 July 2004), Lecture Notes in Computer Science, Vol. 3425, Springer-Verlag, Berlin, 2005, pp. 200–220.

[10] Olson, J.R., and Olson, G.M., *The Growth of Cognitive Modelling In Human-Computer Interaction Since GOMS*, Human-Computer Interaction, Vol. 5, 1990, pp. 221–265.

[11] Vanderdonckt, J., *Visual Design Methods in interactive Applications*, Chapter 7, in M. Albers, B. Mazur (eds.), "Content and Complexity: Information Design in Technical Communication", Lawrence Erlbaum Associates, Mahwah, 2003, pp. 187–203.

[12] Vanderdonckt, J., and Bodart, F., *Encapsulating Knowledge for Intelligent Automatic Interaction Objects Selection*, in Proc. of the ACM Conf. on Human Factors in Computing Systems INTERCHI'93 (Amsterdam, 24–29 April 1993), ACM Press, New York, 1993, pp. 424–429.

[13] Vanderdonckt, J., *A MDA-Compliant Environment for Developing User Interfaces of Information Systems*, in O. Pastor, J. Falcão e Cunha (eds.), Proc. of 17th Conf. on Advanced Information Systems Engineering CAiSE'05 (Porto, 13–17 June 2005), Lecture Notes in Computer Science, Vol. 3520, Springer-Verlag, Berlin, 2005, pp. 16–31.

Chapter 20

IDEALXML: AN INTERACTION DESIGN TOOL
A Task-based Approach to User Interface Design

Francisco Montero and Víctor López-Jaquero
Laboratory on User Interaction & Software Engineering (LoUISE)
Instituto de Investigación en Informática (I3A)
University of Castilla-La Mancha - 02071 Albacete (Spain)
E-mail: {fmontero , victor}@info-ab.uclm.es
Tel: +34 967/599200 – Fax: +34 967/599224 – Web: http://www.i3a.uclm.es

Abstract   Task modeling has become one of the cornerstones of model-based user interface design. In this paper, a task-based approach to user interfaces design is introduced. This approach is supported by a tool, namely IDEALXML, that allows for the animation of the specified user interfaces to generate a *hi-fi* prototype of the future user interface while still in the first development stages

Keywords: Model-based design, Specification animation, Task modeling, User interfaces
design tools, User interface extensible markup language

1.   INTRODUCTION

Nowadays, software engineers use rapid prototyping to discover requirements by analyzing the prototypes built early in the development process and
gathering feedback. In this paper, we address fast *hi-fi* prototyping within a
model-based user interface (UI) environment [17]. This approach is supported
by a powerful visual tool, namely IDEALXML [12,13]. UI design following
the proposed approach is driven by task and domain models using a seamless
mapping technique. The task and the domain models are mapped together
thanks to a set of mappings which express how data from the domain model
is manipulated in the task and how methods from the domain model are executed in tasks. This paper is organized in three sections. First, an overview of
model-based UI generation is presented. Next, UI description languages are
introduced, focusing on UsiXML [10]. Finally, our approach to fast *hi-fi* prototyping is described.

G. Calvary et al. (eds.), Computer-Aided Design of User Interfaces V, 245–252.

2.   USER INTERFACE GENERATION

We can find proposals in the literature that provide frameworks that enable UI development. At the beginning, most of those proposals would generate the UI out of a domain model. However, currently most approaches drive their development out of a task model. Some of these proposals will be introduced in the next sections, describing the pros and cons of both.

2.1   Domain-Based Generation of User Interfaces

Domain model encapsulates the important entities of a particular application domain together with their attributes, methods and relationships. Elements in the domain model possess attributes that are often relevant to UI presentation elements selection. Examples for these attributes are the data type, the range, the minimum and maximum value, etc. Meaningful examples of this strategy in UI generation out of different types of domain models are Janus [2], Vampire [7], OlivaNova [11], Teallach [9] for desktop application, in web-based environments WebRatio [4] and VisualWade [8] and in hypermedia applications OHDM [21]. These domain-based UI generation approaches produce complex UI, because users can see many elements at the same time. Moreover, as long as the user-task is not contemplated, the dialog within the UI is rather limited and constrained, producing UI quite static.

2.2   Task-Based Generation of User Interfaces

Most model-based development approaches define a dialog model by using a task model. ConcurTaskTree (CTT) [16] is a well-accepted notation in the UI research development community used for the specification of task models. Information from the task model is exploited in order to automatically or interactively derive the navigational structure of the application. TERESA [14] exploits structural information as well as temporal relationships in order to generate an *activation set*, which is later used to automatically generate the dialog model and the widgets of presentation model. Task-based design as opposed to domain-based one incorporates information regarding the tasks the user will carry out through the UI as well as the temporal relationships between those tasks. This kind of information allows addressing usability aspects such as UI overload, presentation grouping, etc.

2.3   User Interfaces Prototyping

Some of the main drawbacks of model-based user interface development have been the unpredictability of the final results and the lack of techniques for the evaluation of the final UI given a set of declarative models [15]. To overcome these drawbacks, and some other ones, different techniques have been introduced. One of those techniques introduced is user interface prototyping. Prototyping consists in the creation of a preliminary version of the future UI (prototype) so that the user and the experts can find possible problems in the design of the UI, both from the functional and from the usability points of view. Prototyping techniques fall into two main categories:

1. *Lo-fi* (low-fidelity) techniques: this family of techniques is mostly used in requirements analysis stage to validate the requirements with the user in user-centered approaches.

2. *Hi-fi* (high-fidelity) techniques: they are aimed at the creation of preliminary version of the UI with an acceptable degree of quality. This kind of techniques produces a UI prototype which is closer to the final future one.

Although paper is still the most widely tool used in prototyping, some other tools have been proposed to try to make prototyping faster, easier to change or more accurate. In this sense, sketching tools like SketchiXML [6] or CanonSketch [3] try to replicate the facilities in paper prototyping into a computer. A different point of view is pushed in UI Pilot [19]. *Hi-fi* prototypes could be considered to be better than *lo-fi* prototypes, since they are closer to the final user interface the user will interact with. Nevertheless, a set of disadvantages have been identified [20].

3.   MODEL-DRIVEN DEVELOPMENT IN USER INTERFACES DESIGN

In our proposal, we use models precisely because they actually speed up development and help us to get to a better solution more quickly. Good models clarify design issues and highlight tradeoffs, so design issues can be resolved rapidly. Models also help us to deliver better and more robust systems. In this sense, abstract prototyping was devised because it was found that the sooner developers started drawing realistic pictures or positioning real widgets, the longer it took them to converge on a good design. Abstract models are always much simpler than the real thing. Nowadays, a series of models are used within MB-UID approaches to describe UI. These models need to be stored in a repository so that they can be manipulated by the different tools used during UI generation stages. In most cases these models are stored using an XML-based format. In [22], a review of the most prominent XML-based UI description languages can be found. UIML [1], XIML [18], DiaMODL [11] or UsiXML [10,23] are meaningful examples of these kinds of languages. UsiXML provides an abstract UI model that represents a canonical expression of the renderings and manipulation of the domain concepts and functions in a way that is as independent as possible from modalities and computing platform specifies.

Table 1. Abstract interaction objects and facets in UsiXML and icons used in IDEALXML

Abstract object	Icon		Facet	Icon
Container			Input	
Component			Output	
			Control	
			Navigation	

We are using the abstract UI specification proposed in UsiXML because it provides a reduced set of elements that allow the description of an abstract UI in a platform and modality independent manner. In Table 1 the set of icons used within our tool to represent the different elements of the abstract UI are shown.

4.   FAST GENERATION OF HI-FI USER INTER-FACE PROTOTYPES

One of the advantages of using a formal modeling language to specify the task model, such as CTT, is the ability to simulate the system before it is built. Simulation can help to ensure that the system that is built will match users' conceptual model as well as to help to evaluate the usability of a system at a very early stage. Several task models simulators have been built for CTT. For example, in CTTE the designers can specify a task model, which can be simulated. In IDEALXML, designers can specify a task model and simulate the UI derived from the designed task model in an abstract manner by using CTT, UsiXML and a set of heuristics to transform the task model specification into an abstract UI. Currently, these heuristics are hard coded in IDEALXML application code, but there is an ongoing work to support the use of transformation rules that the designer can modify following approach similar to the one proposed in [10].

4.1   Abstract User Interfaces Prototyping

The previously mentioned hard coded transformation rules are gathered in this section. *Straightforward rules* govern transformations (Table 2):
- Each cluster of interrelated task cases becomes an interaction space in the navigation map, so an abstract task is a container.
- A container also can be an interaction task or an application task if any of them are leaf in a hierarchical task decomposition.
- A component rises when we found an interaction or application task in a hierarchical task decomposition.
- A component can have several facets (input, output, control and navigation). These facets allow the user to interact with a system.

Table 2. From task model to abstract presentation model

Task model	is	Abstract presentation model	
Abstract task	*is*	a container	
Interactive task	*is*	*a leaf:* component	*input*
			output
			control
			navigation
		not a leaf: container	
Application task	*is*	*not a leaf:* container	
		a leaf: component	*output*
			navigation

4.2 Abstract User Interfaces Prototypes Animation

IdealXML supports the animation of the abstract user interface resulting from the designed task model. This animation is grounded in the identification of the *enabled task set* (ETS) [16]. Having identified the ETC for a task model, the next step is to identify the effects of performing each task in each ETS. The result of this analysis is a *state transition network* (STN), where each ETS is a state and transitions occur when tasks are performed. In our proposal, the task model specification is split into states. Each state is a set of interrelated tasks, including temporal relationships between those tasks, usually connected to an *essential use case* [5].

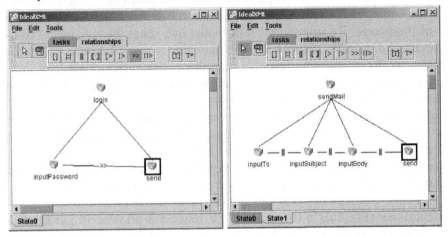

Figure 1. Task model specification in IDEALXML for e-mail sending task

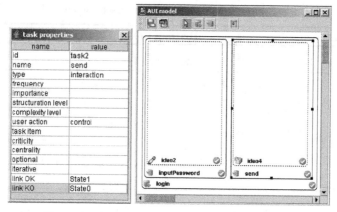

Figure 2. Abstract UI specification out of task model

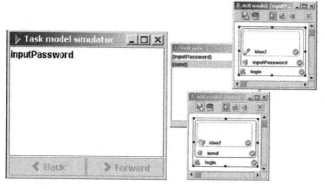

Figure 3. Simulation, ETS and abstract UI specification are available in IDEALXML

In Fig. 1, the task model for sending an e-mail message can be found. Two states have been identified in this case. The first one is related to user identification in the mail server and the second one is related to sending the e-mail message. By splitting the task model into states the task model complexity is drastically reduced and the legibility is really boosted. States are connected by establishing links between them. Two different kinds of links are proposed *linkOK* and *linkKO*. *LinkOK* specifies which state the system should go to when the goal of the current state is successfully achieved. In a similar manner, *linkKO* is state the system should go to when the goal of the current state fails. For example, in Fig. 2, *linkOK* points to the state where the user can send the e-mail (it means that the user password provided was successfully validated) and *linkKO* points to current state (identification state, because the verification of the user password provided failed).

As in CTTE, the designer can simulate task model specification in a textual manner (Fig. 3a). In IDEALXML, the designer is allowed also to animate the specification in a visual manner interacting with the abstract UI. Moreover, at any time designers can select any set of tasks in the task model and get the abstract UI specification for the selected task in a graphical manner.

5. CONCLUSION

A good user interface design is essential to ensure the acceptance of a new software. It is a complex subject, but we can overcome this complexity by raising the level of abstraction in the design by using models. Abstract prototyping is a way to avoid the seduction of attractive prototypes that disguise weak designs. By making better use of modern visual development tools, abstract prototyping can speed up and simplify the design of highly usable systems and help us to produce improved and more innovative software products. In our fast abstract prototyping proposal we address most of the *hi-fi* prototypes shortcomings identified in [20], providing an environment that allows the creation of the prototypes quickly in an abstract level enough to avoid focusing more on *look & feel* than in functional or usability issues and providing prototypes that can be easily modified.

REFERENCES

[1] Abrams, M., Phanouriou, C., Batongbacal, A.L., Williams, S.M., and Shuster, J.E., *UIML: An Appliance-Independent XML UI Language*, Computer Networks, Vol. 31, 1999.

[2] Balzert, H., Hofmann, F., Kruschinski, V., and Niemann, C., *The JANUS Application Development Environment - Generating More than the User Interface*, in J. Vanderdonckt (ed.), Proc. of 2nd Int. Workshop on Computer-Aided Design of User Interfaces CADUI'1996 (Namur, 5–7 June 1996), Presses Universitaires de Namur, Namur, 1996, pp. 183–208.

[3] Campos, P., and Nunes, N., *Canonsketch: a User-Centered Tool for Canonical Abstract Prototyping*, in R. Bastide, P. Palanque, J. Roth (eds.), Proc. of 9th IFIP Working Conf. on Engineering for Human-Computer Interaction EHCI-DSVIS'2004 (Hamburg, 11–13 July 2004), Lecture Notes in Computer Science, Vol. 3425, Springer-Verlag, Berlin, 2005, pp. 146–163.

[4] Ceri, S., Fraternali, P., and Bongio, A., Web Modeling Language (WebML): a Modeling Language for Designing Web Sites, in Proc. 9th Int. Conf. on World-Wide Web (Amsterdam, May 2000), 2000, accessible at http://www9.org/w9cdrom/177/177.html.

[5] Constantine, L.L., and Lockwood, L.A.D., *Software for Use*, Addison-Wesley, Reading, 1999.

[6] Coyette, A., and Vanderdonckt, J., *A Sketching Tool for Designing Anyuser, Anyplatform, Anywhere User Interfaces*, in Proc. of 10th IFIP TC 13 Int. Conf. on Human-Computer Interaction INTERACT'2005 (Rome, 12–16 September 2005), Lecture Notes in Computer Science, Vol. 3585, Springer-Verlag, Berlin, 2005, pp. 550–564.

[7] Eisentein, J., and Rich, C., *Agents and GUIs From Task Models*, in Proc. of 7th ACM Conf. on Intelligent User Interfaces IUI'2002 (San Francisco, 13–16 January 2002). ACM Press. New York, 2002, pp. 47–54.

[8] Gómez, J., *Model-Driven Web Development with VisualWADE*, in N. Koch, P. Fraternali, M. Wirsing (eds.), Proc. of 4th Int. Conf. on Web Engineering ICWE'04 (Munich, 28–30 July 2004), Lecture Notes in Computer Science, Vol. 3140, Springer-Verlag, Berlin, 2004, pp. 611–612.

[9] Griffiths, T., Barclay, P., McKirdy, J., Paton, N., Gray, P., Kennedy, J., Cooper, R., Goble, C., West, A., and Smyth, M., *Teallach: A Model-Based User Interface Development*

Environment for Object Databases, in N.W. Paton, T. Griffiths (eds.), Proc. of 1st Int. Workshop on User Interfaces to Data Intensive Systems UIDIS'99 (Edimburgh, 5–6 September 1999), IEEE Computer Society Press, Los Alamitos, 1999, pp. 86–96.

[10] Limbourg, Q., Vanderdonckt, J., Michotte, B., Bouillon, L., and Lopez, V., *UsiXML: a Language Supporting Multi-Path Development of User Interfaces*, in Proc. of 9th IFIP Working Conf. on Engineering for Human-Computer Interaction EHCI-DSVIS'2004 (Hamburg, July 11–13, 2004), LNCS, Vol. 3425, Springer-Verlag, Berlin, 2005, pp. 200–220.

[11] Molina, P., *User Interface Generation with OlivaNova Model Execution System*, in J. Vanderdonckt, N.J. Nunes, Ch. Rich (eds.), Proc. of ACM Int. Conf. on Intelligent User Interfaces IUI'2004 (Funchal, 13–16 January 2004), ACM Press, New York, 2004, pp. 358–359.

[12] Montero, F., López Jaquero, V., Lozano, M., and González, P., *A User Interfaces Development and Abstraction Mechanism*, in Proc. of V Congreso Interacción Persona-Ordenador Interacción 2004 (Lérida, 3–7 May 2004).

[13] Montero, F., López-Jaquero, V., Vanderdonckt, J., Gonzalez, P., Lozano, M.D., and Limbourg, Q., *Solving the Mapping Problem in User Interface Design by Seamless Integration in IdealXML*, in S.W. Gilroy, M.D. Harrison (eds.), Proc. of 12th Int. Workshop on Design, Specification, and Verification of Interactive Systems DSV-IS'2005 (Newcastle upon Tyne, 13–15 July 2005), Lecture Notes in Computer Science, Vol. 3941, Springer-Verlag, Berlin, 2005, pp. 161–172.

[14] Mori, G., Paternò, F., and Santoro, C., *Tool Support for Designing Nomadic Applications*, in Proc. of the ACM Int. Conf. on Intelligent User Interfaces IUI'2003 (Miami, 12–15 January 2003), ACM Press, New York, 2003, pp.141–148.

[15] Myers, B., Hudson, S.E., and Pausch, R., *Past, Present, and Future of User Interface Software Tools*, ACM Transactions on Computer-Human Interaction, Vol. 7, No. 1, March 2000, pp. 3–28.

[16] Paternò, F., *Model-Based Design and Evaluation of Interactive Applications*, Springer-Verlag, Berlin, 1999.

[17] Puerta, A.R., *A Model-Based Interface Development Environment*, IEEE Software, Vol. 14, No. 4, July/August 1997, pp. 41—47.

[18] Puerta, A.R., and Eisenstein, J., *XIML: A Common Representation for Interaction Data*, in Proc. of ACM Int. Conf. on Intelligent User Interfaces IUI'2002 (San Francisco, 13–16 January 2002), ACM Press, New York, 2002, pp. 216–217.

[19] Puerta, A.R., Micheletti, M., and Mak, A., *The UI Pilot: A Model-Based Tool to Guide Early Interface Design*, in Proc. of ACM Int. Conf. on Intelligent User Interfaces IUI'2005 (San Diego, 10–13 January 2005), ACM Press, New York, 2005, pp. 215–222.

[20] Rettig, M., *Prototyping for Tiny Fingers*, Communications of the ACM, Vol. 37, No. 4. 1994, pp. 21–27.

[21] Schwabe, D., and Rossi, G., *The Object-Oriented Hypermedia Design Model*, Commununications of the ACM, Vol. 38, No. 8, 1995, pp. 45–46.

[22] Souchon, N., and Vanderdonckt, J., *A Review of XML-Compliant User Interface Description Languages*, in J. Jorge, N.J. Nunes, J. Cunha (eds.), Proc. of 10th Int. Conf. on Design, Specification, and Verification of Interactive Systems DSV-IS'2003 (Madeira, 4–6 June 2003), Lecture Notes in Computer Science, Vol. 2844, Springer-Verlag, Berlin, 2003, pp. 377–391.

[23] Vanderdonckt, J., *A MDA-Compliant Environment for Developing User Interfaces of Information Systems*, in O. Pastor, J. Falcão e Cunha (eds.), Proc. of 17th Conf. on Advanced Information Systems Engineering CAiSE'05 (Porto, 13–17 June 2005), Lecture Notes in Computer Science, Vol. 3520, Springer-Verlag, Berlin, 2005, pp. 16–31.

Chapter 21

INTEGRATING MODEL-BASED AND TASK-BASED APPROACHES TO USER INTERFACE GENERATION

Sergio España, Inés Pederiva, and Jose Ignacio Panach
Department of Information Systems and Computation, Valencia University of Technology,
Camino de Vera s/n, 46022 Valencia (Spain)
E-Mail: {sergio.espana, ipederiva, jpanach}@dsic.upv.es – Web: http://oomethod.dsic.upv.es/
Tel.: +34- 96 3877000 ext. 83534 – Fax: +34- 963877359

Abstract   Software Engineering community has been interested in defining methods and processes to develop software by specifying its data and behavior, but disregarding user interaction. Human-Computer Interaction community has defined techniques oriented to the modeling of the interaction between the user and the system, proposing user-oriented software constructions. In this paper, we show how to lay proper bridges between both visions, by integrating a CTT task model into a sound, model-based software development process. This proposal is underpinned by the MDA-based technology OlivaNova Method Execution, which makes software generation a reality, while still taking the user interaction needs into account

Keywords: Code Generation, Functional Requirements, Model-based user interface development environment, Task-based design, User Interface, User Interaction

1. INTRODUCTION

Software Engineering (SE) is considered to be strong in specifying functional requirements, while Human-Computer Interaction (HCI) is centered on defining user interaction at the appropriate level of abstraction. In either case, software production methods that combine the most functional-oriented, conventional requirements specification with the most interaction-oriented, user interface modeling are strongly required.

From an HCI point of view, there is a number of Model-Based User Interface Development Environments (MB-UIDEs) reported in the literature

G. Calvary et al. (eds.), Computer-Aided Design of User Interfaces V, 253–260.

[2]. The first generation aimed to provide run-time environment, as in COUSIN [4] and HUMANOID [15]. The second generation increased the abstraction level, as in MASTERMIND [16]. More recently, some broader frameworks have been proposed, like UsiXML [6,7,10,17] and TERESA [11]. SE has proposed UML-based approaches, for example WISDOM [12] and UMLi [3]. Model transformation technologies (i.e. MDA [8]) make it possible to provide a global software process where the requirements model includes all the relevant aspects of the analyzed problem. These are first projected onto a Conceptual Model and onto the final software product later.

The intended contribution of this paper is to extend a sound software production process with an interaction requirements elicitation. Two basic principles remain constant in the paper:

- Model Transformation is used to automate the conversion of the Requirements Model into the Conceptual Model and then convert this Conceptual Model into the final software application.
- Each modeling step provides appropriate methods to deal properly with the specification of structural, functional and interaction properties.

The approach presented here has been successfully implemented in OlivaNova Model Execution (ONME), an MDA-based tool that generates a software product that corresponds to the source Conceptual Model. This tool should later be enhanced to support our requirements level proposal. The paper is structured as follows. Section 2 introduces a software production process that combines model-based and task-based approaches and exemplified through a case study. Section 3 presents a conclusion and future work.

2.   MODEL-BASED INTERFACE DEVELOPMENT WITH OLIVANOVA MODEL EXECUTION

In this section, we present a complete software production process that combines functional requirements specification [5], user interaction design, and implementation. It is defined on the basis of OlivaNova Model Execution (ONME) [1], a model-based environment for software development that complies with the MDA paradigm [8] by defining models of a different abstraction level. Fig. 21 shows the parallelism between the models proposed by MDA and the models dealt with in OO-Method [13] (the methodology underlying ONME). At the most abstract level, a Computation-Independent Model (CIM) describes the information system without considering if it will be supported by any software application; in OO-Method, this description is called the *Requirements Model*. The Platform-Independent Model (PIM) describes the system in an abstract way, still disregarding the underpinning computer platform; this is called the *Conceptual Model* in OO-Method. ONME implements an automatic transformation of the Conceptual Model into the *source code* of the final user application. This is done by a *Model Compilation* process, with knowledge about the target platform. This step is equivalent to the Platform Specific Model (PSM) defined by MDA.

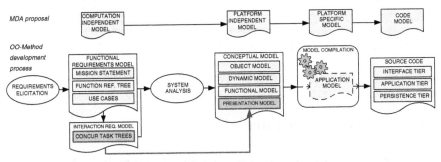

Figure 1. A MDA-based development framework for UI development

2.1 Obtaining Functional Requirements

The first step in the construction of a software system is the requirements elicitation. Its purpose is to specify what the customer needs. In our process, this step is accomplished through the definition of a *Functional Requirements Model* **Error! Reference source not found.**. The requirements model is composed by: a mission statement, a function refinement tree, and a use-case model.

The *Mission Statement* describes the purpose of the system in one or two sentences. The external interactions are partitioned into functions, which are hierarchically structured in a *Functions Refinement Tree (FRT)* where the root is the mission statement, the internal nodes are business activities, and the leaves are use cases. Finally, the *Use Case Model* includes the interaction (decomposed in steps) between the system and an external actor.

In order to explain our proposal, we have chosen an application generated using ONME. The system to be built is *OlivaNova Automatic Tweaking*, part of the ONME suite. It is intended to automate subtle manual changes requested by clients after the code generation. We have simplified the case study, selecting one task of this system: ***Create a version***. In this task, the user must select an existing project and add a new version for it. In Fig. 2 (a), we show part of the FRT in which this task is included. Once we have the FRT, the Use-Case Model can be obtained from the leaves of the tree. Our case study will be centred on the *Create version* use case that corresponds to the leaf that is marked in the FRT. Fig. 2(b) presents the specification of this use case. It consists of a use case description, the actors who can invoke it, the conditions needed to execute it and the list of events which compose it.

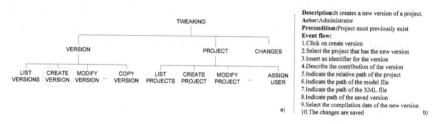

Figure 2. Functional requirements for the Tweaking system

2.2 Eliciting User Interaction

In order to document *interaction requirements*, we propose the use of the *Concur Task Trees* (CTT) notation [14]. The interaction between the user and the system is specified by means of a task model, resulting in a hierarchical task tree in which the tasks have different granularity and are related by temporal operators. A CTT tree is built for each use case. It specifies how the user interacts with the system in order to accomplish the task required. The use case constitutes a high-level task that is decomposed into lower granularity tasks; it is important to define the criterion of decomposition: we propose to reach basic tasks concerning data elements. There is a deep mapping between elements of the use-case specification and elements of its corresponding task model: the steps of the use case involving elemental data manipulation appear as basic tasks of the task tree.

Sometimes this interaction modelling process involves several use cases, which results in their restructuring; that is, the interaction requirements reorganize the functional requirements. These interaction requirements complete the CIM level of our development approach. We have built the task trees with certain structures of tasks that we have observed to be frequent.

Following with the example, Fig. 3 shows the CTT model for the *Create version* use case. The root of the task tree is the use case whose interaction is being modelled. Since this use case has the selection of a project as a precondition, we reuse the *List versions from project* CTT, and we include the *Demand the creation of a new version* interactive task.

We can now identify the mapping between the steps of the use-case specification and the lowest level tasks; i.e., step 5 "Indicate the relative path of the project" has its correspondent interaction task: "Relative path". It is also noticeable that several use cases have been reorganized: the main functionality of *Create version* (the *New version* abstract task) is accessed through the interface of the *List projects* and *List versions* use cases.

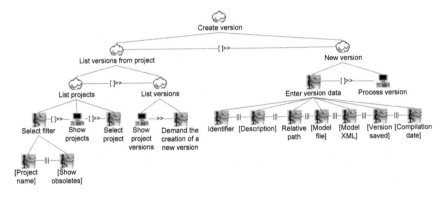

Figure 3. CTT model for the *Create version* use case

2.3 Modelling Data, Behaviour, and Interaction

After the Functional Requirements Model and the CTTs are specified, the data, behaviour, and presentation issues should be modeled. OO-Method defines a PIM called *Conceptual Model* [13] consisting of four models. The *Object Model*, the *Dynamic Model*, and the *Functional Model* can be built using the Functional Requirements Model as input.

Interaction between the system and the user is specified in the *Presentation Model* [9]. It is based on a pattern language which defines three levels of interaction patterns: (1) **Hierarchy of Actions Tree (HAT)**: it organizes the functionality that will be presented to the different users who access the system; (2) **Interaction Units (IUs)**: it represents abstract interface units that the user will interact with to carry out his/her tasks. There are four types of UIs: Service IU, Instance IU, Population IU, and Master/Detail IU; (3) **Elementary patterns (EPs)**: these patterns constitute the primitive building blocks of the UI and allow the restriction of the behaviour of the different interaction units.

Table1. Some matching between CTT and Presentation Model

CTT	Presentation Model
Two abstract tasks related by an *Enabling with information passing* temporal operator	Master / Detail
An abstract task whose name starts with *New* or *Modify*	Service IU
An abstract task whose name starts with *List*	Population IU
An abstract task whose name starts with *Detail*	Instance IU
An interaction task named *Select filter*	Filter
An interaction task named *Select sort criteria*	Order criteria
An interaction task, leaf of a subtree, in a Service IU	Introduction
An interaction task whose name starts with *Demand*	Action

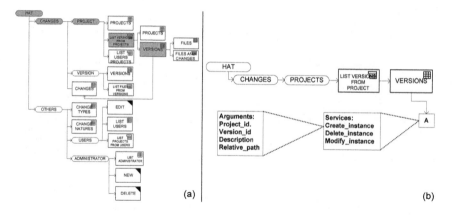

Figure 4. Presentation Model for the Tweaking system

As suggested in Fig. 1, there is a direct mapping between parts of the CTT and parts of the Presentation Model. To do that, we have to define a design pattern for CTT and concrete names for their components. We show some of them in Table 1.

Fig. 4(a) shows the system's first two levels of presentation patterns according to the case study. The patterns that appear highlighted in gray are detailed in (b). Fig. 4(b), shows the services and the arguments of *Create_Instance*. To design this model, we consider the CTT generated in the previous step. In particular, Fig. 4(b) was generated by the definition provided in Fig. 3. The left subtree of the CTT is mapped to a Master/Detail pattern. And, on the other hand, the right side of the tree model is equivalent to a Service IU; its execution will call the *Create_Instance* service. As this service corresponds to a service defined in the Object Model, it turns towards an early model validation, based on the traceability among the Presentation Model and the Use Cases.

2.4   Generating the System

Once we have completed the PIM, the next step is to take advantage of ONME automatic production of the *source code* (Code Model). Nowadays, ONME implements a *Model Compilation* process to automatically transform the information captured in the *Conceptual Model* into a full software system over the following platforms: Visual Basic, C #, ASP. NET, Cold Fusion and Java; using as repository SQL server 2000, ORACLE or DB2. The resulting application is a three-layer application that includes the interface tier, the application tier, and the persistence tier. Some correspondences between PIM elements and their final, concrete widgets for the Visual Basic platform are defined in [9].

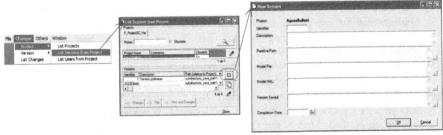

Figure 5. New version window

The result of applying the translation patterns [9] is shown in Fig. 5. The HAT has become the application menu and the *List Version from Project* and *Versions* patterns have been turned into windows. In the *List Versions from Project* window, we can invoke the tasks related to the versions listed by a project. It contains the task to create a version (marked button). Once the button is clicked, the *New Version* window appears to allow the introduction of the information to create a version.

3. SUMMARY AND FUTURE WORK

Software production methods need a complete software production process that properly integrates system functionality, behaviour, and user interaction in the early stages of the system lifecycle. This process should also allow the sketching, modelling, and prototyping of UIs. In accordance with these ideas, we have presented a software production process that starts from requirements elicitation and uses CTT notation based on tasks to build a full software system, not just its user interface. To do this, we embedded the CTT notation in a model-based development approach by respecting its original semantics. The proposed process will be empirically validated in the near future to prove its effectiveness. As a future work, an application that will implement CTT drawing using these proposed patterns will be integrated into the ONME suite. This will allow CTT nodes to be reused easily.

REFERENCES

[1] Care Technologies, accessible at http://www.care-t.com, June 2006.

[2] da Silva, P.P., *User Interface Declarative Models and Development Environments: A Survey*, in Proc. of 7th Int. Workshop on Design, Specification, and Verification of Interactive Systems DSV-IS'2000 (Limerick, 5–6 June 2001), Springer-Verlag Berlin, 2005, pp. 207–226.

[3] da Silva, P.P., and Paton, N.W., *User Interface Modeling in UMLi*, IEEE Software, Vol. 20, No. 4, 2003, pp. 62–69.

[4] Hayes, P.J., Szekely, P., and Lerner, R., *Design Alternatives for User Interface Management Systems Based on Experience with COUSIN*, in Proc. of ACM Conf. on Human Aspects in Computing Systems CHI'85 (San Francisco, April 1985), ACM Press, New ork, 1985, pp. 169–175.

[5] Insfrán, E., Pastor, O., and Wieringa, R., *Requirements Engineering-Based Conceptual Modelling*, Requirements Engineering, Vol. 7, No. 2, 2002, pp. 61–72.

[6] Limbourg, Q., and Vanderdonckt, J., *Addressing the Mapping Problem in User Interface Design with UsiXML*, in Ph. Palanque, P. Slavik, M. Winckler (eds.), Proc. of 3rd Int. Workshop on Task Models and Diagrams for user interface design TAMODIA'2004 (Prague, 15–16 November 2004), ACM Press, New York, 2004, pp. 155–163.

[7] Limbourg, Q., Vanderdonckt, J., Michotte, B., Bouillon, L., and Lopez, V., *UsiXML: a Language Sup-porting Multi-Path Development of User Interfaces*, in Proc. of 9th IFIP Working Conf. on Engineering for Human-Computer Interaction EHCI-DSVIS'2004 (Hamburg, July 11–13, 2004), Lecture Notes in Computer Science, Vol. 3425, Springer-Verlag, Berlin, 2005, pp. 200–220.

[8] Model-Driven Architecture (MDA), accessible at http://www.omg.org/mda, January 2006.

[9] Molina, P., *User Interface Specification: From Requirements to Automatic Generation*, Ph.D. thesis, DSIC, Universidad Politécnica de Valencia, Valencia, March 2003.

[10] Montero, F., López-Jaquero, V., Vanderdonckt, J., Gonzalez, P., Lozano, M.D., and Limbourg, Q., *Solving the Mapping Problem in User Interface Design by Seamless Integration in IdealXML*, in S.W. Gilroy, M.D. Harrison (eds.), Proc. of 12th Int. Workshop on Design, Specification, and Verification of Interactive Systems DSV-IS'2005 (Newcastle upon Tyne, 13–15 July 2005), Lecture Notes in Computer Science, Vol. 3941, Springer-Verlag, Berlin, 2005, pp. 161–172.

[11] Mori, G., Paternò, F., and Santoro, C., *Design and Development of Multidevice User Interfaces through Multiple Logical Descriptions*, IEEE Transactions on Software Engineering, Vol. 30, No. 8, 2004, pp. 507–520.

[12] Nunes, N.J., and Falcão e Cunha, J., *Wisdom: A Software Engineering Method for Small Software Development Companies*, IEEE Software, Vol. 17, No. 5, 2000, pp. 113–119.

[13] Pastor, O., Gómez, J., Insfrán, E., and Pelechano, V., *The OO-Method Approach for Information Systems Modeling: from Object-Oriented Conceptual Modeling to Automated Programming*. Information Systems, Vol. 26, No. 7, November 2001, pp. 507–534.

[14] Paternò, F., Mancini, C., and Meniconi, S., *ConcurTaskTrees: A Diagrammatic Notation for Specifying Task Models*, in Proc. of the IFIP TC13 Int. Conf. on Human-Computer Interaction INTERACT'97 (Sydney, 14–18 July 1997), Chapman & Hall, London, 1997, pp. 362–369.

[15] Szekely, P., *Template-Based Mapping of Application Data to Interactive Displays*, in Proc. of ACM Symposium on User Interface Software and Technology UIST'90 (Snowbird, 3–5 October 1990), ACM Press, New York, 1990, pp. 1–9.

[16] Szekely, P., Sukaviriya, P., Castells, P., Muthukumarasamy, J., and Salcher, E., *Declarative Interface Models for User Interface Construction Tools: the MASTERMIND Approach*, in L.J. Bass, C. Unger (eds.), Engineering for Human-Computer Interaction, Proc. of the IFIP TC2/WG2.7 Working Conf. on Engineering for Human-Computer Interaction EHCI'95 (Yellowstone Park, August 1995), Chapman & Hall, London, 1995, pp. 120–150.

[17] Vanderdonckt, J., *A MDA-Compliant Environment for Developing User Interfaces of Information Systems*, in O. Pastor, J. Falcão e Cunha (eds.), Proc. of 17th Conf. on Advanced Information Systems Engineering CAiSE'05 (Porto, 13–17 June 2005), Lecture Notes in Computer Science, Vol. 3520, Springer-Verlag, Berlin, 2005, pp. 16–31.

Chapter 22

AUTOMATED REPAIR TOOL FOR USABILITY AND ACCESSIBILITY OF WEB SITES

Arnaud Jasselette[1], Marc Keita[1], Monique Noirhomme-Fraiture[1], Frédéric Randolet[1], Jean Vanderdonckt[2], Christian Van Brussel[2], and Donatien Grolaux[2]

[1]*Institut d'Informatique, Facultés Universitaires Notre-Dame de la Paix*
rue Grandgagnage, 21 – B-5000 Namur (Belgium)
E-mail: (aja,mke,mno,fra)@info.fundp.ac.be – Web: http://www.info.fundp.ac.be/DESTINE
[2]*School of Management (IAG), Université catholique de Louvain*
Place des Doyens, 1 – B-1348 Louvain-la-Neuve (Belgium)
E-mail:{vanderdonckt,vanbrussel,grolaux}@isys.ucl.ac.be – Web: http://www.isys.ucl.ac.be/bchi
Tel: +32 10 47{8525, 8391} – Fax: +32 10 478324

Abstract   The need for checking both usability and accessibility of Web sites is widely recognized, approved and recommended by several official organizations. What should really be more recognized or addressed is an equal need for repairing the usability and accessibility defects that have been detected. Within the DESTINE suite, we developed a tool allowing to repair the HTML source code of a page with user interaction. Thanks to an improved version of the Guideline Definition Language (GDL), the accessibility guidelines are not hard-coded, so that our tool can deal with any existing or future standards

Keywords: Accessibility, Automated repair tool, DESTINE, Usability engineering

1.   INTRODUCTION

In our modern world, Internet plays a prevailing role in communication, knowledge and information exchange. Internet expanded almost thanks to the World Wide Web who knew a great expansion these last years. Nowadays, the Web has to be considered as one of the most used and expanded source of information. However, this great amount of data is not always accessible to all users, especially people suffering from a handicap. The awakening of this problem gave birth to the creation of standards and guidelines to follow in the construction of a Web Site. One of the most concrete

261

G. Calvary et al. (eds.), Computer-Aided Design of User Interfaces V, 261–272.
© 2007 *Springer*.

examples of this phenomenon is the e-Europe Action Plan. The e-Europe 2002 forces all public Web Sites from Europe to be accessible to handicapped people. The e-Europe 2005, which is the following action plan, aims at an improvement of quality and Usability and Accessibility (U&A) of the services to the profit of the whole of the citizens. This reviewed plan confirms the adoption of the recommendations made for the U&A to Web Sites. The U&A to the Web and his usability are part of the preoccupations of organisms such as the W3C Consortium who promotes the recommendations for Web Sites to be accessible with the Web Accessibility Initiative (WAI) recommendations and the Web Content Guidelines.

The need for checking the usability and the accessibility of Web sites is thus widely recognized, approved and recommended by several official organizations. Equally recognized, although less addressed, is the desire to support as much as possible the evaluation process through automated tools [12]. What is even less recognized or addressed is an equal need for repairing the usability and accessibility defects that have been detected during the automated evaluation phase. If such a repair process does not exist, the author of the web page could be left out with only a potentially long list of defects, which may be hard to understand and to fix. Indeed, automated evaluation typically performs a summative evaluation (it specifies the type and location of the defects), but not a formative evaluation (it does not provide any feedback on how to fix the detected defects). If the process is not completely supported by a suite of tools, the evaluation conducted before may have little or no impact on the usability and accessibility.

We have designed such an integrated tool where evaluation and repair are parts of the same system. This paper is focused on the repair part. We start with a short overview of the state of the art and on the shortcomings of repair tools in general. Then we present the DESTINE suite, in order to situate the repair tool. Afterwards we shall describe how the software corrects a web page using Guideline Definition Language (GDL) [16] and finally explain how the repair tool interface has been designed. To conclude, we shall emphasize the strengths of the tool regarding to its rivals.

2.   STATE OF THE ART

Research shows the advisability of tools that automatically evaluate and repair Web sites according to ergonomic guidelines, whatever the type of ergonomic guidelines (e.g., usability, accessibility, cognitive walkthrough). Let us cite in particular the work of [6,7,11,13] showing how it is possible and important to systematically and consistently evaluate web site against usability guidelines. Several tools have been developed to automate the evaluation process of a web site according to various techniques. This represents an important research area since it is reported as largely underexplored [12]. They allow evaluating Web Pages from U&A guidelines and informing the evaluator about the different aspects of the site to improve.

Repair tools allow the syntactic correction of ergonomic issues according to U&A guidelines. These tools bring an automatic correction if this is possible; otherwise the user is guided through the correction process and can regulate major conflicts inside the Web page. We can distinguish two types of existing repair tools.

The **first** type can be considered as a plug-in integrated to software, such as a Web page editor. The site author may want to ensure that the site she is creating is "standard compliant". Among these tools we can find:

- Deque Ramp Ascend [9]: this software is compatible with Microsoft Frontpage and Macromedia Dreamweaver authoring environments. They allow validating a web page against the guidelines provided by both Section 508 and W3C WCAG WCAI. The software corrects problems with n-dimensional tables, skips navigation, performs automatic detection and correction of missing alternate tags, and corrects animation graphics so that they do not flash in the 2 to 55 Hertz range.

- Lift [15]: this desktop solution is also intended to produce usable and accessible "Section 508/W3C compliant" web sites within Macromedia Dreamweaver only and focuses on the WCAG Priority 1 and US government section 508 checkpoints. It generates HTML or XML reports from the evaluation performed.

The **second** type of tool is a stand-alone software. It can evaluate a page and may offer some support for correcting portions of a web page which have been evaluated negatively. Modifications and corrections to the document are not done by a Web page editor but by the repair tool itself. The tool can modify the code of the pointed page at any time. That kind of software is less spread than the integrated plug-in, the following list shows the most important of them:

- A-Prompt [17]: based on the WCAG Guidelines or Section 508, this tool guides the user by a completely automated correction in the different stages.

- InFocus [2]: similar to other repair tools, it also evaluates separately guidelines contained in Section 508 and W3C WCAG.

- SWAP [14]: the Semantic Web Accessibility Platform (SWAP) is developed according to the international accessibility standards of the W3C for Internet-accessibility guidelines and worldwide legislation.

There are also some other forms of software products that **combine** both aforementioned types. For Example, the tool AccRepair can be used as stand-alone software or could be integrated in authoring environments like

Microsoft FrontPage. This tool corrects errors concerning the guidelines in the Section 508 and WCAG Compliance Errors.

The main shortcomings that one could identify for the above types of software that stem for developing software for automated evaluation are equally applicable to the development of software for automated repair:

- Repair logic is hard-coded in software: all existing tools which perform some kind of automated repair have their repair algorithms completely built-in the software without any flexibility or modifiability.
- The set of guidelines is predefined: only one or two sets of guidelines are supported, typically the W3C guidelines and the Section 508. A customized set of guidelines, such as a corporate style guide, cannot be supported.
- The underlying guidelines are immutable, so are their repair: the tools only support a single interpretation of each guideline, as well as for automated evaluation as for automated repair. It is not possible to modulate the interpretation of a guideline at evaluation/repair time nor is possible to tailor, to refine this process depending on the context of use.
- Only one set at a time: It is not possible to mix guidelines from different sources in a custom way, with possible optimization of their process. No combination is allowed.

Our goal is obviously to design a software for repairing a web page (or a series of web pages) which have been evaluated negatively, which does not suffer from any of these above shortcomings.

3.   REPAIR TOOLS CLASSIFICATION

Not all guidelines which have been identified as violated for one or several of their checkpoints could be repaired in an automated way. Therefore, different levels of automation could be considered:

- *Fully automated repair*: the software holds all information required to repair the violated guideline.
- *Partial automated repair*: the software does not hold all the information required to repair the guideline, but may assume some hypothesis in order to choose among options. This may give rise to a warning explaining the user why this choice has been made. This typically occurs for syntactical guidelines.
- *Partial interactive repair*: the software may know how to repair the violated guideline, but requires some interpretation from the user to choose among options. This typically arises from more semantic issues.
- *Manual repair with guidance*: the software may know how to repair the violated guideline, but this operation cannot be processed by the software

for several reasons: human decision, incomplete information, need for additional information, need for a consensus, lack of resources (not everything could be implemented), and so on. Therefore, the software may help the designer with some guidance on how to fix the identified defect.

- *Manual repair without any guidance*: the software has identified a violated guideline, but does not know how to fix it.

4.   THE DESTINE ENVIRONMENT

Referring to the repair tool classification presented above, DESTINE consists of a complete environment for evaluating a web page against any previously defined usability and accessibility guideline and a repair tool which executes a partial interactive repair or a partial automated repair depending on the guideline to be processed. As explained before, the repair tool is useful if it is integrated to a suite. DESTINE was a perfect environment for a repair software. We shall first remind the reader about the DESTINE suite before explaining in details our repair tool. DESTINE stands for Design & Evaluation STudio for INtent-based Ergonomic Web sites. The goal of Destine is to help the conception, evaluation and repair of the accessibility quality of web sites. Our tool is based on several bases of ergonomic recommendations and does not need the use of a Web development environment. DESTINE contains five different modules (Fig. 1):

1. *A management tool of usability and accessibility knowledge*: it is responsible for organizing the knowledge bases containing the guidelines: thanks to it, the user can browse and edit any knowledge base.
2. *A Guideline Description Language (GDL) editor*: it allows to formally writing any guideline in the GDL formal language, which is the language used to write the logic evaluation of usability and accessibility guidelines that can be evaluated automatically by a machine.
3. *An Automatic Evaluator of the ergonomic quality of web sites*: it evaluates from the GDL specification the ergonomic quality of pages or web sites and gives a report showing the result of this evaluation. The report allows the user to analyze the quality of his web site but also to correct it manually.
4. *An Ergonomic Repair Tool*: it is aimed at repairing pages where ergonomic problems have been identified by the evaluation tool. The tool gives assistance to the user, which means he controls the repair process. This is the tool the paper will be focused on.
5. *The Multimodal transformation tool*: it is used to transform Web sites originally designed for a computer screen in order to make them compatible with an interactive kiosk.

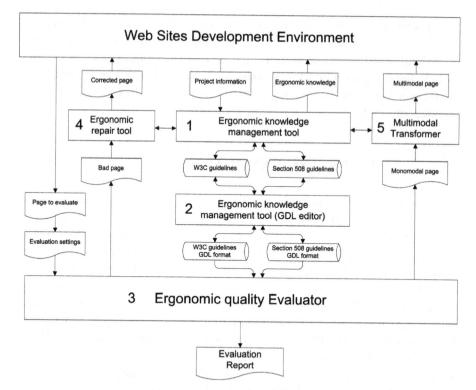

Figure 1. Global architecture of the DESTINE project

DESTINE is a complete suite that can be used at anytime in the development process of Web sites. It can give a knowledge base for the developer, give an evaluation report of the status of his Web site, then repair ergonomic errors and adapt this site to other hardware. One of the advantages of DESTINE is the possibility of an automatic evaluation of ergonomic guidelines or a manual evaluation by the user using the knowledge base of the management tool. Another advantage is the separation between the logic and the evaluation engine, in both evaluation and repair tools.

5.   THE DESTINE REPAIR TOOL

To evaluate automatically and then repair a page, we split ergonomic guidelines in smaller parts that we called "technical checkpoints". A checkpoint can be converted and integrated in a GDL (Guideline Definition Language) [4,5] file which could then be interpreted by our evaluation or repair tool. We shall call a repair candidate an HTML object that is liable to be involved in an ergonomic guideline; a piece of code extracted from the Web page in order to perform the repair according to a technical checkpoint.

5.1   GDL Files for Repair

The main asset of the DESTINE project is the GDL (Guideline Description Language) which allows a clean separation of the definition of usability and accessibility guidelines from the inference engine. We have already presented the format of this language in previous articles [3,4,5]. We chose to follow the same philosophy for the repair tool.

As a reminder, GDL is used to model the estimable aspects of HTML code (e.g., colors, contrast, alternate text for visual content). GDL specifies a suitable structure to formalize an ergonomic guideline in one or more evaluation contexts. Notice that GDL is XML compatible, like other tools using XML structures to automatically analyze the accessibility of Web pages, fore.g., EvalIris [1] or Bobby [8]. The GDL format that is suitable for our evaluation tool, can be used by the repair tool by adding a new "correction guideline" section, as shown in Fig. 2 and Fig. 3.

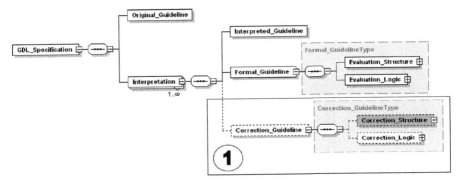

Figure 2. XSD schema of the GDL repair file with its new correction section

The structure is based on the evaluation and allows editing HTML code instead of reading it only. The correction guideline is split between the correction structure, and the correction logic. The former defines the fields to be generated in the interface in order to let the user apply changes during the correction process. Actually, the user interface must be customized for each ergonomic failure the user wants to correct. The latter specifies the way the inference engine will treat HTML data in a bid to correct the Web page content.

Since repairing each guideline depends on the guideline type, the correction structure hold information characterizing what type of correction could be brought to fix the usability defect. For instance, if an alternate tag is missing for an image, the correction structure will require the designer to input a textual description and will feed the HTML code with this information. The designer does not need to know any HTML code since the repair tool itself adds the corresponding portion of code that fixes the defect.

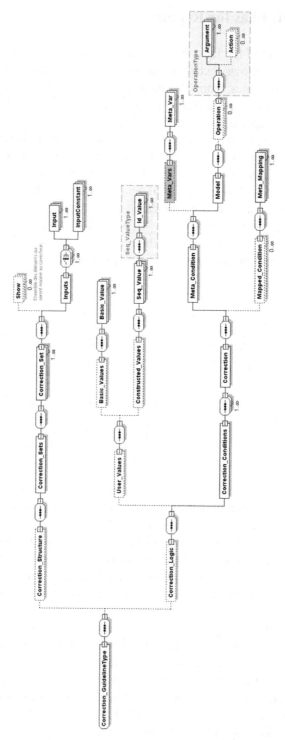

Figure 3. Detail of the correction section

5.2   The Repair Process and the User Interface

The repair process usually takes place in these following steps:

1. The first step consists of selecting the ergonomic guidelines and the Web pages to be repaired. The user selects in the panel 1 a technical checkpoint (Fig. 4, panel 1) and a page that he had previously loaded in the panel 2 (Fig. 4, panel 2).

2. The user chooses if he wants a preliminary evaluation before starting the repair. The preliminary evaluation allows the user to realize the amount of candidates that should be repaired. Notice that the repair process always begins with an evaluation anyway.

3. In a repair process, as soon as an issue is detected, DESTINE adapts its interface (Fig. 4, panel 4) thanks to the correction structure defined in the GDL (Section 5.1) so the user can fix the HTML code.

4. The application checks the new values entered by the user by running the correction logic (Section 5.1) on them.

5. After the changes have been applied to the page, the user can choose to repair the next candidate of the current checkpoint or to restart the process at step 1.

Let us give an example about the easy checkpoint *"Provide an alternative text for images"* [18]. The GDL file specifies to fetch the tag <IMG> and to look if the attribute "alt" is fulfilled. If this is not the case, the GUI is adapted thanks to the GDL specification to allow the user fulfilling the attribute. This process is flexible: at any time, the user can choose which candidate or page he wants to repair according to a guideline. There is no predefined order to apply the correction, the user is free to follow her way and priorities to achieve the pages repair.

In our case the graphic user interface had to be carefully designed. Indeed the repair process is often fastidious and may appear even worse to the user if the interface is not clear and accessible. Unlike the evaluation tool [4] which gives a complete report of the evaluation process, the latter is presented here in a lighter form, briefing the user on the state. The interface is composed by four main panels as illustrated in Fig. 4:

- Panel 1 shows all the usability and accessibility guidelines and their technical checkpoints which can be repaired for a selected page. This panel allows us to launch the repair process or a light evaluation of the currently selected checkpoint.

- Panel 2 displays the set of pages we want to repair.

- Panel 3 shows either the HTML page in a browser with the repair candidate framed or the HTML source code with the repair candidate emphasized).

- Panel 4 contains a set of input fields in order to enter the corrected values to repair the page. This panel also allows the navigation into a technical checkpoint among the repair candidates. It finally gives information about the ergonomic issue and how to fix it.

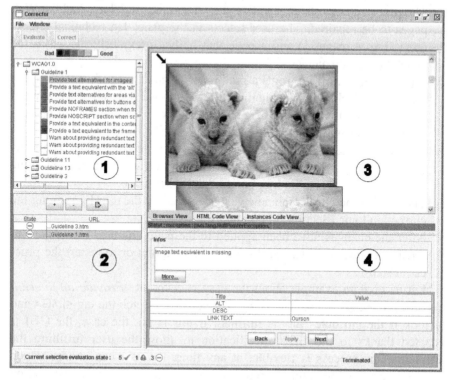

Figure 4. Repair Tool UI

6.   CHARACTERISTICS OF THE TOOL

Let us emphasize what distinguishes this tool from others. As we saw previously in this paper, evaluation and repair processes are quite similar. Indeed, the repair process starts with an evaluation and every correction given by the user needs to be checked until it is valid. The user does not absolutely have to repair, she can just run a partial evaluation independently of his repair process, so he could catch a glimpse of the work to do. The use of GDL files allows a separation between the program and the guidelines expression. That way someone can make a guideline and then evaluate or repair it without having to know anything in programming or having to recompile the application code. Finally, our evaluation tool can deal with problems due to Cascaded Style Sheets, so can our repair tool, unlike most of the existing repair tools. Notice that for the time being, the repair tool can treat CSS files but does not allow correcting them.

7.   CONCLUSION

For the time being, a fully automatic repair process that outputs a perfect Web site is not completely formalizable. There are lots of guidelines which cannot be automatically evaluated and thus repaired, for e.g., the guidelines related to the semantic of Web pages. Moreover, the repair process is a creation process; hence the designer must keep the control on the changes carried out on his pages. However, this restriction is also insoluble among the rival tools. We have shown the repair tool of DESTINE. It is able to repair automated U&A rules. In general, only 44% of the problems can be automatically evaluated for interactive application [10] and only 50% for a Web site [8]. The repair is not completely automatic but the tool can guide the user in his correction. In that point of view we can say the repair process can repair every problem that was automatically detected during the evaluation process but with the interaction of the designer. One of the main advantages of DESTINE stands in the fact that the logic expression of the guidelines to verify and the way to repair them are separated. Each repair technique can be logically defined and just parsed to be treated. This is a largely different approach from those where the repair means are hard-coded (like A-Prompt, X-Act, which is the most recent version of Bobby). In our future work, we are extended our repair tool towards the correction of web pages formatted with Cascading Style Sheets.

REFERENCES

[1] Abascal, J., Arrue, M., Fajardo, I., Garay, N., and Tomas, J., *Use of Guidelines to Automatically Verify Web Accessibility*, Universal Access in the Information Society, Vol. 3, No. 1, 2004, pp. 71–79.

[2] Accessibility solutions SSB, accessible at http://www.ssbtechnologies.com/.

[3] Beirekdar, A., Keita, M., Noirhomme, M., Randolet, F., Vanderdonckt, J., and Mariage, C., *Flexible Reporting for Automated Usability and Accessibility Evaluation of Web Sites*, in Proc. of 10th IFIP TC 13 Int. Conf. on Human-Computer Interaction INTER-ACT'2005 (Rome, 12–16 September 2005), Lecture Notes in Computer Science, Vol. 3585, Springer-Verlag, Berlin, 2005, pp. 281–294.

[4] Beirekdar, A., Vanderdonckt, J., and Noirhomme-Fraiture, M., *A Framework and a Language for Usability Automatic Evaluation of Web Sites by Static Analysis of HTML Source Code*, Chapter 29, in Ch. Kolski, J. Vanderdonckt (eds.), Proc. of 4th Int. Conf. on Computer-Aided Design of User Interfaces CADUI'2002 (Valenciennes, 15–17 May 2002), Kluwer Academics Pub., Dordrecht, 2002, pp. 337–348.

[5] Beirekdar, A., Vanderdonckt, J., and Noirhomme-Fraiture, M., *KWARESMI – Knowledge-based Web Automated Evaluation Tool with Reconfigurable Guidelines Optimization*, in C. Stephanidis (ed.), Proc. of 2nd Int. Conf. on Universal Access in Human-Computer Interaction UAHCI'2003 (Creete, 22–27 June 2003), Vol. 4, Lawrence Erlbaum Associates, Mahwah, 2003, pp. 1504–1508.

[6] Blackmon, M.H., Kitajima, M., and Polson, P.G., *Repairing Usability Problems Identified by the Cognitive Walkthrough for the Web*, in Proc. of the ACM Conf. on Human Aspects in Computing Systems CHI'2003 (Ft. Lauderdale, 5–10 April 2003), ACM Press, New York, 2003, pp. 497–504.

[7] Blackmon, M.H., Kitajima, M., and Polson, P.G., *Tool for Accurately Predicting Website Navigation Problems, Non-Problems, Problem Severity, and Effectiveness of Repairs*, in Proc. of the ACM Conf. on Human Aspects in Computing Systems CHI'2005 (Portland, 2–7 April 2005), ACM Press, New York, 2005, pp. 31–40.

[8] Cooper, M., Limbourg, Q., Mariage, C., and Vanderdonckt, J., *Integrating Universal Design into a Global Approach for Managing Very Large Web Sites*, in A. Kobsa, C. Stephanidis (eds.), Proc. of the 5th ERCIM Workshop on User Interfaces for All UI4ALL'99 (Dagstuhl, 28 November-1 December 1999), GMD Report 74, GMD – Forschungszentrum Informationstechnik GmbH, Sankt Augustin, 1999, pp. 131–150.

[9] Deque Ramp Product page, accessible at http://www.deque.com/products/ramp.html.

[10] Farenc, Ch., Liberati, V., and Barthet, M.-F., *Automatic Ergonomic Evaluation: What are the Limits?*, in J. Vanderdonckt (ed.), Proc. of the 2nd Int. Workshop on Computer-Aided Design of User Interfaces CADUI'96 (Namur, 5–7 June 1996), Presses Universitaires de Namur, Namur, 1996, pp. 159–170.

[11] Gaedke, M., Nussbaumer, M., and Meinecke, J., *An Agile System Facilitating the Production of Service-Oriented Web Applications*, in M. Matera, S. Comai (eds.), "Engineering Advanced Web Applications", Rinton Press, Paramus, 2004.

[12] Ivory, M.Y., and Megraw, R., *Evolution of Web Site Design Patterns*, ACM Transactions on Information Systems, Vol. 23, No. 4, October 2005, pp 463–497.

[13] Luque-Centeno, V., Delgado-Kloos, C., Arias-Fisteus, J., and Alvarez-Alvarez, L., *Web Accessibility Evaluation Tools: a Survey and some Improvements*, in M. Alpuente, S. Escobar, M. Falaschi (eds.), Proc. of First International Workshop on Automated Specification and Verification of Web Sites WWV'05 (Valencia, 14–15 March 2005), Valecnia, 2005, pp. 83–96.

[14] The Semantic Web Accessibility Platform SWAP homepage, accessible at http://www. ubaccess.com/swap.html.

[15] UsableNet web solutions homepage, accessible at http://www.usablenet.com/.

[16] Vanderdonckt, J., Beirekdar, A., and Noirhomme-Fraiture, M., *Automated Evaluation of Web Usability and Accessibility by Guideline Review*, in N. Koch, P. Fraternali, M. Wirsing (eds.), Proc. of 4th Int. Conf. on Web Engineering ICWE'04 (Munich, 28–30 July 2004), Lecture Notes in Computer Science, Vol. 3140, Springer-Verlag, Berlin, 2004, pp. 17–30.

[17] Web Accessibility Verifier A-Prompt, accessible at http://aprompt.snow.utoronto.ca/.

[18] Web Content Accessibility Guidelines 1.0, W3C Recommendation, 5 May 1999, accessible at http://www.w3.org/TR/WAI-WEBCONTENT/.

Chapter 23

AUTOMATING GUIDELINES INSPECTION
From Web Site Specification to Deployment

Joseph Xiong[1], Mouhamed Diouf[2], Christelle Farenc[1], and Marco Winckler[1]

[1]*LIIHS-IRIT, Université Paul Sabatier*
Route de Narbonne, 118 – F-31062 Toulouse Cedex 4 (France)
E-mail: {xiong, farenc, winckler}@irit.fr
Tel.: +33 5 61 55 63 59 – Fax: +33 5 61 55 62 58
[2]*L3A-LaBRI, Domaine Universitaire*
Cours de la Libération, 351 – F-33405 Talence Cedex (France)
E-mail: diouf@labri.fr

Abstract   This work focuses on how we can improve automatic evaluation based on guidelines inspection throughout the life cycle of Web applications by mapping guideline concepts to different artifacts produced during the development process. In order to support such an evaluation approach, we present a tool for automated evaluation based on guidelines reviews

Keywords: Accessibility, Automated usability evaluation, Development process, Ergonomic inspection, Usability, Web sites

1.   INTRODUCTION

Usability evaluation is a complex task that requires knowledge and expertise. For usability experts, most of the evaluation methods are "simple". For non-experts, however, evaluation methods are considered "complex". Usability guidelines may be one way to alleviate this lack of expertise. However, even experts experience difficulties in applying guidelines, at least in the format in which they are conflict with one another because there is a wide gap between the recommendation (e.g., "make the site consistent") and its applications [5]. The SUE inspection method [7] transfers the ergonomic knowledge by guiding novice evaluators through evaluation patterns (called abstract tasks) which tailor the manual inspection. However, such as an approach requires a previous training to employ abstract tasks. In addition, the scope of the evaluation is limited by the coverage of predefined patterns.

273

G. Calvary et al. (eds.), Computer-Aided Design of User Interfaces V, 273–286.
© 2007 Springer.

In order to overcome these limitations of manual inspection, much effort has been devoted in the development of tools supporting the collection and the organization of guidelines [13,14], guiding the inspection [1] and supporting automated guidelines inspection [1,11]. One of the advantages of employing automated tools for guidelines inspection is that no extensive knowledge on ergonomics is required since most the technical details are embedded into the tools. The lack of experts to perform usability evaluations [11] and the high costs of other evaluation methods (e.g., user testing) make automated inspection of guidelines a suitable method for supporting frequent evaluations of Web applications.

Usability evaluation is not only important for identifying problems in the early phases of the development process but also for managing the frequent updates performed over web applications. According to the phase of the development life cycle different categories of guidelines can be employed for supporting design and/or evaluation of User Interfaces (UIs) [6]. In fact, in the over past years, several tools supporting automatic inspection of the HTML/CSS code of Web pages [2] emerged as a valuable approach for improving usability of Web applications [1,3]. However, such tools only can be employed in late phases of development when a UI prototype is available.

In our previous work we have investigated the guidelines verification on specific models (e.g., dialog models [8] and navigation models [16,17]) at particular phases of the life cycle and we have demonstrated the advantages of the guidelines verification over models in early phases of development. In the present work we propose a broader view for automated inspection of guidelines by inspecting all the artifacts produced at different phases throughout the life cycle of Web applications. We present a tool support which demonstrates our approach. The rest of this paper is organized as follows: Section 2 describes requirements for automated inspection of guidelines. Section 3 describes the general architecture of our proposal for automated evaluation using guidelines during the development process. Section 4 provides some examples which demonstrate our approach. Section 5 presents the set of tools dealing with implementation issues. Lastly, we present discussion and future work.

2.   AUTOMATING GUIDELINES INSPECTION

The automation of guidelines verification is a complex process. First of all, it is needed to interpret high-level guidelines and to translate them into more concrete rules where each rule has a unique meaning. In the sequence, concrete rules should be mapped to UIs elements (e.g., navigation elements, text content, graphics, and menus) which can be used as input for automated tools. In addition, before running out with the automation, guidelines should be organized in the way they are useful at each phase of development process [10]. Hereafter, we describe the steps towards the automated inspection of guidelines. The set of guidelines used in this work is issued from W3C/ WAI accessibility initiative (http://www.w3.org/TR/WAI-WEBCONTENT/) and the EvalWeb project [9].

2.1 Guidelines Interpretation

In order to be automated, guidelines have to be described in a precise and non-ambiguous way. Guidelines are expressed in natural language and an interpretation phase is often necessary to translate them into a computing language. Indeed, a rule can be more or less abstract [14] and is not appropriate to an automatic translation in all the cases. If so, rules should be decoded in one or more concrete rules. For example, the rule *"Provide accessible content for visual impaired users"* is too imprecise to be automatically implemented. So it should be interpreted in a more concrete way having a single meaning. For example: *"Provide alternative text for images"*.

Quite often, many concrete rules must be created in order to cover all possible facets a guideline might have with respect to the UI contents or widgets. For example, what does the rule *"Provide accessible content for visual impaired users"* mean for images, menus, buttons, animation, and so on?

The translation process might also create a semantic distance between the original guidelines and the concrete rules created to support automated inspection. Considering the example above, the concrete guideline *"Provide alternative text for images"* only helps to check if a text description is associated to images; this can be considered as a kind of syntactic verification. Currently, there is no available tool supporting the verification of the semantics of alternative text and image's content, thus creating a gap between the rule and what is possible to verify concerning the rule.

2.2 Mapping Guidelines to User Interface Elements

After we have removed possible ambiguities in the guidelines, we must identify which UI elements are concerned. For example, the following accessibility guideline: *"Provide alternative text for images"* will typically address the "IMG" tag and its "ALT" attribute embedded into the HTML. At this point we have two choices: rewrite the rule using a kind of *"algorithms"* processing such UI elements, or alternatively, formally describe ergonomic rule using specific temporal logics such as ACTL [4].

Several guidelines address HTML elements (e.g., images, links, paragraphs, etc.) and their attributes (e.g., link color, textual aid for images, table caption, etc.) that can be easily identified by analyzing the DOM structure of HTML pages (http://www.w3.org/TR/2003/REC-DOM-Level-2-HTML-20 030109/). However, many guidelines refer to abstract elements that are not formally described by HTML tags. For example, the evaluation of the following guideline: *"Include navigational aid pointers across to main sections"* can't be automated because there is no information concerning the elements *"navigational aid"* and *"main sections"*. We can generalize this situation as follows: the guidelines vocabulary used to describe abstract elements (e.g., *"navigational aid"* and *"main sections"*) cannot be automatically translated to the vocabulary (e.g., HTML tags) used to describe the artifacts (e.g., Web pages) being evaluated.

2.3   Development Life Cycle of Web applications

As mentioned before, our main goal is to apply automated inspection at early phase of the development process of the Web applications. So, we had to determine whether we can apply a guideline or not at each phase of the life cycle. Currently, there is no consensus on which phases of development are required, neither which life cycle better describes the development process of Web applications. Despite this, the life cycle for Web development can be generalized as an iterative process [9]. In our work, we follow an iterative design process which is made up of six phases as follow: 1) requirements engineering, 2) Site specification, 3) Site design, 4) Site development, 5) Site usage and evaluation, and 6) Maintenance. This life cycle, called in "O", is presented by Fig. 1. At each phase, several artifacts are produced. For example, the phase 2 (i.e., Site Specification) provides navigation models, data models, and so on, while the phase 3 (i.e., Site design) will provide templates describing the layout of pages. Web pages are produced during the phase 4 (i.e., implementation) and during the phase 5 we can collect reports concerning the usage metrics.

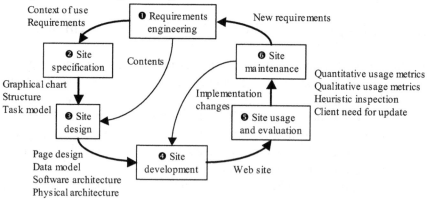

Figure 1. General life cycle of Web applications development

Artifacts describe a set of UI elements on which we might apply ergonomic knowledge. However, the meaning and the applicability of each ergonomic rule can vary according the artifacts take into account; mostly because the ergonomic rules address UI elements which are not described by the artifact. So, according to the artifact available at each step, a different set of guidelines can be applied. This is the basic assumption of our approach for automated evaluation of guidelines, which is presented in the next section.

2.4   Organizing Guidelines for Automated Evaluation

Not all guidelines can be fully automated. According to the degree of automation, we have classified our guidelines as follows:

- **Integrated**: it can be embedded into the design tools thus forcing the designer to respect it. For instance, *"Provide the size of images"*.
- **Automatic**: no human intervention is needed to assess the guideline. For instance, *"Check that all links can be navigated"*.
- **Semi-Automatic**: the system can identify the appropriate elements over the UI but it requires additional information to complete the evaluation. For instance, *"Provide meaningful label for links"*.
- **Manual**: the system cannot determine which UI elements are concerned by a guideline. For instance, *"Don't publish copyrighted material without permission of the owner"*. So, the guideline cannot be automated.

The automation degree depends upon the appropriated mapping of guideline concepts and the artifacts elements available. It is worth noting that a same general guideline could be evaluated manually at a given step (e.g., design phase) and fully automated at the next step (e.g., implementation).

3.   THE GENERAL ARCHITECTURE OF OUR PROPOSAL

Fig. 2 briefly summarizes the general architecture of our approach. At the top, we have the life cycle of Web applications as described in [9]. At each step, we produce some artifacts such as navigation models at the specification phase and templates at the design phase. For example, we produce *"navigation models"* artifacts at the step 2 (i.e., site specification), *"templates"* artifacts at the step 3 (i.e., site design), and so on. The artifacts can vary according to the methods and tools used to specify and create the design. The artifacts are used as source of information to a rule engine enabling the automated processing of guidelines from a database. For the moment, we do not have investigated how we could exploit artifacts produced at the phase of requirements engineering for supporting automated evaluation.

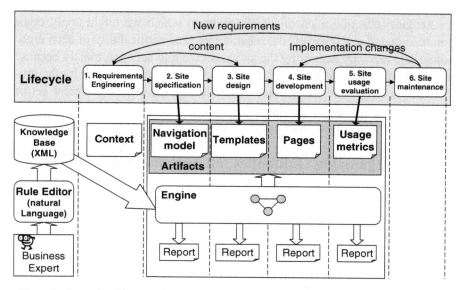

Figure 2. General architecture for supporting automated guideline inspection throughout the development process of Web applications

So, we only are able to cover the phase of specification, site design, site development and site usage. The phase maintenance corresponds to the operation performed to solve problems. Our approach is supported by a guideline editor (at left side in Fig. 2). The knowledge base stores the guidelines as well the corresponding mappings to the artifacts elements. A rule engine (i.e., namely Engine in Fig. 2) uses the guidelines-artifacts mapping information stored in knowledge base to inspect in a seamless way all the artifacts.

In order to solve the mapping-problem between guidelines concepts and artifacts, we have defined a non-ambiguous ontology based on the terms used in the guidelines issued from W3C/WAI accessibility initiative and the EvalWeb project [9]. Then, we have rewritten these guidelines using the terms in such an ontology. The vocabulary contains more than 50 terms related to Web application such as: *"Page"*, *"Link"*, *"Table"*, *"Image"*, *"AudioContent"*, *"Quotation"*, *"NavigationalAid"*, *"NavigationalBar"* *"SiteMap"*, etc. Fig. 3 presents a subset of our ontology concerning the *"navigation mechanisms"* which are used hereafter in our case study.

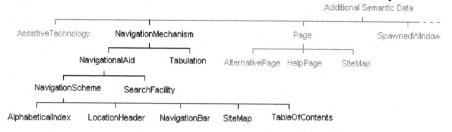

Figure 3. Part of the ontology describing navigation mechanisms

This ontology is used for mapping guidelines to artifacts produced during the development process and thus, allowing the automated evaluation during the whole life cycle of Web applications. For example, in a graph-based navigation model, an arc could be interpreted as a *"link"*. Since the term *"link"* refers to an element in the common ontology, we can from now apply guidelines concerning links over the navigation model. If a guideline term has no representation in a given model, the rule cannot be verified.

Our guidelines are described using XML files which allow the automatic processing by business rule engines such as Drools (http://drools.org/). The XML description includes pointers to the corresponding artifacts and libraries used to run out the inspection.

Fig. 4 shows an example of guideline (e.g., *"Provide persistent links to the home page and high-level site categories"*) translated to the Drools format. Precisely, guidelines described in this way have 3 main parts: a) elements identification, b) test performed to check the guideline, and c) error message if the test fails. The elements identification part contains 3 parameters: *"errorList"* (line 3) which points out to a Java class describing the errors collected during the evaluation; *"page"* (line 6) is the artifact's element assessed in this guideline; and *"domUtils"* (line 9) which refers the library used to run out the inspection over the artifact. In our example, the tests are identified by the *<java:condition>* tag (lines 12 and 13). A condition should contain method calls the library assigned above. Actually, this library has been implemented by the system expert to handle the ontology and the artifacts. Once this library has been implemented, the rule editor is parameterized to use this library. Finally, when a rule satisfies all the conditions the consequence is thrown. In this example, an error is added to the current list of errors (see line 15).

```
1  <!--[26](A) Provide persistent links to the home page and high-level site categories -->
2  <rule name="[26]">
3      <parameter identifier="errorList">
4          <class>error.ErrorList</class>
5      </parameter>
6      <parameter identifier="page">
7          <class>dom.Page</class>
8      </parameter>
9      <parameter identifier="domUtils">
10         <class>util.DomUtils</class>
11     </parameter>
12     <java:condition> domUtils.isLinkedToMainPage(page) !=true </java:condition>
13     <java:condition> domUtils.isLinkedToImportantPages(page) !=true </java:condition>
14     <java:consequence>
15         errorList.addErgoError("\n\nFailed! [26] Provide persistent links to the
16         home page and high-level site categories [A] \n for State: ", state);
17     </java:consequence>
18  </rule>
```

Figure 4. Example of guideline descriptions in Drools format

4.   RUNNING OUT AN EXEMPLE

Our purpose is to evaluate guidelines in every phase of the development process. However, it is worth noting that we do not have the same information about the Web site whether we are at the specification level or at the implementation level for instance. For example, in the specification phase we do not have information concerning the Web page contents whereas this information is fully accessible at the implementation phase. So the rules engine processing guidelines must deal with different artifacts at each step. To illustrate such an approach we present hereafter an example of automated verification at each step of development process.

4.1   At the Specification Phase

Design of web UIs includes design for structure, navigation and appearance. During the specification several models support the design activity (e.g., organizational model, data model, navigation model, etc.). According to the space available, we just present hereafter the navigation model. To deal with the navigation issues we employ the SWC notation [15]. SWC is a typical exemplar of a finite state machine. Fig. 4 shows a view at glance of the elements of SWC notation.

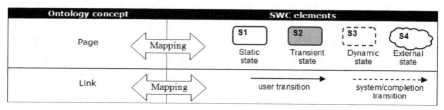

Figure 5. Navigation modeling of the SPIDER Web project Web site

In Fig. 4, at the top level, a compound state named *"SpiderWeb project Web Site"* group all states taking part of the Web site. Rounded-corner rectangles (i.e., *"main intro"*, *"first workshop"*, *"schedule"* and *"publications"*) are *static states* in the SWC notation which means they refer to pages with static content. External or foreign Web sites (i.e., *"Capes"*, *"Cofecub"*, *II-UFRGS"*, *"LIIHS-IRIT"* and *"IHC'2002"*) are depicted by cloud-like symbols (i.e., *external states* in the SWC notation). The labeled transitions from *"t1"* to *"t13"* correspond to the links between pages. Refer to [15] for more details about the notation. As SWC is a navigation model it allows the representation of the concepts such as "page" and "link" by means of the elements "state" and "transition" (Fig. 6). Thus, the state element (static, transient, dynamic or external states) can represent the concept of "page" in our ontology and vice versa. Likewise, a user, system or completion transition will represent the concept of "link".

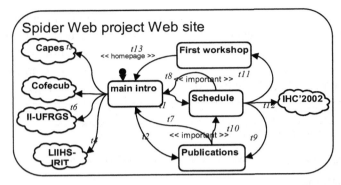

Figure 6. Mapping between the ontology terms and the SWC elements

After having completed the mapping of SWC elements to the ontology, navigation guidelines "*Each page must have a link to it*" can be translated to "*Each state must have a transition pointing to it*".

4.2   At the Design Phase

By the end of the design phase sketches providing the layout and CSS style sheets specifying presentation properties are produced. When drawing the sketches, designers can typically point out where the "*navigation bar*" and "*navigation aids*" should be placed on the Web page. However, a "*navigation bar*" can be implemented in many different ways in the HTML code, for example as a set of links, an image map, a Java script, etc. So, we have to find out a way to map the "*navigationBar*" to any possible HTML elements.

Hereafter, we present a solution based on CSS templates to intermediate the mapping. CSS templates help at describing the locations of content and thus creating a flexible mechanism for pointing elements into the HTML since they are often used for presentation issues. Another possibility for this mapping is XLink (http://www.w3.org/XML/Linking). Let us consider the description of the element "*Navigation Bar*" in a Web page which refers to the identifier "my*NavigationBar*" located in a CSS file (Fig. 7). In that way, we have a particular region on the Web pages called "my*NavigationBar*" on which we apply a particular look & feel.

```
#myNavigationBar {
    position: absolute;
    top: 4em;
    left: 1em;
    background-image: url(/images/background.gif);
}
```

Figure 7. Description of a navigation bar in a CSS template

However, "my*NavigationBar*" has no semantics concerning the ontology: two or more CSS elements having different look & feel (e.g., text-based menu, and image based menu) might have the same semantic (e.g., "*NavigationBar*"). In order to give more flexibility to designers, we employ an XML file for mapping CSS elements and the elements of our ontology (Fig. 8).

```
<?xml version='1.0' ?>
<SemanticData xsi:noNamespaceSchemaLocation="semanticData.xsd"
xmlns:xsi="http://www.w3.org/2001/XMLSchema-instance">
...
    <NavigationalAid type="NavigationBar" selector="#myNavigationBar"/>
...
</SemanticData>
```

Figure 8. CSS description for the identifier "*navigation bar*"

4.3   At the Implementation Phase

At the implementation level, the content of the Web pages is created by developers. So, the evaluation will now be carried out on the HTML code. The mapping between ontology and HTML tags is done by associating tags and ontology terms in a similar way we have done with SWC and CSS elements. Fig. 9 shows how the mapping can be done according some artifacts produced at different steps of development process.

Ontology concept	Specification SWC elements	Design CSS elements	Implementation HTML elements
Page	State	-	<html>
Link	Transition	a: link	<a>
Navigation Aid	-	#myNavigationbar	<a href="..." class="myNavigationbar"

Figure 9. Ontology mapping for the identifier "*navigation bar*" according several artifacts

Besides, we can combine DOM elements, CSS templates, XML files describing templates semantic and SWC models to apply guidelines that could not be checked using each of these artifacts alone. So, we can interpret a guideline according to the mappings done in the early phases between the different models and the ontology. For example: "*Each page must contain <a> elements whose targets lead to each page with a 'homepage' or 'important' semantics*". Like in the previous phase, we manage to distinguish these different pages according to the additional semantic data we add in the XML file. In this step, we can automate evaluation by combination information issued from different artifacts. For example, we can indicate that the "*main intro*" page (Fig. 5) has type "*homepage*" because contrary to the SWC model the DOM model doesn't give information about the type of one page. This mechanism was possible in SWC by means of the stereotype << *homepage* >> [15]. By combining information HTML files and SWC models it is possible to evaluate the guideline "*Each page must contain a link whose targets lead to each page with 'homepage' or 'important' semantics*".

4.4   At the Evaluation (or Deployment) Phase

During the deployment phase the prototype is running so, we should run out the final evaluations before delivering the application to the end users. As mentioned before, the automated evaluation of guidelines does not cover all kind of guidelines. So, at this step, our evaluation tool helps by indicating to the designers the set of guidelines that should be manually inspected and which models and artifacts are concerned by these guidelines. The evaluator is therefore assisted throughout the evaluation with a list of errors/warnings constantly displayed on the screen.

5.   TOOL SUPPORT

The edition of guidelines is supported by an editor and a rule engine inspector integrated into the Eclipse platform as presented in Fig. 10. This editor supports the edition of rules in natural language by giving access to the vocabulary defined by both the ergonomics expert and the system expert in the early phases. In order to be automated, rules entered in natural language are completed with the corresponding mapping to artifacts.

Figure 10. Tool support integrated into the Eclipse platform

Each rule is then stored in a knowledge base in a Drools format as presented by Fig. 4. We also have implemented the knowledge base and the rules engine. The rule engine evaluates guidelines contained in the knowledge base throughout the development process. It takes appropriate models as input according to the phase where the rules set is evaluated. As many models are used from the specification phase to the deployment phase many efforts have to be done to address each model. Indeed, if one ergonomic rule is expressed with a unique language in the rule editor, its evaluation is much more complex: from one model to another one the rule's expression is not the same. After each evaluation a report is generated.

6.   DISCUSSION AND FUTURE WORK

Many studies have shown that careful application of guidelines had positive impact on usability [11]. Automated evaluation of guidelines is a way to employ usability methods on Web design.

This work presented a general architecture and a tool support enabling automated inspection of guidelines in very early phases of development. On one hand, our approach is based on the inspection of artifacts available at each phase of the development process. On the other hand, we propose an ontology enabling the mapping of concepts described in the guidelines and the elements found in the artifacts. The description of guidelines should follow a particular ontology, which requires a compromise between the system expert (which knows all artifacts and models used to build Web applications) and an ergonomics expert. But once the common vocabulary has been established, the guidelines can be described in a computational representation allowing the automated inspection.

The implementation of the corresponding mapping between guidelines and artifacts is very costly, as we have experienced, because we have to code a particular library to every artifact used in the inspection. However, once we have established the mapping to a given model (i.e., navigation model SWC) all new project users can benefit from these models, thus reducing the costs over time. At present we have implemented such an approach for automated checking of guidelines over SWC navigation models, CSS and HTML pages, thus covering the phase from specification to deployment of the Web site.

One of the main drawbacks of our approach is that designers should specify all elements of the UIs at different levels (e.g., model, templates, etc.) and if they miss to clearly identify an element, it will not be checked by our tools. In the future, this task can be alleviated by appropriated authoring environments supporting the design and implementation of Web sites. Future work will include the extension of such an approach for other artifacts produced during the development process. In order to justify the added value of our approach, we intend to compare the results of usability evaluation with our tool with other approaches for usability evaluation.

Even thought the approach for guidelines verification presented here shares a lot of concepts with the Web semantic initiative, no Web semantic technology was used in our implementation. The reason for not using technologies such as RDF, for example, to describe ontology relays on the low performance of currently available rule engines based on the RDF standard. This pragmatic choice was constrained by our industrial partner who sponsors this project.

We have presented here our preliminary results of a method to improve the use of automated tool for guideline inspection throughout the development process of web applications. Our aim is to get more benefits from a tool support helping to apply in an automated manner ergonomic knowledge on the artifacts produced during the design process. Our ongoing work focus on the description of a decision process model that will generalize our contribution and make it in accordance with actual design process and the applicability of quality models such as discussed in [12].

For the moment, we just have employed such as an approach for a few artifacts (i.e., navigation models, templates, CSS and HTML descriptions). Some empirical findings suggest its use on broader set of artifacts, including artifacts related to the structure of the information architecture. We plan to verify this hypothesis in the near future.

ACKNOWLEDGMENTS

This research is partially supported by the WebAudit project, ANRT-CIFRE and Genigraph (http://www.genigraph.fr), Genitech Group.

REFERENCES

[1] Ardito, C., Lanzilotti, R., Buono, P., and Piccinno, A., *A Tool to Support Usability Inspection*, in Proc. of 8th Int. Working Conference on Advanced Visual Interfaces AVI'2006 (Venezia, 23-26 May 2006), ACM Press, New York, 2006, pp. 278–281.

[2] Beirekdar, A., Vanderdonckt, J., and Noirhomme-Fraiture, M., *A Framework and a Language for Usability Automatic Evaluation of Web Sites by Static Analysis of HTML Source Code*, Chapter 29, in Ch. Kolski, J. Vanderdonckt (eds.), Proc. of 4th Int. Conf. on Computer-Aided Design of User Interfaces CADUI'2002 (Valenciennes, 15–17 May 2002), Kluwer Academics Pub., Dordrecht, 2002, pp. 337–348.

[3] Brajnik, G., *Automatic Web Usability Evaluation: What Needs to be Done?*, in Ph. Kortum, E. Kudzinger (eds.), in Proc. of 6th Conf. on Human Factors and the Web HF-Web'2000 (Austin, 19 June 2000), University of Texas, Austin, 2000.

[4] Campos, J.C., and Harrison, M.D., *Formally Verifying Interactive Systems: A Review*, in

Proc. of Eurographics Workshop on Design, Specification and Verification of Interactive Systems DSV-IS'97 (Granada, 4–6 June 1997), Springer-Verlag, Vienna, 1997, pp. 109–124.

[5]   Ivory, M.Y., *Automated Web Site Evaluation: Researchers' and Practitioners' Perspectives*, Kluwer Academic Publishers, Dordrecht, 2003.

[6]   Javaux, D., Colard, M.-I., and Vanderdonckt, J., *Visual Display Design: a Comparison of Two Methodologies*, in A.F. Özok, G. Salvendy (eds.), Proc. of 1st Int. Conf. on Applied Ergonomics ICAE'96 (Istanbul, 21–24 May 1996), Istanbul - West Lafayette, 1996, pp. 662–667.

[7]   Matera, M., Costabile, M.F., Garzotto, F., and Paolini, P., *SUE Inspection: An Effective Method for Systematic Usability Evaluation of Hypermedia*, IEEE Transactions on System, Man and Cybernetics, Vol. 32, No. 1, January 2002, pp. 93–102.

[8]   Palanque, P., Farenc, C., and Bastide, R., *Embedding Ergonomic Rules as Generic Requirements in the Development Process of Interactive Software*, in Proc. of 7th IFIP TC 13 Conf. on Human-Computer Interaction INTERACT'99 (Edinburgh, 30 August- 3 September 1999), IOS Press, Amsterdam, 1999, pp. 408–416.

[9]   Scapin, D. *et al.*, *Conception ergonomique d'interfaces web: démarche et outil logiciel de guidage et de support*, INRIA Technical Report of EvalWeb project, INRIA-Université de Toulouse 1-UCL, Rocquencourt-Toulouse-Louvain, December 1999.

[10] Scapin, D., Leulier, C., Vanderdonckt, J., Bastien, Ch., Farenc, Ch., Palanque, Ph., and Bastide, R., *Towards Automated Testing of Web Usability Guidelines*, in Ph. Kortum, E. Kudzinger (eds.), Proc. of 6th Conf. on Human Factors and the Web HFWeb'2000 (Austin, 19 June 2000), University of Texas, Austin, 2000.

[11] Scholtz, J., and Laskowski, S., *Developing Usability Tools and Techniques for Designing and Testing Web Sites*, in Proc. of the 4th Conf. on Human Factors and the Web HFWeb'98 (Basking Ridge, June 1998).

[12] Seffah, A., Gulliksen, J., and Desmarais, M. (eds.), *Human-Centered Software Engineering: Integrating Usability in the Software Development LifeCycle*, Kluwer Academics Publishers, Dordretht, 2005.

[13] Vanderdonckt, J., and Farenc, C., *Tools for Working with Guidelines*, Proc. of Annual Meeting of the Special Interest Group on Tools for Working with Guidelines TFW-WG'2000 (Biarritz, 7–8 October 2000), Springer-Verlag, London, 2001.

[14] Vanderdonckt, J., *Development Milestones towards a Tool for Working with Guidelines*, Interacting with Computers, Vol. 12, No. 2, 1999, pp. 81–118.

[15] Winckler, M., and Palanque, P., *StateWebCharts: a Formal Description Technique Dedicated to Navigation Modelling of Web Applications*, in J. Jorge, N.J. Nunes, J. Cunha (eds.), Proc. of 10th Int. Conf. on Design, Specification, and Verification of Interactive Systems DSV-IS'2003 (Madeira, 4–6 June 2003), Lecture Notes in Computer Science, Vol. 2844, Springer-Verlag, Berlin, 2003, pp. 61–76.

[16] Winckler, M., Farenc, C., and Palanque, P., *Automatic Evaluation for the Web: How Improve Navigation Guidelines*, in Proc. of ACM CHI'2002 Workshop on Automated Testing (Minneapolis, 21–22 April 2002), ACM, Minneapolis, 2002.

[17] Xiong, J., Farenc, C., and Winckler, M., *Vérification de règles ergonomiques sur un modèle de navigation des applications Web,* in Proc. of 16th Conférence Francophone sur l'Interaction Homme-Machine IHM'2004 (Namur, 30 August-3 September 2004), Presses Universitaires de Namur, Namur, 2004, pp. 259–262.

Chapter 24

REMOTE WEB USABILITY EVALUATION EXPLOITING MULTIMODAL INFORMATION ON USER BEHAVIOR

Fabio Paternò, Angela Piruzza, and Carmen Santoro
ISTI-CNR, Via G.Moruzzi 1,56124 Pisa (Italy)
E-mail: fabio.paterno@isti.cnr.it – Web: http://giove.cnuce.cnr.it/~fabio/
Tel.: + 39 050 3153066 – Fax: + 39 050 3138091

Abstract   In this paper we describe MultiModal WebRemUsine, a tool for remote usability evaluation of Web sites that considers data regarding the user behavior coming from multiple sources. The tool performs an automatic evaluation of the usability of the considered Web site by comparing such data with that contained in the task model associated with the pages (which describes the expected behavior of the user). The results of the analysis are provided along with information regarding the user behavior during the task performance. Using such information, evaluators can identify problematic parts of the Web site and make improvements, when necessary. An example of application of the proposed method is also discussed in the paper

Keywords: Multimodal data, Remote usability evaluation, Web usability

1.   INTRODUCTION

The great penetration of Web sites raises a number of challenges for usability evaluators. In this paper we discuss what information can be provided by automatic tools able to remotely process multimodal information on user behavior gathered from different sources. The collected information ranges from browser logs to videos and eye-tracking data. The approach proposed aims to integrate such data in order to derive the most complete information for analyzing, interpreting, and evaluating the user interactions while visiting a Website. The proposed approach is supported by a tool – MultiModal Web RemUsine, which is able to identify where users interactions deviate from those envisioned by the system design and represented in the related task model. To this end, it exploits the integration of data coming from

287

G. Calvary et al. (eds.), Computer-Aided Design of User Interfaces V, 287–298.

such different sources for better understanding potential problems in task accomplishment. Thus, the evaluator is provided with a more comprehensive picture of the actions performed by the user and, consequently, with more information in order to effectively interpret and evaluate the associated user interface. Moreover, the approach proposed has the remarkable advantage to allow evaluators to identify usability problems even if the analysis is performed remotely, which might contribute to keep at minimum the evaluation costs and allows the users to remain in their familiar environments during the evaluation, improving the trustworthiness of the evaluation itself.

2.   RELATED WORK

While a Web site can easily be developed using one of the many tools available able to generate (X)HTML from various types of specifications, obtaining usable Web sites is still difficult. Indeed, when users navigate through the Web they often encounter problems in finding the desired information or performing the desired task. With over 30 million Web sites in existence, Web sites have become the most prevalent and varied form of human-computer interface, but, at the same time, with so many Web pages being designed and maintained, there will never be a sufficient number of professionals to adequately address usability issues without automation [2]. For these reasons, interest in automatic support for usability evaluation of Web sites is rapidly increasing [1,6], especially as far as the remote evaluation is concerned, because, on the one hand, it is important that users interact with the application in their daily environment, but, on the other hand, it is impractical to have evaluators directly observe users' interactions.

Some studies [8] have confirmed the validity of remote evaluation in the field of Web usability. Some work [3] in this area has been oriented to using audio and video capture for qualitative analysis performed by evaluators on the result of usability testing. Other works have highlighted the importance of performing a comprehensive evaluation able to take into account data derived from multiple sources, and the consequent need to provide analysts from a variety of disciplines (each using distinct sets of skills to focus on specific aspects of the problem) to work cooperatively, in order to adequately gain insight into large bodies of multi-source data [7]. In our case we focus more on quantitative data and provide the support for an intelligent analysis of such data so as to extract useful information for evaluation goals.

3.   THE ARCHITECTURE

Our approach is mainly based on a comparison of planned user behavior and actual user behavior [4]. Information about the planned logical behavior of the user is contained in a (previously developed) task model, while data about the actual user behavior is provided by the other modules (the logging tool, the Web cam and the eye-tracker), which are supposed to be available within the client environment. An overview of the general approach is described in Fig. 1, where we use ovals to indicate data (the colored ovals better highlight the data which are provided to the tool), whereas the rectangles indicate the hardware/software modules aimed at manipulating such data. The eye-tracker provides quantitative data about the gaze of the user during the evaluation session: one of the most relevant measures regards the *scanpaths*, namely the traced routes of the user gaze used to give insights about the navigation strategy followed by the user during the visit of the page. Contextual information is provided by video-based data recorded during the session by a Webcam. The logging tool stores various events detected by a browser, using Javascripts encapsulated in the (X)HTML pages and executed by the browser. When the browser detects an event, it notifies the script which captures the event detected by the browser and adds a temporal indication. Then, a Java applet communicates the log files to the server. The logging tool provides useful information for correctly correlate the data coming from the different sources used in our approach (the eye tracker, the Webcam, etc.), and to this aim some relevant modifications were needed to be implemented. For instance, in order to manage the data associated with the eye-tracker, it is necessary that whenever a scroll event is recorded, also the extent of the shift with respect to the top and bottom corner of the page is recorded as well by the logging tool, so as to reconstruct the actual area that the user was currently looking at. In the same way, in order to correctly manage the correlation between tasks and videos (so as to provide e.g., evaluation about the completion of tasks) it is necessary that the logging tool is able to record the information about starting/ending time of the tasks.

As for the planned user behavior, CTT [5] task models are used to describe it by their graphical representation of the hierarchical logical structure of the potential activities along with specification of temporal and semantic relations among tasks. It is worth pointing out that, with the CTT notation used, the designer might easily specify different sequences of paths corresponding to the same logical behavior just using the same temporal operator, in order to allow the needed flexibility in describing the user behavior: for instance, if two activities should be concurrently performed, (which means that the first one might be performed as the first activity, but also the vice versa is allowed), this behavior is expressed by using the concurrency operator as the right relationship between these two tasks. By comparing the ideal behavior (contained within the task model) with the information coming from logs, videos and the eye tracker, MMWebRemUsine is able to offer the evaluators useful hints about problematic parts of the considered Web site.

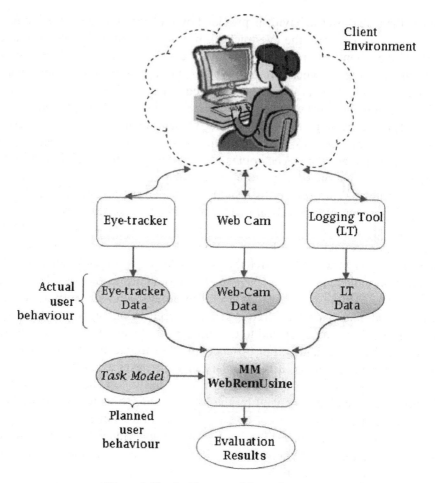

Figure 1. The Architecture of the environment

4.   THE METHOD

The method underlying the tool is composed of two main phases, the preparation and the evaluation.

4.1   The Preparation

The main goal of the preparation phase is to create an association between the *basic tasks* of the task model and the *events* that can be generated during a user session and recorded in log files. This association allows the tool to use the semantic information contained in the task model to analyze the sequence of user interactions stored in the logs. Basic tasks are tasks that cannot be further decomposed and can belong to three different categories according to the allocation of their performance: *user tasks* are internal cognitive activities and this cannot be captured in system logs, *interaction tasks* are associated with user interactions (e.g., click, change) and *system tasks* are associated with the internal browser generated events.

Three types of events can be saved in the logs: user-generated events (e.g., click, change), page-generated events (associated with loading and sending of pages and forms) and events associated with the change in the target task by the user, which is explicitly indicated through selection from the list of supported tasks. Each event should be associated to one task, a task can be performed through different events (e.g., the movement from one field to another one within a form can be performed using either the mouse, or the arrow key or the Tab key). If an event is not associated with any basic task, it means that either the task model is not sufficiently detailed, or the action is erroneous because the application design does not call for its occurrence. An example of association between a task and an event is, for instance, the association between the task "selecting the home page" and the event "Click on the Home button". Once the association between tasks and events has been carried out, it is possible to move on the evaluation.

4.2   The Evaluation

In the evaluation phase the proper automatic analysis is performed: MMWebRemUsine examines the logged data with the support of the task model and provides a number of results also analyzing the data coming from videos and the eye tracker. Such data can provide useful information especially when it is possible to exploit them in an integrated and cross-checking-based approach (as with MMWebRemUsine), for identifying explanations to any problems users might have encountered during the test.

During the test phase all the user actions are automatically recorded, including those associated to goal achievement. The evaluation consists in analyzing such sequences of actions to determine whether the user has correctly performed the tasks as defined in the task model (the user was able to reach the goals and the actions performed were actually useful to reach them) or some errors occurred (e.g., a precondition error, which means that the execution task order did not respect the relations defined in the system design model). In addition to the detailed analysis of the sequence of tasks performed by the user, evaluators are provided with some results giving an overall view of the entire session considered (such as tasks performed correctly, tasks with precondition errors, how many times a task or an error have been performed, tasks never performed, and patterns of tasks). Such information allows the evaluator to identify what tasks are easily performed and what tasks create problems to the user. Moreover, revealing tasks never performed can be useful to identify parts of the application that are difficult to comprehend or reach. On the basis of such information the evaluator can decide to redesign the site in order to reduce the number and complexity of the activities to be performed.

From the semantic log analysis aimed at comparing the actual behavior recorded by the tool with the ideal behavior specified within the task model various types of results can be generated:

- *Success*: the user has been able to perform a set of basic tasks required to accomplish the target task and thus achieve the goal.
- *Failure*: the users starts the performance of the target task but is not able to complete it;
- *Useless uncritical task*: the user performs a task not strictly useful to accomplish the target task but does not prevent its completion.
- *Deviation from the target task*: in a situation where the target task is enabled and the user performs a basic task whose effect is to disable it. This shows a problematic situation since the user is getting farther away from the main goal in addition to performing useless actions.
- *Inaccessible task:* when the user is never able to enable a certain target task.

A further type of information considered regards the task execution duration, calculated for both high level and basic tasks, which can provide information useful to understand what the most complicated tasks are or what tasks require longer time to be performed. It is worth pointing out that longer execution times do not always imply complicated tasks. In some cases download time can be particularly high, and with this regard MMWebRem-Usine provides detailed information, so that evaluators can know its impact on the total performance time. In other cases, when such a long time cannot be explained by a long download, a further cross-checking analysis of additional information provided by the tool (e.g., videos recorded during the session) should be performed in order to find a reasonable motivation for the usability problem (see Section 5).

The data from videos are important because they can provide more "contextual" information during the performance of a task. Indeed, since the evaluation is remotely performed, the evaluator is not in a position to understand if any condition might have disturbed the performance of a task while the user visits the Web site in his/her own environment. For instance, as we pointed out in the previous section, a long time (or, at least, a time longer than expected) for completing a task might not necessarily be brought about by a usability problem or by a high download time: indeed, it may be caused by some external factors (e.g., interruptions occurring in the user's environment during the session). Another useful information that can be gained from videos are user comments, which sometimes can reveal that users are aware of having performed an error but cannot undo the actions.

In order to provide the evaluator with video-based data, an association between task and video is automatically performed by the tool, thanks to the information regarding the start/end time of the different tasks. Indeed, as the whole session is recorded by a Webcam, through such times it is possible to split the video associated with the entire user session into different fragments related to the completion of the various tasks, together with the possibility to activate/stop the visualization of the related video with a suitable player in the tool. In this way, when the evaluators identify e.g., inexplicably long durations for completing a task, they can easily activate the interested fragment of the video to get further data and investigate about the contextual conditions occurred during the concerned period.

While videos provide more "contextual" information regarding users, giving the means for correctly interpreting the user's actions, the eye-tracker provides technical measurements and traces of the visual routes followed by users while visiting a Web site. The data provided by the eye-tracker can be interesting "per se" (e.g., the evaluator can understand the areas of the page that attract or not user attention), but they assume even more importance when compared with the user intention (namely: the target task). Indeed, having in mind the objective the user should achieve, it might be relevant to analyze the areas around the links that should be followed in order to reach such goal according to the task model. For instance, it might be relevant to analyze the extent of time the users spent looking at the areas that attracted their attention (duration of *fixations*), as well as the number of fixations. Long fixations might be a sign of user's difficulty in elaborating the information or a sign of high interest in the information. A high number of fixations on certain areas might indicate that the users are confused and are not able to find the information that they are looking for. Moreover, also a long scan path might indicate that the structure underlying the page is rather complicated. All the data have been automatically integrated within the tool, which is able to offer, e.g., for the various tasks, the related video excerpts and the connected data from the eye tracker (i.e., scan paths and fixations).

5.   AN EXAMPLE APPLICATION

In this section we show an example of application of the proposed evaluation method and of the related tool, which, in its current version, is mainly aimed at being used for usability tests. The Web site we considered (http://www.pisaonline.it) provides information about Pisa, and in Fig. 2 the homepage is shown. The Website is divided into four main sections: "Pisa da

Visitare" (Visit Pisa), "Pisa da Vivere" (Live in Pisa), "Pisa da Studiare" (Study in Pisa) e "Pisa Aziende" (Companies in Pisa). For sake of brevity in Fig. 3 only a simplified version of the task model is visualized, yet detailed enough to highlight the four main tasks for accessing the main sections of the site, together with some tasks that we will refer to in this section.

If we focus more properly on the decomposition of the high level task "Visit Pisa", it is possible to see that one of its sub-tasks provides access to the "Ulisse" subsection, which inherits the name from the title of an airline magazine offering tourist information about Pisa and providing several information about the town, including data about local products (e.g., information about the white truffle, Fig. 3).

Figure 2. The home page of the evaluated Web site

Once having performed the task-event associations it is possible to move to the first step of the proper evaluation phase: the identification of a number of target tasks (the high level activities represented within the task model) to be provided to the test participants at the beginning of the evaluation session. Examples of target tasks considered for the example were "Trova Info su Tartufo Bianco" (Access information about the white truffle), "Trova gradazione alcoolica del Chianti", (Find alcoholic content of Chianti), "Trova ristoranti" (Find restaurant), etc. Once the user selected the interested target task, the environment is in a position to know the intention of the user and automatically identify, within the task model, the *planned* paths that should be followed by the user while carrying out the selected task, which will be used as paragon term for the evaluation. In our test we involved 8 participants aging between 21 and 36. One user selected as target task *"Find information on the white truffle"*, which was a subtask of "Access Ulisse" (see simplified task model in Fig. 3). The analysis of this user trying to carry out this activity reported a number of precondition errors. The logging tool recorded several actions performed by the user, which were judged not necessary when compared with the designer's planned path for achieving the task goal (as it is described in the related task model). In addition, the same user was observed pausing a lot looking at the area of the homepage dedicated to the companies in Pisa (a fixation with a relevant duration was registered by the eye tracker), instead of correctly focusing on the *"Visit Pisa"* section which represents the right route for completing the selected task (see the system task model in Fig. 3). From this it might be derived that the user might have misinterpreted "White Truffle" as the name of a restaurant.

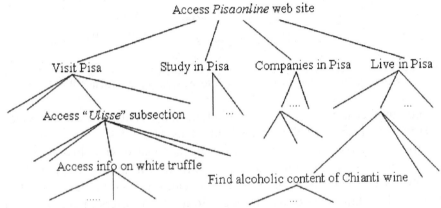

Figure 3. A simplified version of the task model of the PisaOnLine Web site

Moreover, once the same user finally realized the correct section on which looking for the concerned information ("Visit Pisa" section), the evaluation still highlighted –through a long scan path- a possible user difficulty in identifying the right link for accessing the "Access Ulisse" section. Indeed, when referring back to the concerned page, the evaluators noticed that, actually, within this page there are three different links for accessing the Ulisse section (they are highlighted by three circles in Fig. 4): a textual link (with label "Ulisse"), another textual link with a different label ("Alitalia Ulisse"), and also an icon with an image associated to Ulisse. To make things even worse further analysis reported that the information available through the last two links is different from the information reachable through the first link.

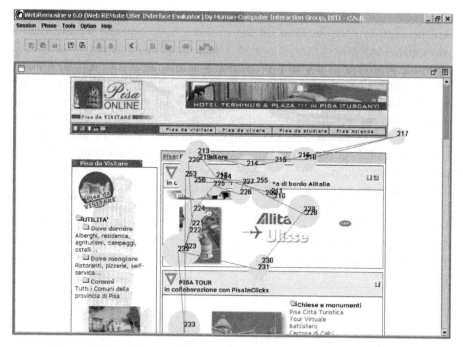

Figure 4. The ambiguity of links related to the section dedicated to "Ulisse"

For another user, who selected "Find alcoholic content of Chianti wine" ("Trova gradazione alcolica del Chianti") as target task, the eye-tracker reported many fixations recorded on the link associated with "Pisa Aziende" ("Companies in Pisa"), rather than, more correctly, within the "Live in Pisa" section, where the link actually is (as you can see from the task model in Fig. 3). This highlighted that the logic followed by users in finding such information was different from that followed by designers.

Moreover, the experiment highlighted that the majority of users did not select the image link associated with the homepage of the PisaOnline Web site (visualized in the top left part of the homepage, see Fig. 5), which was rather surprising due to the relevancy of this page within the entire site. The occurrence of such behavior in almost all users can be interpreted with the fact that the link is rather unclear, and this intuition is reinforced by the image related to the scan path of users on the page (Fig. 5), highlighting that almost all users did not pause on looking at the concerned image link, which might have been confused with a bare decorative image, (especially because it appears on the top part of the page).

In another experiment we analyzed a different site regarding a publishing house and mainly focused on data recorded by videos. Fig. 6 shows the evaluation of task/time performed by the tool, regarding a user who explicitly declared at the end of the task that she was wrong at completing the task.

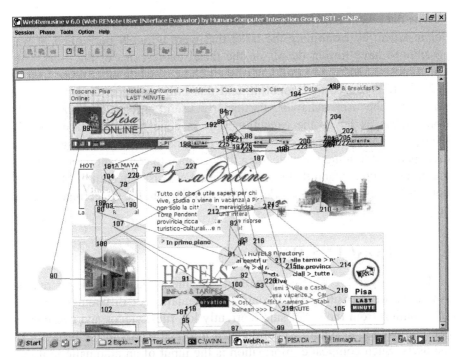

Figure 5. Scan path of "Find Alcoholic Content of Chianti"

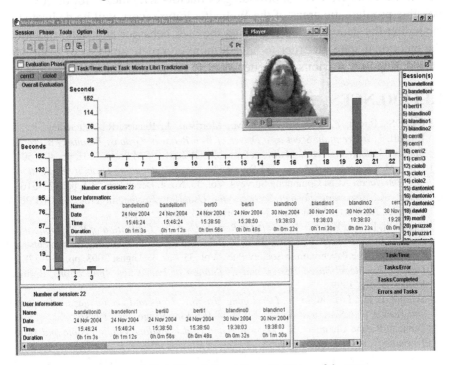

Figure 6. Task/Time Information with Video of the user

The data from the videos were useful to detect some usability problems. For instance, by examining the tasks that were wrongly performed, it was possible to have further details on the facial expressions of the users, who sometimes seemed to be confident of their choices, while other times seemed to be quite confused and doubtful, and this information is important when evaluating the user behavior. Particularly useful information was gained from videos as far as the execution time is concerned, which sometimes seemed to be higher than expected: the analysis of the video revealed that users pause at looking the page, then they happen to comment on it, so this is important to understand that sometimes users are distracted/attracted by portions of the page that are not relevant for carrying out the concerned task, but only by curiosity.

6.   CONCLUSION

In this paper, we propose a method, and the associated tool, for remote evaluation of Websites that, through a combination of different sources of data coming from the client side (currently log files, videos and eye tracker data) allows the evaluator to get detailed information about the behavior of the users. Such composite information is the input of an automatic tool that has shown to be effective in providing evaluators with means for discovering possible problematic areas of the Web site. Future work will be dedicated to extending the data detected regarding the user behavior and state, including the emotional state, in order to have a more complete analysis of what happens during user sessions and better identify the potential usability issues.

REFERENCES

[1] Card, S., Pirolli, P., Van der Wege, M., Morrison, J., Reeder, R., Schraedley, P., and Boshart, J., *Information Scent as a Driver of Web Behavior Graphs: Results of a Protocol Analysis Method for Web Usability*, in Proc. of CHI'2001, ACM Press, 2001, pp. 498–504.

[2] Ivory, M.Y., and Hearst, M.A., *The State of The Art in Automating Usability Evaluation of User Interfaces*, ACM Computing Surveys, Vol. 33, No. 4, December 2001, pp. 470–516.

[3] Lister, M., *Streaming Format Software for Usability Testing*, in Proc. of CHI'2003, Extended Abstracts, ACM Press, New York, 2003, pp. 632–633.

[4] Paganelli, L., and Paternò, F., *Tools for Remote Usability Evaluation of Web Applications through Browser Logs and Task Models*, Behavior Research Methods, Instruments, and Computers, The Psychonomic Society Pub., Vol. 35, No. 3, August 2003, pp. 369–378.

[5] Paternò, F., *Model-Based Design and Evaluation of Interactive Applications*, Springer Verlag, Berlin, 1999.

[6] Scholtz, J., and Laskowski, S., *Developing Usability Tools and Techniques for Designing and Testing Web Sites*, in Proc. of HFWeb'98 (Basking Ridge, June 1998).

[7] Tennent, P., and Chalmers, M., *Recording and Understanding Mobile People and Mobile Technology*, E-social science, 2005.

[8] Tullis, T., Fleischman, S., McNulty, M., Cianchette, C., and Bergel, M., *An Empirical Comparison of Lab and Remote Usability Testing of Web Sites*, in Proc. of Usability Professionals Conference UPA'2002 (Pennsylvania, 2002).